prayer ministry training

Manual

Aim: To produce people who are learning to give and receive ministry

ISBN: 978 1 902750 84 2

Biblical quotations are from the New International Version,
© 1973, 1978, 1984 by the International Bible Society.
Inclusive Language Version.

Published by Alpha International
Holy Trinity Brompton, Brompton Road, London, SW7 1JA.
Email: publications@alpha.org

Contents

Session 1
Theology

Introduction

- This course teaches one particular model for prayer ministry

- It assumes no prior knowledge

- John Wimber visit in 1982

1. Theology

Introducing anything new into church life requires three things: theology, a model and a practice.

a) Jesus' ministry

Mark 1:15
The kingdom of God
The now and the not yet

b) The Twelve

Luke 9:1-2, 6
The nature of power and authority

c) The 72 others

Luke 10:1-2, 8-9, 17-20

d) The Great Commission

Matthew 28:16-20
*'... teaching them to obey
everything I have commanded
you.'*

e) Paul's testimony

Romans 15:17-19
- It is the ministry of Christ
  not 'our' ministry
- We get to play a part in God's
  work
- The compassion of Jesus

Brompton Hospital healing

The secret of ministry is not skill or
experience but obedience

A Basic Model

Introduction

- Values are what hold us together

1. Model values

a) The ministry of the Holy Spirit

- Co-operation with God

- Exodus 14:10, 15-16, 21-22

Preparation

spiritual repentance
faith
power

physical washing
hands, nails
'ministry mints'
teeth
dress

- When we ask the Holy Spirit,
he comes

- Because it is the Holy Spirit's
ministry we go for simplicity and
truthfulness in all aspects of our
prayers for people –
no eccentricities

- The branch must look principally at the vine and not the fruit – our function is to stay close to Jesus

  John 15:1-5
  Luke 10:17-20
  - our relationship with Jesus is the key

b) Biblical authority

- The Spirit of God and the written word of God never conflict

- The truth sets us free

  John 8:32

- Build on biblical truths and promises

  God's love
  Isaiah 30:18
  John 3:16

  Repentance
  Psalm 51
  1 John 1:9

  Fear
  Psalm 91
  Philippians 4:6-7

  Guidance
  Psalm 37:5
  Isaiah 30:21

  Temptation
  1 Corinthians 10:13

c) The dignity of the individual

- confidentiality

- affirm – do not condemn
  (John 3:17)

- faith – somebody must have faith
  (Mark 6:5-6) but do not place
  additional burdens on people

- allow them freedom to come
  back

- avoid all intensity

- same sex:
  men pray with men,
  women pray with women

    - bonding that takes place

    - personal issues that arise

d) Harmonious relationships

*'May they be brought to complete
unity to let the world know that you
sent me and have loved them even
as you have loved me.'*
John 17:23

Lack of unity, love and forgiveness
hinders the work of the Spirit –
beware of comparisons, envy,
criticism etc

*Where no oxen are, the crib is clean;
but much increase is by the strength
of the ox*
Proverbs 14:4 (KJV)

Notes

_____

_____

_____

_____

_____

_____

_____

_____

_____

_____

_____

_____

_____

_____

_____

_____

_____

_____

_____

_____

_____

_____

e) The body of Christ

The Christian community is the place where long-term healing and spiritual growth take place under the protective umbrella of the authority of the church

2. Model practices

a) Pray in relaxed surroundings that are out of earshot, on your own, with one or at most two others

b) If several people are involved, one person should take the lead and be seen to do so with the prayerful help of the others

c) Introduction – names and a short bit of background

Possible questions eg:

- When did you give your life to Christ?

- Have you ever been prayed for to be filled with the Holy Spirit?

- Have you ever prayed in another language?

- What would you like me to pray for?

Smile! Mother Theresa:
'Peace begins with a smile'

Give them your full attention

d) Try to sort out issues of understanding, belief, assurance:

'Am I quite ready to give my life to Christ?'

'I feel unworthy'

'I could never exercise a spiritual gift'

Raise faith with a promise of Jesus (Luke 11:9-13)

Faith is finding a promise of God and daring to believe it

Every gift of God is potentially received by faith and kept by obedience

e) Say how you are going to pray. Check they are still happy. In general remain standing; it is easier to pray, and easier to engage

f) Pray for them!

'Lord, thank you for George/Jane and for your love for him/her… Come now, Lord and fill him/her with your Holy Spirit…'

Then… lay a hand on head/shoulder/chest. Be sensitive where you place your hand.

Notes

Notes

g) Stay facing the person and keep your eyes open; watch their face. Welcome the Holy Spirit when you see signs of his working. Phenomena like sweat/ glow/ eyelids/ tears not essential but they are encouraging

h) Silently ask God what he wants you to say or do

Ask what is happening:

'Do you sense God saying anything/doing anything?'

i) Continue to pray while you think something is happening

j) When you stop praying, make sure the person is happy with what happened. Encourage them to:

- feed on a scripture
- keep in touch
- allow you to pray again for them some time

Warn against increased temptation; refuse to consider that 'nothing has happened'

Go on being filled with the Spirit

Ephesians 5:18

Encourage them by all means that God is good, kind, loving and powerful BUT:

Never advise, suggest, hint or imply discontinuation of any course of treatment or medicine

Never say they have been healed;
let them and their doctor say that

Never give directives eg *'You should
give up your job'*

Never tell them they will get married,
have a baby

If God tells you something, bear in
mind that it is nearly always for your
prayers. If in doubt, consult whoever
is pastorally responsible for the
person you're praying for and/or
whoever is pastorally responsible
for you

k) Whenever you feel the need,
debrief with someone else on the
ministry team and receive prayer
yourself

Notes

Building on the Basic Model

Part 1

Introduction

Importance of operating within our faith

1. Leading someone to Christ

Theology
Humanity is lost without God

a) Isaiah 59:1-2

'Surely the arm of the Lord is not too short to save, nor his ear too dull to hear. But your iniquities have separated you from your God.'

b) Romans 3:23

'...for all have sinned and fall short of the glory of God'.

c) 2 Peter 3:9

'The Lord is not slow in keeping his promise, as some understand slowness. He is patient with you, not wanting anyone to perish, but everyone to come to repentance.'

d) John 3:16

'For God so loved the world that he gave his one and only son, that whoever believes in him shall not perish but have eternal life.'

e) John 3:3

'In reply Jesus declared, "I tell you the truth, no-one can see the kingdom of God without being born again"'

Hence a hunger for:

* meaning and purpose

* forgiveness

* life beyond death

Theology
Jesus died on the cross to reconcile us to God

* Isaiah 53:6
  'We all, like sheep, have gone astray, each of us has turned to our own way; and the Lord has laid on him the iniquity of us all.'

* Romans 6:23
  'For the wages of sin is death, but the gift of God is eternal life in Christ Jesus our Lord.'

* Galatians 2:20
  '... the Son of God, who loved me and gave himself for me.'

Notes

_____

_____

_____

_____

_____

_____

_____

_____

_____

_____

_____

_____

_____

_____

_____

_____

_____

_____

_____

_____

_____

_____

_____

Notes

_____

_____

_____

_____

_____

_____

_____

_____

_____

_____

_____

_____

_____

_____

_____

_____

_____

_____

_____

a) Short introduction – names

When did you give your life to Christ?

ANSWER: I don't think I have

Would you like to? Would you like to ink in what may have been written in pencil?

ANSWER: YES – Proceed joyfully but naturally to c)

b) ANSWER: anything other than YES

Try to sort out issues of understanding, belief, assurance

Am I quite ready?
I feel unworthy
I could never keep it up

Suggest a biblical promise, eg John 3:16: *'God so loved the world…'*

c) Why don't you pray this prayer out loud after me…?

Model
Follow *Why Jesus?* booklet
'What do we have to do?' (p.17)

Sorry, thank you, please

d) I'm now going to pray for you to be filled with the Holy Spirit

PRAY…

e) Follow-up:

- Alpha
- Pastorate
- Homegroup
- Local church
- Contact here

We don't put babies out into the garden to see if they grow!

Need:

Food
(Bible/teaching/encouragement)

Air
(Holy Spirit/God's love)

Friendship
(fellowship/Christian nurture)

2. Praying for someone to be filled with the Holy Spirit

Theology

See Alpha video, 'How can I be Filled with the Holy Spirit?'

Introduction: *'Whoever does not have the Spirit of Christ, does not belong to Christ'* (Romans 8:9)

'Go on being filled with the Holy Spirit.' (Ephesians 5:18)

Notes

_____

_____

_____

_____

_____

_____

_____

_____

_____

_____

_____

_____

_____

_____

_____

_____

_____

_____

_____

_____

_____

Notes

Model

a) Short introduction – names

Have you ever been prayed for to be filled with the Spirit?

ANSWER: No/I'm not sure...

Would you like to? Would you like me to pray again?

ANSWER: YES – proceed joyfully but naturally to c)

b) ANSWER: anything other than YES

Try to sort out issues of understanding, belief, assurance

Am I quite ready?
I feel unworthy
I could never keep it up

Suggest a biblical promise, eg Luke 11:9 *'Ask and it will be given to you'*

c) Let me pray for you...

Relax... why don't you put your hands out and when I lay my hand on you... release your faith and receive

PRAY... lay hands

d) Follow-up as for leading someone to Christ

Warn about possible increased temptation

3. Praying for someone to receive the gift of tongues

Theology

Introduction: *'Follow the way of love and eagerly desire spiritual gifts.'* (1 Corinthians 14:1)

'I would like every one of you to speak in tongues...' (1 Corinthians 14:5)

A form of prayer
1 Corinthians 14:2

Builds up individual
1 Corinthians 14:4

Transcends language barrier
1 Corinthians 14:14

Model

a) Short introduction – names

Have you ever spoken in another language/ tongues/ spirit?

ANSWER: No/I'm not sure...

Would you like to?

ANSWER: YES – proceed joyfully but naturally to c)

b) ANSWER: anything other than YES

Try to sort out issues of understanding, belief, assurance

Notes

Notes

Am I quite ready?
I feel unworthy
I could never keep it up

Suggest a biblical promise, eg 1 Corinthians 14. Raise faith

c) Let me pray for you…

Relax… why don't you put your hands out and when I lay my hand on you… release your faith and receive

PRAY… lay hands

Why don't you just start?...
I might do so too, to cover for you. Start quietly. Encourage them to speak

If getting embarrassed…suggest they start on their own later

Don't listen to yourself
To speak you have to speak!
One language at a time

e) Keep in touch. Persevere. Refuse to doubt that if you ask you receive

Part 2

4. Healing

See Alpha video, 'Does God Heal Today?'

Healing today

a) Simplicity

b) Compassion

  • Mark 1:41

  • Matthew 9:36

c) Words of knowledge

  • pictures

  • sympathy pain

  • impressions

  • hear or see words

  • words formed on tongue

d) Prayer

  • where does it hurt?

  • why does the person have this condition?

  • how do I pray?

  • how are they doing?

  • follow-up

Notes

5. Responding to evil

Example of girl with asthma

Do not say to them *'you've got a demonic spirit'*

Reassure. Pray for protection. Blessing. Peace. Seek advice for after-care

6. Forgiveness

Forgive us our sins as we forgive those who sin against us

Matthew 6:12

How?

- Confess unforgiveness, bitterness

- Repent

- Forgive ... *'with your help and by your grace'*

- Go on forgiving

Illustration of the church bells ringing – forgiveness is a process
Forgiving is part of God's nature – compassion, love, mercy

7. Conclusion

How to get going in prayer ministry:

1. Gather around you a small group where you can pray for people in this way, and receive prayer yourself

2. Persevere

3. Remember that the basis of ministry is our obedience to God's call

Native Bush, Rainbow Springs, Rotorua

*Within these
pages you will find a delightful
collection of 'Charming Places to Stay'.*

Peter Shepherd, publisher of 'Charming Places to Stay'

*Peter Shepherd is proud to present to you
this superb selection of accommodation from
around New Zealand – chosen for their
locations, properties and
the dedication of
their hosts.*

For all enquiries please contact Peter at Travelwise Ltd
Ph: 0064-3-476 1515, Fax: 0064-3-476 1514
email: admin@travelwise.co.nz
www.travelwise.co.nz

Charming
Places to Stay
in New Zealand

year 2012 *edition*

Another Travelwise Publication

Waterfront, Russell, Northland.

Charming
Places to Stay
in New Zealand

A dazzling selection of New Zealand's
finest travel accommodation.

❖ Boutique Accommodation ❖ Lodges ❖ Bed & Breakfasts
❖ Romantic Cottages ❖ Small Hotels ❖ Farmstays
❖ Seaside Escapes ❖ City Apartments ❖ Inns
❖ Homestays ❖ Guest Houses
- and much more.

ISBN 978-0-9864562-2-0

Published by Travelwise Ltd.,
PO Box 6226, Dunedin 9059, New Zealand.
Production and design by Travelwise Ltd.

Printed by Printlink, Wellington, New Zealand.

Distributed by Nationwide Distributors, Christchurch.
Front Cover Photo: Photography, **Bill Nichol**.
Support photos by **Brian Miller** – www.phototrips.info
Furniture and bed linen provided by **'McKenzie & Willis'** Dunedin,
www.mckenzie-willis.co.nz
Accessories provided by the following Dunedin businesses:
Acquisitions, **Arthur Barnett Department Store** and **'McKezie & Willis'** Dunedin

Table of Contents

www.charming-places-to-stay.co.nz

Charming Places to Stay
in New Zealand

"Charming Places to Stay" presents a fabulous choice of travel accommodation. The quality, style and range of showcased properties is outstanding. As the discerning traveller knows, fine accommodation is more than fine property. Above all, the key ingredient for a truly enjoyable stay is hospitality, and this is provided by the hosts.

When compiling this guide book, where possible, we placed as much importance on the character and personality of the hosts as on the properties. Hosts are as varied as their properties – you will encounter those who simply love meeting people and sharing good times while others have taken their style of hospitality to great entrepreneurial heights. Using "Charming Places to Stay" gives you the opportunity to experience the real New Zealand – its people. You may enjoy the company of artists, high country sheep farmers, retired professionals, orchardists, musicians, vintners or writers. While styles of accommodation and hosts vary widely, they all reflect the genuine warmth and friendly hospitality that New Zealanders are known for. Wherever you stay, you will be a welcome guest and your stay a pleasant and memorable one. Enjoy the world's finest hospitality.

"Experience the real New Zealand – its People"

Enjoy unique 'Charming' places to stay.

WHAT TO EXPECT

Travel accommodation in New Zealand has a fine reputation for its standard of services. Guests can expect cleanliness, comfortable beds, a good substantial breakfast and warm, generous hospitality. In addition, your hosts can provide you with first-hand in-depth information about their area. They take pleasure in helping you with your pursuits and travel plans. Their invaluable knowledge can enrich your stay immensely.

WHAT IS EXPECTED OF YOU

Your hosts will do everything in their power to make your stay an enjoyable and memorable one. However, it is important to remember that in most cases you are a guest in a private home. So please consider the little things, like arranging to have a house-key if returning late at night, or asking about the tariffs for toll calls prior to using the telephone. Please let your hosts know in time if you will be late. Thoughtfulness on your part will contribute to a satisfying experience for both host and guest.

WHAT TO DO – HINTS

You will avoid any disappointment by booking ahead, especially during the high summer season. It is also advisable to call your hosts one day in advance to confirm your booking and let them know about your expected time of arrival. Some hosts offer a complimentary pick-up service from coach, plane or train if guests don't have their own transport. Please give your hosts one day's notice if you would like to have an evening meal.

M ost holiday memories are mere
  snapshots – images we treasure, but that
fade with any passing year. But the people we
meet – they become a part of us. They live in us.
They travel with us.

PAM BROWN, b 1928

 ## Boutique Accommodation

Within the world of travel accommodation Boutique Accommodation has been adopted by those hosts whose unique property features reflect a special ambience – period elegance, grace and charm, romance, art, etc. These features are usually enhanced by the hosts' flair for entertainment and hospitality.

 ## Countrystay

Countrystays are often like Homestays. They offer accommodation in a private home. Being in a rural setting, they are associated with all the features and attractions of the countryside. Many Countrystays are close to popular country attractions which offer you the chance to experience rural New Zealand life.

 ## Luxury Accommodation

Luxury Accommodation symbolizes superb facilities, excellent food and an exceptional level of service. Many properties within this category have spectacular settings and offer various additional top class attractions. They represent outstanding accommodation and hospitality.

 ## Guesthouse/Inn

Guest Houses and Inns are usually larger establishments that cater for more guests, but still offer that personalised style of hospitality. They might have several lounge areas and a breakfast room. Guest Houses do not usually offer an evening meal.

Accommodation Categories

Bed & Breakfast

Bed & Breakfast is the umbrella term for the variety of hosted accommodations that include a comfortable bed for the night and a substantial breakfast in the morning. The hosts offer warm and generous hospitality throughout your stay.

Homestay

Homestay is the popular style of accommodation that offers warm and friendly hospitality in a private home. The hosts love meeting people, they enjoy providing their guests with that "home away from home" feeling, knowing that they arrive as strangers but will leave as friends.

Self-contained Accommodation

Self-contained accommodation usually includes a separate entrance, own bathroom. Kitchen and laundry facilities may be included. It can be a self-contained part of the family home or a separate cottage. If breakfast is provided it is either served in the hosts' home, delivered to the doorstep or breakfast provisions provided on the premises.

Farmstay

Farmstays are an ideal way to experience real farm life in New Zealand. An opportunity for you to have hands-on contact with the animals and daily life on a farm. A farm tour may be included. Breakfast is usually taken with the family. Many Farmstays offer lunch and evening meals, as restaurants are often not close by.

How to use this guide – "at a glance"

"at a glance"
Easy Contact Panel
Your hosts: who they are, where they are, and how to make quick contact.

"at a glance"
Tariff Panel
Each tariff indicates the nightly rate. **Double** *indicates the cost for two people sharing one room.* **Single** *indicates the cost for one person occupying a room. A deposit may be required when booking. Tariffs include breakfast unless otherwise stated.* **All prices quoted are in NZ$ – GST inclusive.**
Please confirm details with your host.

"at a glance"
Category Symbols
These quick-to-spot symbols are designed to make selecting your preferred accommodation easy. Particularly helpful for travellers with a limited knowledge of the English language.

"at a glance"
Category Panel
Your hosts' personal description of their category.

"at a glance"
Features & Attractions
Highlighting the main features and attractions in and around this accommodation and locality.

"at a glance"
Location Map
Your hosts' property is indicated by a red dot. Property name is displayed in white box. Maps may be accompanied by a direction panel outlining easy directions.

Clear Address Details
Clear address panel displays essential information, including property address, telephone and fax numbers, e-mail and web site.
NOTE: *When calling from overseas dial New Zealand's international code, 0064, then drop the 0 off the area code (03), for example "Heriot House" 0064-3-477-7228.*

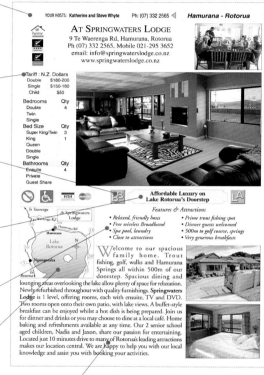

"A Personal Warm Welcome"
These words of welcome have been written personally by your hosts. They describe the features of the accommodation and portray their personality and lifestyle.

🚭 No Smoking

Abbreviations
○ SH – State Highway
h.p. – half price
n/a – not applicable
neg – negotiable
Qty – Quantity
Tce – Terrace

Book direct – Reduce costs
By booking direct with your accommodation host in New Zealand, you make the personal connection right from the start and avoid many additional costs.

www.charming-places-to-stay.co.nz

How to use this guide – Guest room details

Bedrooms

Double = Room with bed for two people
Twin = Room with two beds for two people
Single = Room with bed for one person

Bathrooms

Ensuite = Bathroom adjoining bedroom
Private = Separate bathroom for your use only
Guest Share/Family Share = Bathroom shared
with other guests or host family

Bedrooms	Qty
Double	
Twin	
Single	
Bed Size	**Qty**
King	
Queen	
Double	
King/Single	
Bathrooms	**Qty**
Ensuite	
Private	
Guest Share	

Bed Size	
Super King	*180 x 200cm*
King	*165 x 200cm*
Queen	*150 x 200cm*
Double	*135 x 190cm*
Single	*90 x 190cm*
King Single	*90 x 200cm*

How to use this guide – Category Symbols

 Bed & Breakfast

 Boutique Accommodation

 Countrystay

 Farmstay

 Guest House / Lodge / Inn

 Homestay

 Luxury Accommodation

 Self-contained Accom. & Cottages

How to use this guide – Credit Cards Accepted by Hosts

 Amex – American Express

 Japanese Credit Card

 VISA

 Diners

 Bankcard

 MasterCard

 Maestro

 Eftpos

How to use this guide – Hosts' Associations & Affiliations

 Kiwihost

 Qualmark NZ

 Bed & Breakfast Association New Zealand

 Historic Places Trust

The logo of 'Bed & Breakfast Association New Zealand' assures you of a warm welcome in a private home. Guests are treated as friends of the family and given personal care and time by the hosts. Members' homes are inspected on a regular basis.

Dairies & Supermarkets

Dairies, a long-established feature of the New Zealand landscape, are usually open 7 days a week, from early to late. Like the old general country stores, dairies stock a wide variety of goods. You can normally expect to obtain basic foods and commodities, such as bread, milk, newspapers, confectionery and grocery items.

Because of the extended trading hours, and the benefits of convenient locations, prices are normally slightly higher than those at the supermarket. Some dairies, especially in small communities, also offer Post Shop services.

Supermarkets

Nearly all New Zealand towns and cities have supermarkets.

Supermarkets provide a wider range of goods for one-stop grocery shopping, and have more competitive prices.

Free parking is normally provided, but only for genuine customers - you may be asked to show your receipt. Some supermarkets now have extended trading hours, and most are open 7 days a week.

The Corner Dairy – so much a part of New Zealand's daily life.

Petrol Stations

Also known as 'Service Stations', provide basic commodities for motor vehicles: fuel, oil, air, water, and general motoring accessories. Although petrol stations do not normally provide repair or maintenance services - these are provided by 'Garages' - those that do may have a sign saying 'Mechanic on duty' or 'Repairs carried out'.

Tourist Radio

Tourist Information FM is a service established to provide information to visitors to New Zealand 24 hours a day, and is available in most tourist areas. For English-language broadcasts, tune to 88.2 FM on your radio. For German-language broadcasts, tune to 100.4 FM, and for Japanese-language broadcasts, tune to 100.8 FM on your radio.

Visitor Information Network

Visitor Information Centres are identified by the distinctive green italic *i* logo in conjunction with the Visitor Information logo.

Over 80 of them are located throughout New Zealand. They offer a wide range of services. including travel bookings, tours and accommodation.

The staff, who have unparalleled local and national knowledge are trained and committed to providing accurate and appropriate information to visitors.

Emergency Services

If you require the police, ambulance or fire service, dial 111.
There is no charge for making a 111 call from a public phone box.

Posting a Letter

New Zealand's main postal operator is New Zealand Post with a network of 1000 Post Shops and Post Centres covering the whole country, and 5,000 post boxes where you can post letters. Some outlets combine their normal retail activities with providing New Zealand Post services, especially in smaller towns. Look for the red New Zealand Post logo displayed outside shops.

New Zealand Post Shop

If you need help and cannot get to a Post Shop, you can call New Zealand Post freephone 0800 NZPOST (0800 697 678), 8am to 5.30pm weekdays, or 9am to 12noon Saturdays.

Post Shops

Post Shops offer a wide range of products and services including:
● stamps
● protective packaging
● sending letters and parcels
● sending faxes and telegrams, couriering items overseas or around New Zealand
● stationery, greeting cards, phone cards, gifts (e.g. calendars) and more

Post Shop staff can help you decide which type of packaging will get your parcels delivered as cheaply as possible. A handy Parcel Packaging Guide is also available which contains advice on ways to ensure your parcel arrives safely. Post Shops accept cash, cheque, EFTPOS, MasterCard and VISA for most products and services.

Postal Costs

For sending letters and packages within New Zealand. A standard size letter (maximum 129mm x 235mm) costs 60 cents and takes 2-4 days to be delivered. If you want to get it there faster, FastPost costs $1.20 for a standard size letter which is then delivered by the next working day between major towns and cities. (Rural and remote areas may take a little longer.) You can send parcels from $4.20, depending on size and weight. Items can also be couriered from a Post Shop.

Sending letters and packages overseas. You can ask at the local Post Shop about the best way to package and send items overseas. Options include first class air mail, sea post, registered post and courier. If the value of your item is between $250-1500, then it is recommended that you purchase extra insurance cover from Post Shop.

New Zealand Post website

New Zealand Post has a really excellent website www.nzpost.co.nz You will find it easy to use and packed with helpful and informative advice.

The rural mailbox, a roadside feature throughout New Zealand's countryside.

Money and Banks

Currency

New Zealand has been operating on the decimal currency system with the NZ Dollar as its base since 10 July 1967. Coins in use are: 10c, 20c, 50c, $1 and $2. Bank notes are available in denominations of $5, $10, $20, $50 and $100.

**Automatic Teller Machine
24 hour access.**

Banks

All trading banks are open for business between the hours of 9:30am and 4:30pm. Monday to Friday inclusive, with the exception of public holidays. Automatic Teller Machines (ATMs), operate on a card and pin number system. Cash can be withdrawn 24 hours a day.

Changing Money

Money exchange facilities exist at all banks and at most New Zealand international airports. New Zealand banks buy and sell all major currencies and offer competitive exchange rates which are updated daily.

Travellers' Cheques

Travellers' cheques can also be cashed at Bureaux de Change and hotels or large stores in resorts and larger cities.

Import or export of foreign currency is not subject to any restrictions.

All banks are listed in the Yellow Pages at the back of the local telephone directory.

Credit cards

Payment by any of the international credit cards, including Visa, Master Card, American Express, Diners Club and JCB (Japanese credit card) is widely accepted. Most shops display the card signs in their windows. If in doubt, please check with a sales person before you commence shopping.

EFTPOS (Electronic Transfer of Funds at Point of Sale) is a highly used way of cash payments , which is being used all over New Zealand.

You will find operating EFTPOS machines in shops, museums, supermarkets, petrol stations, to name only a few. Instead of a cash payment, the cash amount is transferred directly from the customer's into the selling company's bank account. The transaction takes place at the counter or check out, where customers swipe their EFTPOS card through the machine and type in their pin number. This convenient way of cash payment can be very handy in remote places or after hours. Many stores with EFTPOS facilities also allow you to withdraw cash when making purchases.

Using the Telephone

The phone system in New Zealand is of a high technical standard and performs efficiently. There are two main service providers, **Telecom** and **Clear**. You will find public telephones throughout the entire country. The majority of public telephones in NZ operate the pre-paid phone card system. Telecom **PhoneCards** are available in NZ$5, NZ$10, NZ$20 and NZ$50 denominations. These can be purchased from many outlets including **NZ Post Shops**, supermarkets, dairies, newsagents, **Visitor Information Centres** and petrol stations. You may find it helpful to purchase a **PhoneCard** even if it is only for emergencies. Increasing numbers of credit card operated phones are now being established which accept major international credit cards. Some public telephones are still coin operated, using 10c, 20c, 50c, NZ$1 and NZ$2 coins. When dialling **Freephone** numbers (commencing with 0800) from public phones you will not require any cards or coins.

Typical public phone booths. Coloured for easy recognition, Yellow for Credit card, Green for PhoneCard, and Blue for Coin.

Telecom PhoneCards available : NZ$5, NZ$10, NZ$20, and NZ$50. They can be easily obtained at many outlets such as Dairies, Post Offices, and Petrol Stations.

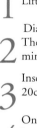

1 Lift handset, do not insert coins.

2 Dial the number you require. The price per minute or part minute will show on screen.

3 Insert coins. Usable coins:10c, 20c, 50c, NZ$1, and NZ$2.

4 Once call is finished replace handset.

5 Unused coins returned, partly used coins not returned.

Using the PhoneCard
1. Lift handset. 2. Insert Card. 3. Dial number.
4. After call, replace handset. 5. Remove card (Don't forget!)

Coins acepted by Coin Phones:– 10c, 20c, 50c, NZ$1 and NZ$2.

e-Phone Card

The *e*-**Phone Toll Card** is an easy and convenient way to use almost any touch tone phone at your own expense. It can be used from a private phone, card phone, credit card phone, cellphone, **Your Yost's Phone**, etc.
Using these prepaid phone cards will make you and your host feel less apprehensive when you use their phone. *e*-**Phone Toll Cards** can be purchased in many dairies, supermarkets and shopping malls.
For detailed information, see website www.prepaidcards.co.nz.

EMERGENCY CALLS......111
Police, Fire, Ambulance
Useful Telephone Numbers

Operator 010
International Operator 0170
National Enquiries 018
International Enquiries....... 0172
International Access Code 00
Australia dialling code 0061
Germany dialling code 0049
Japan dialling code 0081
USA dialling code 001

*"Driving in New Zealand can be a pleasure,
the ever changing scenery is superb."*

On the Road

Driving in New Zealand is a pleasure; the scenery is superb, the roads are generally of a high standard and New Zealanders are helpful and courteous.

However, for your safety and that of other motorists, we urge you to take a little time (New Zealand is patient, it will wait for you) and read the following before you begin driving.

The *New Zealand Road Code* is the definitive guide to correct and lawful driving in New Zealand. It is available at a small cost from the Land Transport Safety Authority. Look in the local telephone directory for the nearest office. A useful leaflet, with English, German and Japanese sections, is *Driving Safely in New Zealand*, also available free of charge from the Land Transport Safety Authority.

Driving: Some Basic Points

Keep Left: In New Zealand we drive on the **left**.
Overseas vistors may find this difficult. – We suggest you take time to adjust and plan your journeys accordingly.

Speed Limit: In general, the maximum speed limit on the open road or motorway / freeway, identifiable by this sign, is 100 kilometres per hour.
In cities and towns, it is 50km per hour. There are exceptions, so watch out for signs (positioned on the left of the road) which may indicate a lower specified speed limit.

Road Signs at Intersections:
Stop: Stop completely, then give way to all traffic.

Give way - Drive slowly. Stop if drivers are approaching from left or right, and give way to all traffic, including those opposite if you are turning left.

Seatbelts: The driver and all passengers (adults and children) - including those sitting in rear seats - must use seatbelts or approved child restraints.

The **New Zealand Automobile Association** (*AA*) offers an excellent service nationwide providing maps, guides and touring information. Freephone 0800 500 444 at any time.

Natural New Zealand

*"The magnificent contrasts and colourful variety
are absolutely breath-taking."*

New Zealand's landscapes are as colourful and diverse as its people. No other country can offer such variety of magnificent scenery in such a comparatively small area. In both islands evergreen native bush abounds. In the North Island there are also exotic forests of huge Kauri trees. A wonderland of hot springs, geysers and boiling mud pools is situated near Rotorua in the centre of the North Island. Therapeutic hot springs are located in parts of both islands, and spectacularly beautiful National Parks with their unspoiled scenery and nature will delight the traveller. The South Island offers scenery on the grand scale: mountains, glaciers, lakes and sweeping coastal beaches. Deep-water fiords slice into the south-west coast, with virgin mountain country in the background. One of the most famous fiords - Milford Sound - is accessible by road as well as by the famed Milford Track, the "most beautiful walk in the world". New Zealand has an abundance of aquatic scenery. Take your pick of spectacular waterfalls, raging torrents, broad rivers, lakes big and small, surfing beaches and rocky coast lines.

South Island West Coast
- Native bush.

"New Zealand – a recreational paradise!"

Waitangi Golf Course - *one of the many superb golf courses you will find in New Zealand.*

Most New Zealanders love sport and the outdoors. Their country's natural features support an abundance of outdoor activities: yachting, golf, rugby and mountaineering, to name only a few. All types of winter sports are practised in both islands and wild game and fish provide excellent hunting and fishing.

www.charming-places-to-stay.co.nz

Tane Mahuta, Waipoua Forest, Northland.

North Island

24

25 - 26
43 - 44
Kaitaia
Kerikeri
Paihia & Russell
Whangarei
45
Dargaville
46
48
AUCKLAND
49 - 66
Whitianga
Thames
Raglan
84
83 - 85
87
86
HAMILTON
Tauranga
Cambridge
Whakatane
Rotorua
109 - 116
117 - 120
125 - 126
121 - 124
Taumarunui
Taupo
New Plymouth
Turangi
Gisborne
127
Wanganui
Taihape
Napier
Hastings
138
Dannevirke
Palmerston North
Levin
Waikanae
Masterton
WELLINGTON
Martinborough

26 - 27
28 - 42
47
70 - 81
67 - 69
82
88 - 90
91 - 92
93 - 94
95 - 96
97 - 108
128
129 - 133
134 - 137
144
139 - 142
143
145 - 152

HOUHORA LODGE

3994 Far North Road, RD 4, Kaitaia
Ph (09) 409 7884, Fax (09) 409 7801, Mobile 021-926 992
email: houhora.lodge@xtra.co.nz
www.topstay.co.nz

Tariff : N.Z. Dollars	
Double	$140-200
Single	$110-140
Child	$30

Bedrooms	Qty
Double	3
Twin	
Single	
Bed Size	**Qty**
Super King	
King	3
Queen	
Double	
Single	6
Bathrooms	**Qty**
Ensuite	2
Private	1
Guest Share	

Your Northern Hideaway
A Fantastic Location

VISA MasterCard bankcard

Features & Attractions

- *Geographical isolation*
- *Fresh garden produce, eggs*
- *Shell collecting*
- *Dig shellfish for dinner*
- *Spectacular, pristine beaches*
- *Wireless internet*
- *Coastal wilderness hiking*
- *Fax, laundry*

We who live on this slim finger of land at the top of New Zealand welcome you, and look forward to sharing its beauty and secret places with you. This is a small part of New Zealand which is different. Come share our home and Max our rescue dog, enjoy the 'good life', home grown vegetables, olive oil, pure water, fresh air, eggs and fruit. Our architect designed home is set in three and a half acres. The beautiful airy pavilion opens to the east and west to fine views and amazing sunrises and sunsets with original New Zealand art adorning the walls. We are delighted to provide advice and assistance for your Far North excursions: 4x4 sightseeing, fishing, walks, trips to famous tourist spots and trips to places that few people visit or even know about (by prior arrangement). A complimentary 4WD trip to view 90 Mile Beach is offered. Dinner if requested. (All rooms are either double or twin.)

AHIPARA TIDES

21 Kotare Street, Ahipara, 90 Mile Beach
Ph (09) 409 2120, Mobile 021-900 555
e-mail: info@ahiparatides.co.nz
www.ahiparatides.co.nz

Tariff : N.Z. Dollars	
Double	$115-165
Single	$115-165
Extra pp	$30

Bedrooms	Qty
Double	1
Twin	
Single	
Bed Size	Qty
Super King	
King	
Queen	1
Double/sofa bed	1
Single	
Bathrooms	Qty
Ensuite	1
Private	
Guest Share	

 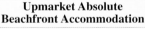

**Upmarket Absolute
Beachfront Accommodation**

DIRECTIONS:
Please telephone for
easy directions
Advance booking recommended

Features & Attractions

- *Absolute Beachfront*
- *Stunning uninterrupted views*
- *Sky TV, wireless broadband*
- *Private off street parking*
- *Incredible sunsets*
- *Lovely appointed unit*
- *Sea view spa pool*
- *Cape Reinga tours arranged*

Your hosts Jackie & Doug extend a warm welcome upon your arrival at **Ahipara Tides**. Just 30 seconds from your covered deck (with BBQ) to the beach. Enjoy the private picnic area adjacent to the beach. Accommodation is pristine clean, modern and very comfortable. We offer all the comforts of home. Enjoy fresh herbs and vegetables from the garden when in season. Relax in style or in the spa pool and enjoy the stunning beauty of 90 Mile Beach and the Tasman Sea. Perfect for two but sleeps four. We can provide a continental breakfast by prior arrangement. We have available an electric golf cart, golf clubs, beach chairs, umbrella, boogie boards and mountain bikes. **Ahipara Tides** is the perfect getaway with many guests reluctant to leave. Guest comments often include, "wow" "stunning" "amazing place to stay" "gorgeous unit" "breathtaking". Seeing is believing. Come and experience our piece of paradise in the Winterless Far North.

BEACH ABODE BEACHFRONT LODGE
11 Korora St, PO Box 134,
Ahipara, 90 Mile Beach
Ph/Fax (09) 409 4070
email: ned.susan@xtra.co.nz
www.beachabode.co.nz

Features & Attractions

- *Secluded beachfront setting*
- *Expansive sea views*
- *Privacy & separate entrances*
- *Impeccably maintained*
- *Qualmark Enviro Silver Rated*
- *Comfortable quality furnishings*

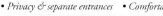

**Elegant Beachfront Retreat
with Spectacular Views**

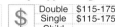

Double	$115-175
Single	$115-175
Child	

Bedrooms	Qty
Double	3
Twin	1
Single	
Bed Size	**Qty**
King	
Queen	3
Double	
Single	2
Bathrooms	**Qty**
Ensuite	3
Private	
Guest Share	

While on holiday in the Far North, Ned and I were captivated by the splendor and expansiveness of 90 Mile Beach. We moved to Ahipara, purchased a private beachfront property and built our beautiful lodge. **Beach Abode** provides everything that we would want in an accommodation; high standard amenities in a scenic location at an equitable price. There are 3 contemporary self-contained waterfront apartments all with private entrances. Open the front door of our apartments and you feel an immediate sense of welcome. Upon entering the apartment, the Tasman Sea draws you out to a covered deck revealing panoramic sea views and landscaped gardens. Apartments are contemporary, pristine, appointed in a warm tropical ambiance. Crisp cotton sheets, Wi-Fi internet, quality comfortable furnishings, fresh coffee, privacy. Scrumptious breakfast available at an additional cost. We hope you consider a retreat at the best kept secret in Ahipara.

MOON GATE VILLA
462 Kerikeri Road, Kerikeri, Bay of Islands
Ph (09) 929 5921, Fax (028) 2551 6088
Mobile 022-079 0210
email: lionel@moongatevilla.com
www.moongatevilla.com

Features & Attractions

- *Stunning house & gardens*
- *Heated swimming pool*
- *Exclusive guest lounge*
- *Free wireless internet*
- *Free airport/coach transfers*
- *Perfect touring location*

**Stylish and Unique Villa
Boutique Accommodation**

Double	$135-275
Single	$170-200
Triple	$305-335

Bedrooms	Qty
Double	3
Twin	
Single	
Bed Size	**Qty**
Super King	2
Queen	1
Double	
King/Single	1
Bathrooms	**Qty**
Ensuite	3
Private	
Guest Share	

Designed in the shape of Cupid's bow by an award winning architect, our house and 1.5 acre gardens feature waterfalls and reflective pools – all within walking distance to Kerikeri cafes, chocolate factory and craft shops. King ensuite rooms offer luxury linens, bar fridge, satellite TV, private indoor and outdoor seating. Enjoy in-house dining, or simply explore the many restaurants Kerikeri is famous for. Minutes away is the historic Stone Store precinct. We are central to wineries, golf courses, waterfall and forest walks, and only 15 minutes to the waterside attractions of Paihia and Russell. A half hours' drive to Northland's famous beaches and diving coast, we make an ideal central base for touring the natural, historic and cultural sights of the Bay of Islands. After a day's touring, relax and enjoy our secluded and romantic gardens.

DIRECTIONS: From State Highway 10, turn at roundabout into Kerikeri Road towards Kerikeri. Watch for the blue (i) information sign.
Our entrance and driveway is 200m meters later on the left.

SWALLOWS RIDGE

32a Rangitane Road, RD1, Kerikeri
Ph (09) 407 5997, Mobile 021-184 2545
email: chris.coakley@xtra.co.nz
www.kerikeribayofislands.co.nz

Tariff : N.Z. Dollars	
Double	$130-230
Single	–
Child up to 10yrs $25-30	

Bedrooms	Qty
Double	3
Twin	
Single	
Bed Size	Qty
Super King	
King	2
Queen	1
Double	
Single	
Bathrooms	Qty
Ensuite	3
Private	
Guest Share	

DIRECTIONS:
Please phone for
easy directions
Booking in advanced
is recommended

Quality Bed & Breakfast
Stunning Views & Great Hospitality

Features & Attractions

- *Sea, rural and inlet views*
- *Relaxed, and peaceful*
- *Solar heated swimming pool*
- *Boating, kayaking and fishing*
- *Wireless Internet*
- *Golf / driving range nearby*
- *Private guest lounge*
- *Shared guest kitchenette*

A warm welcome awaits you at "**Swallows Ridge**"; enjoy spectacular views of the Bay of Islands, Kent Passage and Kerikeri Inlet. Set in 21 acres, our secluded and peaceful location is only 2 minutes drive to Doves Bay Marina and 8 minutes to Kerikeri with its historic Stone Store, craft shops, art galleries, cafés, restaurants and Sunday farmers market. A designated kiwi area, you may hear them at night and perhaps even see them. Meet our chickens, Liz, Doreen and Ruby and ducks George and Mildred. Relax by the swimming pool or your own patio area, watch the world go by, or even a cruise ship. All rooms are ensuite with tea and coffee making facilities. Enjoy a continental or cooked breakfast with freshly laid free range eggs, homemade bread and local produce. Contact us for '*special deals*' throughout the year. We are happy to help you plan your excursions and provide a packed lunch if required. Family room available on request.

ALLEGRA HOUSE

39 Bayview Road, Paihia, Bay of Islands
Ph (09) 402 7932
Mobile 021-082 83603, Skype allegra1957
email: allegrahouse@xtra.co.nz
www.allegra.co.nz

Tariff : N.Z. Dollars	
Double	$145-275
Single	
Child	

Bedrooms	Qty
Double	4
Twin	
Single	
Bed Size	**Qty**
Super King	3
King	
Queen	1
Double	
Single	
Bathrooms	**Qty**
Ensuite	4
Private	
Guest Share	

 Bed & Breakfast with Views
Self-contained Apartment

Features & Attractions

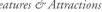

- *Spectacular sea views*
- *Central Paihia*
- *Set amongst native bush*
- *Air conditioned rooms*
- *German & French spoken*
- *Peaceful location*
- *Free wireless Internet*
- *Spa pool nestled in bush*

Allegra House, our spacious, modern home is centrally located, just up the hill from Paihia's wharf, shops and restaurants. We have spectacular views from all rooms over the village to Russell and the Bay of Islands. Luxurious accommodation options are: Bed & Breakfast including continental breakfast, ensuite bathroom, your own tea/coffee making facilities, refrigerator, television and balcony; or Self-catering Apartment with super-king bedroom, large tiled bathroom, fully equipped kitchen and spacious lounge opening onto a large balcony. For your comfort each room has its own air conditioning and the whole house is smoke-free. Enjoy our spa pool nestled in the bush and make use of the barbeque, laundry facilities and internet access.

Plenty of good local information is available to help you choose the best options for your time with us. We can book activities such as sailing, dolphin watching and day trips to Cape Reinga.

ALLVIEW LODGE

30H Sullivans Rd, Paihia, Bay of Islands
Ph (09) 402 8606, Fax (09) 402 8607
Mobile 0274-779 997
email: allviewlodge@xtra.co.nz
www.allviewlodge.co.nz

Tariff : N.Z. Dollars	
Double	$225-275
Single	
Child	

Bedrooms	Qty
Double	2
Twin	1
Single	
Bed Size	Qty
Super King	
King	
Queen	3
Double	
Single	2
Bathrooms	Qty
Ensuite	1
Private	1
Guest Share	

Absolute Beachfront Luxury Accommodation

Features & Attractions

- *Unique location in Paihia*
- *Superb sea and island views*
- *Private beach access*
- *Safe sandy swimming beach*
- *Complimentary Kayaks*
- *Start of coastal walking track*
- *Free Wi-Fi access*
- *Courtesy car to bus/airport (local)*

Showcasing Paihia's best private beachfront location, uninterrupted sea and island views. Architecturally designed for your pleasure and privacy. Stroll along beach to restaurants, cafes and tourist pier, cruise 144 islands, hole in the rock or a 10 mins ferry ride to Historic Russell. Our 1 bedroom suite has 2 queen beds, ensuite with a 2 person bath. Our 2 bedroom suite has 1 queen and 2 single beds, private bathroom. Both suites have large walk-in showers, spacious lounge/dining areas, TV's, garden and patio areas from which dolphins are often seen. Furnishings and fittings are to a high standard. Guests' full laundry and kitchenette adjacent to both suites. Private access is by external stairs or internal lift. A comprehensive breakfast menu is included in tariff served in our conservatory dining area. Local art and sculptures are displayed throughout the Lodge. Friendly Kiwi hosts. Complimentary kayaks, start of coastal walking track. Free Wi-Fi access. Tariff for single, extra person, longer stays, off-peak available on application. "Award 2001 Trip Advisor Certificate of Excellence".

29

APPLEDORE LODGE

624 Puketona Road, Paihia
Ph (09) 402 8007, Mobile 021-165 0072
email: appledorelodge@xtra.co.nz
www.appledorelodge.co.nz

Tariff : N.Z. Dollars	
Double	$175-210
Single	$160-200
Cottage	$200-275

Bedrooms	Qty
Double	4
Twin	2
Single	

Bed Size	Qty
Super King	3
King	
Queen	1
Double	
Single	

Bathrooms	Qty
Ensuite	4
Private	
Guest Share	

  Self-contained Suites & Cottage with Panoramic River Views

Features & Attractions

- *Heated swimming pool*
- *Home made breakfast basket*
- *Wireless internet on site*
- *Trout fishing in our river*

- *Luxuriously appointed accommodation*
- *Spectacular riverside setting*
- *Bush and coastal walking*
- *5 mins drive Paihia & golf*

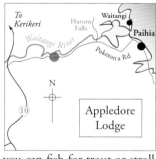

Miniature waterfalls and rapids await your discovery as the Waitangi River gently tumbles past your bedroom window. Tranquility is here to rediscover with our spellbinding riverside setting where you can fish for trout or stroll the riverbank. Set in 2 acres and only 25 metres from the riverbank all our accommodation have magnificent views up and down the Historic Waitangi River are self-contained with ensuite and ranch sliders to private decks. Delight in Janet's special all home made continental breakfast basket delivered and taken at your leisure. Riverside Suite furnished in native rimu and double walk-in shower. Charming Riverside Cottage and Studio are superior and luxuriously appointed with a riverside setting. We enjoy classic cars, golf and travel. With resident ducks, heron, kingfisher, new heated swimming pool, we offer ingredients that all holidays should contain. **Appledore Lodge** is unsuitable for children under 12.

CHALET ROMANTICA

6 Bedggood Close, Paihia, Bay of Islands
Ph/Fax (09) 402 8270, Mobile 027-226 6400
email: info-chalet@xtra.co.nz
www.chaletromantica.co.nz

Tariff : N.Z. Dollars	
Double	$135-299
Single	$115-265
Child	$25

Bedrooms	Qty
Double	3
Twin	1
Single	
Bed Size	**Qty**
Super King	2
King	
Queen	2
Double	
Single	2
Bathrooms	**Qty**
Ensuite	3
Private	1
Guest Share	

 Central Town Bed & Breakfast and Apartments

Features & Attractions

- *Central location with sea views*
- *Café's & restaurants nearby*
- *Stroll to beach and water activities*
- *Heated pool, spa, mini gym*
- *TV, CD, DVD, and phone in rooms*
- *Laundry facilities, internet*
- *Tour desk on site*
- *Francaise and German spoken*

Spoil yourself and experience the magic of **Chalet Romantica**. Nestled above Paihia Beach with unsurpassed views over the Bay and township, spectacular by day and night. Each upstairs room has its own balcony, superb sea views, quality furnishing and fittings, wireless internet, crisp linen and extra comfy beds.

A delicious breakfast with home baked breads and farm fresh eggs will await you in our conservatory overlooking the Bay. Spend your days exploring or relax on your balcony, swim in our heated pool, soak in the hot spa or work out at our gym. What better way to re-charge the batteries! Bird lovers will be thrilled with lots of native birds visiting our garden and surroundings. Excellent restaurants, shops and "the Bay of Islands Dolphin and Cruise Departure Piers" are just a stroll from us.

Bay View Suite

19 Bayview Road, Paihia
Ph (09) 402 6628, Fax (09) 402 5366
email: carl.lucas@xtra.co.nz
www.charmingaccommodation.co.nz

Features & Attractions

- *Welcome Basket*
- *Quality & comfort*
- *Warm hospitality*
- *Privacy*
- *Elevated site*
- *Magic sea & village views*

Self-contained Central Paihia		Double $150-190
		Single
		Child

Elevated setting for privacy and to capture sea view. Enjoy the sea views with twinkling lights at night and ever-changing water views by day. Accommodation is fully self-contained and serviced daily. Extra luxuries include robes, slippers, plunger coffee, iron. The tariff includes a generous continental breakfast, served in your suite so you can enjoy it at your leisure. A five minute walk takes you to all the local attractions, beaches and quality restaurants. We offer a courtesy pickup and delivery service. A complimentary wine and welcome basket awaits you upon arrival. Bookings essential, two nights minimum stay.

DIRECTIONS: At 19 Bayview Road proceed to top of driveway. Bookings essential.

Bedrooms	Qty
Double	1
Twin	
Single	
Bed Size	**Qty**
King	
Queen	1
Double	
Single	
Bathrooms	**Qty**
Ensuite	1
Private	
Guest Share	

Typical Northland beach.

DECKS OF PAIHIA

69 School Road, Paihia
Ph (09) 402 6146, Fax (09) 402 6147
Mobile 021-278 7558
email: info@decksofpaihia.com
www.decksofpaihia.com

Features & Attractions

- *Quiet, central location*
- *Sun-drenched decks / pool*
- *Lovely sea views*
- *Private ensuites each room*
- *All suites air-conditioned*
- *Free wireless Internet in each room*

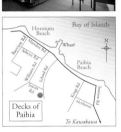

$	Double	$165-245
	Single	-
	Child	-

Luxury Bed & Breakfast

Bedrooms	Qty
Double	3
Twin	
Single	
Bed Size	Qty
Super King	3
Queen	
Double	
Single	
Bathrooms	Qty
Ensuite	3
Private	
Guest Share	

Contemporary designed home, completed October 2005. Three guest suites all with private ensuite bathrooms. All suites offer your own tea/coffee making facilities, TV/DVD, air conditioning, refrigerator, and open out on to sheltered, sun drenched decks overlooking swimming pool.Private garden area allows the opportunity for a lazy afternoon in the sun beside the pool. Quiet peaceful central Paihia location, with off street parking. Very comfortable interiors, stylishly furnished. Guest lounge located adjacent to suites area offers extended living space in which to relax, with a comprehensive DVD and book library. Philip and Wendy have enjoyed many years in the hospitality industry and are happy to share their home, and their extensive knowledge of the Bay of Islands and Northland with you.

GUADALEST

37 Bayview Road, Paihia
Ph/Fax (09) 402 7996
email: remmy@slingshot.co.nz
www.guadalest.co.nz

Features & Attractions

- *Spectacular views*
- *Infinity pool*
- *Luxury suites*
- *All ensuite*
- *Modern furnishings*
- *Central location*

$	Double	$250-350
	Single	-
	House	$1000 p/n

 **Luxury Bed & Breakfast**

Bedrooms	Qty
Double	2
Twin	
Single	
Bed Size	Qty
Super King	2
Queen	
Double	
Single	
Bathrooms	Qty
Ensuite	2
Private	
Guest Share	

Guadalest offers a very warm welcome to guests. For the first time, this prestigious family home is available for Bed & Breakfast holiday accommodation.
Overlooking the Bay of Islands it has stunning views from a sun-drenched patio featuring an infinity pool and barbecue area – the perfect spot in which to relax and unwind. All rooms have a super king bed, lounge area, ensuite bathroom and breath-taking sea views. The main living area is open plan, spacious and modern. Delicious cooked or continental breakfast is available. Take advantage of local knowledge as we are happy to make reservations on the many trips and tours in the area. There is ample off-street parking or courtesy car pick up/drop offs. **Guadalest** is situated only a three minute stroll from Paihia town centre, shops, wharf, cafés, restaurants and bars. Please direct all enquires to owner and host Jan Ward.

MARLIN HOUSE
15 Bayview Road, Paihia,
Bay of Islands
Ph (09) 402 8550, Mobile 021-038 0674
email: marlinhousebnb@xtra.co.nz
www.marlinhouse.co.nz

Tariff : N.Z. Dollars	
Double	$145-190
Single	$145-190
Child	

Bedrooms	Qty
Double	2
Twin	1
Single	
Bed Size	**Qty**
Super King	
King/Twin	2
Queen	1
Double	
Single	
Bathrooms	**Qty**
Ensuite	3
Private	
Guest Share	

 It is the Small Things that Make us Different

Features & Attractions

- *Own private entrance*
- *Stylishly furnished suites*
- *Tiled ensuites all rooms*
- *4 min easy walk to wharf*
- *Stunning views of the Bay*
- *Quiet central location*
- *Secure off street parking*
- *Free wireless Internet*

DIRECTIONS
Please phone for easy directions.
Advance booking recommended.

Marlin House is a comfortable colonial-syle home set in a subtropical garden with ample off-street parking. Substantial decks provide stunning views over the Bay of Islands. An easy four minute walk to the beach, wharf, cafés, restaurants and central Paihia. **Marlin House** offers three generous sized suites, each with a private entrance, a sitting and dining area, ensuite, fridge, microwave and TV. Tea/coffee making facilities are also provided. With Rogers restaurant/chef experience we look forward to treating you to a special breakfast which will ensure a great start to the days many activities this region has to offer. Tailored excursions or activities can be organised. Lunch hampers and evening meals are available by arrangement.

MOREPORK RIVERSIDE LODGE

846 Puketona Road, Paihia
Ph (09) 402 5577, Fax (09) 402 5575
Mobile 021-986 687
email: moreporklodge@xtra.co.nz
www.moreporklodge.co.nz

Tariff : N.Z. Dollars	
Double	$145-205
Single	$125-170
Child	

Bedrooms	Qty
Double	3
Twin	
Single	
Bed Size	**Qty**
King	2
King/2 Singles	1
Queen	
Double	
Single	
Bathrooms	**Qty**
Ensuite	3
Private	
Guest Share	

Quality Bed & Breakfast with Kiwi Hospitality

Morepork Riverside Lodge

Puketona Rd   Paihia
Opua
Kawakawa
To Whangarei

DIRECTIONS: 8.4 km from the Waitangi/
Puketona Road roundabout on Paihia waterfront.
Driveway on the right
with white 'navigation' stones.

Features & Attractions

- *4 acres of bush & gardens*
- *Yummy full breakfast*
- *Gourmet evening meals*
- *Knowledgeable Kiwi hosts*
- *Free wifi, wheelchair access*
- *Expansive rural views*
- *Tame alpacas, sheep, goat*
- *7mins drive Paihia/Waitangi*

Welcome to our home set in 4acres on the Waitangi River. Stroll through our native bush & gardens, home to many NZ birds including Moreporks. Feed our friendly farm animals and meet our personable cat, Panpoot. All our rooms have an ensuite (one with a large corner bath), TV, DVDs, Teas, Coffee & Refrigerator. Our two river side rooms have their own deck with river/rural views and a sofa. Puketona guests have their own table & chairs on the BBQ deck, also with river and rural views. We'll happily advise you on local attractions and places to dine. Perhaps you'd like a pre-breakfast walk with Paul while Barbara prepares your full breakfast? We offer 3-course gourmet meals or single-course light meals. We are both "Kiwi" born & bred and have travelled throughout NZ, the Pacific and some parts of Europe.

TARLTON'S LODGE & RETREAT

11 Sullivans Road, Paihia
Ph/Fax (09) 402 6711
email: stay@tarltonslodge.co.nz
www.tarltonslodge.co.nz

Tariff : N.Z. Dollars	
Double	$170-325
Single	$170-325
Child	–

Bedrooms	Qty
Double	2
Twin/Double	3
Single	
Bed Size	Qty
Super King	3
King	
Queen	2
Double	
King Single	
Bathrooms	Qty
Ensuite	5
Private	
Guest Share	

 Awake to the Best Seaviews in Paihia

Features & Attractions

- *All rooms fantastic sea views*
- *Infinity Swimming Pool*
- *Generous Cooked Breakfast*
- *Air Conditioning all rooms*
- *Wireless Broadband Internet*
- *Fridge, Tea-Coffee making all rooms*
- *Luxurious Bedrooms-Quiet & Peaceful*
- *Guest Laundry & iron*

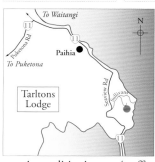

Paihia's most spectacular sea and island views await your discovery at **Tarlton's Lodge & Retreat**. All this plus an infinity swimming pool. All our B&B rooms have private decks and entrances, air conditioning, tea/ coffee making, fridge, all designed and furnished to the highest standard with full-sized armchairs that you can really relax in and enjoy the fabulous views. Spoil yourself in Hobson's Suite with its own private lounge and super-king bedroom plus spa pool. During the day relax and sunbath by our fabulous infinity pool set in this peaceful subtropical location. The **Retreat** is a fabulous self-contained open plan 1-2 bedroomed apartment. This can sleep 2-4 people. All this is just waiting for you to spoil yourself. **Tarlton's Lodge** is situated just an 8 minute walk or 2 minute drive to the centre of Paihia close to the amenities and tours but away from the hustle and bustle. Pictures of all five rooms can be seen on our website.

WINDERMERE
168 Marsden Road, Paihia
Ph (09) 402 8696, Fax (09) 402 5095
Mobile 021-115 7436
email: office@windermere.co.nz
www.windermere.co.nz

Tariff : N.Z. Dollars	
Double	$120-190
Single	$100-180
Child	

Bedrooms	Qty
Double	2
Twin	
Single	
Bed Size	**Qty**
Super King	
King	
Queen	2
Double	
Single	2
Bathrooms	**Qty**
Ensuite	2
Private	
Guest Share	

Bed & Breakfast
Self-contained Accommodation

Features & Attractions

- *Great views & location*
- *Spacious sunny units*
- *Own private entrance*
- *Wireless Internet & Freeview TV*
- *Walk to town or golf course*
- *Spa pool & decks*
- *Sky T.V.*
- *Spectacular sunsets*

Windermere is a large modern family home set in a bush setting and yet located right on one of the best beaches in the Bay of Islands. Superior accommodation is provided with suites having their own ensuite, kitchen facilities and 'Freeview' television.

For longer stays one suite has its own laundry, dryer and fully equipped kitchen. The other suite has microwave and refrigerator only. Each suite has its own decks (a barbeque is provided) which you can sit, relax and enjoy the view enhanced by spectacular sunsets.

Jill and Richard would welcome your company to enjoy our own little part of paradise. **Windermere** is the jewel in the Bay of Islands.

BELLROCK LODGE

22 Chapel Street, Russell
Ph/Fax (09) 403 7422
Mobile 021-0263 7446
email: bellrockbandb@xtra.co.nz
www.russellbnb.co.nz

Tariff : N.Z. Dollars	
Double	$150-220
Single	POA
Child	n/a

Bedrooms	Qty
Double	4
Twin	
Single	
Bed Size	**Qty**
Super King	4
King	
Queen	
Double	
King Singles	8
Bathrooms	**Qty**
Ensuite	4
Private	
Guest Share	

**Best Views in Russell
Luxury, Spacious & Good Food**

Features & Attractions

- *Fully equipped kitchenette*
- *Airconditioning*
- *5 min walk to village wharf*
- *Close to 2 swimming beaches*
- *Luxury ensuite rooms*
- *Each room has private entrance & deck*
- *Continental or cooked breakfast on request*
- *Off street parking & free WiFi*

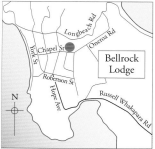

DIRECTIONS: Russell Rd brings you into Russell, it becomes Hope Ave, veers to left into Florance Ave, turn right into Matauwhi Road, pass Christ Church on your left into Baker St, turn right into Chapel Street which ends at our driveway.

For the best views in Russell come to **Bellrock Lodge** which is on the hill overlooking the bay and the lovely village of Russell,

we are only a 5 min stroll to the village and wharf. Luxury en-suite rooms with private entrance and French doors leading out of your room onto your private patio. The rooms can either have twin beds (2 singles) or a super king bed. Each room has: Freeview TV, DVD player, Radio/CD/iPod dock, air conditioner. Spacious bathrooms with large shower, two hand basins, bidet, toilet, heated towel rail and lovely soft towels. Off street parking and free WiFi. Enjoy a drink on your private patio while watching the sunset. Spacious guest lounge/dining room has SKY TV, fully equipped bar and barbeque facilities on deck. Our delicious generous servings of Continental or choice of cooked breakfasts should keep you going till dinner.

BAY OF ISLANDS COTTAGES

92A Te Wahapu Road, Russell, Bay of Islands
Ph (09) 403 7757
email: info@bayofislandscottages.co.nz
www.bayofislandscottages.co.nz

Tariff : N.Z. Dollars	
Double	$220-275
Single	$200-240
Child	enquire

Bedrooms	Qty
Double	3
Double/Twin	1
Single	

Bed Size	Qty
Super King	
King	1
Queen	3
King/Single	1
Single	1

Bathrooms	Qty
Ensuite	4
Private	
Guest Share	

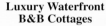

**Luxury Waterfront
B&B Cottages**

Features & Attractions

- *Delicious breakfasts*
- *Sea view from every cottage*
- *Sub-tropical organic garden*
- *Private beach with dinghy*
- *Broadband, digital TV*
- *Forest & coastal walks*
- *Kiwi protection zone*
- *Dinner by arrangement*

Welcome to our four luxury eco cottages in a secluded waterfront location. Each cottage has close sea views from wide sunny terraces and is surrounded by beautiful gardens and tree ferns. The interiors are spacious, comfortable and welcoming with fresh modern styling. Art and vintage pieces add individuality and cotton bed linen, luxury eco toiletries, and fresh flowers all help make your stay something to look forward to. Breakfast is a special event as guests gather around our large terrace table to enjoy good food and conversation. Where possible our food is organic and homemade, with the addition of the best local produce. Russell village is just seven minutes away by car and we can help you with bookings, maps and suggestions for local sightseeing. Alternatively our dinghy and kayaks are available anytime for fishing or a paddle out in the bay.

La Veduta

11 Gould Street, Russell Bay of Islands
Ph/Fax (09) 403 8299
email: laveduta@xtra.co.nz
www.laveduta.co.nz

Features & Attractions

* Spectacular views of the Bay
* 5 mins. walk to town
* Unique stylish bedrooms
* Tours and cruises arranged
* French and Italian spoken
* Excellent restaurants nearby

**Quality Boutique Homestay
Bed & Breakfast**

Double	$180-240
Single	$150-180
Child	

DIRECTIONS:
Please phone for easy directions.

Enjoy our mix of traditional European culture in the midst of the beautiful Bay of Islands, historic heartland of New Zealand. **La Veduta** is the perfect "pied-a-terre" for your Northland holiday. We offer our guests a warm welcome, taking care of your smallest needs.

All our bedrooms are individually styled, offering full sea views. You may be served a delicious cooked breakfast on the balcony overlooking the Bay of Russell. Enjoy complimentary afternoon tea. Relax and delight in the sunset over the bay. **La Veduta** is only a few minutes walk from the township, wharf, sandy beaches and restaurants.

Bedrooms	Qty
Double	4
Twin	1
Single	
Bed Size	**Qty**
King	2
Queen	1
Double	2
King/Single	2
Bathrooms	**Qty**
Ensuite	3
Private	2
Guest Share	

The White House

- Te Wharema -
7 Church Street, Russell, Bay of Islands
Ph/Fax (09) 403 7676, Mobile 021-241 1010
email: info@thewhitehouserussell.com
www.thewhitehouserussell.com

Features & Attractions

* Luxury Historic accommodation
* Flat 2 min stroll to waterfront
* Free WI-FI throughout & SKY TV
* Breakfast served until noon
* Complimentary port & sherry
* Spa pool, gardens & BBQ

**Luxuries of a Hotel
Comfort of a Home**

Double	$195-325
Single	$175-290
Child	

The Historic **'White House'** Russell
Luxury Bed & Breakfast Accommodation

Come and have a truly unique stay with us in one of Russell's oldest houses (circa 1840). A beautifully restored villa with plenty of character.

She features three well appointed rooms with super-king size beds and fresh new ensuites along with guest lounge and full kitchen.

Indulge in absolute luxury ideally situated in the heart of Russell with 12 midday check-out. Enjoy a dip in the spa pool, read a book on the shaded sundeck or wander to the waterfront.

DIRECTIONS:
Upon entering Russell, turn
right into Church St,
past NZ's oldest church,
go straight across the next junction.
We are about 20m on your right.

Bedrooms	Qty
Double/Twin	3
Twin	
Single	
Bed Size	**Qty**
Super King	3
Queen	
Double	
Single	
Bathrooms	**Qty**
Ensuite	3
Private	
Guest Share	

Ounuwhao "Harding House"
Historic B & B Guestlodge
Matauwhi Bay, Russell, Bay of Islands
Ph (09) 403 7310, Fax 09 (403 8310) Mobile 027-414 1310
email: thenicklins@xtra.co.nz
www.bedandbreakfastbayofislands.co.nz

Tariff : N.Z. Dollars	
Double	$240-350
Single	$150-200
Child	$45

Bedrooms	Qty
Double	6
Twin	2
Single	

Bed Size	Qty
Super King	1
King	1
Queen	4
Double	
Single	4

Bathrooms	Qty
Ensuite	6
Private	2
Guest Share	

 Boutique Accommodation & Self-contained Accommodation

Features & Attractions

- *Detached garden suite*
- *Safe, sandy swimming beaches*
- *Swimming with the dolphins*
- *Hearty, healthy gourmet breakfasts*
- *Historic Russell Village*
- *Sea and island excursions*
- *Coastal and bush walks*
- *Historic homestead*

When visiting Historic Russell take a step back into a bygone era. Spend some time with us in our delightful nostalgic, immaculately restored villa (circa 1894). Enjoy wrap-around verandahs in summer and the large guest lounge with open fire in winter. Each room has traditional wallpapers and paint work with handmade patchwork quilts and fresh flowers to create a lovingly detailed, traditional romantic interior. Breakfast is served in our farmhouse kitchen around the large kauri dining table. It is an all homemade affair, from the fresh baked bread to the yummy daily special and the jam conserves. Our 1930's self-contained cottage is set in park-like grounds for your privacy and enjoyment. With two bedrooms, two bathrooms, large lounge and sunroom and fully self-contained kitchen, it is ideal for people wanting peace and time out. Breakfast is available if required. We look forward to meeting you soon.

DIRECTIONS:
We are on the main road from
the vehicular ferry, in Matauwhi Bay
1 km from Russell Village.

EXPERIENCE OUR HISTORIC BED & BREAKFAST,
ENJOY A WORLD OF DIFFERENCE.

VILLA DU FRESNE

23 Du Fresne Place, Tapeka Point, Russell
Ph/Fax (09) 403 7651, Mobile 021-636 121
email: villadufresne@xtra.co.nz
www.villadufresne.co.nz

Features & Attractions

- *Spectacular 180° waterviews*
- *Spacious & private*
- *Historical birthplace of NZ*
- *Bush & coastal walks*
- *Off-street parking*
- *Free wireless Broadband*

DIRECTIONS: Travel through Russell Village and up Flagstaff Hill. Turn left down to Tapeka Pt then right into Du Fresne Place. No 23 is the last r.o.w drive on your right before beach.

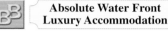

Absolute Water Front Luxury Accommodation

	Double
Villa	$210-280
Roberton	$180-210

Bedrooms	Qty
Double	1
Twin	1
Single	
Bed Size	**Qty**
Queen	1
Super King/Twin	1
Double	
Single	
Bathrooms	**Qty**
Ensuite	2
Private	
Guest Share	

Just 2 km over the hill from Russell is beautiful Tapeka Point, with 2 beaches and spectacular views out to the islands of the Bay. Villa Du Fresne is a Mediterranean-style villa with 2 accommodation options. The Villa has 1 or 2 bedrooms, and is fully self-contained like a home away from home, complete with basic pantry and full breakfast supplies. The Roberton Room is the king/twin suite that has tea/coffee making facilities, fridge etc, and a continental breakfast. There are 2 entrances. Your hosts live in a separate wing so you are ensured of privacy. Happy to help with tours or cruises from Russell, or you can just relax and enjoy the fully glassed terrace overlooking the water. Piano and log fire in Villa lounge. There is a BBQ and lots of outdoor furniture, beach umbrella and plenty of towels and linen. Villa for extra 2 persons $50 per person. Not suitable for children under 10 years.

VILLA RUSSELL

2 Little Queen Street, Russell, Bay of Islands
Ph/Fax (09) 403 8845, Mobile 027-492 8912
email: info@villarussell.co.nz
www.villarussell.co.nz

Features & Attractions

- *Spectacular views of the bay*
- *2 minutes walk to town*
- *Free wireless Broadband*
- *Sail the bay with us too*
- *Delicious breakfasts included*
- *Tours and cruises arranged*

DIRECTIONS:
Travel through Russell Village into Queen St. 50 metres ahead is our sign and white picket fence with driveway at the bottom of Flagstaff Hill.

Luxury Bed & Breakfast with Sailing Option

	Double	$185-320
	Single	
	Child	

Bedrooms	Qty
Double	3
Twin	1
Single	
Bed Size	**Qty**
Super King	2
Queen	1
Double	
King/Single	2
Bathrooms	**Qty**
Ensuite	3
Private	
Guest Share	

Enjoy a welcoming visit to **Villa Russell**, 2 minutes from the beach and Russell's restaurants, yet totally private and secluded. Relax with magnificent views of Russell's bay and wharf from the deck of our beautifully restored 1910 villa, or from our guest cottage with spacious guest rooms, with ensuite and large verandah. Imagine having breakfast while surrounded by mature native trees and birdsong. A short walk takes you to Long Bay surf beach or historic Flagstaff hill and native bush. Your suite is complete with tea/coffee making facilities, refrigerator, microwave, TV/DVD, laundry facilities. Off Street parking provided. You may also be greeted by our friendly family dog. Make your stay even more special with a sailing charter on our 11.6M yacht Kingfisher or 15M Kama Lua to further explore the beautiful sights the Bay of Islands has to offer.

42

HORSE SHOE MANOR AT JARVIS FARMSTAY

6984D SHI, Pakaraka, Bay of Islands
Ph (09) 405 9606, Mobile 021-259 1120
email: baystay@igrin.co.nz
www.nzbaystay.com

Tariff : N.Z. Dollars	
Double	$130-150
Single	$75
Child	u9 1/2 price

Bedrooms	Qty
Double	3
Twin	1
Single	1
Bed Size	**Qty**
Super King	
King	
Queen	2
Double	1
Single	3
Bathrooms	**Qty**
Ensuite	1
Private	3
Guest Share	

 VISA MasterCard

**Charming Countrystay
"Middle of Everywhere"**

Features & Attractions

- *15mins to Russell, Waitangi, BOI*
- *Free wireless internet*
- *Golf course nearby*
- *Thermal pools - 10mins*
- *Dolphin cruises and tours*
- *Wine trails*
- *Dinner parties*
- *Musical soirees*

The middle of everywhere en route SH 1. A gateway for touring North (Cape Reinga 90 mile beach) & West coast – Gaint Kauri tree. Opononi's Hokianga harbour, and to the Bay of Islands. Swim with the dolphins, sailing & fishing. Ngawha hot springs, vineyards and Farmers market. Share the sunset at our homely, pet friendly Farmstay. Winnie the Pooh B & B sign at our gate. Stroll in the fabulous subtropical palm/water gardens and orchards. while dinner is prepared by the 'Patron'. Dinner is served in the conservatory or Al fresco on the deck with local wine. Breakfast includes home made conserves, an orchard bowl of fruitfullness, (parsley scrambled eggs a 'specialty'). Queensize 4 poster bed suite overlook this bird lovers haven. "Treetops Cottage" a s/c studio for a quiet retreat, has a unique family basement to sleep 4. Dinner available on request. Free wireless broadband available click on www.nzbaystay.com for Northland weather reports and local links info.

43

TEN ON ONE COUNTRY HOMESTAY

5 Ludbrook Road, Pakaraka, Bay of Islands
Ph (09) 405 9460, Fax (09) 405 9461
Mobile 027-227 6001
email: ten.on.one@ihug.co.nz
www.tenonone.co.nz

Features & Attractions

- *Hearty breakfast*
- *Evening meals available*
- *Laundry service/iron avail*
- *Courtesy airport & coach pick up and return*
- *Clean swimming pool*

DIRECTIONS:
At intersection of SH 10 and SH
1 travel 80 mtrs north on SH 1.
We are first house on the left
(use Ludbrook Road entrance)

**Affordable & Relaxing
Country - Homestay**

Double	$127
Single	$88
Child	half price

T o all our visitors a warm and friendly greeting, the Bay of Islands awaits you. Our farmlet is situated in central Bay of Islands and is fifteen minutes from most towns and attractions including Paihia, Waitangi, Russell, Kerikeri and the Hokianga region. We have exciting attractions to interest you. Would you like to visit Cape Reinga, cruise to Cape Brett (Hole in the Rock), see a 2000-year-old Kauri tree (Tane Mahuta), visit famous Waitangi and treaty house, historical Russell Town, glow worm caves, waterfalls, swimming, paragliding, tramping, horse riding, fishing, golf? Northland can genuinely lay claim to the most compact and diverse scenic orientated wonderland in New Zealand, come and judge for yourself. For your safety our modern home meets all fire and safety regulations. Enjoy our friendly home, feed the animals, collect the eggs, relax around the swimming pool or enjoy a barbeque.

Bedrooms	Qty
Double	4
Twin	1
Single	
Bed Size	Qty
King	
Queen	4
Double	1
Single	2
Bathrooms	Qty
Ensuite	4
Private	1
Guest Share	

Charming
Places to Stay
in New Zealand

"Charming Places to Stay is a lovely book, the best presented of all the B&B books we have ever seen, it is crisp, clear and every advert looks enticing. We have stayed all over the world and it is by far and away the most accurate book we have ever used as well."

Robin and Linda Spiller, Cornwall, UK

44

KAURI HOUSE LODGE

60 Bowen Street, Dargaville
Ph/Fax (09) 439 8082, Mobile 027-454 7769
email: kaurihouselodge@orcon.net.nz
www.kaurihouselodge.co.nz

Tariff : N.Z. Dollars	
Double	$225-300
Single	$200
Child	

Bedrooms	Qty
Double	2
Twin	1
Single	
Bed Size	**Qty**
Super King	1
King	1
Queen	
Double	
King/Single	1
Bathrooms	**Qty**
Ensuite	3
Private	
Guest Share	

**Luxury Historic
Bed & Breakfast**

Features & Attractions

- *Kauri villa over 5000 sq ft*
- *Farm bush walk included*
- *Free wireless Broadband*
- *Summer swimming pool*
- *Peaceful & tranquil location*
- *Beach, lakes & bush walks*
- *Historic homestead*
- *Close to Waipoua Forest*

N
Grey St.
Bowen St.
Kauri
House
Lodge
Jervois St.
14
To Whangarei
12
To Auckland

Original features of this 1880s style villa include the detailed verandah balustrading, stained glass, pressed ceilings, sash windows and native Kauri panelling. Completed in 1910 by a leading bushman as a spacious family residence, **Kauri House** now offers three private ensuite guest rooms and three lounge rooms – a billiard room, library and television lounge – furnished with antiques. Only three kilometres from the township of Dargaville, with many nice restaurants. **Kauri House** is set in three hectares of garden with abundant native birdlife including fantails, wood pigeons and seasonal tui. A swimming pool provides relaxation and exercise in summer only. Nearby is Doug's forty hectare farm on which he runs steers. This land includes sixteen hectares of protected native bush. "Perfect accommodation, good host, these things make holidays worthwhile" *Frank & Annie, Holland* "Fantastic house and timber furniture, best we've seen" *Gary & Trish, Australia*

PALM HOUSE

669 Pahi Road, Paparoa
Ph (09) 431 6689, Mobile 027-688 8296
email: palmhouse@paradise.net.nz
www.palmhousepahi.co.nz

Features & Attractions

- *Close to Matakohe Museum*
- *Home cooked dinners*
- *Complimentary kayak*
- *Golf course nearby*
- *In house & s/c garden cottage*
- *Excellent restaurant nearby*

**On the River
Bed & Breakfast**

Double	$120
Single	$75
Child	$55

Hector and Jenny are renowned for their relaxed, friendly hospitality; delicious meals of fine local produce, accompanied by fine New Zealand wines.

Enjoy staying at peaceful Pahi. Stroll along the tideline or stand on the wharf and watch the fish jump. Just two hours from Auckland, thirteen kilometres from the famous Matakohe Museum and en route to the spectacular Kauri Forest.

Signposted on the main Highway 12, travel seven kilometres down Pahi Road and reach **Palm House.**

Bedrooms	Qty
Double	2
Twin	1
Single	
Bed Size	**Qty**
King	
Queen	2
Double	
King Single	2
Bathrooms	**Qty**
Ensuite	1
Private	
Guest Share	1

www.phototrips.info

Mangawhai Lodge
"A ROOM WITH A VIEW"
4 Heather Street, Mangawhai Heads, Northland
Ph (09) 431 5311
email: info@seaviewlodge.co.nz
www.seaviewlodge.co.nz

Tariff : N.Z. Dollars	
Double	$175-250
Single	$165-190
Child	

Bedrooms	Qty
Double	5
Twin	6
Single	8
Bed Size	**Qty**
Super King	
King	
Queen	2
Double	
King Single	3
Bathrooms	**Qty**
Ensuite	3
Private	2
Guest Share	

Stylish, Contemporary Seaview Accommodation

Features & Attractions
- *Beaches, fishing & kayaking*
- *Arts ,crafts & wine trails*
- *Bird sanctuary*
- *Chocolate factory*
- *Free WiFi & off street parking*
- *Walk to cafés, shops & harbour beach*
- *Adjacent golf course*
- *2 hours to International Airport*

Mangawhai Lodge map

Mangawhai Lodge, at the beach village of Mangawhai Heads offers spectacular sea & island views. Just 80 minutes drive north of Auckland, 50 minutes from Whangarei and 2 hours from both Bay of Islands and Auckland's International Airport. We provide the perfect retreat for rest, relaxation and base to discover the treasures of North Auckland and Northland. Relax in the stylish B&B guest rooms (all with bathrooms) opening to private verandas and views with a gourmet breakfast included. Choose the quality self-contained apartment, suitable for short and long stays offering sea views, verandas with optional breakfast. Walk to cafes, golf and harbour beach. Spend your days exploring beaches, walkways, kayaking, swimming, fishing, surfing, artisan galleries and vineyards.
Visit our website for seasonal specials, group packages and hot deals. Mangawhai Lodge is a great base for Rugby World Cup games in Auckland and Whangarei. Free wifi and off street parking.

EBBTIDE

36 Kanuka Road, Sandspit
Ph (09) 425 8681, Mobile 021-238 3850
email: stay@ebbtide.co.nz
www.ebbtide.co.nz

Features & Attractions

- *Peace & tranquility*
- *Stunning beaches*
- *Ferry to Kawau Island*
- *Goat Island Marine Reserve*
- *Sumptuous breakfast*
- *Dinner by arrangement*

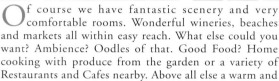

Luxurious Homestay
Warm Hospitality

	Double	$160-190
	Single	$130
	Child	-

Of course we have fantastic scenery and very comfortable rooms. Wonderful wineries, beaches and markets all within easy reach. What else could you want? Ambience? Oodles of that. Good Food? Home cooking with produce from the garden or a variety of Restaurants and Cafes nearby. Above all else a warm and friendly welcome.

Feel at home and join us for a cup of tea or a glass of wine. Wander in the gardens and play with the dog, who loves visitors. Or just sit and enjoy the changes as the tide ebbs and flows.

Bedrooms	Qty
Double	2
Twin	
Single	
Bed Size	**Qty**
Super King	1
Queen	1
Double	
King Single	2
Bathrooms	**Qty**
Ensuite	2
Private	
Guest Share	

WARKWORTH COUNTRY HOUSE

18 Wilson Road, RD 1, Warkworth
Ph/Fax (09) 422 2485, Mobile 027-600 1510
email: info@warkworthcountryhouse.co.nz
www.warkworthcountryhouse.co.nz

Features & Attractions

- *Private entrance and patio*
- *Each room with ensuite*
- *TV in each room, WiFi available*
- *Generous breakfasts*
- *Near regional parks*
- *2 acres of bush and garden*

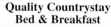

Quality Countrystay
Bed & Breakfast

	Double	$120-150
	Single	$95-110
	Child	

Warkworth Country House is situated on the fringe of Warkworth historic township. We have sheep and cows as neighbours with views of the rolling countryside towards the Mahurangi estuary. Bird life is abundant in our 2 acres of garden and bush. Warkworth is the ideal place for a peaceful and relaxing weekend getaway. After a leisurely breakfast, enjoy a stroll through the groves of kauri and bush at the Warkworth museum and Parry Kauri Park just 500 metres up the road. Drive into Warkworth for coffee or to Matakana for lunch at the wineries and potteries in the area. Beaches, Kawau Island, Scandrett or Tawharanui Regional parks are within easy reach. Let us make your stay enjoyable and refreshing.

DIRECTIONS: Approaching Warkworth from Auckland turn right into McKinney Rd signpost Warkworth Museum/Parry Kauri Park,then turn left into Wilson Road.

Bedrooms	Qty
Double	1
Twin	1
Single	
Bed Size	**Qty**
King	
Queen	1
King/Single	
Single	2
Bathrooms	**Qty**
Ensuite	2
Private	
Guest Share	

THE AMBERS LUXURY B&B

146 Pine Valley Road, Silverdale, Auckland
Ph (09) 426 0015, Fax (09) 426 3287
email: gerard@the-ambers.co.nz
www.the-ambers.co.nz

Tariff : N.Z. Dollars	
Double	$250
Single	$160
Child	$80

Bedrooms	Qty
Double	3
Twin	1
Single	

Bed Size	Qty
Super King	2
King	3
Queen	
Double	
Single	

Bathrooms	Qty
Ensuite	4
Private	
Guest Share	

Charming European Country House

Features & Attractions

- *Georgian country house*
- *Elegant & Romantic*
- *Close to golf, Snow Planet*
- *Orewa Beach close by*
- *Private and tranquil*
- *Superb healthy breakfast*
- *Pre dinner wine & canapés*
- *Wireless internet/email*

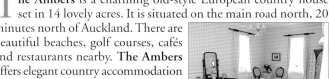

The **Ambers** is a charming old-style European country house set in 14 lovely acres. It is situated on the main road north, 20 minutes north of Auckland. There are beautiful beaches, golf courses, cafés and restaurants nearby. **The Ambers** offers elegant country accommodation inclusive of European-style cooked breakfast. Guests have full use of the library which features a large comfortable desk, hundreds of books and fast broadband, internet access. We have four double bedrooms, three with their own ensuites. Choose from our elegant "Regency Room" or French-style "Blue Room" both on the 1st floor, or our romantic attic suite with antique clawfoot bath. The two attic rooms make an ideal family suite. A recent addition has been the "Gite"; a self-contained unit in the garden, ideal for a quiet weekend away. We look forward to welcoming you into our home.

DIRECTIONS: From South take Motorway Silverdale exit, turn left onto SH17, then immediately right into Pine Valley Rd. We are 300m down the hill in the first bend. From North on Motorway turn right into SH17. From Orewa cross Motorway into SH17. Proceed as above.

The Ambers Luxury B&B

49

BAYVIEW MANLY BED & BREAKFAST

1 Beach Road Manly Village, Whangaparaoa Peninsula
Hibiscus Coast, North Auckalnd
Ph/Fax (09) 428 0990, Mobile 027-280 8346
email: bayviewmanly@xtra.co.nz
www.bayview-manly.co.nz

Features & Attractions

• *Auckland Airport 1hr South*	• *Wireless Internet Access*
• *Bay of Islands 3hrs North*	• *Guest lounge & patio*
• *Rotorua 3hrs South*	• *Golfing, bird sanctuaries*

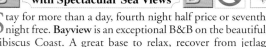
Quality Bed & Breakfast with Spectacular Sea Views

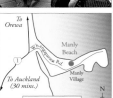

	Double	$145-195
	Single	$135-185
	Child	

Stay for more than a day, fourth night half price or seventh night free. **Bayview** is an exceptional B&B on the beautiful Hibiscus Coast. A great base to relax, recover from jetlag and take in the wide range of nearby attractions. Ideal for international arrivals/departures. Midway between Rotorua and Pahia. Set above Manly beach and adjacent to Manly Village's excellent restaurants. Uncrowded beaches, golf courses, bush walks, ferries to Tiritiri Matangi bird sanctuary, Auckland City, Kawau Island. Sailing, kayaking, vineyards, charter fishing, indoor snow skiing etc. Two rooms with balconies and seaviews. All equipped with TVs and fridges. Complimentary bottle of wine and nibbles on arrival. Hosts Carolyn, Arnold and Steven will help make your stay a happy one.

Bedrooms	Qty
Double	3
Twin	1
Single	
Bed Size	**Qty**
King/Twin	1
Queen	2
Double	
Single	
Bathrooms	**Qty**
Ensuite	2
Private	1
Guest Share	

THE SHEEP & SHAG

6A Roberts Road, Matakatia, Whangaparaoa
Ph (09) 428 5256, Mobile 021-645 485
email: info@sheepandshag.co.nz
www.sheepandshag.co.nz

Features & Attractions

• *Panoramic views*	• *Private entrances & patio*
• *20m solar-heated pool*	• *Golf, swimming, boating*
• *Purpose-built in 2001*	• *Tiritiri bird sanctuary*

Superior Bed & Breakfast Self-contained Apartment

	Double	$145-165
	Single	$125
	Child	neg

Relax around the pool in our sunny, modern facility, on a lifestyle block on the beautiful Hibiscus Coast. Approximately 30 min. from downtown Auckland and close to shops, restaurants, beaches and golf courses.
The Sheep and Shag is a luxurious contemporary home with panoramic views. The separate accommodation wing is on one level with external access to each room, plenty of off-street parking (boats welcome) and a 20 metre solar heated swimming pool. Guest lounge with Wifi, Sky TV, DVD, and guest laundry available. Discounts for long term stays. Early check-in or late checkout by arrangement.

Bedrooms	Qty
Double	3
Twin	
Single	
Bed Size	**Qty**
King	
Queen	3
Double	
Single	2
Bathrooms	**Qty**
Ensuite	3
Private	
Guest Share	

MILFORD HOUSE

34 Milford Road, Milford, Auckland 0620
Ph (09) 486 6033, Mobile 021-104 7301
email: jimliz44@hotmail.com
www.milfordbbnewzealand.com

Features & Attractions

- *Walk to cafés, restaurants, shops*
- *Beach at end of road*
- *10 min to Auckland city*
- *Broadband*
- *All dietrary needs catered for*
- *Guest lounge/ dining rooms*

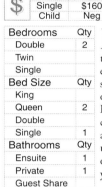

$	Double	$175-185
	Single	$160
	Child	Neg

**Boutique Bed & Breakfast
Convenient Location**

Bedrooms	Qty
Double	2
Twin	
Single	
Bed Size	**Qty**
King	
Queen	2
Double	
Single	1
Bathrooms	**Qty**
Ensuite	1
Private	1
Guest Share	

Milford House is a 'very convenient place to stay'. Situated in the heart of Milford it is close to all the places that will make your holiday/business sojourn a pleasurable experience. We have two large queen bedrooms, each with seated bay windows and TV. Relax in your own lounge with open fire (in winter) and big screen TV. Delicious continental/ English breakfasts are served in the dining room or private courtyard. Selections of teas/coffees, fresh fruit and biscuit bars are always available. Milford has many cafes/ restaurants, plus up market shopping mall, shops, beach, banks and transport only a few steps away. Liz and Jim look forward to welcoming you to **Milford House** for your relaxing, enjoyable stay.

'MY PLACE'
BED & BREAKFAST

2/35 Calypso Place, Rothesay Bay,
North Shore City, Auckland
Ph/Fax (09) 479 4408, Mobile 027 859 5235
email: slowtravel@xtra.co.nz
www.slowtravel.co.nz/auckland-bed-and-breakfast/

Features & Attractions

- *Stunning 180° views*
- *Luxurious, sunny*
- *Private sitting room*
- *Glorious sunrises*
- *Close to travel links*
- *Tour guide available*

$	Double	$150-190
	Single	$115-145
	Child	n/a

**Stylish Homestay in
Peaceful Garden Setting**

Bedrooms	Qty
Double	1
Twin	
Single	
Bed Size	**Qty**
Super King	1
Queen	
Double	
King / Single	2
Bathrooms	**Qty**
Ensuite	1
Private	
Guest Share	

Welcome to '**My Place**' – the perfect spot to stop, relax and enjoy all Auckland has to offer. Set in North Shore's glorious East Coast Bays, you're just minutes away from gorgeous beaches that look out to the gulf's magical islands. Walk the coastal paths, soak up the atmosphere at local cafes, and meander your way through your holiday. I love the idea of slow travel – taking the time to enjoy every pleasure on your journey. And at '**My Place**', that's what you'll do – a stylish home away from home in your private suite with panoramic views, delicious cooked or continental breakfast made from the finest local produce, as well as the bonus of a personal tour guide if you need it. Discover Auckland's natural beauty, food, wine, markets, art, shopping… whatever your heart desires. So come and enjoy '**My Place**'.

DIRECTIONS: '**My Place**' Bed and Breakfast can be found on Google Maps. Just type in '**My Place**' Bed and Breakfast, Calypso Place, North Shore, Auckland

COATESVILLE LAVENDER HILL

11A Beacon Road, Coatesville, Auckland
Ph/Fax (09) 412 5275
Mobile 021-728 051
email: tricia@lavenderhill.co.nz
www.lavenderhill.co.nz

Features & Attractions

- *Wine trails*
- *Close to city*
- *Country markets*
- *A range of leisure activities*
- *Wedding venues*
- *Swimming - West & East coasts*

VISA
MasterCard
AMERICAN EXPRESS
eftpos
bankcard
JCB

Luxury Bed & Breakfast

Double	$150-200
Single	$100-120
Child	$50

Bedrooms	Qty
Double/Twin	4
Twin	
Single	

Bed Size	Qty
S King/Twin	4
Queen	
Double	
Single	

Bathrooms	Qty
Ensuite	3
Private	1
Guest Share	

Coatesville Lavender Hill is nestled amongst eight acres of organic lavender, olive and lemon groves. We have four spacious bedrooms, which can be set up as double or twin rooms. Each room has its own ensuite bathroom. The upstairs bedrooms have views to the Auckland City skyline. Continental breakfast is included in the room rate or, if you prefer, a cooked breakfast menu is available. Lunch, dinners and BBQs can be catered for if pre-arranged. Tea and plunger coffee are complimentary and Italian espresso coffees can be made on request (a small charge applies). Guests are welcome to use the spa and swimming pools at the B&B. We provide wireless internet. During your stay you are welcome to browse our gift shop, visit our distillery, or just relax and enjoy the peaceful views of Riverhead Forest and the Upper Harbour.

'Kiwis' love their coffee culture.

BIRDWOOD HOUSE

12A Moore St, Hillcrest, North Shore, Auckland
Ph (09) 418 1612, Fax (09) 480 0407
Mobile 027-477 7722
email: barbie@birdwood.co.nz
www.birdwood.co.nz

Tariff : N.Z. Dollars	
Double	$150-170
Single	$130-150
Child	n/a

Qty	Bedrooms
3	Double
	Twin
	Single

Qty	Bed Size
	Super King
	King
2	Queen
1	Double
	Single

Qty	Bathrooms
2	Ensuite
1	Private
	Guest Share

           Elegant Bed & Breakfast Accommodation

DIRECTIONS:
From motorway just north of Harbour Bridge, take exit 421, drive to top of Onewa Rd, turn right into Birkenhead Ave. Moore St. is 1st on right after lights at Pupuke Rd. 12A is 150m down the hill on the left.

Features & Attractions

- *Native bush and birds*
- *Breakfast our speciality*
- *Quiet, tranquil location*
- *Sunny verandas & courtyard*
- *City 10min., bus close by*
- *Elegant, well appointed bedrooms and guest lounge*
- *Bush walks, golf course, beaches*

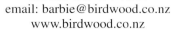

Barbie Bell, ex Birdwood House Parnell, and husband Dr David Scott, invite you to share their newly renovated **Birdwood House** in Hillcrest on Auckland's North Shore. The colonial farmhouse style villa, wrapped with verandas, and a courtyard, is set amongst native bush and birds. Guests are offered three tastefully furnished bedrooms with best quality beds and cotton bed linen, wool duvets, underlays and pillows, TV, robes and tea/coffee. The modern bathrooms are tiled, with under-floor heating and one has a claw-foot bath. Breakfast, served in our formal dining room, or on the veranda, has an emphasis on home-made cuisine, an elegant gourmet affair with linen napkins, candles and silver cutlery, described by a previous guest as "A dinner-party at breakfast time!" More than fifteen good restaurants less than five minutes away. Enjoy a port wine while listening to music or reading a book from our library. Barbie will be delighted to reacquaint herself with previous **Birdwood** guests.

PANORAMA HEIGHTS BED & BREAKFAST

42 Kitewaho Road, Swanson, Waitakere City
Ph (09) 832 4777
email: nzbnb4u@clear.net.nz
www.panoramaheights.co.nz

Features & Attractions

- *Dinner on request*
- *30 min to Auckland city*
- *Kumeu Wineries 16km*
- *45 min to Airport*
- *Train to city*
- *Shopping centres 10 min*

	Double	$200
	Single	$180
	Child	

Bed & Breakfast With a Little Indulgence

Bedrooms	Qty
Double	2
Twin	1
Single	
Bed Size	**Qty**
King	
Queen	2
Double	
Single	2
Bathrooms	**Qty**
Ensuite	3
Private	1
Guest Share	

Paul and Allison invite you to visit and share our extremely special location high in the Waitakere Ranges with tranquility, privacy and magnificent panoramic views across Native Rainforest to Auckland City and Rangitoto Island beyond. Explore 250km walking/hiking trails in surrounding Regional Park, West Coast beaches, (Piha, Karekare, Bethells, Muriwai) Wineries, two scenic golf courses. Train to city is nearby. Excellent quality accommodation is here for you to enjoy. Your hosts who reside next door, encourage relaxation while we spoil you. Unwind on the deck or in the spacious lounge. If time permits, let us take you on a bush walk and show some of the local flora and fauna. We serve a delicious '**Panorama**' breakfast in the dining room. *You'll love it here.*

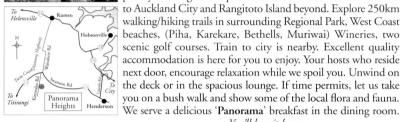

EASTVIEW

2 Parkside Road, Hobsonville, Auckland
Ph (09) 416 9254,
Mobile 027-437 3400
email: enquiries@eastview.co.nz
www.eastview.co.nz

Features & Attractions

- *Stunning day and nightime views*
- *Quiet and restful location*
- *Extra person discounts*
- *Delightful local restaurants*
- *15 min. to Auckland City*
- *Divine breakfasts*

	Double	$120-134
	Single	$80-100
	Child	$30

Bed & Breakfast/ Homestay With Panoramic Views

Bedrooms	Qty
Double	2
Twin	1
Single	
Bed Size	**Qty**
King	
Queen	2
Double	
Single	2
Bathrooms	**Qty**
Ensuite	
Private	2
Guest Share	

Eastview, so easy-to-find from the airport and travel routes north and south, is located ideally for exploring Auckland. Just the place to unwind at the end of a long journey or a day of sightseeing. Relax in the comfort of **The Marina Suite**, bathed in all-day sun, opening onto a colourful garden. This area has two bedrooms (one queen, one twin), a private bathroom and a comfortable lounge (with studio kitchen). **Rosie's Retreat** offers a queen-size bedroom plus private bathroom. An inviting sunny lounge is available for your use and a log fire for winter evenings. From **Eastview** discover superb beaches, rainforest-clad hills, gannet colonies, golf courses, thermal pools or harbour excursions. Handy to Kumeu wineries (popular wedding venues). Marina close by… catch a ferry to the city.

DIRECTIONS: **From city/south** take SH16. Turn right T-intersection onto Hobsonville Rd.
SH18. 6th street on right Westpark Drive, 2nd left Parkside Road.
From north take SH18 Greenhithe/Upper Harbour highway into Hobsonville Rd.

THE BIG BLUE HOUSE

103 Garnet Road, Westmere, Auckland
Ph (09) 360 6384, Mobile 021-884 662
email: info@thebigbluehouse.co.nz
www.thebigbluehouse.co.nz

Features & Attractions

- *Close to city centre*
- *Panoramic views*
- *Swimming pool & spa*
- *Spacious comfortable rooms*
- *Near Ponsonby cafés & restaurants*
- *Adjacent to zoo & parks*

$	Double	$150-180
	Single	$80-140
	Child	$10-20

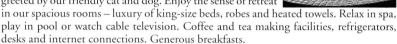

Be 'At Home' in Comfort

Bedrooms	Qty
Double	2
Twin	
Single	1
Bed Size	**Qty**
King	2
Queen	
King/Single	1
Single	1
Bathrooms	**Qty**
Ensuite	1
Private	
Family Share	2

Kate and Lynne warmly invite you to share their unique Homestay B&B close to central city and harbour. Be greeted by our friendly cat and dog. Enjoy the sense of retreat in our spacious rooms – luxury of king-size beds, robes and heated towels. Relax in spa, play in pool or watch cable television. Coffee and tea making facilities, refrigerators, desks and internet connections. Generous breakfasts.

Take an easy stroll to cafés, restaurants, Auckland Zoo or Western Springs Park. Shop at nearby Ponsonby or hop on the bus to city centre (15 minutes). We have a range of rooms to suit your needs. The very large 'Seaview Room' with ensuite, king bed (extra single) suits couples or families. The 'Mountview Room', large with king bed and shared bathroom (own basin and facilities) provides a very comfortable option. The 'Hideaway Room' offers a cosy retreat for the single traveller.

-"Make yourself at home!"

BRAEMAR ON PARLIAMENT STREET

7 Parliament Street, Auckland
Ph (09) 377 5463, Fax (09) 377 3056
Mobile 021-640 688
email: braemar@aucklandbedandbreakfast.com
www.aucklandbedandbreakfast.com

Features & Attractions

- *In downtown Auckland*
- *Walk to city attractions*
- *Non smoking indoors*
- *Heritage building*
- *Projector Television*
- *Pet poodles*

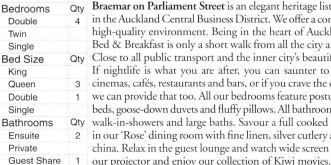

$	Double	$250
	Single	$180
	Suite	$350

Heritage Home in the Heart of Auckland

Bedrooms	Qty
Double	4
Twin	
Single	
Bed Size	**Qty**
King	
Queen	3
Double	1
Single	
Bathrooms	**Qty**
Ensuite	2
Private	
Guest Share	1

Braemar on Parliament Street is an elegant heritage listed home in the Auckland Central Business District. We offer a comfortable high-quality environment. Being in the heart of Auckland, our Bed & Breakfast is only a short walk from all the city amenities. Close to all public transport and the inner city's beautiful parks. If nightlife is what you are after, you can saunter to theatres, cinemas, cafés, restaurants and bars, or if you crave the quiet life, we can provide that too. All our bedrooms feature posturepaedic beds, goose-down duvets and fluffy pillows. All bathrooms feature walk-in-showers and large baths. Savour a full cooked breakfast in our 'Rose' dining room with fine linen, silver cutlery and bone china. Relax in the guest lounge and watch wide screen TV from our projector and enjoy our collection of Kiwi movies.

A Woodlands Retreat

18 Waiatarua Road, Remuera, Auckland
Ph (09) 524 6990
email: *jude.harwood@xtra.co.nz*
www.charmingaccommodation.co.nz

Tariff : N.Z. Dollars	
Double	$145-175
Single	$110
Child	n/a

Bedrooms	Qty
Double	2
Twin	1
Single	

Bed Size	Qty
Super King	
King	1
Queen	1
Double	
Single	2

Bathrooms	Qty
Ensuite	1
Private	1
Guest Share	

 Bed & Breakfast in Native Woods

Features & Attractions

- *Secluded, peaceful woodland setting*
- *On bus route*
- *Divine breakfasts*
- *Handy to Auckland airport*
- *Solar heated swimming pool*
- *Close to Ericcson stadium*
- *Wi Fi Internet*
- *Swim before breakfast*

Our three bedrooms overlook the solar heated swimming pool and lush native greenery. The ensuite king-sized room opens out to a private conservatory, and a private entrance to the pool. The 'Pool Room' with a private bathroom, opens directly to the pool – have a swim before breakfast. The smaller 'Deck Room' opens to the pool area, suitable for two friends, as it is a twin room. Each room has a coloured TV, tea/coffee making facilities, pool towels, heated towel rails, and hairdryers. A guest refrigerator is provided. The rooms are very quiet and secluded. Safe off-street car parking provided. Breakfasts are very special – we use fresh seasonal fruit, then a cooked breakfast of your choice, home-made jams and preserves, herbal teas/teas or percolated coffee, cereals, freshly squeezed juices, muesli.

Visitors book comments 2010: "*A magic stay – such a stunning place and superb hosts*", "*Wow, what a wonderful start to our Honeymoon – you spoilt us*", "*Gorgeous breakfast, great, divine hosts*", "*PERFECT, first class, I mean 11/10!!*", "*Tres Bon – Magnifique!!*"

Join us for a glass of New Zealand wine by the pool. Arrive as a guest and leave as a friend.

ArtHotel - The Great Ponsonby

30 Ponsonby Terrace, Ponsonby, Auckland
Ph (09) 376 5989, Fax (09) 376 5527
email: info@greatpons.co.nz
www.greatpons.co.nz

Tariff : N.Z. Dollars	
Double	$245-400
Single	$200-320
Child	

Bedrooms	Qty
Double	5
Twin	6
Single	
Bed Size	Qty
Super King	6
King	
Queen	5
Double	
Single	
Bathrooms	Qty
Ensuite	11
Private	
Guest Share	

A Small Art Hotel

Features & Attractions

- *Fast, free wifi*
- *Ipod docks in each room*
- *Easy stroll to 50+ restaurants*
- *Link bus passes every 10 mins.*
- *Walk or bus to city attractions*
- *Relax in garden or courtyard*
- *Off street parking*
- *Help with travel plans*

Delightful small hotel providing bed and breakfast. Just two minutes stroll to Ponsonby's vibrant cafés and shops, five minutes by taxi to the harbour and city centre. Breakfasts are legendary. Eleven rooms of varying size and price. All have everything you could need and have modern New Zealand and Pacific artworks. Courtyard studios are much bigger than villas and spacious suites and penthouse are twice as large again. The sitting room is a place to read, listen to the extensive CD collection or have a drink with friends. There is no tv. They are in the bedrooms. Ponsonby, is one of the earliest areas of Auckland and is also the trendiest part of town, a place where Aucklanders come to eat, to drink coffee and to have fun. Close to the city centre so, **The Great Ponsonby**, set in a large, beautiful garden is in the best place from which to explore Auckland. The hosts are committed to the environment and are passionate about sustainability. The first accommodation provider to extensively use eco products for guest amenities, laundry and cleaning and first Guest and Hosted to achieve an Enviro Gold award. For your city bus-route information go to www.linkbus.co.nz/tickets-and-timetables/route-information.php

ASCOT PARNELL

St Stephens Avenue, Parnell, Auckland
Ph (09) 309 9012, Fax (09) 309 3729
email: info@ascotparnell.com
www.ascotparnell.com

Tariff : N.Z. Dollars	
Double	$245-385
Single	$245-325
Child	n/a

Bedrooms	Qty
Double	
Twin	3
Single	

Bed Size	Qty
Super King	1
King	
Queen	2
Double	
Single	

Bathrooms	Qty
Ensuite	3
Private	
Guest Share	

  Bed & Breakfast in a 'Charming' atmosphere

Features & Attractions

- *Walk to all city attractions*
- *3 Luxury suites w/bathrooms*
- *50+ restaurants @ 300m*
- *Airport meet & greet*
- *Everthing on 1 floor*
- *Free wireless internet*
- *Secure indoor parking*
- *Garden, city & sea views*

Parnell Village, near downtown Auckland has an elegant, contemporary and quiet 'small B&B hotel' in a top central location at a moment's stroll from cafés, restaurants, and city attractions. Built amidst the sub-tropical gardens of this historic neighbourhood,

DIRECTIONS: From airport take road No. 20 motorway to Auckland city, exit at Queenstown Road, follow Auckland centre. Follow Manukau Road (Road No 12) to Parnell. Turn right at the Cathedral of the Holy Trinity into St. Stephens Avenue. The **Ascot Parnell** is 300m down on your left.

Ascot Parnell offers 3 generous suites, with large windows, garden or harbour views. Guest-rooms are beautifully appointed with queen or super-king beds, a luxury European bathroom, TV, climate control, free wireless internet and telephone. The spacious guest-lounge opens to a large, sunny balcony with spectacular harbour- and city skyline views. Breakfast is sumptuous with such choices as fresh organic fruit and yoghurt, Belgian crépes, French toast, gourmet omelettes made to order. Your friendly and helpful hosts and their aristocratic, well-mannered Salukis, will make certain your stay will be perfect. Ask for Bart to 'meet & greet' you at the airport. Top Tripadvisor listing.

58

OMAHU LODGE

33 Omahu Road, Remuera, Auckland
Ph/Fax (09) 524 5648, Mobile 021-954 333
email: info@omahulodge.co.nz
www.omahulodge.co.nz

Tariff : N.Z. Dollars	
Double	$230-325
Single	$170-200
Child	

Bedrooms	Qty
Double	4
Twin	1
Single	1
Bed Size	**Qty**
Super King/Twin	1
King	1
Queen	2
Double	
Single	2
Bathrooms	**Qty**
Ensuite	4
Private	1
Guest Share	

 A Boutique Resort

Features & Attractions

- *Spacious, private setting*
- *Solar-heated pool*
- *Spa, sauna, central heating*
- *Minutes to central city*
- *Walk to restaurants/cafés*
- *Parnell, Newmarket 5 min*
- *Free Wi Fi • 2010/11 Travellers Choice Award - Tripadvisor*

[map: To City, Market Road, Motorway, Remuera Road, Great South Road, Omahu Road, Omahu Lodge, To South]

Omahu Lodge offers luxury Bed & Breakfast accommodation with total privacy in a peaceful residential setting. The Lodge is very spacious with beautifully appointed bedrooms all with ensuites, fine bed linen, heated towels, bathrobes, slippers, hair dryers, ironing and tea/coffee facilities. Rooms have views of Cornwall Park, Mt Hobson, Mt St John and the eastern suburbs. Relax in the large lounge amongst the antiques or in the separate entertainment room with a large plasma television, DVD and CD player or enjoy the solar heated pool, sauna or spa. **Omahu Lodge** is a boutique resort. The city centre and Auckland's renowned harbour are just 10 minutes away by car. Remuera, Parnell and Newmarket's exclusive shopping, restaurants and antique shops are only minutes away. Walks in Cornwall Park, Mt Hobson and Mt St John add to the peaceful ambience of the suburban setting. A full sumptuous breakfast is served in the conservatory overlooking the pool, on the patio beside the pool or room service is available. Please refer to www.tripadvisor.com for guest comments.

The view from our balcony

AKARANA'S NAUTICAL NOOK - SAILING

23B Watene Crescent, Okahu Bay, Orakei, Auckland
Ph (09) 521 2544
email: nauticalnook@bigfoot.com
www.nauticalnook.com

Features & Attractions

- *Complimentary sailing!*
- *Free wireless internet*
- *Swimming beach 100m*
- *Perfect central location*
- *Pay cash 7.5% discount*
- *Early 'am' check-in available*

Homestay Bed & Breakfast
Harbour Yacht Sailing

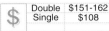

	Double	$151-162
	Single	$108

Friendly, relaxed, beachside hospitality overlooking park & harbour, 4.8km from downtown. 100m from Okahu Bay, fringed by Pohutukawa trees, for swimming and picnics. Gourmet cooked breakfast, served at Captain's Table. Stroll along picturesque promenade to Kelly Tarlton's Underwater World, Mission Bay beach (cafes and bars). Bus at door to Downtown, ferry terminal, museums, Eden Park (rugby) and Vector Arena. Unwind for 2-7 day stopover - our home is your home. Heaps to do in and around Auckland. Enjoy the thrill of a complimentary sail on the sparkling harbour on our 10.2m yacht. We have a wealth of local knowledge and international travel experience and can assist with sightseeing and travel planning. Take taxi or shuttle-van to our door. Welcome! Check our excellent website.

Bedrooms	Qty
Double	2
Twin	
Single	
Bed Size	**Qty**
King/Twin	2
Queen	
Double	
Single	
Bathrooms	**Qty**
Ensuite	2
Private	
Guest Share	

New Zealand has a vibrant café life

PARITAI DRIVE LUXURY ACCOMMODATION

163a Paritai Drive, Orakei, Auckland
Ph (09) 215 3217
Mobile 021 867 072
email: luxuryparitaidrive@gmail.com
www.charmingaccommodation.co.nz

Tariff : N.Z. Dollars	
Double	$250-350
Single	$250
Child	POA

Bedrooms	Qty
Double	2
Twin	
Single	
Bed Size	**Qty**
Super King	
King	2
Queen	
Double	
Single	
Bathrooms	**Qty**
Ensuite	3
Private	
Guest Share	

Luxury 4 U
The "No 1" Address in Auckland

Features & Attractions

- *1km to Kelly Tarltons*
- *Famous beaches 1-4km*
- *Auckland city 4.5km*
- *Mission Bay, cafés, movies*
- *Harbour cruises*
- *Relax, recover in luxury*
- *Magnificent views*
- *Gourmet breakfast experience*

163a **Paritai Drive** is Auckland's No. 1 prestigious address with magnificent views to the sky tower, city lights at night and Hobson Bay. The accommodation is apartment style sheer luxury! 1- 4km to world famous beaches and attractions, cafés, restaurants and bars.

Your hosts Delma and John Harrison have owned and operated some of the most successful bars, restaurants and pubs in Auckland. With 30 years experience, they are famous for their hospitality. Delma is a qualified chef, so breakfast will be a gourmet experience! Everything your heart desires is in Auckland - the city is alive! Complimentary N.Z. champagne awaits you on arrival.
You won't be disappointed!

DELAMORE LODGE

83 Delamore Drive, Matiatia, Waiheke Island
Ph (09) 372 7372
Fax (09) 372 7382
email: reservations@delamorelodge.com
www.delamorelodge.com

Tariff : N.Z. Dollars	
Double	$915-1315
Single	$915-1315
Apartment	$1800

Bedrooms	Qty
Suites	4
2-Bedroom Apartment	1

Bed Size	Qty
Super King	4
California King	2
Queen	
Double	
Single	

Bathrooms	Qty
Ensuite	
Private	6
Guest Share	

 Luxury at its Finest

Features & Attractions
- *Vineyard - Wine Tours*
- *Great fishing*
- *Excellent golf*
- *Art Tours*
- *Kayaking*
- *White sand beaches*
- *Jacuzzi, sauna & swimming pool*
- *Health and beauty therapy rooms*

Advance booking
highly recommended

Inspired by hours spent on the land, the timeless romance of the Mediterranean, and the image of a Maori bone fishhook (matau), local architect Ron Stevenson together with the owner, Roselyn Barnett-Storey, has designed a remarkable building that affords breathtaking views, sensuality, and a oneness with its unique environment. A sweeping stairway links the dramatic entrance directly to the library, and on to the spacious guest lounge and dining area. From the library you can also wander into the central courtyard which features a tropical rock pool and waterfall, a deep, cave-like Jacuzzi, a sauna, health and beauty therapy rooms, and a wine cellar. The courtyard in turn cascades into the striking, Italian-style fireplace and outdoor dining area which is flanked by the lounge and the four luxurious suites. Our newly completed Infinity swimming pool overlooking the Hauraki Gulf completes the picture of relaxation and luxury, soak in the Jacuzzi and then flow into the pool for a glass of champagne….luxury at its finest!

❖ Also we have a stunning luxury two bedroom apartment now available.

HILLPARK HOMESTAY

16 Collie Street, Hillpark, Manurewa, Auckland
Ph (09) 267 6847, Fax (09) 267 8718
Mobile 021-207 2559
email: stay@hillpark.co.nz
www.hillpark.co.nz

Tariff : N.Z. Dollars	
Double	$110
Single	$70
Child	$25

Bedrooms	Qty
Double	1
Twin	2
Single	

Bed Size	Qty
Super King	
King	
Queen	1
Double	
Single	4

Bathrooms	Qty
Ensuite	1
Private	
Guest Share	1

        Bed & Breakfast Homestay

Features & Attractions

- *Friendly, helpful hosts*
- *Near to airport –15 min.*
- *Manukau City Centre*
- *Regional botanic garden*
- *Pacific events centre*
- *Tipapa events centre*
- *Close to motorway Nth/Sth*
- *Dinners available $20 pp*

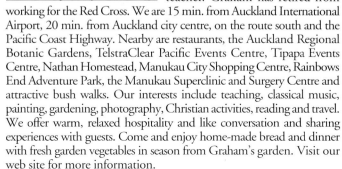

Welcome to our sunny, spacious home in Hill Park, a quiet, pleasant suburb of Manurewa, where our friendly Tonkinese cat will greet you. The beds are comfortable, with electric blankets and wool underlays. Katrine is an occasional primary school relief teacher. Graham has retired from working for the Red Cross. We are 15 min. from Auckland International Airport, 20 min. from Auckland city centre, on the route south and the Pacific Coast Highway. Nearby are restaurants, the Auckland Regional Botanic Gardens, TelstraClear Pacific Events Centre, Tipapa Events Centre, Nathan Homestead, Manukau City Shopping Centre, Rainbows End Adventure Park, the Manukau Superclinic and Surgery Centre and attractive bush walks. Our interests include teaching, classical music, painting, gardening, photography, Christian activities, reading and travel. We offer warm, relaxed hospitality and like conversation and sharing experiences with guests. Come and enjoy home-made bread and dinner with fresh garden vegetables in season from Graham's garden. Visit our web site for more information.

DRURY HOMESTEAD

349 Drury Hills Rd, RD1, Drury
Ph (09) 294 9030, Fax (09) 294 9035
Mobile 021-157 6531
email: druryhomestead@gmail.com
www.charmingaccommodation.co.nz

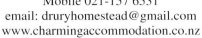

Tariff : N.Z. Dollars	
Double	$140
Single	$90
Child	neg

Bedrooms	Qty
Double	3
Twin	1
Single	

Bed Size	Qty
Super King	
King	
Queen	3
Double	
King/Single	2

Bathrooms	Qty
Ensuite	3
Private	1
Guest Share	

Drury Homestead

**Country Paradise
Bed & Breakfast**

Features & Attractions

- *Quiet, rural setting*
- *Native bush & stream*
- *5 min. off State Highway 1*
- *Discount for 3 days plus*
- *Character-filled colonial home*
- *Nearby local restaurants*
- *Carolyn's breakfast highly recommended*
- *Central Auckl. 35min/ Airport 20min*

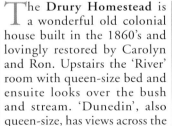

The **Drury Homestead** is a wonderful old colonial house built in the 1860's and lovingly restored by Carolyn and Ron. Upstairs the 'River' room with queen-size bed and ensuite looks over the bush and stream. 'Dunedin', also queen-size, has views across the countryside. 'Cape Reinga' has twin king/single beds and private bathroom complete with shower, toilet and clawfoot bath. Downstairs the 'Lily' room has kitchen facilities, queen bed and ensuite and with its own entrance and veranda, is ideal for longer stays. We discount for stays 3 days and over. A cot and pullout beds are available.

We are situated on a rural block minutes from the motorway, 35 minutes from Auckland central and 20 minutes from the airport. We love our lifestyle here and would like to make your stay truly memorable. Family cat and dog.

REGIS PARK BED & BREAKFAST
91 Beatty Road, Pukekohe
Ph/Fax (09) 238 7193, Mobile 021-936 017
email: eview@slingshot.co.nz
www.regispark.com

Tariff : N.Z. Dollars	
Double	$140-180
Single	$120-160
Child	

Bedrooms	Qty
Double	4
Twin	
Single	

Bed Size	Qty
Super King	1
King	1
Queen	2
Double	
King Single	2

Bathrooms	Qty
Ensuite	1
Private	1
Guest Share	1

 Luxury Bed & Breakfast and Self-contained Unit

Features & Attractions

- *Delightful Pukekohe country setting*
- *20-30 mins from Auckland Int'l Airport*
- *Touch of elegance*
- *Guest lounge*
- *Breakfast options*
- *Glenbrook Vintage Railway*
- *Hunua Falls*
- *6 nearby golf courses*

Here you will find true NZ hospitality with a warm friendly and relaxing environment. Enjoy every home comfort with a touch of elegance - offering four beautifully presented bedrooms - all with their own individual style and points of difference. Relax in the comfort of one of our delightful lounges offering large LCD TVs and DVD. There is also an option of a self contained unit available, comprising of large lounge, dining, kitchen, bedroom and ensuite for those wishing to have a complete home away from home at a weekly rate of $630. For breakfast enjoy a fresh fruit platter, cereals and yoghurt, toast and spreads. Available on request we also offer a gluten free or cooked breakfast option. Enjoy our delightful Pukekohe country setting with the convenience of being only 20-30 minutes from Auckland International Airport and Manukau City.

WESTWIND HOMESTAY B&B

228 North Road, Mangatarata, Thames
Ph (07) 867 3305, Fax (07) 867 3356
Mobile 021-803 293
email: beds@westwindhomestay.co.nz
www.westwindhomestay.co.nz

Tariff : N.Z. Dollars	
Double	$140-160
Single	$90
Child	neg.

Bedrooms	Qty
Double	2
Twin	
Single	
Bed Size	**Qty**
Super King	2
King	
Queen	
Double	
King/Single	
Bathrooms	**Qty**
Ensuite	2
Private	
Guest Share	

DIRECTIONS: From north: Take exit 477, travel 35km south/east on SH2. Take RH fork at Coromandel intersection, continue for 5km on SH2. At Tirau/Tauranga turn off go straight ahead 100m on SH27. Turn right into North Road. Travel 2.28km.

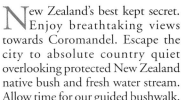

Rural Bed & Breakfast
1 Hour South of Auckland Airport

Features & Attractions

- *Fluffy pancake breakfast*
- *Native bushwalk & tour*
- *Woodturning workshop*
- *Insect screens*
- *Close to Miranda seabirds*
- *Only 1 hour to airport*
- *Complimentary afternoon tea*
- *Spacious guest rooms*

New Zealand's best kept secret. Enjoy breathtaking views towards Coromandel. Escape the city to absolute country quiet overlooking protected New Zealand native bush and fresh water stream. Allow time for our guided bushwalk. Expect to be pampered from the moment you arrive. Charming hosts will serve complimentary afternoon tea/real coffee plus extras. Collect healthy seasonal fruit, vegetables and free range eggs on the garden walk. Visit friendly pigs, chooks and beef cattle, Ian's Woodturning workshop and Linda's Paua studio. Choose fluffy pancakes for breakfast with great coffee. Stretch out in the SuperKing-size beds and cuddle up with soft feather duvets for the best nights sleep ever. Gateway to Coromandel's exciting white sandy Beaches, Rotorua's Thermal wonderland, Miranda seabird centre. Golf just down the road. Plenty to amuse and inspire. **Westwind** will not disappoint. Only 1 hour south of Auckland Airport.

BONNIEBRAE FARMSTAY

556 State Highway 27, Ngatea
Ph/Fax (07) 867 3387, Mobile 021-255 8005
email:rhyshilda@xnet.co.nz
www.charmingaccommodation.co.nz

Tariff : N.Z. Dollars	
Double	$120
Single	$85
Child	neg.

Bedrooms	Qty
Double	1
Twin	1
Single	

Bed Size	Qty
Super King	
King	1
Queen	1
Double	
Single	2

Bathrooms	Qty
Ensuite	2
Private	2
Guest Share	

Quality Farmstay
Spectacular Views

Features & Attractions

- *Gateway to Coromandel*
- *Dinner by arrangement*
- *Auckland airport 1hr*
- *Delicious homebaking*
- *Relaxed family atmosphere*
- *Many tourist attractions nearby*
- *Private entrances & ensuites*
- *Experience award-winning farm*

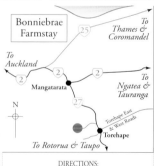

DIRECTIONS:
See map. We are on SH27 - Gate 556
(either 5.5 km south of Mangatarata,
or 2km north of Torehape).

This is a farmstay not to be missed. A beautiful 450 acre rolling sheep and beef farm with amazing views and also winners of

the Environmental Wildlife Habitat Enhancement Award. We farm Romney ewes and Dairy grazers. We offer home-grown lamb, beef,

pork, produce from our vegetable garden and delicious home-baking. Try our free-range eggs for breakfast or home-made yoghurt and preserved fruits from our organic orchard. Both rooms have been crafted from trees grown on our farm, they also have TV, radio, hairdryers and tea/coffee making facilities. Bar fridge also available for your use.

This farm has fenced wetland and duck ponds all beautifully planted, native bush and natural streams. Try **Bonniebrae Farmstay** for a very warm and welcoming Scottish/Kiwi experience.

68

THE HEIGHTS BED & BREAKFAST

300 Grafton Rd, Thames, Coromandel Peninsula
Ph (07) 868 9925
Mobile 021-150 9642
email: info@theheights.co.nz
www.theheights.co.nz

Tariff : N.Z. Dollars	
Double	$199-230
Single	$189-215
Child	

Bedrooms	Qty
Double	2
Twin	
Single	
Bed Size	Qty
Super King	1
King	1
Queen	
Double	
Single	
Bathrooms	Qty
Ensuite	2
Private	
Guest Share	

  The Views Go On Forever...

Features & Attractions

- Beaches, fishing, sea
- Hot Water Beach
- Hiking, eco-tours, birds
- Ancient kauri groves
- Arts, crafts, dining
- Historic gold rush towns
- Scenic railroads
- Explore the Coromandel

Photos can't do justice to our panoramic views of sea, mountains and historic Thames. The short climb to Te Moana Room gives you the best views in the house, while gardenview Te Koru Room has a cosy fireplace and patio hot tub. Relax in luxury with your own private deck or patio, private entrance, ensuite, king bed, fine linens, tea making, fridge, TV/DVD, free WIFI and guest lounge. A warm welcome from our friendly cats and special touches like homemade cookies, turndown service and breakfast in our romantic garden make a memorable stay. (We're Qualmark 4 Star Plus B&B, Qualmark Enviro Silver accredited, and Finalists in the 2010 and 2011 AA Spirit of Hospitality Awards.) Discover the spectacular coastal drive, ancient kauri groves, great hiking, historic towns, crafts, fine dining, plus every imaginable way to enjoy the sea. Only 1.5 hours from Auckland, **The Heights** is ideal for your first or last night in NZ or as a home base for exploring the Coromandel.

DIRECTIONS: From SH25 in Thames, at BP turn onto Bank St. which becomes Parawai. Left at Grafton Rd. **The Heights** is on the right, across from Millington Pl.

KAEPPELI'S BED & BREAKFAST
40 Gray Avenue, Kuaotunu, RD 2, Whitianga
Ph (07) 866 2445, Mobile 027-656 3442
email: paradise@kaeppelis.co.nz
www.kaeppelis.co.nz

Features & Attractions
- *Atemberaubende Assicht*
- *Echt hausgemachtes Brot*
- *Ausgezeichnetes Essen*
- *Quiet, peaceful setting*
- *Unbeatable sea views from all rooms*
- *Breakfast in 'Panoramic Gazebo'*

Panoramic Coastal Paradise

Double	$130-190
Single	$95-140
Child	neg

Country living in style and comfort, with glorious sea views, privacy and character. Quiet sunny rooms with private decks. Tea & coffee making facilities. TV/DVD in each room. Kitchenette & BBQ for Guests use. Short walk to the beach. Beautiful bush walk. Breakfast is served in our panoramic gazebo or guests dining room, both with wonderful views. Jill's Swiss style bread makes a pleasant change from toast. A unique peaceful haven off the main road where you can relax and enjoy the natural beauty and tranquility of Kuaotunu. A nature lover's paradise. Choice of clean, safe, white, sandy beaches, fishing, tennis, kayaking, swimming, arts, crafts, cafés, golf and horse trekking all nearby. Children welcome. Pets to pamper. Ideal for exploring the Coromandel Peninsula. Swiss/German spoken. And our view? Simply the best!

DIRECTIONS:
In Kuaotunu west turn off SH 25 into Bluff Rd, across bridge, first left into Gray Ave, end of Gray Ave up hill on tar sealed driveway approx. 800 metres.

Bedrooms	Qty
Double	2
Twin	2
Single	
Bed Size	**Qty**
King	2
Queen	
Double	
Single	4
Bathrooms	**Qty**
Ensuite	4
Private	
Guest Share	

New Zealand has so many wonderful beaches.

KUAOTUNU BAY LODGE

8 State Highway 25, Kuaotunu
Ph/Fax (07) 866 4396
Mobile 027-601 3665
email: muir@kuaotunubay.co.nz
www.kuaotunubay.co.nz

Tariff : N.Z. Dollars	
Double	$295-310
Single	$270
Child	

Bedrooms	Qty
Double	3
Twin	1
Single	
Bed Size	**Qty**
Super King	
King	
Queen	3
Double	
King/Single	2
Bathrooms	**Qty**
Ensuite	3
Private	1
Guest Share	

**Boutique Accommodation &
Self Service Accommodation**

Features & Attractions

- *Affordable luxury*
- *Panoramic views*
- *Purpose-built*
- *Overlooking safe beach*
- *Golf nearby*
- *Central to all activities*
- *Decks own entrance*
- *2.5 hrs Auckland airport*

DIRECTIONS:
Just 18 km north of
Whitianga on State Highway 25.
Please phone for bookings
and easy directions.

Welcome to our elegant beach house, set in four hectares of bush and pasture, offering panoramic views of the Peninsula and Mercury Island. Savour a generous breakfast watching the waves. The safe, sandy beach is just a short walk through the garden. Central to all activities a two or three day stay allows time to explore the whole peninsula. Bush/beach walks, kayaking, horse riding all within easy reach.

A choice of fine dining in Whitianga or at the local Golf Club. Having enjoyed this property since 1972 we offer our guests affordable luxury and a true 'Kiwi' experience. A tastefully decorated self-service unit is also available.

LEIGHTON LODGE

17 Stewart Place, Opito Bay, Whitianga
Ph (07) 866 0756
Mobile 027-230 0656 or 021-210 7608
email: welcome@leightonlodge.co.nz
www.leightonlodge.co.nz

Tariff : N.Z. Dollars	
Double	$160-200
Single	$130-145
Child	$25-35

Bedrooms	Qty
Double	2
Twin	
Single	
Bed Size	**Qty**
Super King	
King	
Queen	2
Double	1
Single	
Bathrooms	**Qty**
Ensuite	1
Private	1
Guest Share	

 **Bed & Breakfast
Self-contained Haven**

Features & Attractions

- *View of Mercury Islands*
- *Peace and tranquility*
- *Swimming boating & diving*
- *Special dinners*
- *Local gourmet seafood*
- *Maybe see the dolphins*
- *Outdoor fire & Pizza oven*
- *Great local fishing*

Leighton Lodge

Share the tranquil and peaceful environment of our Opito Bay paradise just two minutes walk from the stunning white sands of the beach. Our spacious deck commands panoramic views of the Great Mercury Islands. Enjoy local walks to the historic Maori Pa site,to Crayfish Bay or a beach ramble (our dog Kiri might lead the way). Enjoy safe swimming, diving, fishing and boating or play golf at a nearby course. From Opito Bay, explore the wider area. Cathedral Cove, Hot Water Beach, Coromandel Town or New Chum Beach. Alternatively, sit under a Pohutukawa tree with your book. Opito is a great place to release that city life stress. The tranquility will invigorate you.
We offer you either our Pacific Room, a large double bedroom with ensuite, or the privacy of the self contained Seahorse Suite. Sample the local seafood and Maire's delicious home cooked dinners. Picnic lunches can be prepared by arrangement. We are a non smoking family.

72

At Parkland Place

14 Parkland Place, Whitianga
Ph (07) 866 4987, Fax (07) 866 4946
Mobile 021-404 923
email: parklandplace@wave.co.nz
www.atparklandplace.co.nz

Features & Attractions

- *Very quiet and peaceful*
- *Close to beach*
- *Internet WiFi*
- *Close to town activities*
- *Two golf courses nearby*
- *Many marine activities*

$	Double	$165-225
	Single	
	Child	neg

Luxurious Bed & Breakfast
Quiet Location

Bedrooms	Qty
Double	5
Twin	1
Single	
Bed Size	**Qty**
Super King	3
Queen	2
Double	
King Single	2
Bathrooms	**Qty**
Ensuite	5
Private	
Guest Share	

Enjoy European hospitality in Whitianga's most luxurious hotel style B&B. Maria, a ships chef from Poland and NZ husband Guy, a master mariner, will make your stay a memorable experience. A single level purpose built house with private entry for guests. Large luxuriously appointed rooms with ensuite, quality linen, TV and writing desk. Magnificent continental breakfast. Superb dinner or BBQ by arrangement. Sunny, private picturesque outdoor area with spa pool. Large guest lounge with refreshment bar and satellite TV. Situated next to reserves and farmland ensures peace and quiet with no road noise and a few minutes level scenic stroll to the beach. Friendly hosts will help you plan your stay and make any bookings required. You will not regret coming.

DIRECTIONS: Take SH 25 to Whitianga. Drive through township along Buffalo Beach Road for 4 km.
Turn left into Centennial Drive, then first left into Parkland Place.

Charming **Places to Stay** in New Zealand

"Superb! ...independent travellers, whether from overseas or locals, should never travel New Zealand without a copy of this guide..."

Colin Moore, NZ Herald.

Buffalo Beach Luxury B&B

68 Buffalo Beach Road, Whitianga
Ph (09) 215 3217, Mobile 021 867 072
email: luxurybuffalobeach@gmail.com
www.charmingaccommodation.co.nz

Tariff : N.Z. Dollars	
Double	$180-250
Single	$250
Child	POA

Bedrooms	Qty
Double	2
Twin	
Single	
Bed Size	**Qty**
Super King	
King	
Queen	2
Double	
Single	
Bathrooms	**Qty**
Ensuite	2
Private	
Guest Share	

Luxury & Fun
29 Steps to Heavenly Buffalo Beach

Features & Attractions

- *Spectacular location*
- *Enjoy luxury and fun*
- *Gourmet breakfast experience*
- *30 years of hospitality knowledge*
- *29 steps to famous Buffalo Beach*
- *1 km walk or taxi to town centre*
- *Cafés, shops, restaurants, exciting tours*
- *NZ's No 1 Deep Sea Fishing Club*

68 **Buffalo Beach** Road is one of Whitianga's most spectacular accommodation spots. only 29 steps to famous Buffalo Beach, a 1km walk or taxi to the town centre where cafés,

restaurants, exciting shops and a comprehensive selection of world famous tours to Cathedral Cove, glass bottom boat trips, banana boats and Whitianga charter cruises await you.

Mercury Bay fishing club is recognised as the No.1 deep sea fishing club in New Zealand. (Entry to this club can be arranged) With over 30 years experience, hosts Delma and John Harrison have owned and operated many of the most successful restaurants, bars and pubs in Auckland. They are famous for their hospitality. Delma is a qualified chef, so breakfast will be a gourmet experience!

CAROLYN'S ON PARKLAND

13 Parkland Place, Whitianga
Ph (07) 866 2292, Fax (07) 866 2291
Mobile 0274 838 020
email: relax@carolynsonparkland.co.nz
www.carolynsonparkland.co.nz

Tariff : N.Z. Dollars	
Double	$195
Single	$175
Child	

Bedrooms	Qty
Double	1
Twin	
Single	

Bed Size	Qty
Super King	
King	
Queen	1
Double	
Single	

Bathrooms	Qty
Ensuite	1
Private	
Guest Share	

Upmarket Boutique B&B
Relax, Unwind, Rejuvenate

Features & Attractions

- *Private & Tranquil*
- *Tropical gardens*
- *Short stroll to beach*
- *Delicioius home baking*
- *Hot tub to relax & unwind*
- *Amazing 1 1/2 & 2 hr massages*
- *Wireless internet access, Sky TV*
- *Fish, cruise, kayak & more*

DIRECTIONS:
From SH 25 Whitianga
turn left onto Buffalo Beach Rd, then left
into Centennial Drive at Brophy's beach
and then 1st left into Parkland Place.

Relax and unwind in the beautiful and tranquil surroundings of this upmarket B&B with sunny decks, tropical gardens, a few minutes stroll to the beach and bordering a scenic reserve. With only one guest room with ensuite you will enjoy total peace and privacy and is ideal for the romantic getaway. The guestroom opens to sunny decks and tropical gardens. Sky TV, internal access garaging, complimentary tea and coffee facilities add to the comforts of your stay. **Carolyn's** specialties include delicious continental breakfasts and home baking, with dinner by arrangement. Specialty diets are also catered for. To add to the delights of your stay indulge in one of Carolyn's amazing 1½ or 2 hour massage treatments or relax and soothe the soul in the outdoor hot tub. Total bliss!! **Carolyn's on Parkland** is a truly memorable experience!!

COSY CAT COTTAGE
41 South Highway, (town end),Whitianga, Mercury Bay
Coromandel Peninsula
Ph (07) 866 4488, Fax (07) 866 4488
email: cosycat@xtra.co.nz

 www.cosycat.co.nz

Features & Attractions

- *Picturesque cottage*
- *Amusing catty decor*
- *A-la-carte breakfast*
- *Separate self-contained cottage*
- *Comfortable guest lounge*
- *Helpful, friendly service*

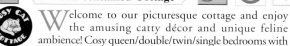

Bed & Breakfast
Self-contained Cottage

	Double	$105-125
	Single	$70-90
	Child	

Bedrooms	Qty
Double	2
Twin	1
Single	1
Bed Size	**Qty**
King	
Queen	2
Double	
Single	2
Bathrooms	**Qty**
Ensuite	2
Private	1
Guest Share	

DIRECTIONS:
1 km south of
the town centre.

Welcome to our picturesque cottage and enjoy the amusing catty décor and unique feline ambience! Cosy queen/double/twin/single bedrooms with ensuite/private bathrooms are available all year. Delicious a-la-carte breakfasts are complimentary and teas or coffees can be served when required. An easy drive may take you to Hot Water Beach, Cathedral Cove and other fascinating places. Friendly and helpful service is assured and you will probably like to meet Honey the cat and perhaps visit the "cat hotel" in the garden. A self-contained cottage is also available with two queen bedrooms, bathrooms and kitchen.

You're never far from water in New Zealand.

FERRY LANDING LODGE

1169 Purangi Road, Ferry Landing, Whitianga
Ph (07) 866 0445, Fax (07) 866 0792
Mobile 021-253 7244
email: info@ferrylandinglodge.co.nz
www.ferrylandinglodge.co.nz

Tariff : N.Z. Dollars	
Double	$180-260
Single	–
Extra person	$50-60

Bedrooms	Qty
Double	5
Twin	
Single	
Bed Size	**Qty**
Super King	
King	2
Queen	3
Double	
Single	2
Bathrooms	**Qty**
Ensuite	
Private	3
Guest Share	

 VISA **MasterCard**

Unique Historic Location
At Waters Edge

Features & Attractions

- *Guided Walk included in tariff*
- *Special organic breakfast*
- *Passenger Ferry - 2 min walk*
- *Cathedral Cove - 12 min drive*
- *Hot Water Beach - 12 min drive*
- *Peaceful garden / bush setting*
- *Wireless broadband*
- *90+ tripadvisor reviews*

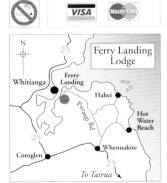

Ferry Landing Lodge, on the Coromandel Peninsula, is just a stones' throw from Whitianga shops and restaurants, and minutes from some of the most spectacular beaches in NZ. Experience genuine 'Kiwi' hospitality, peaceful surroundings and beautiful views in a convenient location. Bush walks, swimming, kayaking and fishing…on your doorstep. Take the ferryboat, enjoy fine dining, spectacular sunsets and a romantic walk home in the moonlight. Rob's local knowledge and heritage is matched in enthusiasm by Pam's energy and creativity in the garden and the kitchen. Breakfast includes fresh seasonal fruit from the garden, homemade muesli, preserves, jams and oven-baked muffins. Guided Historic Walk (Also available to the public). Rob, as a direct descendant of the first European settlers in Hahei, is passionate about the region. Join him on his daily bush walk to Historic Whitianga Rock. Visit the oldest stone wharf in NZ and view evidence of Maori fortifications, while following in the footsteps of Capt. Cook. Learn about early European settlement and the Kauri industry in Whitianga.

MUSSEL BED

892 Purangi Road, Cooks Beach, Whitianga
Ph (07) 866 5786, Fax (07) 866 5706
Mobile 027-234 8747
email: welcome@musselbed.co.nz
www.musselbed.co.nz

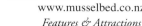

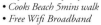

Features & Attractions

- *Hot Water Beach & Cathedral Cove 10mins*
- *Walk to "Go Vino Café" & "Eggsentric Café"*
- *Shakespeare Reserve walking track close by*
- *Kayak to Lonely Bay*
- *Cooks Beach 5mins walk*
- *Free Wifi Broadband*

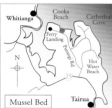

Bed & Breakfast Cottage Accommodation

Double	$175-275
Single	$150-225
Extra PP	$75

Bedrooms	Qty
Double	4
Twin	2
Single	
Bed Size	**Qty**
King	
Queen	4
King Single	2
Single	2
Bathrooms	**Qty**
Ensuite	5
Private	1
Guest Share	

"**Mussel Bed**" is just around the corner from Cathedral Cove and Hot Water Beach and only a short walk to beautiful Cooks Beach. Catch the little ferry to Whitianga and don't miss the very special "Lost Spring" for a hot swim & spa! Our guest wing has 3 luxurious suites each with tiled ensuites and private decks with TV/DVD, bathrobes, beach towels and home baking to tempt you everyday. Try our new breakfast menu of home-made muesli, honey & yoghurt with fresh fruit parfaits, a "daily hot dish" with freshly baked muffins, home-baked bread & pastries. **Mussel Bed Cottage** is self catering with a special breakfast hamper. Chris and Paul look forward to making your stay a special one!

FLAXHAVEN LODGE
995 Purangi Rd, Flaxmill Bay, Whitianga
Ph (07) 866 2676, Fax (07) 866 2396
Mobile 021-286 1088
email: welcome@flaxhavenlodge.co.nz
www.flaxhavenlodge.co.nz

Tariff : N.Z. Dollars	
Double	$210-260
Single	$200-230
Child	

Bedrooms	Qty
Double	2
Twin	
Single	
Bed Size	**Qty**
Super King	1
King	
Queen	1
Double	
King/Single	
Bathrooms	**Qty**
Ensuite	2
Private	
Guest Share	

**Luxury Coastal
B&B Accommodation**

Features & Attractions

- *Centrally located*
- *4 safe sandy beaches all within a short stroll*
- *Close to cafes restaurants*
- *Historic bush walks*
- *Boating kayaking fishing*
- *Purpose-built 2005*
- *Internet wi-fi*

Flaxhaven Lodge is set in 1.5 acres of gardens and green spaces, nestled alongside picturesque Flaxmill Bay. It is surrounded by tranquil countryside and native bush yet only minutes to Whitianga town via the quaint passenger ferry. Within a few minutes walk are 4 beautiful beaches each one different. Walk also to our local well-known "Eggcentric" restaurant, or experience superb eateries along Whitianga waterfront. Famous Cathedral Cove and Hot Water Beach are a 15 min. drive away. Purpose-built luxury accommodation is designed for guest relaxation, privacy and comfort with quality linens, fittings, private entrances and patios. Our Cottage has a queen bedroom, ensuite, livingroom and kitchenette. The private guest wing has a superking bedroom, sitting room with fridge/tea/coffee making, ensuite and separate toilet. Enjoy special breakfasts in our sunny kitchen with home-grown organic and free-range produce where possible. We will welcome you with warmth, help you unwind with refreshments and share with you our home and this beautiful part of the Coromandel coast.

79

Mercury Orchard Bed & Breakfast

141 Purangi Road, Whitianga
Ph (07) 866 3119, Fax (07) 866 3115
email: relax@mercuryorchard.co.nz
www.mercuryorchard.co.nz

Tariff : N.Z. Dollars	
Double	$165-185
Single	$120-140
Child	$20

Bedrooms	Qty
Double	2
Twin	
Single	1
Bed Size	**Qty**
Super King	
King	1
Queen	1
Double	
Single	2
Bathrooms	**Qty**
Ensuite	2
Private	
Guest Share	

   Peaceful Garden Cottages

 VISA MasterCard

Features & Attractions

- *Outdoor bath, swimming pool*
- *Private deck with BBQ*
- *Tranquil garden setting*
- *Bush walks*

- *Golf course nearby*
- *Hot Water Beach and Cathedral Cove 8min.*
- *Delicious breakfast*

DIRECTIONS:
14 km north of Tairua turn
into Hot Water Beach Road.
Please phone for further
directions.

Paua Bach and **Fig Tree Cottage** are nestled amongst 5 acres of peaceful country gardens and orchard. Two self-contained garden cottages, country-style luxury with French doors opening out into the orchard, crisp cotton bed linen, bath robes, fresh fruit, flowers and candles. Special to **Paua Bach** is an old fashioned outdoor bath. Watch the variety of our birdlife while enjoying a full breakfast brought out onto your private deck. Freshly squeezed orange juice, in-season fruit, home made muesli and our own free-range eggs.

Quiet and relaxing, perfect for that special anniversary or as a restful stay. The area is well known for crafts and gardens. Local activities include swimming, diving, bush walking, tramping, horse riding, fishing, kayaking, scenic boat cruises and golf. Cathedral Cove, Cooks and Hot Water Beaches are 7-8 min. drive. There are several good restaurants close by, alternatively BBQ your evening meal Kiwi style. We normally have fresh produce available from our garden. Meet our friendly sheep, kunekune pig, donkey, and two small dogs.

HOT WATER BEACH BED & BREAKFAST

48 Pye Place, Hot Water Beach
Ph (07) 866 3991, Fax (07) 866 3291
Mobile 027-479 9620
email: TKnight@xtra.co.nz
www.hotwaterbedandbreakfast.co.nz

Tariff : N.Z. Dollars	
Double	$180-260
Single	$160-240
Child	

Bedrooms	Qty
Double	2
Twin	
Single	
Bed Size	**Qty**
Super King	
King	
Queen	2
Double	
Single	
Bathrooms	**Qty**
Ensuite	2
Private	
Guest Share	

**Sea View
Bed & Breakfast**

Features & Attractions

- Spectacular beach views
- Close to Cathedral Cove
- Several cafés nearby
- Hot springs, easy walk
- Quality assessed accom.
- Kayak and boat trips
- Guests billiard table
- Fridge in rooms

Welcome to our modern beach house, enjoy delicious breakfasts on our huge sunny deck overlooking the sea and islands. On the beach below, dig a natural hot pool, swim, surf and boogie board. Go for a bush walk observing the native bird life or view the glittering night sky and glowworms.

We are happy to advise you about kayak-boat trips to Cathedral Cove viewing spectacular sea caves and blowholes also golf, diving, fishing and winery visits. Back at our home relax on the deck with coffee, tea or a cold drink and maybe the dolphins will come into the bay to play.

Your hosts Gail and Trevor Knight, are relaxed and easy going and we are members of the Bed and Breakfast New Zealand Association. We and our sociable dog and cat, look forward to welcoming you to our home.

DIRECTIONS:
Follow Hot Water Beach Road from State Highway 25 . Continue past Beach Shop. We are 50 metres on the right uphill.

81

WAIHI BEACH LODGE

170 Seaforth Rd, Waihi Beach,
Southern Coromandel
Ph (07) 863 5818, Fax (07) 863 5815
Mobile 021-657 888
email: info@waihibeachlodge.co.nz
www.waihibeachlodge.co.nz

Tariff : N.Z. Dollars	
Double	$295-350
Single	
Child	

Bedrooms	Qty
Double	4
Twin	
Single	
Bed Size	**Qty**
Super King	
King	3
Queen	1
Double	
Single	
Bathrooms	**Qty**
Ensuite	3
Private	1
Guest Share	

   Luxury Coastal Accommodation

Features & Attractions

- *Stunning sea and rural views*
- *Short 2 minute stroll to beach*
- *Four golf courses within 30mins*
- *Five local cafés*
- *Wireless internet connection*
- *Less than 2hrs - Auckland*
- *Central location for Coromandel*
- *Close to Karangahake Gorge*

Waihi Beach is a friendly seaside resort and one of the safest surf beaches in New Zealand and the gateway to both the Coromandel and Bay of Plenty. Our central location provides you with the flexibility to see the Coromandel and Rotorua from one base and we are only I ½ hrs from Auckland Airport. Surrounded by natural beauty, **Waihi Beach** offers a whole range of leisure opportunities from beach and gorge walks to golf and fishing. Or, if you prefer, relax and experience the many sea views available from the Lodge with a book from our

DIRECTIONS:
From North: Turn off SH2 to Waihi Beach, turn right at
roundabout, 1½ km on right
after shopping village. Cnr Seaforth Rd and Hanlen Ave
with main entrance off Hanlen
Ave. From South: Turn off SH2 to
Waihi Beach, turn left at roundabout,
400m on left. Proceed as above.

library. We have 3 king bedrooms with ensuites and a modern studio apartment with a queen size bed. 3 rooms have private entrances. All rooms are furnished with quality beds, cotton linen, bath robes, toiletries, hair dryers, televisions, DVD players and fridges. Scrumptious full breakfasts are served in the dining room or alfresco on one of the decks. **Waihi Beach** has great cafés for evening dining.

82

ARBOR LODGE

126c Woodcock Rd, Tamahere, Hamilton
Ph (07) 856 3820, Fax (07) 856 3825
Mobile 021-554 846
email: admin@arborlodge.co.nz
www.arborlodge.co.nz

Features & Attractions

- *Private country setting*
- *Midway Hamilton & Cambridge*
- *Hamilton gardens/river walks*
- *Lovely gardens*
- *Golf courses nearby*
- *Mystery Creek 6 mins*

Double	$145-185	
Single		
Child		

Self-contained Bed & Breakfast

Bedrooms	Qty
Double	1
Twin	
Single	
Bed Size	**Qty**
King	
Queen	1
Double	
Single	
Bathrooms	**Qty**
Ensuite	1
Private	
Guest Share	

Arbor Lodge is set in landscaped gardens on 11 acres and is ideally situated for Hamilton, Cambridge and Mystery Creek, the "Fieldays" venue. The location makes a convenient base for day trips to Rotorua, Waitomo Caves and beaches at Raglan and Tauranga. Guests can enjoy private, self-contained accommodation in a peaceful, country setting. Relax by the pool in summer or wander around the delightful gardens. The spacious air-conditioned studio offers adjoining dressing room, ensuite and well equipped kitchenette with fridge, microwave and complimentary beverages. Also included are wireless internet access, CD/radio, TV, DVD (selection of films), sofa and breakfast table for two. Continental breakfast and fresh fruit are provided in the room.

SAXON LODGE 'THE ORGANIC PLACE'

Rural No 266, Peacockes Road, RD 2, Hamilton
Ph (07) 843 3497, Fax (07) 843 3473
email: saxonlodge@ihug.co.nz
www.charmingaccommodation.co.nz

Features & Attractions

- *Dawn chorus*
- *Stylish one storey home*
- *Great gardens & orchard*
- *Comfortable beds*
- *Campervan facilities*
- *Handy to city & airport*

Double	$150	
Single	$130	
Child	$50	

Delightful Organic Homestay

Bedrooms	Qty
Double	
Twin	2
Single	
Bed Size	**Qty**
King	
Queen	
Double	
Single	4
Bathrooms	**Qty**
Ensuite	
Private	1
Guest Share	

Saxon Lodge, 'The Organic Place'

Saxon Lodge, is set on two acres just south of Hamilton. You wake up to the 'dawn chorus' – the birds greeting you and the morning. After a morning cup of herbal tea you can collect fresh eggs from our hens (the girls) and pick in season fruit for your breakfast. Our dog Sophie (a Pembroke corgi) and our cat Tara will help! You may have to chase the wild ducks, rabbits and pukekos (a native bird) out of your way! The house, designed by a local architect, is a stylish New Zealand single storey home with high raked timber ceilings and brick veneer. We love it and would like you to enjoy it too.

WATERS EDGE

100E Greenslade Road, Raglan
Ph (07) 825 0567, Fax (07) 825 0562
Mobile 027-648 6803
email: info@watersedge.co.nz
www.watersedge.co.nz

Features & Attractions

- *Stunning water views*
- *Beautiful garden setting*
- *Free wifi and satellite tv*
- *Visit Waitomo Caves*
- *Many artisans and cafés*
- *Surf, kayak, swim or laze!*

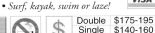

DIRECTIONS: Greenslade Road is 9 km past Te Uku SH23 on your right hand side, immediately after completing left hand bend signposted by 75km road sign

Waterfront Self-contained Cottage & Apartment

	Price
Double	$175-195
Single	$140-160
Child	

Comfort, peace, privacy, and helpful friendly hosts welcome you to romantic Moonlight Bay. Choose from two private holiday havens, nestled in extensive peaceful gardens and native bush, meandering down to the water. A New Zealand style beach cottage or modern apartment, furbished with flair and ambience (candles, fresh flowers, books, beverages and special touches, with breakfast option for weary travellers). Enjoy Raglan's many cafés, eclectic shops, artisan trail, world famous surf and attractions, golf course and gorgeous beaches, bush and mountain walks. Take a picnic and explore the harbour and waterfalls in our kayaks, fish from our dinghy, book a fishing charter or surf lesson. Relax on sun soaked decks or a scenic sunset cruise . . . leave refreshed and rested!

Bedrooms	Qty
Double	2
Twin	
Single	1
Bed Size	**Qty**
King	
Queen	2
Double	
Single	2
Bathrooms	**Qty**
Ensuite	1
Private	1
Guest Share	

KUA MAKONA

142 Reid Rd, Ngahinepouri, Ohaupo, Waikato
Ph (07) 825 2852, Fax (07) 825 2852
Mobile: 027-496 0064
email: themarcrofts@xtra.co.nz
www.charmingaccommodation.co.nz

Tariff : N.Z. Dollars	
Double	$135-155
Single	$100
Child	$50

Bedrooms	Qty
Double	2
Twin	1
Single	
Bed Size	**Qty**
Super King	
King	
Queen	2
Double	
Single	2
Bathrooms	**Qty**
Ensuite	1
Private	
Guest Share	1

VISA   MasterCard

 Countrystay Deer Farm

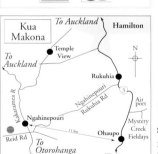

Features & Attractions

- Deer farm
- Elegant home, formal garden
- Quiet and relaxing
- Swimming pool & spa pool
- Central North Island location
- Auckland & Rotorua 1½ hr
- Fieldays & Kiwi House close by
- Waitomo Caves 40 minutes

Quiet rural setting with homestyle welcome. Centrally situated for tourist attractions, 90 minutes from Auckland Airport, Rotorua & Taupo. Waitomo Caves 40 minutes, Kiwi House 20 minutes away. National Fieldays, V8's and Hamilton Airport all close proximity. Transfers to and from Airport or Hamilton can be arranged.

We run a deer finishing unit. Surrounding district has traditional dairy and beef farms as well as a diverse range of horticulture. Award winning Viligrad vineyard close by and superb country golf course just down the road. Relax by a cozy fire in the formal lounge in the winter or cool off beside the pool in the summer or unwind in the outdoor spa pool. French doors open out into

the garden from all the tastefully furnished bedrooms. Laundry, Internet facilities and cot available. Cooked or continental breakfast included, dinner by request $65pp

ABSEIL BREAKFAST INN

709 Waitomo Caves Road, Waitomo Caves
Ph (07) 878 7815
email: abseilinn@xtra.co.nz
www.abseilinn.co.nz

Tariff : N.Z. Dollars	
Double	$140-180
Single	$130-140
Child	

Bedrooms	Qty
Double	3
Twin	1
Single	
Bed Size	**Qty**
Super King	
King	
Queen	4
Double	
Single	1
Bathrooms	**Qty**
Ensuite	4
Private	
Guest Share	

**Rural Splendour
Romantic Accommodation**

Features & Attractions

- *At the Waitomo Caves*
- *Blackwater rafting*
- *Bush walks*
- *Close to restaurants*
- *Spectacular rural views*
- *Romantic themed rooms*
- *Canopied queen beds*
- *Helen rocks*

DIRECTIONS:
Turn opposite the
Red Rabbit shearing shed.

Wanted: Guests full of the joy of life for the delightfully bijou **Abseil Breakfast Inn**. Applicants must have a hearty appetite for a leisurely breakfast of local delicacies – after all breakfast is our middle name. Mingling with other guests is required (in the guest lounge, on the deck or at the communal dining table in the morning) – can your tall stories better Helen's? Enjoyment of sunsets behind stunning rural scenery an advantage; wine glass in hand optional. Having an adventurous attitude towards the bedroom aspect of the stay is an essential; these are themed to the utmost skill and imaginative reach of the hostess, including the **Farm Room** with its spectacular views out over the Waitomo Valley, the **Bush Room** with its magnificent canopy, the **Swamp Room** with its bath built for two and a range of bath oils and candles, and the hairy but cuddly **Cave Room**. You must be adventurous – overly faint of heart will not make it up the driveway. And above all you must 'Approach with Enthusiasm'. Recommended by most good guide books and chance-met strangers. Fodor's pick 2010.

GLENELG
6 Curnow Place, Cambridge
Ph (07) 823 0084
email: glenelgbnb@ihug.co.nz
www.charmingaccommodation.co.nz

Features & Attractions

- *Ensuite accommodation*
- *Warm hospitality*
- *Quiet, peaceful setting*
- *Hamilton Airport 15 min*
- *Spa and air bath*
- *5 min to Lake Karapiro*

Double	$120	
Single	$85	
Child	$30	

Quiet Rural Outlook
B&B - Homestay

Bedrooms	Qty
Double	3
Twin	1
Single	
Bed Size	**Qty**
King	
Queen	3
Double	
King Single	2
Bathrooms	**Qty**
Ensuite	3
Private	1
Guest Share	

Cambridge, 15 km from Hamilton and 1 hour from Rotorua, is famous for its picturesque old English atmosphere and known as the "Town of Trees". If you are looking for a "Home away from Home", restful and away from the hustle, bustle and traffic noise, **Glenelg** is the place for you to be. We have a new, modern home in a quiet, peaceful setting with 200 roses in our garden. Breakfast is either cooked or continental with a menu to choose from – evening meals by prior arrangement. Guest laundry and off-street parking is available. We are in comfortable driving distance from the main tourist attractions: Mystery Creek Events Centre 10 min, Rotorua 1 hour, Waitomo Caves 45 min, Auckland or Taupo 2 hours.

Map: To Cambridge, Town Centre, To Rotorua, Golf Course, Waikato River, Cook St, Shakespeare St, Leamington Medical Centre, Browning St, To Karapiro, To Te Awamutu, Mystery Creek, Lamb St, To Karapiro, Milton St, Cowley Drive, Murray St, Cowley Drive, Glenelg, Curnow Place

---

RIVERSONG BED & BREAKFAST COUNTRYSTAY
213 Horahora Road, Tirau, Sth. Waikato
Ph/Fax (07) 883 1477, Mobile 027-642 3239
email: riversong.bb@xtra.co.nz
www.charmingaccommodation.co.nz

Features & Attractions

- *Relaxed rural setting*
- *Antiques, arts & crafts*
- *Water sports & golf*
- *Maungatautari Ecological Island*
- *Waikato River Trails*
- *Mystery Creek - Fieldays 30 min.*

Double	$110-140	
Single	$100	
Child	neg	

Bed & Breakfast Countrystay
Self-contained Accommodation

Bedrooms	Qty
Double	3
Twin	2
Single	
Bed Size	**Qty**
Super King	1
Queen	1
Double	1
KingSingle	2
Bathrooms	**Qty**
Ensuite	1
Private	1
Guest Share	1

You are assured a warm welcome at **Riversong** situated in the heart of the beautiful South Waikato with Lake Karapiro views. We are an ideal base for touring the central North Island, only 45 mins from Rotorua, Tauranga 50 mins, Hamilton Airport 30 min. Our cosy, fully equipped two bedroom unit (one queen and one twin) will ensure your comfort and privacy. Tariff for two bedroom unit $140 per night, $15 each extra person. The main house has three bedrooms, one double with ensuite, one twin and one double with private bathroom. Breakfast is full cooked or continental. Dinner by prior arrangement. Tea and coffee facilities in all rooms. Guest comments: *"Brilliant" home from home/ Excellent Hosts/Wonderful Hospitality/We'll be back.*

DIRECTIONS: Heading south turn right off SH 1. 500m south of Route 29 (Tauranga) Riversong is 2.13 km on left opposite lake. Right hand driveway.

Map: Riversong, To Matamata, To Tauranga, To Cambridge, Hamilton & Auckland, Lake Karapiro, Tirau, To Rotorua, To Arapuni, To Taupo

B&B@PANORAMA COUNTRY LODGE

901 Pacific Coast Highway (SH2), Katikati
Ph/Fax (07) 549 1882, Mobile 021-165 5875
email: mckernon@xtra.co.nz
www.panoramalodge.co.nz

Tariff : N.Z. Dollars	
Double	$180-200
Single	$140-150
Child	neg

Bedrooms	Qty
Double	2
Twin	1
Single	
Bed Size	**Qty**
Super King	
King	1
Queen	1
Double	
Single	2
Bathrooms	**Qty**
Ensuite	4
Private	1
Guest Share	

**Quality Bed & Breakfast
with Magnificient Sea Views**

VISA MasterCard

Features & Attractions

- *Stunning views/spectacular location*
- *Home cooked gourmet breakfasts*
- *Swimming pool/landscaped gardens*
- *Wireless Internet*
- *Beach, cafes & wineries close by*
- *Relaxed hospitality/room service*
- *Fabulous sun and moon risings*
- *Elegant and spacious rooms*

Discover the difference and experience a memorable stay at our wonderful rural retreat with spectacular views of the ocean from

each room, perfectly situated, just minutes to Waihi Beach or Katikati. Relax in spacious beautifully furnished private

suites, each with big beds, fine linens, french doors to swimming pool and terrace, TV, DVD, lounging and dining area, tea/coffee-making facilities, air-conditioning, robes and slippers, toiletries, gourmet breakfast served either in suite, terrace or dining room. Wander around 4ha of kiwifruit and avocado orchards, landscaped gardens, feed "our boys" the Alpacas. Great base for exploring the Coromandel or Rotorua, golf, fishing, wineries, lots to see and lots to do, come and have fun in the sun! We love it here...so will you! "*The view, the breakfast overlooking the bay, Barbara's hospitality, Phil's fabulous tour of the estate, the lovely room, the ambiance.......Panorama Lodge - we loved it all*" Pat & Jay Tressler, Illinois, USA

Cotswold Lodge Countrystay

183 Ongare Point Road, Katikati
Ph (07) 549 2110, Fax (07) 549 2109
email: relax@cotswold.co.nz
www.cotswold.co.nz

Tariff : N.Z. Dollars	
Double	$165-175
Single	$130
Child	

Bedrooms	Qty
Double	2
Twin	1
Single	

Bed Size	Qty
Super King	
King	
Queen	2
Double	1
Single	1

Bathrooms	Qty
Ensuite	3
Private	
Guest Share	

**Country Bed & Breakfast
– with a little Luxury**

Features & Attractions

- *Stunning country scenery*
- *Peace & tranquillity*
- *Hot tub for relaxation*
- *Abundant birdlife*
- *Scenic walks from Lodge*
- *Laundry available*
- *Wireless Internet*
- *Tours can be arranged*

To Waihi
Cotswold Lodge
Woodlands Rd
Kauri Pt. Rd
Ongare Pt. Rd
N
Willoughby Rd
Lindeman Rd
Tauranga Harbour
Katikati

We offer warm Kiwi hospitality and a little luxury in our rural home, just 8 min. north of Katikati Mural town and 15 mins.from Waihi Beach. Auckland is 2 hours away. Quality accommodation overlooking kiwifruit and avocado orchards, with views to the Kaimai Ranges. Expect to be pampered on arrival with a welcome cuppa and refreshments and rejuvenated by the time you leave. All rooms with ensuite bathroom, quality furnishings, hairdryers, bathrobes, etc. Guest refrigerator, tea and coffee facility available. Evening meals by prior arrangement. Watch the sunset while relaxing in the spa. Pétanque in the garden. Short stroll through the orchards and down to the harbour. Short distance by car to restaurants, golf, wineries, walking tracks, museum, beaches, arts and crafts, gardens, etc. Come and enjoy our piece of paradise or make us a base to explore the beautiful Bay of Plenty. – We have a friendly Labrador. We look forward to meeting you.

TRANQUILITY LODGE

325 Rea Rd, Katikati, Bay of Plenty
Ph (07) 549 3581, Fax (07) 549 3582
Mobile 027-452 2960
email: info@tranquilitylodge.co.nz
www.tranquilitylodge.co.nz

Tariff : N.Z. Dollars	
Double	$170
Single	$135
Child	

Bedrooms	Qty
Double	2
Twin	
Single	
Bed Size	**Qty**
Super King	
King	2
Queen	
Double	
Single	
Bathrooms	**Qty**
Ensuite	2
Private	
Guest Share	

     Tranquility at its Best

Features & Attractions

- *Generous warm hospitality*
- *Supper with a wee dram*
- *Open fire for winter warmth*
- *Laundry available*
- *Scrumptious breakfasts*
- *Peaceful & private*
- *Relaxed rural valley*
- *Farm animals & pets*

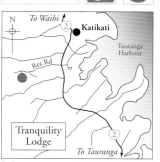

Nestled in a peaceful valley, warm kiwi hospitality and superior Bed & Breakfast accommodation await you. Get away from the crowds, and take time out to enjoy Katikati and it's surrounding areas. Have a seat on our large deck

and relax to the tune of birdsong and the stream while viewing the stunning Kaimai ranges, or play Petanque beside the courtyard. Each king suite is sumptuously furnished, has it's own private entry and deck where you can relax and enjoy the view of our lifestyle farm, pets and gardens. Bathrobes, slippers, toiletries and hairdryers are supplied in each ensuite. For the cooler evenings sit by the open log fire and toast marshmallows. First class 18 hole golf course, day spa, bird gardens, antiques, crafts, museum, art, bush walks, beaches, winery, cafés and so much more all within a few minutes drive.
We are a wheelchair friendly home.

VILLA COLLINI

36 Kaiate Falls Road, Welcome Bay, Tauranga
Ph/Fax (07) 544 8322, Mobile 021-047 8394
email: margrit@naturetours-nz.com
www.villacollini.co.nz

Tariff : N.Z. Dollars	
Double	$140-180
Single	$110-140
Child	neg

Bedrooms	Qty
Double	2
Twin	
Single	
Bed Size	Qty
Super King/Twin	1
King	
Queen	1
Double	
Single	
Bathrooms	Qty
Ensuite	1
Private	
Guest Share	1

**Quality Bed & Breakfast
with Panoramic Views**

Features & Attractions

- *Simply superb breakfasts*
- *Very quiet hilltop location*
- *Close to Kaiate waterfalls*
- *Park-like garden*
- *Tauranga/beach 15min.*
- *Gourmet cuisine*
- *Panoramic views*
- *Wir sprechen deutsch*

"Paradise means different things to different people, but for us Villa Collini is as close as it gets" Guest comment.

Enjoy spectacular panoramic views of Mt. Maunganui and the sea in a quiet, relaxing atmosphere. Get spoiled with a warm welcome and great hospitality, gourmet Mediterranean dinners ($45per person), comfortable beds, generous continental breakfast with homemade breads, croissants, cereals, cheese, sliced cold meat, Italian coffee etc.

Relax in our park-like garden or walk the endless beaches of Papamoa. Our location is an ideal base for Rotorua, Tauranga or White Island. We both have travelled world- and nationwide, so there is a lot to talk about. "Come as a stranger and leave as a friend".

91

MILLERS HAVEN HOMESTAY
147 Belk Road South, Pyes Pa, Tauranga
Ph/Fax (07) 543 5335, Mobile 021-258 8270
email: millershaven@actrix.co.nz
www.charmingaccommodation.co.nz

Features & Attractions
- *Country charm & birdlife*
- *Outdoor spa & laundry facility*
- *Guest lounge/kitchenette*
- *Between Rotorua & Tauranga*
- *Delicious breakfast*
- *Complimentary beverage & snacks*

Bed & Breakfast Homestay

Double	$120-150
Single	$100
Child	poa

Welcome to our recently built homestay, conveniently situated between Tauranga and Rotorua. Guest lounge with a small kitchenette, which includes a fridge, microwave, and tea/coffee facilities etc. Outside spa, Freeview TV, Email available.

The homestay boasts real country tranquillity, nestled close to an untouched piece of New Zealand bush, with abundant bird life. Your hosts, Simon and Renu, would love to spend time with you, and suggest any activities using their local knowledge. Maybe visiting a waterfall or a boat trip on Tauranga harbour. As past dairy farmers we have a deep love for this country, and will strive to make your visit memorable. Feel free to wander over our eight acre lifestyle farm and gardens.

Bedrooms	Qty
Double	1
Twin	1
Single	
Bed Size	**Qty**
King	
Queen	1
Double	
King/Single	2
Bathrooms	**Qty**
Ensuite	2
Private	
Guest Share	

HILLTOP APARTMENT
105 Fourth Avenue, The Avenues, Tauranga
Ph (07) 578 1614, Fax (07) 578 9168
Mobile 021-610 546
email: anneor@eol.co.nz
www.hilltopapartment.co.nz

Features & Attractions
- *Victorian charm*
- *Quiet central location*
- *Fully self contained*
- *Spacious lounge dining for 6*
- *Near shops and restaurants*
- *Popular holiday destination*

 **Luxury Self-contained Historic Apartment**

Double	$225
minimum 2 nights	
extra person $50	

The west wing of this large Victorian Villa is a fully self-contained 3 bedroom apartment suitable for a family, a group of friends or a small business group. Built in 1895, its recent quality restoration has accommodated all modern facilities yet retained the charm and elegance of the colonial era. The homestead apartment is spacious, has its own private parking and entrance and is fully equipped for travellers requiring short term, self-catering, and private luxury accommodation. Starter breakfast provided first day. The region has a reputation as one of the countries premiere holiday destinations. Glittering white sand on the countries premier beaches, beautiful harbours, crystal clear mountain waters, a large horticultural and farming hinterland and a lifestyle that is the envy of other New Zealanders. Everything you need for your holiday can be found here - sun, surf, seaside cafes, endless activities, attractions – and a great welcome by the friendly 'Bay' inhabitants.

Bedrooms	Qty
Double	2
Twin	
Single	1
Bed Size	**Qty**
King	
Queen	2
Double	
Single	1
Bathrooms	**Qty**
Ensuite	1
Private	
Guest Share	1

POHUTUKAWA BEACH B&B & COTTAGE

693 State Highway 2, (RD 4, Whakatane), Pikowai/Matata
Ph (07) 322 2182, Fax (07) 322 2186
Mobile 027-699 4978
email: joe@prinztours.co.nz
www.beachbnb.co.nz

Tariff : N.Z. Dollars	
Double	$100-140
Single	$100
Child	

Bedrooms	Qty
Double	1
Twin	2
Single	

Bed Size	Qty
King	
Queen	1
Double	
King Single	4
Single	

Bathrooms	Qty
Ensuite	1
Private	1
Guest Share	

 Coastal Country Stay and Cottage

Features & Attractions

- *Cottage SC from $150*
- *Outdoor pool*
- *Organic farm*
- *100 metres to beach*
- *Respite Care*
- *Coaching/counselling on request*
- *German spoken*
- *Guided tours*

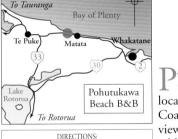

DIRECTIONS:
Directly on State Highway 2. Just 8 km
west of Matata, 34 km east of Te Puke.

Pohutukawa **Beach B&B and Cottage** are set in a picturesque location on and above the Pacific Coast Highway offering great ocean views. Glance up from the breakfast table and sea marine volcano White Island. Sometimes dolphins and  whales pass by close to shore. Visit the nearby geothermal attractions or just relax in our garden, by the pool or on the farm. We have an organic cattle farm and orchard. The dogs are friendly and the cats sleepy. We also run Prinz Tours Ltd, and do guided tours for groups New Zealand wide.

For people who want to have more time out on respite care we offer family counselling and health/life coaching on site. Wir sprechen deutsch. We are looking forward to welcoming you in our house for a holiday or wellness retreat.

93

FOTHERGILLS ON MIMIHA
B&B and COTTAGE
84 Mimiha Road, Pikowai/Matata
Ph/Fax (07) 322 2224, Mobile 027-460 5958
email: info@fothergills.co.nz
www.fothergills.co.nz

Tariff : N.Z. Dollars	
Double	$150
Single	$125
Child	$10-25

Bedrooms	Qty
Double	2
Twin	2
Single	

Bed Size	Qty
Super King	
King	
Queen	2
King Single	2
Single	2

Bathrooms	Qty
Ensuite	1
Private	2
Guest Share	

 Self-contained B&B and Mimiha Cottage

Features & Attractions

- *2 bdrm self-contained B&B suite*
- *2 bedrm fully equipped cottage*
- *Covered carparks, own entrances*
- *Rural peaceful location*
- *Glorious large country garden*
- *Spa pool*
- *Home grown produce & preserves*
- *Handy to SH2 and beach*

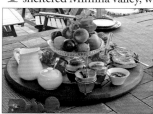

You'll find us just off SH2 and the beach, in the beautiful, peaceful, sheltered Mimiha valley, with farmland, nature and lovely views. Our stylish 2-bedroomed B&B suite is upstairs; private, self-contained and separated from the house by a carport. Beautiful, home-made, home-grown breakfasts are our specialty. **Mimiha Cottage** is a self-contained 2-bedroomed home with everything provided; pets by arrangement. The garden attracts regular visits from birds including kereru, tuis, quail, fantails and bellbirds, viewable from the shaded outdoor BBQ area. Our large 2-hectare country garden makes this a garden-lover's paradise, and we're friendly and hospitable – winners 2010 Spirit of Hospitality award. Use this as a base for trips to Tauranga and Mount Maunganui, Rotorua, Whakatane and White Island, all within an hour. Go walking, play petanque, enjoy a luxurious spa. Free WiFi available. Come and enjoy this slice of heaven!

DIRECTIONS: Approx halfway between Te Puke and Whakatane, Mimiha Rd turns off SH2 5km north west of Matata.

OCEANSPRAY HOMESTAY

283A Pohutukawa Ave, Ohope, Bay of Plenty
Ph (07) 312 4112, Fax (07) 312 4192
Mobile 027-286 6824
email: frances@oceanspray.co.nz
www.oceanspray.co.nz

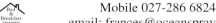

Tariff : N.Z. Dollars	
Double	$150-170
Single	$100-120
Child	neg

Bedrooms	Qty
Double	2
Twin	1
Single	
Bed Size	Qty
Super King	
King	1
Queen	1
Double	
Single	2
Bathrooms	Qty
Ensuite	1
Private	1
Guest Share	

Quality Beachfront Homestay

Features & Attractions

- *Absolute beachfront*
- *Separate downstairs apartment*
- *Ocean views from upstairs decks*
- *Safe swimming beach*
- *Generous hospitality*
- *Tourist attractions & golf nearby*
- *Free wireless internet*
- *Peaceful beachside retreat*

A warm invitation to share in our slice of paradise at **Oceanspray Homestay** – a beachfront property 100metres from the beach. Our downstairs private self contained apartment has three attractively furnished bedrooms, lounge/kitchen and two bathrooms(one is an ensuite).

Enjoy the view of the ocean from our upstairs decks, and our warm hospitality, with complimentary wine, and home baking on your arrival. Comprehensive breakfast provisions are supplied into the apartment for self help. We offer an excellent standard of accommodation, with quality linen, bathroom toiletries, use of laundry facilities, wireless internet, and BBQ. All the comforts of home with a great selection of books, toys, DVDs and beach gear(two kayaks) make this an ideal family holiday retreat. We have two very sociable cats – Barnaby and Cleo.

We look forward to ensuring your stay is a memorable one.

CRESTWOOD BED & BREAKFAST
2 Crestwood Rise, Whakatane
Ph (07) 308 7554, Mobile 027-624 6248
email: pandjmckechnie@xtra.co.nz
www.crestwood-homestay.co.nz

Features & Attractions
- *Warm, sunny, spacious rooms*
- *Free wireless internet*
- *Home baking on arrival*
- *Safe, flat off road parking*
- *Ideal for group of up to four*
- *One party booking only*

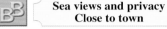

Sea views and privacy
Close to town

Double	$150
Single	$130
Child	

Bedrooms	Qty
Double	1
Twin	1
Single	
Bed Size	**Qty**
King	
Queen	1
Double	
Single	2
Bathrooms	**Qty**
Ensuite	
Private	1
Guest Share	

Situated above the town with spectacular ocean and bush views yet only 5 minutes drive to the wharf for White Island volcano trip, dolphin watching, fishing charters, town, restaurants, scenic walks and the night sky observatory. Guest entrance to private, quiet upstairs suite of rooms with a cosy sitting room, writing desk, phone, tv, comfy sofas and lots of room to spread out. Bathroom with separate toilet. Also the extra bedroom is ideal for family or friends when travelling as a group.

The double room and lounge open to a sunny balcony for you to enjoy the expansive views. There is also a small kitchenette with bench space, refrigerator, coffee/tea facilities. Breakfast with homemade muesli, jams and fruit off our trees in season is served downstairs overlooking the garden. Our interests are rugby, trout fishing the rivers and lakes. Janet is a radio operator for Coastguard.

Charming
Places to Stay
in New Zealand

"Simply the best B&B Guide I've come across anywhere. Superb choice of places, so easy to use, a delightful book. I eagerly recommend it to all travellers to New Zealand."

G. Wallis, Hampton, England

AT SPRINGWATERS LODGE

9 Te Waerenga Rd, Hamurana, Rotorua
Ph (07) 332 2565, Mobile 021-295 3652
email: info@springwaterslodge.co.nz
www.springwaterslodge.co.nz

Tariff : N.Z. Dollars	
Double	$190-210
Single	$160-190
Child	$60

Bedrooms	Qty
Double	4
Twin	
Single	
Bed Size	**Qty**
Super King/Twin	4
King	
Queen	
Double	
Single	
Bathrooms	**Qty**
Ensuite	4
Private	
Guest Share	

Affordable Luxury on
Lake Rotorua's Doorstep

Features & Attractions

- *Relaxed, friendly hosts*
- *Free wireless Broadband*
- *Spa pool, laundry*
- *Close to attractions*
- *Prime trout fishing spot*
- *Dinner guests welcomed*
- *500m to golf course, springs*
- *Very generous breakfasts*

Welcome to our spacious family home. Trout fishing, golf, walks and Hamurana Springs all within 500m of our doorstep. Spacious dining and lounging areas overlooking the lake allow plenty of space for relaxation. Newly refurbished throughout with quality furnishings and linen, your comfort is guaranteed. **Springwaters Lodge** is 1 level, offering 4 guest rooms, each with ensuite, TV and DVD. Two rooms open onto their own patio, with lake views. A buffet-style continental breakfast can be enjoyed whilst a hot dish is being prepared. Join us for dinner and drinks or you may choose to dine at a local café. Complimentary home baking and refreshments available at any time. Our 2 senior school aged children, Nadia and Jaxon, share our passion for entertaining. Located just 10 to 15 minutes drive to many of Rotorua's leading attractions makes our location central. We are happy to help you with our local knowledge and assist you with booking your activities.

A PANORAMIC COUNTRY HOMESTAY

144 Fryer Rd, Hamurana, Rotorua
Ph/Fax (07) 332 2618, Mobile 021-610 949
email: panoramahomestay@xtra.co.nz
www.panoramahomestay.co.nz

Tariff : N.Z. Dollars	
Double	$200-300
Single	$150
Child	$60

Bedrooms	Qty
Double	2
Double/Twin	1
Single	

Bed Size	Qty
Super King	1
King	1
Queen	1
Double	
Twin	2

Bathrooms	Qty
Ensuite	2
Private	1
Guest Share	

**Peaceful Luxury
Country Homestay**

Features & Attractions

- *Private and peaceful retreat*
- *Close to all major attractions*
- *15 min. from Rotorua i-Site*
- *Magnificent lake views*
- *Relaxed & friendly hospitality*
- *Spacious ensuite rooms*
- *Phone & email facilities*
- *Heated outside spa pool*

DIRECTIONS:
Take SH 5 to roundabout. Travel north
around lake through Ngongotaha towards
Hamurana. Turn left into Fryer Rd and
travel 1.5km to **Panorama** driveway
on your right (No 144).

Aptly named, **Panorama** is your ideal base to stay near Rotorua's many attractions. Take in the magnificent views overlooking

Lake Rotorua and legendary Mokoia Island, Mt. Tarawera and surrounding country-side. Feel the peace and tranquility as you relax under the stars in the outdoor heated massage spa pool, then curl up in front of the log fire in winter. You may prefer an energetic

game of tennis or take in fantastic walks before you stretch out on the extra large beds in **Panorama's** peaceful surrounds for a perfect nights' sleep. The large house is centrally heated and wheelchair accessible. The 3 spacious luxury bedrooms have private bathrooms/ensuites containing toiletries, heated towel rails, hairdryers, shaving points and heaters. The large, comfortable inner-spring beds are warmed with electric blankets, woollen underlays, and feather quilts in winter. Only 15 min. from Rotorua, smoke free and away from sulphur smells.

124 ON BRUNSWICK BED & BREAKFAST

124 Brunswick Drive, Brunswick Park,
Rotokawa, Rotorua
Ph (07) 345 9430, Mobile 027- 454 9037
email: reservations@124onbrunswick.co.nz
www.124onbrunswick.co.nz

Tariff : N.Z. Dollars	
Double	$160-200
Single	$140-160
Child	neg

Bedrooms	Qty
Double	3
Twin	
Single	
Bed Size	**Qty**
Super King	
King	1
Queen	2
Double	
King Single	1
Bathrooms	**Qty**
Ensuite	3
Private	
Guest Share	

**Semi Rural Kiwi Homestead
Boutique Bed & Breakfast**

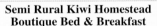

Features & Attractions

- *Guests reading room*
- *Free snacks and refreshments*
- *Guests kitchenette*
- *Free wireless Broadband*
- *Panoramic rural & lake views*
- *Great base to explore*
- *Warm relaxed atmosphere*
- *Great Kiwi hospitality*

Map showing Lake Rotorua, To Tauranga, 33, 36, 30, Ngongotaha, To Whakatane, To Auckland, 5, Rotorua City, 124 on Brunswick, To Taupo

Lindsey and Jonathan welcome you to **124 on Brunswick Bed & Breakfast**. This award winning Kiwi homestead was specially designed as a bed and breakfast and is situated in 2 acres of rural Brunswick Park. The guest lounge with kitchenette and each of the 3 guest bedrooms with en-suites have French doors leading out to a covered verandah with panoramic rural and lake views. We have a 4 star Qualmark rating and a Enviro Bronze Qualmark rating for sustainability. We have planted around 3000 native plants and trees on our property to offset carbon footprints. Jonathan is a professional photographer and his photographs are on display though out the homestead. Rotorua is the premier cultural and tourism destination in NZ and **124 on Brunswick Bed & Breakfast** provides a great base in which to explore the many attractions that this beautiful region has to offer. We are 5 minutes drive from Rotorua Airport and 15 minutes from the city centre.

THE RISING TROUT

15 Waana Street, Mourea, Rotorua
Ph (07) 362 4858, Mobile 021-187 4349
email: risingtrout@xtra.co.nz
www.risingtrout.co.nz

Features & Attractions

- *Trout fishing*
- *Lakeside home*
- *Genuine kiwi hospitality*
- *Kayaking*
- *Warm sunny home*
- *15min to town*

Affordable Lakeside B&B

Double	$165-185
Single	$120
Child	

T he Rising Trout is our lakeside home where a warm kiwi welcome awaits our many guests. We are located on beautiful Lake Rotorua situated at the top of the lake very close by world renowned fishing spot - the Ohau Channel. Serenity, birdlife and wonderful sunsets are features of this tranquil spot. Accommodation consists of two well appointed queen rooms each with ensuite, luxury bedding, glorious views, tea making facilities plus all other usual comforts of home including access to an extensive home library. We provide a complimentary happy hour and of course a special breakfast. Close by attractions include fishing, kayaking from a cross the front lawn, lakeside golf and white water rafting whilst many other famous Rotorua visitor sites are but a short drive. We love it here. So will you.

Bedrooms	Qty
Double	2
Twin	
Single	
Bed Size	**Qty**
King	
Queen	1
Double	1
Single	
Bathrooms	**Qty**
Ensuite	2
Private	
Guest Share	

ROBERTSON HOUSE

70 Pererika Street, Rotorua
Ph (07) 343 7559, Mobile 021-136 0719
email: info@robertsonhouse.co.nz
www.robertsonhouse.co.nz

Features & Attractions

- *Old world charm*
- *Perfect central location*
- *Beautiful cottage garden*
- *Warm & friendly hosts*
- *All activities easily arranged*
- *Quiet & relaxing*

Charming Bed & Breakfast Homestay

Double	$150-195
Single	$120-160
Triple	$255

O ur historic home, only two minutes drive from the city centre, was built by one of Rotorua's forefathers in 1905. Under the auspices of the Historic Places Trust it has been carefully renovated, retaining its colonial charm.

Relax in its warm, comfortable atmosphere, or take time out on the veranda and enjoy our old English cottage garden resplendent with colour and fragrance, citrus trees and grape vines.

Our friendly hosts are happy to assist with information and bookings for Rotorua's many Maori cultural, and sightseeing attractions.

Robertson House – a historic colonial villa, carefully restored, is warm and inviting with a peaceful cottage garden.

Bedrooms	Qty
Double	4
Twin	1
Single	
Bed Size	
Super King	1
Queen	2
Double	2
Single	2
Bathrooms	**Qty**
Ensuite	5
Private	
Guest Share	

CITY LIGHTS BOUTIQUE LODGE

56c Mountain Road, Rotorua
Ph/Fax (07) 349 1413
Mobile 027-577 6644
email: stay@citylights.net.nz
www.citylights.net.nz

Tariff : N.Z. Dollars	
Double	$179-299
Single	$149-249
Child	

Bedrooms	Qty
Double	3
Twin	
Single	
Bed Size	Qty
Super King	
King	
Queen	3
Double	
Single	
Bathrooms	Qty
Ensuite	3
Private	
Guest Share	

**Luxury Modern
Bed & Breakfast**

Features & Attractions

- *Warm and friendly hosts*
- *Spa pool, gym and sauna*
- *Guest lounge with computer*
- *Close to all attractions*
- *Only 8 minutes to city*
- *Quiet peaceful location*
- *Complimentary internet/Wifi*
- *Beautiful views over Rotorua*

City Lights is a new **Boutique Lodge** set in 2 acres on Mount Ngongotaha in the beautiful city of Rotorua. We offer a luxury Bed and Breakfast experience with spectacular views over the city. With just 3 en-suite guest rooms we can offer a top class service as well as privacy. We have fantastic facilities including a guest lounge with computer station, FREE wireless broadband internet, real fire and heat pump/air conditioner. We have plenty of off road parking and garage parking can be arranged. All bedrooms have en-suite bathrooms with bathrobes, luxury toiletries, tea/coffee, bottled water, wall mounted LCD TV, CD/Radio, and hairdryer. Other facilities include a gym, outdoor spa, and infrared sauna. We have 2 mountain bikes available to guests at no charge. We welcome the chance to help you plan the most from your trip. Attractions and restaurant advice freely given and bookings can be made by your hosts on request. We look forward to welcoming you to stay.

CLASSIC TRESCO
THERMAL OASIS B&B ROTORUA
3 Toko Street, Victoria, Rotorua
Ph/Fax (07) 348 9611, Mobile 027-710 4883
email: stay@trescorotorua.co.nz
www.trescorotorua.co.nz

Tariff : N.Z. Dollars	
Double	$120-250
Single	$80-120
Child	

Bedrooms	Qty
Double	4
Twin	1
Single	1
Bed Size	Qty
Super King	
King	1
Queen	3
Double	1
Single	2
Bathrooms	Qty
Ensuite	3
Private	1
Guest Share	1

 Your Private 100% Natural Mineral Pool

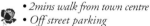

Features & Attractions
- *Private 100% thermal mineral pool*
- *Continental & full cooked breakfast*
- *Free Wi-fi*
- *Sky digital LCD TV*
- *2mins walk from town centre*
- *Off street parking*
- *Free pick up/drop off*
- *Tresco was built in 1925*

DIRECTIONS: From the north take the SH 5 toward Rotorua City. Turn left into Malfroy Road, about 100m right into Toko St. and Tresco B&B is on your left. From the south take the SH 5 or SH 30 into Fenton St. Just before the Shell Petrol Station, turn left into Victoria St, and first left into Toko St. Tresco B&B is on your right.

Classic **Tresco** offers Rotorua's only Qualmark 4 Star B&B with a 100% real geothermal private hot pool heated from the volcano. On a quiet street and just 2 mins walk to the City, with your own parking. You'll enjoy and relax with your private geothermal hot pool [39-42C] and geothermal central heating in the winter. You're also close to all the activities, restaurants, cafes, spa resorts, convention centres, Museum and Galleries. The warmest welcome

is from **Tresco**. Your hosts will not only know vast information but also offer discount vouches for activities and parks that you will enjoy. We can arrange tours and bookings as we have intimate knowledge of all local activities. Visit our web site. Email us to ask your questions. Our courtesy transport will collect you from the Rotorua International Airport and Bus Terminals with no cost at all.

KOURA LODGE LAKE ROTORUA

Owners: David and Gina Wells
209 Kawaha Point Road, Rotorua
Ph (07) 348 5868, Fax (07) 348 5869
email: stay@kouralodge.co.nz
www.kouralodge.co.nz

Tariff : N.Z. Dollars	
Double	$345-645
Single	
Extra pp	$100

Bedrooms	Qty
Double	7
Twin	3
Single	
Bed Size	**Qty**
Super King	
King	6
Queen	3
Double	
King Single	4
Bathrooms	**Qty**
Ensuite	All
Private	All
Family Share	1

Genuine Lawn to Lake Luxury

To Hamilton
Kawaha Point
Kawaha Point Rd
Kawaha Point Rd
Fairy Springs Rd
Koutu Rd
Koura Lodge Rotorua
Ranger Rd
Old Taupo Road
Lake Rd
Lake Rotorua
N
City Centre

DIRECTIONS: From north, take
SH 5 towards Rotorua City. Turn left
into Kawaha Point Road, left into Koutu
and right again. Travel to Lodge at end.
From city, take SH 5 north. Turn right
into Kawaha Point Road. Then as above.

Features & Attractions

- *Championship tennis court*
- *Buffet & cooked breakfasts*
- *5 minutes from City centre*
- *Sauna & spa facility*
- *Fishing & hot pool trips, canoes*
- *Comp. email, WiFi available*
- *On-site massage*
- *Complimentary off-street parking*

Koura Lodge is situated on the tip of Kawaha Point, nestled in sub-tropical gardens, only five minutes drive from the City Centre, yet secluded from traffic noise and sulphur fumes. **The Lodge** offers a range of double accommodation as well as family suites and a two bedroom apartment, all with private ensuites, veranda seating and spectacular lake views. **Koura Lodge** is minutes from three well-known golf courses, mountain bike and walking trails and dozens of restaurants. **Koura Lodge** also offers floatplane, jetboat and fishing excursions, departing from the private jetty.

MAPLE HOUSE

154A Tarawera Road, Lynmore, Rotorua
Ph/Fax (07) 345 8434
email: j.nicol@actrix.co.nz
www.maplehouse.co.nz

Tariff : N.Z. Dollars	
Double	$150
Single	$100
Child	$25

Bedrooms	Qty
Double	1
Twin	1
Single	

Bed Size	Qty
Super King	
King	
Queen	1
Double	
Single	2

Bathrooms	Qty
Ensuite	
Private	1
Guest Share	

**Homestay
Bed & Breakfast**

Features & Attractions

- *Beautiful gardens*
- *Delicious breakfasts*
- *Quiet nights*
- *Free laundry facilities*
- *Scenic forest walks*
- *Spacious bathroom*
- *Close to major attractions*
- *Redwoods & glow worms nearby*

DIRECTIONS:
Route 30 East 2.5km (towards airport).
Turn right at roundabout onto
Tarawera Road. Maple House
is 154A, just past Hilton Road.

You've found it! Walk in, relax and experience genuine New Zealand hospitality in a warm, quiet, well appointed home. Choose from a comfortable queen or twin bedroom with spacious private bathroom and separate toilet. After a busy day you will enjoy the tranquillity of the sunny lounge, share refreshments on the garden patio or curl up beside a cosy fire in Winter. Across the road is Whakarewarewa Forest with scenic trails, magnificent redwoods, tree ferns and glow worms. Just five minutes to airport, town centre, restaurants, golf courses, or the luxury of thermal spa facilities. Use your hosts' wide local knowledge of scenic, thermal, adventure and cultural activities to help you plan a memorable visit. We have travelled and worked extensively overseas. Joan loves gardening, walking, museum guiding, entertaining, theatre. Barry, avid reader and rugby follower, enjoys company and a red wine! Once you've shared the wonders of Rotorua, you'll want to return again and again bringing your friends!

*"**Your beautiful home and exceptional hospitality made Rotorua a memorable stay!**"* – guest comment.

CLOVER DOWNS ESTATE

175 Jackson Road, Ngongotaha, Rotorua
Ph (07) 332 2366, Fax (07) 332 2367
Mobile 021-712 866
email: reservations@cloverdowns.co.nz
www.accommodationinrotorua.co.nz

Tariff : N.Z. Dollars	
Double	$250-350
Single	$235-335
Child	neg

Bedrooms	Qty
Double	3
Twin	
Single	

Bed Size	Qty
Super King	2
King	1
Queen	
Double	
Single	

Bathrooms	Qty
Ensuite	3
Private	
Guest Share	

**Fine Country
Bed & Breakfast Retreat**

Features & Attractions

- *Secluded, peaceful rural retreat*
- *Spacious home like comfort*
- *Telephone & wireless internet*
- *Laundry facilities available*
- *Tourist attractions nearby*
- *Trout fishing trips available*
- *Children welcome*
- *Deer and Ostrich farm tour*

DIRECTIONS:
Take State Highway 5 to roundabout. Travel north around lake, through Ngongotaha on Hamurana Road. Take third left into Central Road, then turn right into Jackson Road. Travel 1.75km to **Clover Downs** on left.

Welcome to **Clover Downs,** a luxury Bed & Breakfast retreat in stunning rural surroundings near Rotorua. **Clover Downs** is a unique place to stay.

Just 15 minutes drive north from Rotorua in the secluded country setting of Ngongotaha, it is a Bed & Breakfast farmstay experience like no other, catering for single travellers, couples and families. Large comfortable rooms provide you with a place to rest and relax in peace and tranquillity, while sheep, ostrich and deer graze on the green paddocks surrounding the house.

Your hosts, Mike and Sharon, can help arrange activities so that you can experience all that Rotorua has to offer – geothermal wonderlands with geysers and bubbling mud pools, the rich Maori culture, excellent trout fishing, sightseeing and other exciting pursuits. We strive to exceed our guest's expectation through an affable blend of warmth, generosity and attention to detail.

DEER PINE LODGE
255 Jackson Road, Ngongotaha, Rotorua
Ph (07) 332 3458, Fax (07) 332 3458
Mobile 027-312 0338
email: deerpine@xtra.co.nz
www.charmingaccommodation.co.nz

Tariff : N.Z. Dollars	
Double	$95-110
Single	$80-90
Child	Neg.

Bedrooms	Qty
Double	4
Twin	1
Single	
Bed Size	**Qty**
Super King	
King	3
Queen	1
Double	
Single	2
Bathrooms	**Qty**
Ensuite	5
Private	
Guest Share	

 **Farmstay Bed & Breakfast
Self-contained Accommodation**

Features & Attractions

- *Quiet, peaceful surroundings*
- *Beach 30 minutes away*
- *Architecturally designed units*
- *Beautiful views of lake*
- *Tourist attractions nearby*
- *Telephone & Email facilities*
- *Horse riding close by*
- *No sulphur smells*

Deer Pine Lodge — map: To Hamurana, Jackson Rd, Central Rd, Oturoa Rd, Dalbeth Rd, Ngongotaha, Lake Rotorua, To Hamilton, To Rotorua.

DIRECTIONS: Please phone or write for brochure and easy directions.

Welcome to **Deer Pine Lodge**. Come and relax in peaceful, quiet countryside surroundings with lovely views of Lake Rotorua and wake up to the singing of the birds. During your stay you are most welcome to have a look at the sheep and take photographs. Our property is surrounded with trees, planted by New Zealand Forest Research. The nearby city of Rotorua is fast becoming New Zealand's most popular tourist destination. Our bed/breakfast units/ rooms are private with ensuite, television, radio, refrigerator, microwave, heaters, electric blankets on all beds and tea/coffee making facilities. There are heaters and hair dryers in bathrooms. Our two-bedroom fully self-contained units, designed by prominent Rotorua architect Gerald Stock, each have a private balcony, carport, sundeck, ensuite, spacious lounge, kitchen, also laundry facilities, television, radio, heaters etc (cot/highchair available). Smoke detectors fitted in all bedrooms and lounges, fire extinguishers installed in all kitchens. We hold the NZ Certificate in Food Hygiene, which ensures high standards of food preparation and service. An evening meal with pre-dinner drinks is available by prior arrangement. Hosts John and Betty, originally from Scotland, have travelled extensively overseas and have many years experience in hosting. We look forward to your stay with us.

NGONGOTAHA LAKESIDE LODGE

41 Operiana Street, Ngongotaha, Rotorua
Ph/Fax (07) 357 4020, Mobile 027-385 2807
email: lake.edge@xtra.co.nz
www.lakesidelodge.co.nz

Tariff : N.Z. Dollars	
Double	$220-250
Single	$200-220
Child	neg

Bedrooms	Qty
Double	2
Twin	
Single	
Bed Size	**Qty**
Super King	
King	1
Queen	1
Double	
Single	
Bathrooms	**Qty**
Ensuite	2
Private	
Guest Share	

'Inviting - Relaxing - Affordable'

DIRECTIONS:
From Rotorua drive through Ngongotaha Village,
cross over railway line, then first
right into Wikaraka Street, then left
into Okana Cresent, left again
into Operiana Street.
We are on the right.

Features & Attractions

- *Absolute lake edge*
- *Guest lounge*
- *Scenic flights from property*
- *Activities arranged*
- *Fly fishing in lake & stream*
- *Fishing gear provided*
- *Free wireless internet*
- *Sulphur free*

We invite you to stay at our award winning Bed & Breakfast, perfectly located at the shore of Lake Rotorua. Arrive to the aroma of home baking and coffee and make yourselves at home. Settle in and enjoy stunning panoramic views, fly fishing, bird watching, great food and warm hospitality. Quiet, peaceful and close to major attractions, only 10 min. to town and away from the sulphur fumes. The guest floor has two well appointed ensuite bedrooms with superior beds, that guarantee you a restful night's sleep, and the generous, special breakfasts set you up for another fun filled day. Feed the ducks, paddle the canoe or kayak, experience the thrill of fly fishing at the mouth of the famous Waiteti Stream and have your catch pan-fried for breakfast or smoked with pre dinner drinks. **Lakeside Lodge**, your perfect B&B choice. Ideal as a base for central island touring or for the longer stay. Free use of all fishing gear, canoes, kayaks and BBQ. Off-street parking, wireless internet and laundry service. We promise you a great stay!

YOUR HOSTS: **Philippa and Richard Cain**   Ph: (07) 333 2720

LAKE OHAKURI FARMSTAY
912 Poutakataka Road, Ngakuru, Rotorua
Ph/Fax (07) 333 2720
email: lakeohakurifarmstay@xtra.co.nz
www.lakeohakurifarmstay.co.nz

Tariff : N.Z. Dollars	
Double	$120-150
Single	$95-120
Child	

Bedrooms	Qty
Double	2
Twin	1
Single	1
Bed Size	Qty
Super King	
King	
Queen	2
King/Single	1
Single	2
Bathrooms	Qty
Ensuite	2
Private	
Family Share	1

**Delightful Farmstay
Bed & Breakfast**

Features & Attractions

- *Mountain & lake views*
- *Proximity to Rotorua / Taupo*
- *Cottage & homestead accommodation*
- *Dairy stock*
- *Spacious country garden*
- *Local thermals*
- *Tourist attractions nearby*
- *Hearty cooked breakfast*

Lake Ohakuri Farmstay offers peace and tranquility in a spacious, rural garden setting with magnificent views of the lake and volcanically formed hills. You can sit and enjoy these views from the dining room table while you have a hearty, cooked breakfast with all the trimmings or take a walk around the garden and paddocks to really take it all in. A tour of the dairy farm is available by arrangement and we have a laundry service available for a small charge. We have a separate cottage with en suite or either a queen room or twin room with en suite in the house. These homestead rooms also have their own lounge. We have some wonderful, local attractions to visit which include Wai-O-Tapu, Waimaungu Thermal reserve, Waikite Thermal Mineral Swimming Pools, plus all the other Rotorua/Taupo attractions within easy driving distance. A three course dinner is available by prior arrangement and we do our best to use home grown or local produce. We look forward to welcoming you to our piece of paradise.

MINARAPA LODGE

620 Oruanui Road, Taupo
Ph (07) 378 1931
Mobile 027-355 5232
email: info@minarapa.co.nz
www.minarapa.co.nz

Tariff : N.Z. Dollars	
Double	$155-185
Single	$120-150
Child	poa

Bedrooms	Qty
Double	2
Twin	2
Single	
Bed Size	**Qty**
Super King	
King/Twin	1
Queen	2
Double	
Single	2
Bathrooms	**Qty**
Ensuite	2
Private	1
Guest Share	

Countrystay
Bed & Breakfast

Features & Attractions

- *Tree-lined drive*
- *Park-like grounds*
- *Tennis and billiards*
- *Peace, privacy, space*
- *Tourist attractions nearby*
- *Dinner by arrangement*
- *German spoken*
- *Lifestyle farming*

Wind your way along a wonderful tree-lined drive into rural tranquillity. **Minarapa**, our 11-acre country retreat is 12 minutes north of Taupo, 45 minutes from Rotorua, within easy reach of golf courses and major attractions, including Huka Falls, Wairakei Terraces, Orakei Korako and other thermal areas. **Minarapa** offers space and character aplenty. Downstairs relax in the large guest lounge/billiard room with television and refrigerator. Upstairs retire to one of the guestrooms – spacious, light, appointed with a view to your comfort, each with individual style. Two rooms have ensuite bathroom, balcony, TV and tea/coffee facilities. They overlook our park-like grounds where you may play tennis, wander among colourful tree-sheltered gardens, cross the pond and stream to visit our friendly farm animals or simply sit and enjoy the birdsong. In addition to continental or cooked breakfast, dinner with wine is available on request ($40-50pp). Barbara spricht fliessend Deutsch.

SOUTH CLARAGH & BIRD COTTAGE
3245 Poihipi Road, Taupo

Ph (07) 372 8848, Fax (07) 372 8047
Mobile 021-125 3263
email: welcome@countryaccommodation.co.nz
www.countryaccommodation.co.nz

Features & Attractions
- *Taupo's best kept secret*
- *Comfortable, relaxed atmosphere*
- *Deluxe continental breakfast* • *Friendly farm animals*
- *On routes to/from Waitomo to Rotorua, Tongariro*

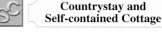

Countrystay and Self-contained Cottage

	Double	$110-160
	Single	$30-90
	Child	$15-50

DIRECTIONS: Easy to find from whichever direction you come. Contact us by phone/email/fax or check our website for map.

Turn into our leafy driveway and relax...

Guest accommodation in our charming, centrally heated farm house consists of two ensuite rooms, one with a shower, the other is a deluxe room which has a cast iron claw-foot bath which can accommodate two people. Both rooms have their own private entrance and decking area overlooking our lucious gardens which cover three acres surrounding the farm house. A special continental breakfast is provided with our own breads, organic blueberries, raspberries and yoghurt. If you would like to be a bit more independent, why not stay in our charming 1950's cottage, nestled amongst the trees in its own little forest. It is very secluded and access is down its own leafy track, leading through the forest. The cottage is fully self-contained and has one double bed, a bed settee in the lounge, it's own BBQ and heated outdoor spa, great if more accommodation is needed.

Bedrooms	Qty
Double	3
Twin	
Single	
Bed Size	Qty
King	
Queen	3
Double	1
Single	
Bathrooms	Qty
Ensuite	2
Private	
Guest Share	

TWYNHAM AT KINLOCH
84 Marina Terrace, Kinloch, Lake Taupo
Ph (07) 378 2862, Fax (07) 378 2868
Mobile 027-285 6001
email: twynham.bnb@xtra.co.nz
www.twynham.co.nz

Features & Attractions
- *Three minute stroll to Lake*
- *Dinner by arrangement*
- *Short 15 min drive to Taupo*
- *Walking tracks and golf galore*
- *Coffee, cake and relaxation*
- *Compl. kayak/fishing tackle*

Country Village Accommodation

	Double	$155-195
	Single	$145-175
	Child	POA

DIRECTIONS: Driving north out of Taupo on SH 1 take the Te Kuiti/Kinloch turn-off on left (Poihipi Road). Follow Kinloch signs to village.

Nestled within large private gardens in the picturesque lakeside village of Kinloch - **Twynham** is a haven for fresh air, good coffee and relaxation and unequaled as a base for exploring the delights of the Taupo region, plus the more strenuous delights of golf (adjacent), fishing (five minutes), water sports, snow skiing, bush and mountain walks. Hearty breakfasts, wholesome dinners and warm welcomes assure guests of an enjoyable stay. Guest accommodation is a private wing with bedrooms, bathrooms and elegant lounge. Laundry service available. Elizabeth has a wide knowledge of the volcanic and geothermal history of the region. Paul is a New Zealand Kennel Club Judge and golf, music, dog sports and travel are family interests. We are owned by one friendly dog Saxon. Pets are welcome by arrangement.

Bedrooms	Qty
Double	2
Twin	1
Single	
Bed Size	Qty
Super King	
King	1
Queen	1
King/Single	2
Bathrooms	Qty
Ensuite	1
Private	1
Guest Share	

ACACIA BAY LAKEFRONT

21 Te Kopua Street, Acacia Bay, Taupo
Ph (07) 378 8449, Fax (07) 378 8449
Mobile 027-481 8829
email: bibbys@taupohomestay.com
www.taupohomestay.com

Tariff : N.Z. Dollars	
Double	$250-420
Single	$250-350
Child	$20-50

Bedrooms	Qty
Double	3
Twin	1
Single	
Bed Size	**Qty**
Super King	2
King	
Queen	1
Double	
King/Single	2
Bathrooms	**Qty**
Ensuite	3
Private	
Guest Share	

To Auckland — Poihipi Rd — Kaihua Rd — Norman Smith St — Taupo — Acacia Bay Lakefront — Te Kopua St. — Wakeman Rd — Lake Taupo

**Absolute Lakefront
Luxury Accommodation**

Features & Attractions

- *Luxurious silk & cotton bedding*
- *Private beach & jetty*
- *Generous breakfasts*
- *Quiet and relaxing*
- *Uninterrupted panoramic views*
- *Boat fishing, sightseeing trips*
- *Close to all major attractions*
- *Hot pool and golf nearby*

Paeroa Lakeside Homestay set on the lake edge with private beach, native bush and gardens, in sheltered Acacia Bay, with panoramic views of Lake Taupo and beyond. A warm, welcoming environment waits – comfort, private facilities, spacious lounge areas and outdoor living. Guest areas and beds are warm, comfortable and tastefully decorated. Television and tea/coffee facilities in rooms, email and laundry service available. Retired sheep farmers, we enjoy living in our peaceful, private home beside the beach next to a bushwalk, just minutes from the town centre. Three golf courses, thermal areas, restaurants,

boating, fishing and all major attractions, and within easy driving distance from mountains, National Park, extensive thermal areas and wineries. Amongst our interests are travel, golf, gardening, fishing, hospitality, having travelled and fished extensively overseas. Guided fishing and sightseeing experiences available from John's new 30 foot cruiser. The catch can be smoked or may be cooked for breakfast. A welcome tea or coffee on arrival. We assure you of a memorable stay. Please email, fax or phone for bookings. **Free Wi Fi Internet available.**

SCENIC HEIGHTS LODGE

24 Scenic Heights, Acacia Bay, Taupo
Ph (07) 376 5866, Mobile 027-494 9873
email: scenicheightslodge@gmail.com
www.scenicheightslodge.co.nz

Tariff : N.Z. Dollars	
Double	$375
Single	
Child	n/a

Bedrooms	Qty
Double	2
Twin	
Single	
Bed Size	**Qty**
Super King	2
King	
Queen	
Double	
Single	
Bathrooms	**Qty**
Ensuite	2
Private	
Guest Share	

**Peaceful Secure Hideaway
with Stunning Lake Views**

Features & Attractions

- *Peaceful, secure hideaway*
- *Quality ensuite bedrooms*
- *Lake & mountain views*
- *Taupo centre 5-min. drive*
- *Lake & river trout fishing*
- *International golf courses*
- *Pool with swim jets*
- *High-speed broadband*

DIRECTIONS:
From SH 1 just north of Taupo, turn west into Norman
Smith St. Turn left into Acacia Bay Rd and pass Acacia
Bay Shops. Take 2nd left into Scenic Heights and travel
to Lodge at end. 5 minutes from town.

Scenic Heights Lodge is a classically designed 2-suite Boutique Lodge designed for the discerning traveller seeking a peaceful,

secure hideaway. Nestling on a headland amongst mature gardens just above the lake, the lodge maximizes views over Taupo and Mt Tauhara. Acacia Bay is 5min. drive from Taupo and the Lodge is 5 min. walk from local restaurant. The **Lodge** has two super-king

ensuite guest rooms opening to terraces, one with garden views and the other overlooking the pool and to the lake beyond. Facilities include pool with swim jets, extensive terracing, large guest lounge, home theatre/den with 50-inch plasma screen, and high speed broadband facilities. Tariffs include full English or continental breakfast. Your Kiwi hosts have years of experience in hospitality and know the Taupo area well. Boots, the cat on site.

TE MOENGA LODGE

60 Te Moenga Park, Acacia Bay, Taupo
Ph (07) 378 0437, Fax (07) 378 0438
Mobile 027-452 1459
email: info@temoenga.com
www.temoenga.com

Tariff : N.Z. Dollars	
Double	$160-305
Single	$130-225
Child	POA

Bedrooms	Qty
Double	1
Double/Twin	3
Single	

Bed Size	Qty
S. King/Twin	3
King	
Queen	1
Double	
Single	

Bathrooms	Qty
Ensuite	4
Private	
Guest Share	

Private Chalets and Bed & Breakfast

Features & Attractions

- *Luxury private chalets*
- *Peace, privacy & luxury*
- *Secure off-street parking*
- *Nearby restaurant*
- *Magnificent panoramic views*
- *7 minutes drive from town*
- *Separate guest entrances*
- *Wireless Internet access*

DIRECTIONS: Follow directions to Acacia Bay. Take 1st street on right, Reeves Rd and continue on to **Te Moenga** Park to end.

Climb the tree-lined road to the homestead on the hill. Close the door on the everyday and relax on a deck so far above the lake that it seems you're looking down from the sky. Enjoy being apart and above, just for a while. These are moments to treasure. **Te Moenga Lodge** will be the high point of your time in Taupo. Choose a studio for two with ensuite, television and tea and coffee making facilities. Enjoy use of a spacious guest lounge overlooking the nightlights of Taupo. Breakfast in the sun at a table as big as the view. For the ultimate in luxury, choose a private chalet with king/twin beds, a separate lounge, television, tea and coffee making facilities and stylish bathroom with a spa bath. A breakfast basket is delivered daily. From your chalet's private deck, own the breath-taking view for the length of your stay. We invite you to experience these special qualities of our stunning rural retreat.

ABOVE THE LAKE - TAUPO
46 Rokino Road, Taupo
Ph (07) 378 8738, Mobile 021-840 469
email: windsor-charters@xtra.co.nz
www.taupostay.com

Features & Attractions

- *Spectacular lake views*
- *Private garden, hot tub*
- *Centrally located*
- *Modern guest suites*
- *Air conditioned*
- *Charter boat fishing*

Boutique Bed & Breakfast **Lake Fishing/Cruising with Hosts**		
Double	$170-225
Single	$160-215
Child	POA

Plan some days in Taupo, experience all that is here. 'Above the Lake' is located in the heart of Taupo, convenient for restaurants and shopping and has well appointed rooms with tea/coffee facilities, fridge, Sky TV, air-conditioning, hair drier and toiletries.

On arrival, relax with your hosts over a glass of wine and enjoy the breathtaking lake views, with a backdrop of snow-capped volcanoes, or soak in the spa pool in the secluded 'English' garden. Breakfast in the contemporary dining room, overlooking both lake and garden, full cooked or continental served. Trout fishing from the MSA registered charter boat, Fish'N'Fun is an option and could be the highlight of your Taupo vacation.

Bedrooms	Qty
Double	3
Twin	
Single	
Bed Size	**Qty**
Super King	1
Queen	2
Double	
Single	
Bathrooms	**Qty**
Ensuite	1
Private	1
Guest Share	

RIVE GAUCHE
128 Ferndale Way, Taupo
Ph (07) 377 6167, Mobile 021-050 6735
e-mail: *lynnejim4@clear.net.nz*
www.rivegauchetaupo.co.nz

Features & Attractions

- *1 hectare of gardens & vineyard*
- *Wifi internet & satellite TV*
- *Quiet, convenient location*
- *3 mins to town centre*
- *Genuine Kiwi hospitality*
- *Fluent French spoken*

Boutique Accommodation **and Independent Studio**		
Double	$1780-245
Single	$160-180
Child	$30-50

Rive Gauche is a 4 year old home set in 1ha of gardens and developing vineyard overlooking the Waikato River near Huka Falls. We offer quality accommodation with ensuite bathrooms, independent access and kitchenette with fridge providing tea/coffee making facilities. Be assured of a warm welcome, share a drink with us in our main lounge or garden courtyard and discuss your plans and the various breakfast options available. Our studio is the perfect place for a special weekend getaway or a relaxing longer stay; gorgeous views, proximity to walkways, fridge, microwave, satellite TV, courtyard barbeque area, and laundry facilities available on request. We are close to Wairakei International golf course and walking distance to a neighbourhood restaurant.

Bedrooms	Qty
Double	3
Twin	
Single	
Bed Size	**Qty**
King	2
Queen	1
Double	
Kint/Single	1
Bathrooms	**Qty**
Ensuite	3
Private	
Guest Share	

DIRECTIONS: When coming from Taupo, turn right into Huka Falls Rd, left into Clearwater Lane, right into Ferndale Way.

KARAKA COTTAGE
42 Gillies Avenue, Taupo
Ph (07) 378 4560, Fax (07) 378 3145
Mobile 027-496 9432
email: karaka@rugsoriental.com
www.charmingaccommodation.co.nz

Tariff : N.Z. Dollars	
Double	$275-350
Single	$225-250
Child	Free

Bedrooms	Qty
Double	3
Twin	
Single	

Bed Size	Qty
Super King	
King/Twin	1
Queen	2
Double	
Single	

Bathrooms	Qty
Ensuite	3
Private	
Guest Share	

**Delightful Boutique
Self-contained Cottage**

Features & Attractions

- *Swimming pool*
- *BBQ available*
- *Thermal hot pools 2km*
- *Guided fishing*
- *Restaurants 1-2km*
- *Golf matches arranged*
- *Lake Taupo 5km walk*
- *Orakei Korako Cave & Thermal Park*

Directions From north on SH 1, turn left
into Tamamutu St. Travel to "T" junction
and turn right into Gillies Ave. Cottage
200m on right. From south, on SH 1,
turn right into Rifle Range Rd,
then right into Gillies Ave.

Centrally located in Taupo, **Karaka Cottage** is set in a quiet garden with mature trees. The cottage, adjacent to the main house, has been purpose built to provide total guest privacy. The deck from the cottage opens directly to the swimming pool, giving a relaxed atmosphere. Single parties can be accommodated in the super-king/twin bedroom of the self-contained cottage with its fully equipped kitchen for self-catering. Breakfast provisions are supplied for the cottage, or served in the dining room of the house or alfresco in the landscaped garden. Two bedrooms, both with ensuite bathrooms, are also available for guests in the house. Oriental rugs are a feature of both cottage and house. Dinner can also be provided by arrangement.

B&B @ Number Ten

10 Coprosma Crescent, Botanical Heights, Taupo
Ph/Fax (07) 378 6823, Mobile 021-237 2405
email: stay@bnbnumberten.co.nz
www.bnbnumberten.co.nz

Features & Attractions

- *Panoramic view of lake*
- *Relaxed, friendly hospitality*
- *Groundfloor guestrooms*
- *Free wifi*
- *Full breakfast*
- *Close to thermal hot pools*

 Bed & Breakfast Homestay

Double	$175-195
Single	$130-150
Child	

Are you looking for a Bed and Breakfast in Taupo that offers fun and a relaxed atmosphere? If so, then **B&B @Number Ten** is the place for you. We have fabulous views of Lake Taupo, a quiet, well furnished, modern home with a separate guest area. Both groundfloor guest rooms are warm and sunny each with ensuite and French doors leading out onto a courtyard. We love good food, good company and love to hear of your travel adventures, especially over a glass of wine before you go to dinner. We are happy to help you make the most of your time in Taupo, there is so much to see and do.

DIRECTIONS: Travelling south or north along Lake Terrace, turn onto Napier SH 5, 1st right onto Arrowsmith Ave, 2nd left onto Botanical Heights Dr then left onto Magnolia Rise then right onto Coprosma Cres.

Bedrooms	Qty
Double	2
Twin	
Single	
Bed Size	**Qty**
S King/Twin	1
Queen	1
Double	
Single	
Bathrooms	**Qty**
Ensuite	2
Private	
Guest Share	

Moselle

3 Te Hepera St, Taupo
Ph (07) 377 2922, Fax (07) 377 2290
Mobile 021-072 9975
email: ragevelvin@xtra.co.nz
www.moselletaupo.com

Features & Attractions

- *Free wireless facilities*
- *Top quality linen, Sky TV*
- *Golf courses near by*
- *Full cooked breakfast in dining room*
- *Walking distance to the Lake*
- *Full laundry/kitchen facilities*

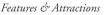 **Self-contained Boutique Accommodation**

Double	$180-200
Single	$160
Child	

Hosts Anne and Grahame Velvin welcome you to **Moselle Bed and Breakfast**, situated in a quiet cul de–sac. Guest accommodation is upstairs in the Aqua Room with a view of the lake, king bed or twin singles, ensuite and Sky TV. The Tulip Room has twin single beds and a private bathroom with spa bath. All guests served a breakfast of their choice in the dining room. Free wireless internet facilities. We are members of the Wairakei International Golf Course and will arrange your game there. Fishing trips also easily arranged. A 90 minute drive to the Ski fields, a three minute drive to the Thermal Hot Pools and a short stroll to the Lake. **Moselle** also offers a self contained unit.

Bedrooms	Qty
Double	3
Twin	
Single	
Bed Size	**Qty**
King	2
Queen	
Twin Singles	2
Singles	2
Bathrooms	**Qty**
Ensuite	2
Private	1
Guest Share	

DIRECTIONS: Travelling south on State Highway 1 take the second left turn after the Napier State Highway 5 turn-off, onto Shepherd Road, then first right into Te Hepera Street.

KAHOTEA HOUSE

32 Kahotea Drive, Motuoapa, Lake Taupo
Ph (07) 386 5523
Mobile 027-481 5320
email: kahoteahouse@xtra.co.nz
www.kahoteahouse.co.nz

Tariff : N.Z. Dollars	
Double	$135-155
Single	$135
Child	n/a

Bedrooms	Qty
Double	3
Twin	
Single	
Bed Size	**Qty**
Super King	
King	
Queen	3
Double	
Single/Bunks	2
Bathrooms	**Qty**
Ensuite	3
Private	
Guest Share	

The Bed & Breakfast Experience

Features & Attractions

- *Relaxing, private, quiet*
- *Fishing, also with a guide*
- *Tramping, golf, skiing*
- *Tokaanu hot pools*
- *Stunning lake views*
- *Photographers paradise*
- *Tongariro crossing*
- *Free internet, drying room, own TV*

K**ahotea House** is located in the heart of the playgrounds of the central plateau. With 180 degree views from the slopes of Motuoapa overlooking Lake Taupo. Your hosts Richard and Shirley-Ann offer warm hospitality and a comfortable stay in their tranquil home with a traditional, full english or nutritious, continental breakfast. Evening meals are available by prior arrangement.

Water activities include guided fly fishing on the famous local rivers for beginners or experts. Our guide is a member of NZPFGA and will provide equipment and a picnic lunch. Lake fishing is also an option. Other water activities include kayaking, rafting and water skiing, do it yourself boat hire. The central plateau's range of activities also include the Tongariro crossing tramp, skiing, snowboarding, cycling and golf at the famous Wairakei International, Kinloch and local courses.

Turangi

FOUNDERS @ TURANGI
253 Taupahi Road, Turangi
Ph (07) 386 8539, Fax (07) 386 8534
Mobile 027-485 4000
email: chris@founders.co.nz
www.founders.co.nz

Features & Attractions

- *Tongariro Alpine Crossing*
- *White water rafting*
- *Fly fishing, lakes and rivers*
- *Kayak, swim, golf, ski*
- *Walks local & National Park*
- *Historic thermal area, pools*

Bed & Breakfast Homestay	Double	$180
	Single	$120
	Child	

Peter and Chris Stewart offer you a warm welcome to their home on the border of Tongariro National and World Heritage Park. Close to Lake Taupo and a short stroll to the Tongariro River, this is the perfect place to visit if you love the outdoors. The Tongariro Alpine Crossing, trout fishing, white water rafting, golf, walks nearby and in the National Park, lake cruises, flights over the volcanoes, hunting and skiing.

Breakfast in our sunny dining room is a great start to your day. We happily cook early breakfast for Tongariro Crossing adventurers. A short drive to lakeside restaurants or a stroll to town makes dining a pleasure. Enjoy comfortable, relaxed hospitality in this place for all seasons.

Bedrooms	Qty
Double	4
Twin	
Single	
Bed Size	**Qty**
King	
Queen	3
Double	
King Single	2
Bathrooms	**Qty**
Ensuite	4
Private	
Guest Share	

Turangi

THE BIRCHES
13 Koura Street, Turangi
Ph (07) 386 5140, Fax (07) 386 5149
Mobile 021-136 4264
email: tineke.peter@xtra.co.nz
www.thebirches.net.nz

Features & Attractions

- *Tongariro River 2 min. stroll*
- *Fly-fishing, rafting*
- *Quiet, peaceful setting*
- *Skiing, golf, tramping*
- *Thermal pools*
- *Special breakfasts*

Bed & Breakfast Homestay	Double	$170
	Single	$140
	Child	

Close to the world-renowned Tongariro River we welcome you to our attractive residence, set in park-like surroundings on a quiet street. This unique location is ideally situated for many outdoor pursuits such as fly fishing, skiing, tramping, golf and rafting.

We offer superior and spacious ensuite accommodation with TV and coffee/tea making facilities in a separate part of the house. Your Dutch/Canadian hosts have considerable international experience through living in Canada, the Netherlands, France, Belgium and Singapore and can speak Dutch and French.

Dinner by prior arrangement.

Bedrooms	Qty
Double	1
Twin	
Single	
Bed Size	**Qty**
King	
Queen	1
Double	
Single	
Bathrooms	**Qty**
Ensuite	1
Private	
Guest Share	

TUI LODGE
196 Taupahi Road, Turangi
Ph (07) 386 0840, Fax (07) 386 0843
Mobile 027-441 1625
email: tui-lodge@xtra.co.nz
www.tui-lodge.co.nz
Features & Attractions

- *Personalised Maori culture tours*
- *Excellent Fly fishing*
- *Tongariro crossing and short walks*
- *Whakapapa ski fields*
- *Tokannu thermal area 5 min.*
- *Rafting 4x4 & horse trekking*

	Double	$270
	Single	$170
	Child	–

Luxury Accommodation
Bed & Breakfast

Bedrooms	Qty
Double	4
Twin	
Single	
Bed Size	**Qty**
King	4
Queen	
Double	
Single	
Bathrooms	**Qty**
Ensuite	4
Private	
Guest Share	

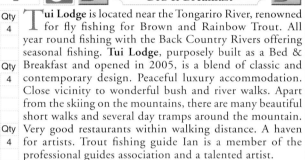

Tui Lodge is located near the Tongariro River, renowned for fly fishing for Brown and Rainbow Trout. All year round fishing with the Back Country Rivers offering seasonal fishing. **Tui Lodge**, purposely built as a Bed & Breakfast and opened in 2005, is a blend of classic and contemporary design. Peaceful luxury accommodation. Close vicinity to wonderful bush and river walks. Apart from the skiing on the mountains, there are many beautiful short walks and several day tramps around the mountain. Very good restaurants within walking distance. A haven for artists. Trout fishing guide Ian is a member of the professional guides association and a talented artist.

www.phototrips.info

Omori Lake House

31 Omori Rd, Omori, Turangi
Ph/Fax (07) 386 0420, Mobile 021-667 092
email: stay@omorilakehouse.co.nz
www.omorilakehouse.co.nz

VISA
MasterCard

Features & Attractions

- *New specialist-built luxury lodge*
- *Kiwi hospitality at its best*
- *Kiwi cuisine with dining options*
- *Panoramic views*
- *Volcanic landscape*
- *World-class trout fishing*

Boutique Lodge

Double	$175
Single	$155
Child	

We invite you to experience Kiwi hospitality at its best. Our new Boutique Accommodation is set high above Omori with stunning views looking across to Taupo. There are two luxury guest rooms with super king size beds, ensuite bathrooms, tea/coffee facilities and private deck. One room suits less abled with handrails and wet floor shower while the other has its own bath. Raewyn loves to cook – eating well is part of the experience. Enjoy barbeques in summer or sit at the large rimu table for Kiwi cuisine with Kiwi classics on the menu. Special diets can be catered for. Omori, on the south west of the lake, is close to a variety of activities including world renowned fly fishing, bush, the Tongariro Alpine crossing and other walks, thermal hot pools and ski slopes.

Bedrooms	Qty
Double	2
Twin	
Single	
Bed Size	**Qty**
Super King	2
Queen	
Double	
Single	
Bathrooms	**Qty**
Ensuite	2
Private	
Guest Share	

Willsplace

145 Omori Road, Omori, Turangi
Ph/Fax (07) 386 7339, Mobile 027-228 8960
email: b.g@willsplace.co.nz
www.willsplace.co.nz

Features & Attractions

- *Private suite*
- *Bush & lakeside walks*
- *Children welcome*
- *Fabulous lake views*
- *Good fishing & boating*
- *Close to National Park*

 Lakeside Bed & Breakfast

Double	$140-160
Single	$110-130
Child	neg

Our home overlooks the beautiful southwest corner of Lake Taupo. Just off the beaten track, yet only 10-15 minutes to Tokaanu Hot Thermal Pools, Turangi shops and restaurants and Tongariro River. Forty minutes to World Heritage Tongariro National Park. We offer you a superior, comfortable two-bedroom suite for your use alone with own entry and safe parking. Separate living area with tea-making facilities, refrigerator, microwave, TV. A spacious bathroom with bath and shower. Laundry and Internet available. Private patio overlooking the lake. Start the day with a full breakfast at a time to suit you. After your day's activities, with prior arrangement, you can come home to a delicious home-cooked dinner. Discount for three or more nights.

DIRECTIONS:
From Turangi take SH 41.
After 14 km turn right into Omori Rd.
Drive 2.5 km towards lake, small uphill
climb. 2nd house on right.

Bedrooms	Qty
Double	2
Twin	
Single	
Bed Size	**Qty**
King	
Queen	2
Double	
Single	2
Bathrooms	**Qty**
Ensuite	
Private	1
Guest Share	

93 By the Sea

93 Buller Street, New Plymouth
Ph (06) 758 6555, Mobile 027-230 3887
email: pat@93bythesea.co.nz
www.93bythesea.co.nz

Tariff : N.Z. Dollars	
Double	$160-200
Single	$110-150
Child	$20-70

Bedrooms	Qty
Double	2
Twin	1
Single	
Bed Size	Qty
Super King	
King	1
Queen	1
King/Single	1
Single	
Bathrooms	Qty
Ensuite	1
Private	1
Guest Share	

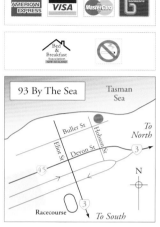

**Garden Setting, Near Seaside
City Central**

Features & Attractions

- *Central yet peaceful*
- *Off-street parking*
- *Ensuite or private spa bathroom*
- *Private guest entrance*
- *Adjacent Coastal Walkway*
- *National Park nearby*
- *Dinner by prior arrangement*
- *Laundry facilities available*

DIRECTIONS:
Please phone for easy directions.

'**93 By the Sea**' is a supremely comfortable revitalised 1930's bungalow within easy walking distance (up to 1.5 kilometres) to City Centre shops restaurants and all facilities. You can leave your car at home. Choose either the Ginkgo Suite –king/twin single bed(s)-private entrance-spacious lounge-spa bathroom or the Rimu room-totally cosy with queen bed –shower ensuite. Neither will disappoint. Enjoy my especially prepared breakfasts in the North facing Dining area inside or out) whilst viewing the garden and the sea. This is a wonderfully relaxing spot, especially on an evening after a day enjoying Taranaki's delights. Lets us spoil you.

Two websites that might help you plan your stay are www.taranaki.co.nz and www.newplymouthnz.com

COTTAGE BY THE SEA

66 Lower Turangi Road, RD 43,
Waitara, New Plymouth
Ph (06) 754 4548, Mobile 027-630 0737
email: cottagebythesea@clear.net.nz
www.cottagebythesea.co.nz

Tariff : N.Z. Dollars	
Double	$155-195
Single	$145-185
Child	

Bedrooms	Qty
Double Units	4
Twin	
Single	
Bed Size	**Qty**
Super King	
King	1
Queen	3
Double Sofabed	2
Single	
Bathrooms	**Qty**
Ensuite	4
Private	
Guest Share	

Spectacular Sea Views
Quiet Garden Setting

Features & Attractions

- *Expansive gardens and lawns*
- *20min. north of New Plymouth*
- *Breakfast optional extra*
- *Peacefull and private*
- *Near cafés, gardens, golf*
- *Coastal walks, art/crafts*
- *BBQ, DVDs & movies*
- *Everchanging seaviews*

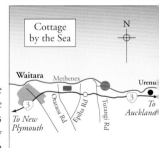

DIRECTIONS:
Nearest Town: New Plymouth
- about 25km north,
just a 20min drive.
1/2 km off State Highway 3
between Waitara and Urenui

Find yourself, lose yourself - the choice is yours. Peacefulness and privacy are our specialty - a perfect atmosphere to unwind. Lose yourself in the everchanging seaviews, or find yourself in our tranquil sunken garden. Hear the sounds of the waves and chorus of birds. Wander down 100 handcrafted steps to the secluded blacksand beach or relax with a book on your patio. Treat yourself to the magnetism that brings guests back again and again.

Two cottages, nestled in their own gardens, each sleeps 2 - 4. Two boutique, open-plan suites, each sleeps 2. All have kitchens and ensuites. Regrettably our property is not suitable for children. Please go to our website for more photos and details.

GLEN ALMOND HOUSE

18C Glen Almond Street, New Plymouth
Ph (06) 758 2920, Mobile 021-054 1555
email: sleep@glenalmondhouse.co.nz
www.glenalmondhouse.co.nz

Tariff : N.Z. Dollars	
Double	$100-180
Single	$90-145
Child	neg

Bedrooms	Qty
Double	2
Twin	1
Single	

Bed Size	Qty
Super King	
King	2
Queen	
Double	
Single	2

Bathrooms	Qty
Ensuite	
Private	2
Guest Share	1

**Boutique
Bed & Breakfast**

DIRECTIONS:
From city follow SH 45 towards
Oakura, along Devon Street West
(1 km), turn left at Belt Road, up the
hill, 50m turn right, Glen Almond St,
driveway on right 100m.

Features & Attractions

- *Secluded location*
- *Wireless internet*
- *Balcony with sea views*
- *Aromatherapy massage*
- *Character house with original features*
- *10 min walk to coastal walkway*
- *Warm & friendly atmosphere*
- *Private drawing room*

Indulge yourself in total comfort and pleasure at **Glen Almond House**! Located minutes from the city, tucked down a private driveway with a peaceful, sunny enclosed garden and courtyard for your enjoyment. Enjoy stunning sea and city views from this fully restored historic home. Share in the elegance of a bygone era. For your comfort the residence is centrally heated and offers two generous size double bedrooms with king-size beds and a twin bedded room, all furnished with high quality linen, with two private and one shared bathrooms. The **Balcony Room** overlooks the city and coastline, enjoys all day sun, enjoy a quiet drink on the private verandah.

The **Glyndwr Room** is on the ground floor for ease of access. We are a Kiwi/Welsh couple who are well seasoned travellers and who know what is needed to make your stay memorable. We offer you our convivial company, delicious home-made breads and muffins, a choice of hearty, healthy breakfasts and more...! Anne is a London trained beauty therapist specialising in aromatherapy massage. So for total body and mind relaxation you can be pampered with a massage of your choice. Ideal after a hard day of sightseeing!

123

VILLA HEIGHTS BED & BREAKFAST

333 Upland Road, New Plymouth, Taranaki
Ph (06) 755 2273, Mobile 027-416 4131
email: villaheights@xtra.co.nz
www.villaheights.co.nz

Tariff : N.Z. Dollars	
Double	$160-200
Single	$110-130
Child	$35

Bedrooms	Qty
Double	3
Twin	
Single	
Bed Size	**Qty**
Super King	
King	2
Queen	1
Double	
Single	1
Bathrooms	**Qty**
Ensuite	3
Private	
Guest Share	

Quiet & Peaceful Setting
Gracious Victorian Villa

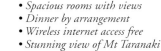

Features & Attractions

- *15 minutes to city*
- *Peaceful rural setting*
- *Full cooked breakfast*
- *Warm hospitality*

- *Spacious rooms with views*
- *Dinner by arrangement*
- *Wireless internet access free*
- *Stunning view of Mt Taranaki*

DIRECTIONS:
Please telephone for easy directions.

John and Rosemary warmly welcome you to their beautiful restored 1900's Victorian villa. Set in lovely gardens with stunning views of mount Taranaki countryside to the sea. Delight awaits those who appreciate finely crafted timbers. Panels and ceiling are of rich glowing New Zealand natives. Spacious quality rooms. Guests have their own private lounge with sky TV. Tea and coffee facilities, fresh home baking. Full breakfast. Open fires in winter. Off street parking. Evening meal by arrangement with complimentary wine. Special rates for staying more than one night. Free pick up from airport and bus terminal. Enjoy a friendly welcome, great hospitality with special touches to make your stay memorable.

We are just 15 minutes drive from New Plymouth city beaches, golf courses, beautiful gardens restaurants and the lovely coastal walkway. Egmont National park is just 30 minutes drive.

FERNLEAF B&B AND FARMSTAY

58 Tunanui Rd, Owhango, Taumarunui
Ph (07) 895 4847, Fax (07) 895 4837
Mobile 027-362 2993
email: fernleaf.farm@xtra.co.nz
www.fernleaffarmstay.co.nz

Features & Attractions

- *Beautiful country setting*
- *Ruapehu skifields*
- *Midway Auckland/Wellington*
- *Dinner by arrangement*
- *Enjoy our friendly pets*
- *Log fire in winter*

Double	$100-140
Single	$80-100
Child	neg

**Bed & Breakfast
Farmstay**

Bedrooms	Qty
Double	3
Twin	1
Single	
Bed Size	Qty
King	
Queen	2
Double	1
Single	2
Bathrooms	Qty
Ensuite	2
Private	1
Guest Share	1

Relax in the tranquil Tunanui Valley midway between Auckland and Wellington. Just 500m from SH 4, close for convenience, far enough away for peace and quiet.
We are the third generation to farm **Fernleaf** and our Romney flock has been recorded for eighty years.
Take a stroll across the farm and take in the awesome views from various vantage points, the mountains Ruapehu, Ngaruahoe, Tongariro and in the far distance Taranaki.
Enjoy our generous country hospitality, wonderful breakfasts, our beautiful dalmatian, friendly cats and pet lambs in season.
Dinner by arrangement.

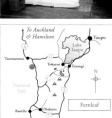

MOUNTAIN HEIGHTS LODGE

State Highway 4,
National Park Village
Ph (07) 892 2833, Fax (07) 892 2850
email: info@mountainheights.co.nz
www.mountainheights.co.nz

Features & Attractions

- *Private guest wing*
- *Tongariro Alpine Crossing*
- *Soak in the hot spa*
- *15 minutes to ski fields*
- *Spacious, self contained accomm*
- *Delicious breakfasts*

Double	$145-175
Single	$120-150
Child	neg

**Bed & Breakfast
Self-contained Accomm.**

Bedrooms	Qty
Double	2
Twin	2
Single	
Bed Size	Qty
King	
Queen	2
Double	2
Single	2
Bathrooms	Qty
Ensuite	4
Private	
Guest Share	

Mountain Heights is situated on the edge of Tongariro National Park, a Dual World Heritage Area. An ideal place from which to explore the mountains and volcanoes of the Central Plateau. Activities abound for all abilities, including the world renowned **Tongariro Alpine Crossing,** classed as the best one-day walk in New Zealand. Excellent mountain bike rides, horse trekking, canoeing the Whanganui River and scenic flights across the volcanoes.
For the less strenuous, enjoy the comfort of our centrally heated lodge. Soak in the hot spa or relax in front of the log fire with a good book or a game of chess. After a good night's sleep enjoy a delicious breakfast with freshly baked bread.

SPIRAL GARDENS

101 Raurimu Road, Raurimu, Owhango
Ph (07) 892 2997, Fax (07) 892 2653
Mobile 027-475 3482
email: spiralgardens@xtra.co.nz
www.spiralgardens.co.nz

Tariff : N.Z. Dollars	
Double	$110-175
Single	$110-140
Child	$30-50

Bedrooms	Qty
Double	4
Twin	
Single	

Bed Size	Qty
Super King	
King	
Queen	3
Double	4
Single	

Bathrooms	Qty
Ensuite	3
Private	1
Guest Share	

Homestay - Bed & Breakfast & Self-contained Cabin

Features & Attractions

- *Location, Location, Location*
- *Skiing, golf, tramping*
- *Discover hidden treasures*
- *Dinner by arrangement*
- *Central to activities/attractions*
- *Fishing, hunting, biking*
- *Families welcome*
- *Vegetarians catered for*

Our home overlooks the Piopiotea Stream and a magnificent stand of native bush. We are five minutes north of National Park Village, gateway to the Tongariro and Whanganui National Parks. The Whakapapa ski area is a 25 minute drive. Transport to the world renowned Tongariro Crossing day walk is available at National Park Village. We can organise any of the adventure activities on offer in the Central Plateau area, horse treks, river rafting, guided hunting and fishing tours. Our luxury suites feature a queen bed, ensuite or private bathroom, a double bed settee, casual chairs and table, writing bureau and refrigerator.

We have central heating throughout in winter. Coffee and tea making facilities are on hand for guest use in our family kitchen and we encourage you to use the lounge and decks in casual relaxation. The cabin is small and cosy with a pot belly fire, stereo, television, private deck and carport and self-catering.

TARATA FISHAWAY LODGE
Mokai Road, Mokai Valley, Taihape
Ph (06) 388 0354, Fax (06) 388 0954
Mobile 027-279 7037
email: fishaway@xtra.co.nz
www.tarata.co.nz

Tariff : N.Z. Dollars	
Double	$120-220
Single	$65-180
Child under 12	$40

Bedrooms	Qty
Double	9
Twin	
Single	

Bed Size	Qty
Super King	
King	4
Queen	5
Double	
Single	3

Bathrooms	Qty
Ensuite	5
Private	1
Guest Share	

DIRECTIONS:
Central North Island –
Turn off SH 1, 6 km south
of Taihape, at the Gravity
Canyon Bungy and
Ohotu signs. Follow signs
for 14 km to the Bungy
Bridge. We are 6 km past
here on Mokai Road.

 **River Retreat - Honeymoon Suite
Fishingstay - Farmstay**

Features & Attractions

- *Trout fishing and scenic rafting*
- *Visit LOTR, Middle Earth*
- *6km past Bungy & Flying Fox*
- *'Mini' Golf (with a difference)*
- *Swimming & spa pools*
- *Bush walks & spotlight safari*
- *Camp outs*
- *Clay-bird shooting*

We are very lucky to have a piece of New Zealand's natural beauty. **Tarata** is nestled in bush in the remote Mokai Valley where the picturesque Rangitikei River meets the rugged Ruahine Ranges. We have the wilderness and unique trout fishing right at our doorstep. Stephen offers guided fishing and rafting trips for all ages. Raft down the gentle crystal clear waters of the magnificent Rangitikei River, visit Middle Earth and a secret waterfall, stunning scenery you will never forget. Our spacious home and our large garden allow guests private space to relax and unwind. Whether it is by the pool on a hot summer's day with a book, soaking in the spa pool after a day on the river or enjoying a cosy winter's night in front of our open fire with a glass of wine. Come on a farm tour meeting our many friendly farm pets and experience our 'nightlife' on our spotlight safari. Stay in our homestead or in **Tarata's** fully self-contained 'River Retreats' where you can enjoy a spa bath with 'million dollar views' of the river and relax on the large decking amidst native birds and trees. Peace, privacy and tranquillity at its best! We will even deliver a candle light dinner to your door. Approved pets welcome. We think **Tarata** is truly a magic place and we would love sharing it with you.

BEST BEACH VIEW

8 Tuahine Cres, Wainui, Gisborne
Ph (06) 868 9757
Mobile 027-356 6229
email: bestbeachview@xtra.co.nz
www.charmingaccommodation.co.nz

Tariff : N.Z. Dollars	
Double	$150
Single	$100
Child	

Bedrooms	Qty
Double	2
Twin	
Single	

Bed Size	Qty
Super King	
King	
Queen	2
Double	
Single	

Bathrooms	Qty
Ensuite	2
Private	
Guest Share	

Bed & Breakfast Homestay

Features & Attractions

- *Good parking*
- *Quiet location*
- *Stunning sea views*
- *One of NZ's nicest beaches*
- *8 minute walk to restaurant*
- *One of NZ's best golf courses*
- *Tennis courts, horse trekking*
- *Excellent Wineries*

Annabel Reynolds, your host, welcomes you to a peaceful, comfortable and memorable stay from an elevated section, with breathtaking and panoramic views of Wainui Beach. Unwind with a swim or a walk on the beach which is right on your doorstep. Gisborne is quickly being discovered as a jewel of the East Coast.

The city is beautiful with different species of palm trees lining the streets and a great selection of cuisine from excellent cafés and restaurants on the water and in the CBD. The city has its own charm and is very beautiful with beaches and rivers running through it and surrounding it. There are wineries to visit and Eastwood Hill Arboretum is internationally recognised as having the greatest selection of oak trees in Australasia. Gisborne is a tremendous experience and staying at Wainui Beach at Annabel's **Best Beach View B&B** will remain a special memory.

COBDEN GARDEN HOMESTAY

1 Cobden Crescent, Bluff Hill, Napier
Ph (06) 834 2090, Fax (06) 834 1977
Mobile 027-695 1240
email: info@cobden.co.nz
www.cobden.co.nz

Features & Attractions

- Quiet, private surroundings
- Extensive views
- Guest computer provided
- 10 minute walk to city centre
- Guest laundry facilities
- Off-road parking & easy access

Double	$200-240	
Single	$170-210	
Child	$50	

Boutique Homestay Bed & Breakfast

Bedrooms	Qty
Double	3
Twin	
Single	
Bed Size	**Qty**
Super King	2
King	1
Double	
Single	5
Bathrooms	**Qty**
Ensuite	3
Private	
Guest Share	

We invite you to stay in our quiet, sunny colonial villa on Bluff Hill. Relax in a spacious room with ensuite. Feel pampered in king or twin single beds with fine cotton linen, duvets, electric blankets, plump pillows and robes. Enjoy lounge seating, TV, heater, fan, tea/coffee making facilities and complimentary refreshments in your room. Unwind with a walk around our ½ acre garden or take in the view from our verandah, guest lounge or upstairs sunroom. Prior to indulging your taste-buds at a local restaurant join us on the verandah or in the lounge for complimentary tasting of local wine and produce. Choose your breakfast from our menu of local foods and home-made delights. We make every effort to make your stay extra special and memorable. When booking, please advise of any special dietary requirements. Three unobtrusive cats in residence.

MAISON BÉARNAISE BED & BREAKFAST

25 France Road, Bluff Hill, Napier
Ph (06) 835 4693, Fax (06) 835 4694
email: info@maisonbearnaise.co.nz
www.maisonbearnaise.co.nz

Features & Attractions

- Quiet location, views
- Colourful gardens
- 10 min walk to city
- Wineries, golf, fishing nearby
- Single level home
- Emails, wireless internet

Double	$160-220	
Single	$120-170	
Child		

Quality Homestay Bed & Breakfast

Bedrooms	Qty
Double	2
Twin	
Single	
Bed Size	**Qty**
King	
Queen	2
Double	
Single	
Bathrooms	**Qty**
Ensuite	2
Private	
Guest Share	

A warm invitation to share our charming oasis of ever changing colourful gardens. Christine, Napier born, is happy to assist with local and national sightseeing advice. Both large guest rooms are privately appointed with ensuite bathrooms, have comfortable queen beds, armchairs, heating, fan, hairdryers, tea/coffee making facilities, telephone, DVD television. You may prefer to sit back in the light and airy guest lounge with a book, magazine, newspaper or board games email access is available here. Our sunny, private courtyard provides opportunities to relax or savour the delicious breakfast choices including homemade and local produce. Napier city is a ten minutes walk and the historic suburb of Ahuriri, with many fine restaurants is a two minute drive from here. Off-street parking, laundry service available. Welcome, unwind, our wish is you feel at home.

DIRECTIONS: North on Marine Parade. Left Coote Road. Right Thompson Road. Left France Road (first driveway on left).

Seaview Lodge
5 Seaview Terrace, Napier
Ph (06) 835 0202,　Mobile 021-180 2101
email: cvulodge@xtra.co.nz
www.aseaviewlodge.co.nz

Features & Attractions

- *Overlooking Pacific Ocean*
- *3 min walk to city centre*
- *Across from heated pools*
- *Quiet, elevated location*
- *Off-street parking*
- *Free Wi Fi access*

Quality, Central City Bed & Breakfast

	Double	$170-180
	Single	$130-140
	Child	n/a

Seaview Lodge is a lovingly renovated, spacious late Victorian home. This inner city, beachside Bed and Breakfast offers a warm welcome and spectacular views over the city and ocean. Enjoy your continental breakfast of fresh croissants and fruit salad on the lower verandah while watching the waves break on the shore. At the end of the day relax in the comfortable guest lounge or on the large upstairs balcony and enjoy a glass of local wine while watching the sun set. A spacious single and a double room share the large guest lounge with TV and tea/coffee making facilities. The other double/twin room has its own lounge area including TV.

The 2008/2010 edition of Lonely Planet guide recommended **Seaview Lodge** as their pick for Napier.

Bedrooms	Qty
Double	1
Twin/Double	1
Single	1
Bed Size	**Qty**
SuperKing/Twin	1
King	1
Queen	
King/Single	1
Bathrooms	**Qty**
Ensuite	1
Private	2
Guest Share	

Villa Vista
22A France Road, Bluff Hill, Napier
Ph/Fax (06) 835 8770
Mobile 027-435 7179
email: accommodation@villavista.net
www.villavista.net

Features & Attractions

- *Cape & ocean views*
- *Sumptuous breakfasts*
- *Museum & art galleries*
- *Art Deco attractions*
- *Wineries*
- *15 min walk to city centre*

VISA

MasterCard

Bed & Breakfast

	Double	$145-160
	Single	$110-125
	Child	

Villa Vista is a beautiful turn-of-the century Edwardian villa with fantastic uninterrupted views of Cape Kidnappers, Te Mata Peak and the Pacific Ocean, located 15 min. walk and 3 min. drive from the CBD. We offer 3 large, private rooms, situated on the top floor. One double room has a balcony. Every room has delightful views, en-suite, TV, coffee/tea making facilities, air conditioning, hair dryer and bathrobes. Continental and cooked Kiwi breakfast is served in the spacious dining room. A variety of home-made delicacies will set you up for a busy or relaxing day in all that Hawke's Bay has to offer, such as wineries, Art Deco tours, gannet colonies.

~ Welcome to Napier, Hawke's Bay.

Bedrooms	Qty
Double	2
Twin	1
Single	
Bed Size	**Qty**
King	
Queen	3
Double	
Single	1
Bathrooms	**Qty**
Ensuite	3
Private	
Guest Share	

DIRECTIONS:
Port end Marine Parade,
Coote Road, right into Thompson
Road, left into France Road, house on
your right.

KERRY LODGE & GARDEN COTTAGE
7 Forward Street, Greenmeadows, Napier
Ph (06) 844 9630, Fax (06) 844 1450
Mobile 027-493 2874
email: stay@kerrylodge.co.nz
www.kerrylodge.co.nz

Tariff : N.Z. Dollars	
Double	$180-260
Single	$130-60
Child	$60

Bedrooms	Qty
Double	2
Twin	2
Single	

Bed Size	Qty
Super King	1
King	2
Queen	1
Double	
Single	2

Bathrooms	Qty
Ensuite	1
Private	1
Guest Share	1

**Bed & Breakfast
Homestay**

Features & Attractions

- *Spacious rooms*
- *Quiet location*
- *Off-street parking*
- *Wheel chair accessible*
- *Tranquil, spacious gardens*
- *Caring, informative hosts*
- *Close to wineries, restaurants*
- *Laundry available*

DIRECTIONS: From Napier, travel along Kennedy Rd & Gloucester St until Greenmeadows, turn right into Avenue Rd, then left into Forward St

We are situated in the heart of Taradale, just ten minutes from Napier, 15 minutes from Hastings and only minutes away from New Zealand's two oldest wineries, Church Road Winery and Mission Estate Winery - ideally placed for all Hawke's Bay activities. Our premises include a fully self contained two bedroom cottage and two large bed and breakfast rooms

in the main house. We are situated on a quiet back section in half an acre of gardens and our pool is the perfect place to unwind after a day's sightseeing. We love living in Hawke's Bay and enjoy supporting the many local growers, producers and businesses. Because it is one of the sunniest and warmest areas in New Zealand, Hawke's Bay is a wonderful place to visit and holiday in - with fabulous world class vineyards through to stunning Art Deco architecture. We look forward to sharing it with you.

Mission Vista

359 Church Road, Greenmeadows, Napier
Ph/Fax (06) 844 5727, Mobile 027-452 0725
email: mission.vista@xtra.co.nz
www.missionvista.co.nz

Tariff : N.Z. Dollars	
Double	$120-200
Single	$100-120
Child	neg

Bedrooms	Qty
Double	3
Twin	1
Single	1
Bed Size	**Qty**
Super King/Twin	1
King	
Queen	2
Double	1
Single	2
Bathrooms	**Qty**
Ensuite	1
Private	1
Guest Share	

Bed & Breakfast
Self-contained Apartment

Features & Attractions

- *Personalized trips organised*
- *Halfway Napier/Hastings*
- *Cafés & restaurants nearby*
- *4 golf courses within 30 min.*
- *Pottery Design Studio workshop on site*
- *Art deco attractions*
- *36 wineries within 30 min.*
- *Sky Digital TV, Wireless internet*

We have a luxurious self-contained apartment, plus a spacious queen and twin accommodation with lounge, kitchenette and bathroom - with stunning views from both balconies over the vineyard up to the Mission Estate Winery. All have tea and coffee making facilities. Enjoy a continental or fully cooked breakfast. Ideally situated for a Hawke's Bay getaway holiday, we are 5 min. from the airport, and 10 min. from Napier/Hastings. If needed we will pick you up from any public transport. Fine and casual dining is available within walking distance. In close proximity are shops, golf course, garden centres and the Mission and Church Road Wineries. As we are both experienced tour guides and 4th generation Napierites we are more than happy to organise specialized tours and to share our knowledge and love of the Bay. Our Pottery Ceramic Design Studio workshop is on site. Drop in for a chat whilst we are working, we are happy to direct you to all the things to do for a relaxed or busy holiday and help make it a great time for you to remember.

132

OMARUNUI HOMESTAY

69 Omarunui Road, Waiohiki, Napier
Ph/Fax (06) 844 9396, Mobile 021-071 0159
email: kate.ladson@slingshot.co.nz
www.omarunuihomestay.co.nz

Features & Attractions

- *Quiet, relaxing location*
- *Very spacious room*
- *Small, solar heated pool*
- *Close to wineries, restaurants & shops*
- *Free Wi Fi & Laundry facilities*
- *Cooked or continental breakfasts*

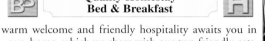

$		
Double	$150-160
Single	$110-130
Child	

**Quality Homestay
Bed & Breakfast**

Bedrooms	Qty
Double	1
Twin	
Single	
Bed Size	**Qty**
Super King	1
Queen	
Double	
Single	
Bathrooms	**Qty**
Ensuite	1
Private	
Guest Share	

A warm welcome and friendly hospitality awaits you in our home, which we share with our two friendly cats, Sooty and Tiddles. We live in a quiet, semi-rural location set in an acre of lovely, private gardens containing many subtropical plants and panoramic views over the local vineyards, distant hills and mountains.

Our accommodation is a spacious, sunny room with ensuite, a super king bed and a roomy, comfortable sitting area. The ensuite has a large, modern shower, toiletries and hair dryer. A private patio leads to the garden and there is complimentary tea/coffee in the room together with a small fridge.

We would be happy to offer you helpful, friendly advice on things to do and places to eat. Start your day with a delicious breakfast and join us for a pre-dinner glass of wine and nibbles in the evening.

WHINFIELD COUNTRY B&B

615 Puketapu Road, Taradale, Napier
Ph (06) 844 8623, Fax (06) 844 8623
email: whinfield@xtra.co.nz
www.charmingaccommodation.co.nz

Features & Attractions

- *Peaceful lifestyle*
- *Art Deco attractions*
- *Food & wine trails*
- *Two ensuite rooms*
- *Fishing and swimming*
- *Outdoors chess board*

$		
Double	$140
Single	$85
Child	$50

**Countrystay
Bed & Breakfast**

Bedrooms	Qty
Double	1
Twin	1
Single	
Bed Size	**Qty**
Super King	1
King Single	1
Queen	
Single	1
Bathrooms	**Qty**
Ensuite	2
Private	
Guest Share	

Whinfield is a comfortable country home with spectacular river views. Our accommodation offers two ensuite rooms in a separate cottage in the garden. Enjoy breakfast on the terrace of the main house and then have a game of chess on the outdoor board or stroll down to the river to fish or walk along the bank, past vineyards and deer farms.

We are only five minutes away from excellent restaurants and shops in Taradale and 5 minutes from the golf course. The Art Deco attractions of Napier are just 20 minutes away. We are happy to help plan your activities . At the end of the day, join us for a glass of wine and some home-grown olives.

We are retired farmers grazing a few cattle and have chooks and a cat.

DIRECTIONS: Take Puketapu Rd at roundabout in Taradale - Whinfield is 6.15 km on left.

WAIWHENUA FARMSTAY
ANNIES COTTAGE
808 River Road, Hastings
Ph (06) 874 2435, Fax (06) 874 2465
Mobile 027-479 4094
email: info@waiwhenua.co.nz
www.waiwhenua.co.nz

Tariff : N.Z. Dollars	
Double	$150-250
Single	$100
Child	$50

Bedrooms	Qty
Double	1
Twin	2
Single	
Bed Size	Qty
Super King	
King	
Queen	1
Double	
Single	4
Bathrooms	Qty
Ensuite	
Private	1
Family Share	

 Unique Farmstay

Features & Attractions

- *Extensive sheep, beef & deer farm*
- *Families & children welcome*
- *Historic homestead & cottage*
- *Relaxing swimming pool*
- *Trout fishing onsite*
- *Informative farm tours*
- *Fresh farm-style meals*
- *Bush and farm walks*

The perfect place to experience a genuine farmstay and friendly rural hospitality at **Annies Cottage**. Come and join us on our extensive 440 ha sheep, beef and deer farm. We offer guests a home away from home. Enjoy a guided farm tour, fish in our trout-filled river, or just relax in the total privacy at **Annies Cottage**. We provide three comfortable bedrooms and a fully self contained kitchen and laundry facilities. Suitable for individuals or families seeking total privacy and interested in the outdoor life. Two night stay recommended

DIRECTIONS:
Turn off SH 50 that goes between Napier and Hastings at Omahu (Fernhill in some maps) into Taihape Rd. Travel 35 km to River Road (Right). Travel 8km on River Road. Annies Cottage #744/746 white mail box right hand side.

however longer stay options also available. Enrich your stay by including other outdoor activities at our backdoor: hunting and fishing (guide available), bush and farm walks, garden tours, jet boating and extensive mountain hikes, plus many attractions in the greater sunny Hawkes Bay area. Sleeps up to six people at $150-250 per night. Meals can be provided by prior arrangement. Please bring all provisions with you as we have no shops nearby. Advanced bookings recommended.

OPTIONS

92 Simla Avenue, Havelock North, Hawke's Bay
Ph/Fax (06) 877 0257, Mobile 027-653 7270
email: gr.duff@xtra.co.nz
www.charmingaccommodation.co.nz

Tariff : N.Z. Dollars	
Double	$130-150
Single	$100-120
Child	neg

Bedrooms	Qty
Double	2
Twin	1
Single	

Bed Size	Qty
Super King	
King	1
Queen	1
Double	
Single	3

Bathrooms	Qty
Ensuite	1
Private	1
Guest Share	

Bed & Breakfast
Homestay

DIRECTIONS:
OPTIONS is easy to find.
Please ring for directions.
Advance booking recommended

Features & Attractions

- *Wine, gannets & Art Deco - all within 30minutes*
- *Near Te Mata Peak – views*
- *Internet with wireless connection*
- *Swimming pool & spa*
- *Laundry facilities*
- *Mini petanque court*
- *Private patios*

ptions is halfway between the centre of Havelock North village and Te Mata Peak which at 399 metres is the best place to start sightseeing in Hawkes Bay. The wineries, Cape Kidnappers with the gannets, and Napier with its Art Deco buildings are all within thirty minutes of **Options.**

Options offers friendly hospitality and guests are accommodated within our home in either a large double bedroom with king-size bed and ensuite, or a suite with a double room with queen-size bed, a twin room, a private bathroom and separate lounge. The internet is available to guests and all rooms have wireless connection.

In its elevated position, **Options** has lovely views and with the private patios there is a choice of sun or shade. The pool, heated to extend the summer season, and spa offer respite after a day's sightseeing. During winter the fire is welcoming.

A delicious breakfast of your choice is served inside or outside depending on the weather. In the village there is a range of restaurants available. Sharing an evening meal with us, at an additional cost, is a great way to learn about our area.

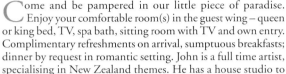

THE LOFT ART STUDIO
AND PREMIUM BED & BREAKFAST
10 Woodford Heights, Havelock North
Ph (06) 877 5938, Mobile 021-474 729
email: theloft@hawkesbayhomestay.co.nz
www.hawkesbayhomestay.co.nz

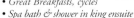

Features & Attractions

- *Refreshments on arrival*
- *Email, wireless, skype*
- *Private sitting room with TV*
- *TV in bedrooms*
- *Great Breakfasts, cycles*
- *Spa bath & shower in king ensuite*

Premium Homestay
Bed & Breakfast

	Double	$160-200
	Single	$140-180
	Child	neg

Bedrooms	Qty
Double	2
Twin	
Single	
Bed Size	**Qty**
King	1
Queen	1
Double	
Single	
Bathrooms	**Qty**
Ensuite	2
Private	
Guest Share	

Come and be pampered in our little piece of paradise. Enjoy your comfortable room(s) in the guest wing – queen or king bed, TV, spa bath, sitting room with TV and own entry. Complimentary refreshments on arrival, sumptuous breakfasts; dinner by request in romantic setting. John is a full time artist, specialising in New Zealand themes. He has a house studio to visit. Use our intimate courtyard or deck at your leisure. Just minutes to the picturesque village of Havelock North with cafes, restaurants, and boutique shopping. We are central to the many world renowned local wineries – Craggy Range, Te Mata Estate, Black Barn, to name but a few; Cape Kidnappers with one of the largest mainland gannet colonies in the world. There is so much to see in Hawke's Bay, which makes **The Loft Art Studio and Bed & Breakfast** the perfect base from which to explore. Tour bookings available. Tariff adjustable with seasons and options chosen.

THE WHITEHOUSE

14 Woodford Heights, Havelock North
Ph (06) 877 0522
Mobile 021-143 8109
email: info@thewhitehousebandb.co.nz
www.thewhitehousebandb.co.nz

Tariff : N.Z. Dollars	
Double	$155-215
Single	–
Child	neg

Bedrooms	Qty
Double	2
Twin	
Single	

Bed Size	Qty
Super King	
King	1
Queen	1
Double	
Single	

Bathrooms	Qty
Ensuite	1
Private	1
Guest Share	

Luxury Accommodation
Homestay Bed & Breakfast

Features & Attractions

- *Stunning views*
- *Close to village*
- *Great wine/food district*
- *Boutique shopping*
- *Refreshments, homebaking on arrival*
- *Wonderful breakfast selection*
- *Relax outdoors in the spa*
- *Hire Mazda MX5 roadster*

Welcome to **The Whitehouse,** an adventure with a difference. Karin and Doug offer luxury Bed & Breakfast accommodation in the heart of Havelock North and only minutes from the cities of Hastings and the Art Deco Capital of Napier. These locations offer you boutique shopping and a range of casual and fine dining, also short drives to many wonderful wineries that make this region so very special.

We offer two luxury suites, 'Woodford' and 'Iona', refreshments and homebaking on arrival. Then relax on the decks or in the spa pool with your wine and soak up the stunning views. Hire for a day the new Mazda MX5 Roadster and enjoy what Hawkes Bay has to offer; Wineries, Golf, Art Deco, Cape Kidnappers. We also have bikes for guests.

ASHLEY PARK

SH 3, Waitotara, South Taranaki
Ph (06) 346 5917, Fax (06) 346 5861
email: ashley_park@xtra.co.nz
www.ashleypark.co.nz

Features & Attractions

- *Peaceful country setting*
- *Pet farm animals & aviaries*
- *Park, lake & farm walks*
- *Antique and tea-shop*
- *Swimming pool*
- *Tennis and mini golf*

$	Double	$100-140
	Single	$100
	Child	

 Farmstay Bed & Breakfast and Self-contained Chalets

Bedrooms	Qty
Double	1
Twin	2
Single	
Bed Size	**Qty**
King	
Queen	1
Double	
Single	4
Bathrooms	**Qty**
Ensuite	1
Private	
Guest Share	1

R elax and enjoy the peace of the country with views of Mt. Egmont. Hand-feed our pet farm animals, stroll around the park and lake or take a more strenuous farm walk. Be tempted with Devonshire teas in the antique shop, and a visit to our 'memory lane' museum. Partake in a round of mini golf or tennis. Dinner available.

I look forward to welcoming you into my home.

Guests comment – *"Feels like we belong here, very welcoming and friendly".*

Charming
Places to Stay
in New Zealand

"Charming Places to Stay is a lovely book, the best presented of all the B&B books we have ever seen, it is crisp, clear and every advert looks enticing. We have stayed all over the world and it is by far and away the most accurate book we have ever used as well."

Robin and Linda Spiller, Cornwall, UK

COUNTRY PATCH B&B

18 Kea Street, Waikanae
Ph (04) 293 5165, Fax (04) 293 5164
Mobile 027-296 3716
email: stay@countrypatch.co.nz
www.countrypatch.co.nz

Tariff : N.Z. Dollars	
Double	$175-260
Single	
Child	$30-35

Bedrooms	Qty
Double	3
Twin	1
Single	
Bed Size	**Qty**
Super King/Twin	2
King	
Queen	1
Double	
Single	2
Bathrooms	**Qty**
Ensuite	3
Private	
Guest Share	

**Self-contained
Bed & Breakfast**

Features & Attractions

- *Delightful country style*
- *Magnificent views*
- *Cosy and comfortable*
- *Good restaurants close by*
- *2 minutes drive from SH 1*
- *Wellington commuter train 2 min*
- *Villa has large verandah and
  wheelchair access*

It's the little extras... that keep guests staying an extra night. Our visitor book glows with appreciative accolades. Two delightful self-contained accommodation sites...

Country Patch Studio, with its own entrance and deck, has a queen bed with ensuite and twin beds on the mezzanine floor of the kitchen-lounge.

Country Patch Villa has an open fire and large verandah with magical views. It is wheelchair accessible and the two bedrooms, each with ensuite, have super-king beds that can unzip to make twins.

Set on 2½ acres in the Waikanae foothills with breathtaking views over the Kapiti Coast and historic Kapiti Island, the property is handy to Wellington and the Manawatu. Bush walks can be enjoyed from over the back fence. Hosts Brian and Sue display an infectious hospitality. **A treat you can't beat!**

AWATEA LODGE

19 Hadfield Rd, Peka Peka, Waikanae
Ph (04) 293 2404, Mobile 027-242 7572
email: brent@awatealodge.co.nz
www.awatealodge.co.nz

Features & Attractions

- *Restful, friendly atmosphere*
- *Panoramic views/sunsets*
- *Private spa pool*
- *Gourmet breakfast*
- *Bush or beach walks*
- *Spinning/weaving studio*

**A Relaxing Farmstay
Bed & Breakfast**

Double	$165
Single	$90-100
Child	

We welcome you! Take time to relax and enjoy eight acres of garden and beautiful natural surroundings. Unwind in the hammock on the deck, or walk around the farm and meet the friendly alpacas and llamas. A spectacular way to enjoy a beautiful Kapiti Island sunset is to either stroll up the back hill or wander along the beach - or you may just prefer to 'chill-out' in the spa pool. Local eco-tourism includes coastal, river and bush walks, or a special day trip to the Kapiti Island. Other popular attractions include the 'Kapiti Arts Trail' Maori Arts gallery and golf courses. Our specialty is 'slow food' using where possible our own fresh organic produce. We can prepare delicious home-made dinners and hampers on request. A cooked or continental breakfast is included in the tariff.

Bedrooms	Qty
Double	1
Twin	1
Single	
Bed Size	**Qty**
King	
Queen	1
Double	
Single	2
Bathrooms	**Qty**
Ensuite	
Private	1
Guest Share	

RIVERSTONE GARDEN

111 Ngatiawa Road, Waikanae, Kapiti Coast
Ph (04) 293 1936
email:eppie@riverstone.co.nz
www.riverstone.co.nz

Features & Attractions

- *Rural self-contained*
- *Local dining out*
- *River and bird song*
- *Bush and local walks*
- *Shops, beach, Lindale*
- *Golf and car museum*

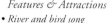

**Rural Cottage
Bed & Breakfast**

Double	$130
Single	$90
Child	$45

The cottage has self-contained accommodation with bedrooms, bathroom, lounge and kitchenette. Courtyard and barbecue area with views of river and bush. Continental or full breakfast. Paul is an engineer and writer, and Eppie sketches and paints. Laundry facilities. Local café, pottery and birdpark with river walks and you can swim in the river. There are more restaurants in Waikanae village, six minutes drive, and in Paraparaumu, ten minutes towards Wellington. Craft shops and boutiques at Lindale and general shopping at Paraparaumu. Beaches and swimming pools in both centres. The capital city Wellington is forty-five minutes away and has the airport, inter-island ferries, shops, galleries and museums. Internet available.

Bedrooms	Qty
Double	1
Twin	1
Single	
Bed Size	**Qty**
King	
Queen	1
Double	
Single	2
Bathrooms	**Qty**
Ensuite	
Private	1
Guest Share	

DIRECTIONS: Turn off SH 1 across railway lines onto Akatarawa Road. At 5km turn left before small church into Ngatiawa Road. 1km to **Riverstone** on left.

(HELEN'S) WAIKANAE BEACH B&B/HOMESTAY

115 Tutere St, Waikanae Beach, Kapiti Coast
Ph (04) 902 5829, Fax (04) 902 5840
Mobile 021-259 3396
email: waikanaebeachbandb@paradise.net.nz
www.waikanaebeachbandb.co.nz

Tariff : N.Z. Dollars	
Double	$160-180
Single	$140-160
Child	neg

Bedrooms	Qty
Double	2
Twin	
Single	
Bed Size	Qty
Super King	
King	
Queen	2
Double	
Single	1
Bathrooms	Qty
Ensuite	1
Private	1
Guest Share	

A Relaxing Seaside Homestay/ Bed & Breakfast

DIRECTIONS:
On SH1, travelling north from Wellington, turn left into Te Moana Road after crossing the Waikanae River Bridge. Follow the road down, keeping left where road splits. Upon reaching T-intersection at the end of the road, turn left into Tutere Street.

Features & Attractions

- *Warm, friendly hospitality*
- *Good local restaurants*
- *Direct beach access*
- *Tea/coffee making facilities*
- *Awesome sea views and sunsets*
- *Dinner by arrangement (off-season only)*
- *Paraparaumu Beach Golf Club - Ranked in the world's top 100 golf courses*

Helen's open-plan home by the sea is the perfect location to relax and unwind. Enjoy direct access to a long, sandy beach with spectacular views of Kapiti Island, and the Tararua mountains. During the day, walk/cycle along the banks of the Waikanae River, or take a leisurely stroll along the beach towards sunset. Marvel at the incredible night sky and later, drift off to sleep to the soothing sounds of the ocean. In the morning, enjoy a delicious breakfast (continental or full).

Do plan to stay at least two nights! **Helen's** is a wonderful location for a honeymoon, or just a romantic weekend away, and do let her know if you are celebrating a special occasion. To make a booking, or for more information and suggestions of what to do and see on the Kapiti Coast, please visit her website www.waikanaebeachbandb.co.nz.

OCEAN RETREAT

94 The Esplanade, Raumati South, Paraparaumu
Ph (04) 902 1210, Fax (04) 902 1210
email: stay@oceanretreat.co.nz
www.oceanretreat.co.nz

Tariff : N.Z. Dollars	
Double	$150
Single	$150
Child	

Bedrooms	Qty
Double	1
Twin	
Single	
Bed Size	Qty
Super King	
King	
Queen	1
Double	
Single	
Bathrooms	Qty
Ensuite	1
Private	
Guest Share	

**Absolute Beachfront
Bed & Breakfast**

Features & Attractions

- *Ocean/beach/island views*
- *Right on the beachfront*
- *Swim/kayak/bike/walk*
- *QEII Park on doorstep*
- *Lovely sunsets/nightsky*
- *Far infrared sauna*
- *Lots to see, do & enjoy!*
- *2min SH1 45min Wellington*

Take a break at **Ocean Retreat**. Whether travelling, attending a special occasion, or just needing a break away, you will be welcomed here at **Ocean Retreat**. We have a new home right on the beachfront. Sit and relax, enjoy endless ocean views, safe swimming, sandy beaches, or walk to QEII Park. Take the mountain bikes, ride the trails, try out the kayak. You have ocean views from your ensuite bedroom and patio. The comfortable bedroom has a queen bed, TV/DVD/video/CD, tea making facilities and fridge. The far infrared sauna is also available to our guests by appointment. With plenty of wonderful cafés and restaurants nearby you're spoilt for choice. Shop at local markets, Coastlands or Lindale; see a movie, play golf, enjoy Southwards Car Museum, Nga Manu Bird Sanctuary, horse riding, visit antique and craft shops, wineries and potteries. It's all here for you! Need a retreat? Come stay with us. **Ocean Retreat**. You're very welcome!

THE MARTINBOROUGH CONNECTION

80 Jellicoe Street, Martinborough, Wairarapa
Ph (06) 306 9708, Fax (06) 306 9706
Mobile 027-438 1581
email: martinboroughconnection@xtra.co.nz
www.martinboroughconnection.co.nz

Tariff : N.Z. Dollars	
Double	$135-145
Single	$115-120
Child	$15

Bedrooms	Qty
Double	4
Twin	
Single	
Bed Size	**Qty**
Super King	
King	
Queen	4
Double	
Single	
Bathrooms	**Qty**
Ensuite	4
Private	
Guest Share	

VISA **MasterCard** **bancard** **e** **eftpos**

Historic Bed & Breakfast
Boutique Accommodation

Features & Attractions

- *Restored heritage building*
- *Guest lounge, open fire*
- *Sky TV, wireless internet*
- *Lovely outdoor area*
- *6 minute walk to cafés*
- *Wine tours arranged*
- *Cape Palliser Lighthouse*
- *Fur seal colony 55 min*

Your visit to the wine village of Martinborough, one hour's drive "over the hill" from Wellington, will be enhanced by your stay at **The Martinborough Connection**. Built in 1889, originally as a boot store and home, the property has been beautifully renovated and converted to a B&B, retaining its original character and charm.

Open your bedroom door to a sunny veranda and garden. Commence your day with a scrumptious breakfast using fresh fruit and local products. Spend your day sampling Martinborough's award-winning wines or alternatively visit an olive grove, take part in the various adventure activities or a walk. Stay an extra day and ensure that you visit Cape Palliser with its spectacular coastline, lighthouse, and fur seal colony. Or relax at the property. Sip a wine in front of the open fire in the guest lounge, or outside in the lovely garden, on the deck or the garden swing under the willows. Our interests include travel, sport, bridge, art and wine. We look forward to hosting you.

143

LLANDAFF COUNTRY RESIDENCE

183 Upper Plain Road, Masterton
Ph/Fax (06) 378 6628, Mobile 021-359 562
email: llandaff@xtra.co.nz
www.llandaff.co.nz

Tariff : N.Z. Dollars	
Double	$110-130
Single	$70-120
Child	$25

Bedrooms	Qty
Double	4
Twin	1
Single	
Bed Size	**Qty**
Super King	
King	1
Queen	2
Double	1
Single	1
Bathrooms	**Qty**
Ensuite	1
Private	
Guest Share	3

      Delightful Rural Retreat

Features & Attractions

- *Gracious 1880 Homestead*
- *Horse drawn vehicles*
- *Wine trails*
- *Nearby attractions*
- *Country cooked breakfast*
- *Peaceful country atmosphere*
- *Majestic gardens*
- *Bicycles,croquet and petanque*

Elegantly restored homestead boasts beautiful native NZ timbers, old pull-handle toilets, open fire in lounge surrounded by large gardens and 130 year old trees. Explore the historic hayloft and stables, washhouse, produce shed, gardener's shed, pavilion and dove cote or wander the farm and feed the animals. Bike riding, croquet and petanque are also available to guests. **LLandaff Country Residence** gives peace and tranquillity to the visitor, yet is located in the centre of a huge range of Wairarapa pursuits - river and sea fishing, canoeing and swimming, bush and farm walks, horse-riding, garden visits, wine tasting (35 minutes to Martinborough), antiques, crafts, historic places and the National Wildlife Centre (20 minutes away). **LLandaff Country Residence** is less than 5 minutes to town, vineyards and restaurants, yet is located 1 km off the road in quiet countryside.

144

Beach Haven

26 Pukerua Beach Road, Pukerua Bay, Porirua
Ph (04) 239 9384, Mobile 021-375 074
email: Pukerua.Glass@xtra.co.nz
www.charmingaccommodation.co.nz

Tariff : N.Z. Dollars	
Double	$175-190
Single	$175
Child	–

Bedrooms	Qty
Double	1
Twin	1
Single	

Bed Size	Qty
Super King	1
King	
Queen	
Double	
King Single	2

Bathrooms	Qty
Ensuite	1
Private	
Guest Share	1

To Paraparaumu
Beach Haven
Paekakariki
Pukerua Bay
N
Plimmerton
To Porirua

**Boutique Bed & Breakfast
Stunning Sea Views**

Features & Attractions

- *Native bush garden*
- *Beaches, coastal walks*
- *Modern, spacious guest wing*
- *Guest lounge, open fire*
- *Off-street parking*
- *Near SH1, 30 mins ferry*
- *10 min walk to trains*
- *German spoken*

Pukerua Bay is a charming coastal village only 30 minutes north of Wellington on SH1. A perfect stopover if you are travelling on a Cook Strait ferry and a peaceful place to stay when visiting Wellington.
Our region has a variety of bush walks and nature reserves. Easy access to events in Wellington by train or road. Unwind amongst native bush in our quiet garden. Take a walk on the beach. Ideal for 1-4 people, the guest wing in our spacious home has 2 bedrooms with stunning views of the sea and Kapiti Island. The main bedroom has a balcony and ensuite.
The guest lounge has a large deck for summer and an open fire for winter. We also run an art glass studio, which you are welcome to visit. Evening meals on request. Laundry facilities available.

145

BOATING CLUB POINT BED & BREAKFAST

Whale Cottage, 9 Gordon Road, Karehana Bay,
Plimmerton, Wellington
Ph (04) 233 9690, Mobile 027-354 8832
email: lizpeter@actrix.co.nz
www.charmingaccommodation.co.nz

Features & Attractions

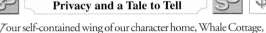

- *Superb sea panorama*
- *Unique décor*
- *Beach, bush & coastal walks*
- *1 min. walk to safe beach*
- *Ensuite spa bath*
- *No stairs, extra sofa bed*

**Panoramic Sea View,
Privacy and a Tale to Tell**

Double	$130
Single	$100
Child	Half price

You self-contained wing of our character home, Whale Cottage, has breathtaking views of harbour and sea – all top windows in the photo are yours. Rest in your comfortable rooms or fill your spa bath to unwind. The house has a unique nautical décor of NZ maritime history, ship fittings, curiosities and seagoing books. Your sitting-room has a telescope, easy chairs, double sofa-bed, TV/DVD, m/w, coffee beans+grinder, tea and breakfast (continental, self-service). One party at a time. Parking at your door. Free laundry. 3 mins along sea front from SH1 Plimmerton traffic lights (north of Porirua). Wellington 25mins away – we can help plan your visit. Enjoy the ever-changing blues of the sea. Relax watching the boats or go fishing from the jetty. At night a thousand pretty lights shine across the harbour. Good village cafés and takeaways.

"Incredible sunsets..gracious hosts..so peaceful.." California *"the ambience, the sound of the waves, the yummy breakfasts.."* UK *"..most comfortable bed ever!!.."* Austria

Bedrooms	Qty
Double	1
Twin	
Single	1
Bed Size	Qty
King	
Queen	1
Double	
Single	1
Bathrooms	Qty
Ensuite	1
Private	1
Guest Share	

AQUAVILLA SEASIDE BED & BREAKFAST

16 Steyne Avenue, Plimmerton, Wellington
Ph (04) 233 6321, Mobile 027-555 3123
email: info@aquavilla.co.nz
www.aquavilla.co.nz

Features & Attractions

- *A few steps to the beach*
- *Off-street parking*
- *Easy access to Wellington*
- *Gourmet breakfast*
- *Charming village setting*
- *Spa pool in courtyard*

**Seaside Self-contained
Bed & Breakfast**

Double	$180
Single	$160
Child	$50

Breathe deep the sea-scented air and treat yourself, mind, body and soul at our seaside haven. In the gorgeous garden of our character villa, your architecturally-designed accommodation complete with spa pool set in a courtyard at your door. You will find comfort and serenity at this special retreat. Guests enjoy crisp cotton sheets, flowers and home-made biscuits.

Catch the train or drive to Wellington, New Zealand's capital city, in 20 mins. Golf, beach and bush walks - all close by. Also galleries, shopping, windsurfing and ocean swimming. We enjoy preparing a delicious breakfast for you. Watch the sun-set, before strolling to a selection of cafés. restaurants and takeaways. We look forward to sharing **Aquavilla** and our charming village with you. We have both travelled widely and enjoy meeting new people. Liz has particular expertise in the hospitality industry here and abroad.

Bedrooms	Qty
Double	1
Twin	
Single	2
Bed Size	Qty
King	
Queen	1
Double	
Single	2
Bathrooms	Qty
Ensuite	
Private	1
Guest Share	

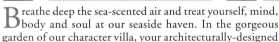

CHERSWUD B&B

121 Helston Road, Johnsonville, Wellington
Ph (04) 477 6767, Mobile 021-060 7815
e-mail: stay@cherswud.com
www.cherswud.com

Tariff : N.Z. Dollars	
Double	$120
Single	$80
Child	–

Bedrooms	Qty
Double	2
Twin	1
Single	

Bed Size	Qty
King	
Queen	2
Double	
King Single	1
Single	1

Bathrooms	Qty
Ensuite	
Private	2
Guest Share	

**A delightful home away from home
Just 10 minutes from the ferry**

Features & Attractions

DIRECTIONS:
Ten minutes from the inter-island ferry,
12 minutes from the central city, and
two minutes off State Highway 1 at the
Johnsonville exit. Please phone or
email for directions and maps.

- *Ferry 10 minutes away*
- *Warm sunny bedrooms*
- *Private bathrooms*
- *Beautiful conservatory*
- *Warm helpful hospitality*
- *Delicious meals*
- *Gluten-free options*
- *Free broadband internet*

We're delighted to welcome you to **Cherswud**, our authentically restored 1919 home located just ten easy minutes from the Interislander ferry and two minutes off State Highway 1 at the Johnsonville exit. Our accommodation includes two lounges, a conservatory and sunny deck overlooking a lovely sheltered garden, two warm and bright queen rooms with very comfortable beds, electric blankets, feather duvets, and well-stocked bookcases. Each bedroom has its own private bathroom, one with a spa bath and massage shower. A twin room is also available if required. We host a maximum of two parties at any one time. On the menu are delicious meals, including homemade bread and gluten-free options. Help yourself to tea and coffee in the kitchen at any time. Dinner (pre-arranged) is served with New Zealand wine, although several restaurants are within 12 minutes' walk. Free broadband internet plus free transfer of photos from digital cameras to CD. Warm, welcoming hospitality. A genuine "home away from home".

HARBOUR LODGE WELLINGTON

200 Barnard Street, Wadestown, Wellington
Ph (04) 976 5677, Mobile 021-032 6497
email: lou@harbourlodgewellington.com
www.harbourlodgewellington.com

Tariff : N.Z. Dollars	
Double	$180-270
Single	$160-250
Child	neg

Bedrooms	Qty
Double	4
Twin	
Single	
Bed Size	**Qty**
Super King	
King	4
Queen	
Double	
Single	
Bathrooms	**Qty**
Ensuite	4
Private	
Guest Share	

Luxury
Bed & Breakfast

Features & Attractions

- *Fabulous harbour views*
- *Sauna*
- *Spa pool*
- *Beautiful bush setting*
- *2 km to central city*
- *Close to ferry & stadium*
- *Rooms with balconies*
- *Large lounge with woodburner*

Harbour Lodge is situated on a quiet hillside amongst beautiful native bush, with all day sun and sweeping harbour views, yet only three minutes drive from central Wellington, Wellington Stadium and the ferry terminal. Admire the fabulous views of Wellington Harbour from the large sunny deck. Idly watch as the ferries curve in and out of the harbour and the yachts drift by. Treat yourself to a sauna or spa, or on cooler evenings warm up around a crackling fire in the spacious guest lounge.

DIRECTIONS:
From north - take Hawkestone Street exit off motorway. Turn right onto bridge, right again onto Tinakori Road. Follow signs to Wadestown (3rd on left), follow Wadestown Road up hill for 2 min, turn right into Sefton Street (changes name to Barnard Street). Look for our sign on left. Drive down driveway to the bottom.

The guest rooms have been refurbished to the highest quality with king size beds and snowy white linen. Each room has a private bathroom and views to the native bush-clad hills or harbour. Cable television, tea /coffee making facilities are available in each room.
Let your stresses be gently lulled away in the luxurious comfort of this beautiful lodge.
You might never want to leave.

Ngaio Homestay

56 Fox Street, Ngaio,
Wellington
Ph (04) 479 5325
email: enquiries@ngaiohomestay.co.nz
www.ngaiohomestay.co.nz

Tariff : N.Z. Dollars	
Double	$150-170
Single	$110-130
Child	neg.

Bedrooms	Qty
Double	2
Twin	1
Single	2
Bed Size	Qty
Super King	
King	
Queen	1
Double	1
Single	4
Bathrooms	Qty
Ensuite	3
Private	1
Guest Share	

**Homestay
Self-contained Accommodation**

Features & Attractions

- *Family home atmosphere*
- *Safe, quiet surroundings*
- *Off-street parking*
- *Extensive views*
- *2 min walk to local train station*
- *Ferry 5 min, city 10 min by car*
- *Internet facilities available*
- *Music salon*

DIRECTIONS: From ferry take north exit, left at first traffic lights – Ngaio Gorge Road, at roundabout take Ottawa Road fork, at shops turn left Awarua Street – Fox Street is second on right. Use driveway at No.56.

Welcome to Wonderful Wellington! Share your visit with us and enjoy helpful personal hospitality! Our unusual multi-level open plan chracter home (built 1960) is in the suburb of Ngaio. Guests may leave their car here and take the train to CBD (10mins). Our double room has tea/ coffee facilities, quality bedding, tiled ensuite and French doors opening onto a deck and private "jungle" garden. Breakfast is continental. Evening meals an optional extra. Adjacent to our property, two self-contained apartments, one with queen bed one with twin beds, comfortable, convenient, tastefully furnished and recently redecorated. Each apartment has a couch with a fold-out bed in lounge, fully equipped kitchen, shower, bath, laundry facilities, Free view TV and internet (small fee). Perfect for relocating or longer stays. Weekly tariff offered. There is a large garden with trees, birds and views. Jennifer plays harp at home and live piano music daily in NZ's top department store. Compliment from guest:"This is a home where there is beautiful music, art and love". Please phone before 11am or after 3pm or fax or email.

149

HOMESTAY AT EVANS BAY

4/378 Evans Bay Parade, Evans Bay, Wellington
Ph (04) 386 1504, Fax (04) 386 1503
Mobile 021-043 5683
email: leishas@xtra.co.nz
www.homestayevansbay.co.nz

Tariff : N.Z. Dollars	
Double	$190-250
Single	$180-230
Extra pp	$75

Bedrooms	Qty
Double	1
Twin	1
Single	
Bed Size	**Qty**
Super King	
King	
Queen	1
Double	
King/Singles	2
Bathrooms	**Qty**
Ensuite	1
Private	1
Guest Share	

 Luxury Homestay/Bed & Breakfast with Stunning Harbour Views

Features & Attractions

- *Collected from airport*
- *5 min. from city & airport*
- *Drive to the door*
- *Off street parking*
- *City bus in front*
- *Gourmet breakfast*
- *Wireless Internet facilities*
- *Stylish & comfortable home*

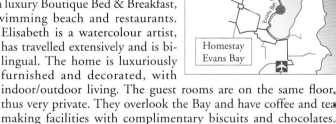

H**omestay at Evans Bay** is a luxury Boutique Bed & Breakfast, overlooking the bay, swimming beach and restaurants.

Elisabeth is a watercolour artist, has travelled extensively and is bilingual. The home is luxuriously furnished and decorated, with indoor/outdoor living. The guest rooms are on the same floor, thus very private. They overlook the Bay and have coffee and tea making facilities with complimentary biscuits and chocolates. You are welcomed with drinks and hors d'oeuvres and we serve an extensive gourmet breakfast at your convenience, either in the dining room or alfresco in our private rose garden.

There are electric blankets on the beds, robes and quality toiletries, hair dryers and heated towel rails in the bathroom. SKY television, small library and music in bedrooms.

Negotiable terms and 'out-of-season rates'. See our web site.

Highly rated by the New York Times Travel.

AT THE BAY

Marine Drive, Sorrento Bay,
Eastbourne, Wellington
Ph/Fax (04) 568 4817, Mobile 027-568 4817
email: at.the.bay@ihug.co.nz
www.charmingaccommodation.co.nz

Tariff : N.Z. Dollars	
Double	$120-165
Single	$90-135
Child	neg.

Bedrooms	Qty
Double	1
Twin	
Single	1
Bed Size	**Qty**
Super King	
King	
Queen	
Double	1
Single	1
Bathrooms	**Qty**
Ensuite	
Private	1
Guest Share	

**Homestay
Bed & Breakfast**

Features & Attractions

- *Awesome harbour & city views*
- *Bush and beachfront setting*
- *Sleep to lapping waves*
- *Awaken to birdsong*

- *Relaxed peaceful atmosphere*
- *Friendly hosts and cat*
- *20 min to ferry and CBD*
- *Single party bookings*

Jennifer, Ken and our neighbour's friendly cat look forward to giving you a warm welcome to our homestay, **At the Bay**. It is nestled amongst native bush on the beachfront at Sorrento Bay. Share with us the magical views of Wellington's picturesque harbour and city, and the tranquillity of lapping waves in the evening and birdsong in the morning.

We invite you to join us for a drink on a deck in summer, or in front of a cosy fire in winter. We are on the bus route and only twenty minutes by vehicle from Wellington's CBD, close enough to enjoy the vibrancy of the city but far enough away to relax from its hustle and bustle. Cafés and shops are close by in Eastbourne Village and historic Petone.

We hope to make your stay a memorable one, where you arrive as strangers but leave as friends. No smoking inside, please.

NATURE'S TOUCH GUEST HOUSE

25A Happy Valley Rd,
Owhiro Bay, Wellington
Ph/Fax (04) 383 6977, Mobile 027-559 0966
email: info@naturestouchguesthouse.com
www.naturestouchguesthouse.com

Features & Attractions

- *Nautical theme B&B*
- *Seaviews & stream sounds*
- *Spacious suite & views*
- *Gourmet breakfast*
- *Japanese meals available*
- *Wireless BYO computer*

**Luxury Suite
with Sea Views**

Double	$140-170
Single	$120-140
Child	$15-45

The Terrace Tunnel
End of SH ①
Wellington City
Brooklyn Rd
Ohiro Rd
N
Nature's Touch
Happy Valley Rd
Owhiro Bay PDE

DIRECTIONS:
Feel free to give us a call
for easy directions.

"Warm welcome and delightful hospitality in beautiful craftsmanbuilt home. Spacious, comfortable suite with stunning views. Convenient location. Superb cuisine, both Western and Japanese. A true gem." – *Margaret, Australia.* "**Nature's Touch Bed & Breakfast** *was the best B&B that we experienced in New Zealand during our trip in March 2008. The food was amazing. The breakfasts outdid any other B&B by a long shot, and the Japanese meal was great."* – *Don and Julie, Canada.* A warm welcome from us! We are a nautical themed B&B and just a short stroll to the beach. Only 10 mins drive to the city, 15 mins drive (almost straight line) to the ferry terminal and the airport driving along the coast. Upper Boat Bedroom (Luxury Suite) is for you to enjoy whole of upstairs and sea views as well as privacy. Enjoy tranquility.

Bedrooms	Qty
Double	1
Twin	
Single	
Bed Size	**Qty**
Super King	1
Queen	
Double	
Single	
Bathrooms	**Qty**
Ensuite	
Private	1
Guest Share	

Charming Places to Stay in New Zealand

"Superb! ...independent travellers, whether from overseas or locals, should never travel New Zealand without a copy of this guide..."

Colin Moore, NZ Herald.

You can book online at –www.charmingplacestostay.co.nz

".... and now for the South Island."

South Island

155 - 157
158 - 159
160 - 165
169 - 173
166 - 168
186

Takaka
Nelson

176
177 - 180
Picton

186
174 - 175
187

Westport

Blenheim

181 - 185
174

Murchison

Hanmer
Springs
Kaikoura

187 - 191

Greymouth

197 - 201
202 - 203
204

192 - 193
226
194

Hokitika

CHRISTCHURCH

204 - 207
208 - 222

195 - 196

Methven

222 - 225
227 - 228

Haast

Geraldine
Fairlie

Tekapo

238 - 241
242

Wanaka

Twizel

Timaru

229 - 230
231 - 233
236 - 237
234

243 - 250
253 - 261

Cromwell

Oamaru

235
272

251
251 - 252
262 - 270
271

Queenstown

Te Anau

Alexandra

DUNEDIN

273
274
275 - 290

Gore

Balclutha

291
294
292 - 293
295 - 298
274

INVERCARGILL

Stewart
Island

TWIN WATERS LODGE
30 Totara Ave, Collingwood, Golden Bay
Ph (03) 524 8014, Fax (03) 524 8054
Mobile 027-242 8778
email: twin.waters@xtra.co.nz
www.twinwaters.co.nz

Tariff : N.Z. Dollars	
Double	$200-250
Single	$175-195
Child	

Bedrooms	Qty
Double	3
Twin	1
Single	
Bed Size	**Qty**
Super King	
King	
Queen	3
Double	
Single	2
Bathrooms	**Qty**
Ensuite	4
Private	
Guest Share	

Bed & Breakfast Homestay

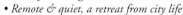
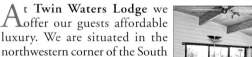

Features & Attractions

- *Close to Farewell Spit, Wharariki Beach, Heaphy Track, Aorere Valley*
- *Wildlife viewing: waders, birds, seals*   • *Restaurants close by*
- *Remote & quiet, a retreat from city life*   • *Long, sandy beach close by*

At **Twin Waters Lodge** we offer our guests affordable luxury. We are situated in the northwestern corner of the South Island amongst some of the best and most varied scenery and outdoor activities New Zealand has to offer. Our purpose-built lodge nestles harmoniously on a finger of land between a wildlife estuary and the shining blue waters of Golden Bay. Imagine drifting off to sleep to the sound of the sea and waking to birdsong provided by our resident tui and bellbird population. Before joining us for breakfast you can enjoy tea or coffee on your private deck, in the guest lounge or one of the surrounding decks with views up to bush-clad hills. Our lodge features curved wooden ceilings, walls of glass and offers four ensuite rooms; three queen and one twin. Our resident barista will be happy to make coffee of your choice at breakfast and after dinner.

FERNTOWN LODGE

112 Collingwood Puponga Road, Golden Bay
Ph (03) 524 8731, Mobile 027-223 1053
email: stay@ferntownlodge.co.nz
www.ferntownlodge.co.nz

Tariff : N.Z. Dollars	
Double	$200
Single	$200
Extra pp	$50

Bedrooms	Qty
Double	1
Twin	
Single	1
Bed Size	**Qty**
Super King	1
King	
Queen	
King/Single	1
Single	
Bathrooms	**Qty**
Ensuite	
Private	1
Family Share	

Enjoy the Great Outdoor Boutique Accommodation

Features & Attractions

- *Discreet and private with oversized jet spa & all amenities*
- *Kayaks/bikes/BBQ available*
- *Private bush & nature walks*
- *Award-winning chef for villa or lodge-hosted meals*
- *Great base for 'Farewell Spit', 'Heaphy Track' and countless activities and adventures*
- *3 mins drive from Collingwood*

Ferntown Lodge offers boutique adventure lodge accommodation, kayaking, bush walks, native bird life and access to the many local attractions and activities in Golden Bay, New Zealand. Whether you are looking for a bit of adventure, are on your honeymoon, or just need a bit of time out, we offer a truly unique Kiwi experience. The park-like grounds contain one of New Zealand's finest virgin lowland totara forests. Without even leaving the lodge, you can experience the wonderful hidden walks amongst the serene native bush and bird life, take a paddle through the property's many tranquil waterways, or venture into the river for some trout fishing, then just relax in the privacy of your own villa. Cooked breakfast avaiable on request. Your hosts will be Brian and Judy who have many years of hospitality experience in ownership of such places as the famous Cardrona Hotel. Continental breakfast included. Reservations essential.

DIRECTIONS: 3 minutes drive from Collingwood, or 25 minutes from Takaka, Golden Bay. Please phone for easy directions.

HERON'S REST B & B

23 Gibbs Road, Collingwood, Golden Bay
Ph/Fax (03) 524 8987, Mobile 027-247-1790
email: be@herons-rest.co.nz
www.herons-rest.co.nz

Tariff : N.Z. Dollars	
Double	$110-130
Single	$75-90
Extra pp	$15

Bedrooms	Qty
Double	2
Twin	1
Single	2
Bed Size	**Qty**
Super King	
King	
Queen	2
Double	
Single	2
Bathrooms	**Qty**
Ensuite	2
Private	
Hosts Share	1

Bed & Breakfast & Self-contained Accommodation

Features & Attractions

- *Panoramic views of mountains & sea*
- *Farewell Spit Eco Tours/bird-watching*
- *Pottery & Pacific Carver's Studio*
- *4 min. bush walk to eateries, beach*
- *Friendly & welcoming hosts*
- *Landscaped, private gardens*
- *Large deck with BBQ facility*
- *Spacious lounge; TV*

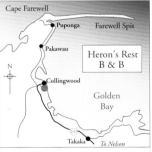

S ituated in a unique, unspoilt location, your welcoming hosts enjoy making guest stays comfortable and memorable. We offer home-made and locally-produced foods and complimentary drinks. Hairdryer, laundry and wireless internet available. A wide choice of outdoor activities caters for all fitness levels. Excellent walks. Farewell Spit, Abel Tasman and Kahurangi National Parks are nearby, as is access to the Heaphy Track. Guests can follow the trail of Golden Bay's artisan outlets sampling, en route, our interesting cafes and restaurants (including The Mussel Inn), or merely relax on the deck and at nearby sandy beaches, or in the garden. **Heron's Rest** is a peaceful location, yet very convenient, via our bush track, to amenities in Collingwood.

DIRECTIONS: Just before Collingwood township, turn right up Lewis St, left into Washington Rd, then left into Gibbs Rd. Proceed to end, taking left fork of (LEVEL) gravel road - to end . We're on the headland overlooking Collingwood.

In addition, our charming cottage nestled up in the trees sleeps 3 comfortably, offering a double and single bed/s, all with sea views. It has an ensuite bathroom, hairdryer, private deck with gas BBQ, giving outdoor dining options. It has superb sea/mountain/estuary views, TV, most kitchen appliances including fridge and microwave; we provide breakfasts.

THE BAY LODGE

36 Bay Vista Drive, Pohara, Takaka
Ph (03) 525 9198, Mobile 027-227 7672
email: welcome@thebaylodge.co.nz
www.thebaylodge.co.nz

Tariff : N.Z. Dollars	
Double	$170-240
Single	$160-220
Child	

Bedrooms	Qty
Double	2
Twin	1
Single	

Bed Size	Qty
Super King	1
King	1
Queen	1
Double	
King/Single	2

Bathrooms	Qty
Ensuite	3
Private	
Guest Share	

**Luxury Accommodation
Exclusive Photo Safaris**

Features & Attractions

- *Gateway to Abel Tasman NP*
- *Walk to beach, art studios & cafés*
- *Stunning seaviews, private decks*
- *Superb coastal walks & beaches*
- *Private photo safaris*
- *Outdoor spa, swimming pool*
- *Tennis & golf nearby, wireless internet*
- *Luxury bedding, kitchenette, tea/coffee*

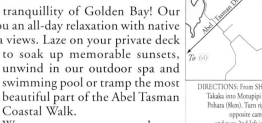

DIRECTIONS: From SH60 turn right on entry to
Takaka into Motupipi St and follow signs to
Pohara (8km). Turn right up Richmond Rd
opposite camping ground
and turn 2nd left into Bay Vista Dve.

Escape to the beauty and tranquillity of Golden Bay! Our elevated location offers you an all-day relaxation with native birdsong and unsurpassed sea views. Laze on your private deck

to soak up memorable sunsets, unwind in our outdoor spa and swimming pool or tramp the most beautiful part of the Abel Tasman Coastal Walk.

We assure you a warm welcome and enjoy chatting over a welcoming drink. All suites are tastefully decorated with first class facilities to assure you a great night's rest. Breakfast options vary from a generous breakfast hamper in the privacy of your room to a full gourmet surprise in our panoramic dining room. For a wonderful day out take part in our private Golden Bay Photo Safari. Rated as one of the best nature & wildlife experiences in New Zealand ! We look forward to meeting you at our Lodge!

SHADY REST

139-141 Commercial Street, Takaka, Golden Bay
Ph (03) 525 9669, Mobile 027-734 5623
email: stay@shadyrest.co.nz
www.shadyrest.co.nz

Tariff : N.Z. Dollars	
Double	$150-230
Single	$115-150
Extra pp	$45

Bedrooms	Qty
Double/Twin	5
Twin	
Single	1
Bed Size	Qty
S.King/Twin	5
King	
Queen	
Double	
King/Single	1
Bathrooms	Qty
Ensuite	3
Private	2
Guest Share	1

VISA **MasterCard**

  Fine Accommodation
Quality Bed & Breakfast

Features & Attractions

- *Character home*
- *Luxury outdoor bath*
- *Internet access & wireless*
- *5 min. walk to town, cafés, etc*
- *Abel Tasman National Park*
- *Beautiful walks and beaches*
- *Whariki Beach a must see*
- *Friendly, colourful locals*

Welcome to **Shady Rest**. If you're looking for a homely spot in the Takaka township, then this is the place for you.

Shady Rest is the hundred year old grand historic doctor's residence, situated on Takaka's main street, set back from the road amongst tall and beautiful native trees.

Whether you're on a family holiday or on business, you will be well looked after by your hosts Mark and Janice. **Shady Rest** features beautiful, spacious rooms, a cosy TV lounge, use of our fully equipped kitchen and all the B&B comforts you'd expect.

We offer a generous, cooked breakfast to suit your tastes. Cups of tea, relaxing ambience and a perfect base from which to explore Golden Bay's friendly community and breath taking natural beauty. Take an easy five minute stroll to the local shops, cafés and excellent restaurants.

Relax at the end of the day by enjoying a glass of wine and soaking in our luxury outdoor bath.

Staying at **Shady Rest** will make your holiday in this paradisiacal corner of New Zealand a truly rewarding experience.

Please enquire for winter rates.

SPLIT APPLE LODGE

370 Kaiteriteri-Sandy Bay Road, Motueka
Ph/Fax (03) 527 8502, Mobile 027-439 4009
email: stannards@xtra.co.nz
www.splitapplelodge.co.nz

Tariff : N.Z. Dollars	
Double	$180-210
Single	
Child	

Bedrooms	Qty
Double	6
Twin	
Single	
Bed Size	Qty
Super King	
King	
Queen	6
Double	
King/Single	3
Bathrooms	Qty
Ensuite	6
Private	
Guest Share	

**Peaceful Hideaway with
Panoramic Views**

Features & Attractions

- *Peace and tranquillity*
- *Purpose built*
- *Abel Tasman Nat. Park 10 mins*
- *Expansive deck area*
- *Separate guest facilities*
- *Available for functions*

W arm and friendly hospitality awaits you at **Split Apple Lodge**, a purpose built Bed & Breakfast, nestled amongst five acres of native bush and pines. Views of either the sea or the mountains will amaze you from every window of this tsunami safe lodge. Peaceful and private, we maintain a pet and children free environment for the comfort of our guests. Continental breakfast is included in the tariff and a hearty home cooked dinner is available between May and October.

Full laundry facilities, wireless internet, garden walks and use of moutain bikes are also offered. **Split Apple Lodge** is ten minutes from a host of activities for guests to enjoy including kayaking, sailing, moutain biking or, not far away, sky diving, trout fishing and wine tours. All this and arguably the sunniest weather in New Zealand, will make this a holiday to remember.

Bellbird Lodge
Sandy Bay Road, Kaiteriteri, Motueka
Ph (03) 527 8555, Fax (03) 527 8556
Mobile 021-057 1470
email: stay@bellbirdlodge.com
www.bellbirdlodge.com

Tariff : N.Z. Dollars	
Double	$250-325
Single	$200-275
Child	

Bedrooms	Qty
Double/Twin	2
Twin	
Single	
Bed Size	Qty
Super King	2
King	
Queen	
Double	
Single	4
Bathrooms	Qty
Ensuite	1
Private	1
Guest Share	

Luxury Boutique Bed & Breakfast with Panoramic Sea Views

DIRECTIONS:
From Kaiteriteri Beach follow
the road up the hill towards Marahau for
approx 1.5 km.
At the **Bellbird Lodge** sign,
turn right into our private road.
We are the 3rd house.

Features & Attractions

- *Panoramic sea views*
- *Relaxed and friendly*
- *Spacious and comfortable*
- *Lounge with TV, video, CD & piano*
- *WIFI, phone, fax available*
- *Laundry and barbeque*
- *Art, craft and wine trails*
- *Winter specials*

Welcome to **Bellbird Lodge**, where warm friendly hospitality, superb food and fine accommodation await you. Nestled on the hillside in a tranquil setting with panoramic sea views, **Bellbird Lodge** is close to Kaiteriteri Beach with its stunning golden sands, the gateway to Abel Tasman National Park. The tastefully furnished guest rooms are on the ground floor and have either ensuite or private bathrooms. All have tea/coffee making facilities, hairdryers, electric blankets, bathrobes and have sea or bush views and outdoor terraces. Wake to the songs of bellbird and tui and marvel at the sunrise over Tasman Bay. Enjoy a delicious buffet breakfast with fresh local produce and homemade muesli, bread and preserves and featuring a hot gourmet special of the day, served in the dining room or alfresco on the terrace. The area has much to offer all year round. Walk the coastal track, take a scenic cruise, water taxi or kayak and discover the unspoiled beauty of the Abel Tasman National Park. Excellent restaurants are a few minutes drive away. Dinner available by prior arrangement (May-October). We look forward to welcoming you soon.

BAYVIEW B & B

2 Bayview Heights, Kaiteriteri, Motueka
Ph/Fax (03) 527 8090, Mobile 021-130 6873
email: book@kaiteriteribandb.co.nz
www.kaiteriteribandb.co.nz

Features & Attractions

- *Gateway to Abel Tasman*
- *Kayaking trips organised*
- *Hiking trips arranged*
- *Sea views from your room*
- *Golden sand beaches*
- *Restaurants close by*

Purpose Built B&B with Views to Die for

Double	$175-205	
Single	$155-175	
Child		

We welcome you to paradise. Kaiteriteri Beach, the gateway to the Abel Tasman National Park with the most beautiful coastline in New Zealand and the sunniest weather. Here we can offer you Bed & Breakfast at its best. Your rooms are large and beautifully furnished with extensive views of the bay. You have a comfortable sitting area, outside terrace, ensuite with heated towel rail and hair dryer, fridge, tea/coffee making facilities, radio, flat screen TV and DVD player. Laundry, phone/fax and wireless broadband also available. You are welcome to share our living area, terraces, extensive collection of books or be as private as you wish. Kayak adventures and water taxi services leave from our pristine beach. We recommend a minimum 2 night stay to explore this unique area.

DIRECTIONS: 8km north of Motueka on HW60 turn right into Kaiteriteri Rd. After 4km take 2nd right into Cederman Drive. **Bayview** is 200mtrs on right.

Bedrooms	Qty
Double	1
Twin/Double	1
Single	
Bed Size	**Qty**
King	1
Queen	
Double	
King/Single	1
Bathrooms	**Qty**
Ensuite	2
Private	
Guest Share	

WALL STREET ACCOMMODATION

6 & 8 Wall Street, Kaiteriteri, Motueka
Ph/Fax (03) 527 8338, Mobile 021-216 6440
email: stay@kaiteriteribnb.co.nz
www.kaiteriteribnb.co.nz

Features & Attractions

- *Abel Tasman National Park*
- *Wireless internet*
- *German & French spoken*
- *Nearby golden sanded beaches/restaurants*
- *Private guest entrance, courtyard, carpark*
- *Sea-kayaking & water taxi 2 mins*

Quality Bed & Breakfast

Double	$135-190	
Single	$130-170	
Child	$50	

Our two modern stylish homes are in a peaceful bush setting, centrally located to explore Abel Tasman National Park, Golden Bay and Nelson environs. Kayak companies and water taxis for hiking into the Abel Tasman Park are just a short drive away. We are only minutes to golden-sanded Kaiteriteri beach and restaurants and a mini-general store are close by. We offer 3 Queen rooms and 1 Twin room - choose from B&B or Room only. All rooms are separate from the main house and have their own courtyard/deck and private entry, tea & coffee making facilities, TV or DVD. Guest lounge, chemical-free natural swimming pool, car parks and wireless internet available. German and French spoken by Hans.

DIRECTIONS: Please phone for easy directions.

Bedrooms	Qty
Double	3
Twin	1
Single	
Bed Size	**Qty**
King	
Queen	3
Double	
Single	2
Bathrooms	**Qty**
Ensuite	2
Private	1
Guest Share	

FRASER HIGHLANDS
177 Riwaka - Sandy Bay Rd, Motueka
(Main route to Abel Tasman Park),
Ph (03) 528 8702, Mobile 027-315 0688
email: fraserhighlands_nz@hotmail.com
www.fraserhighlands.co.nz

Tariff : N.Z. Dollars	
Double	$110-180
Single	$110-160
Child	$15

Bedrooms	Qty
Double	2
Twin	
Single	1
Bed Size	**Qty**
Super King	
King	
Queen	2
Double	
Single	2
Bathrooms	**Qty**
Ensuite	2
Private	
Guest Share	

 Spectacular Views Tasman Bay Bed & Breakfast

To Takaka
Marahau
60
Sandy Bay
N
Riwaka
Motueka
Fraser Highlands
Nelson
60

DIRECTIONS:
Riwaka-Sandy Bay Rd. - 2nd driveway on
left up hill on main route to Marahau.

Features & Attractions

- *Abel Tasman National Park*
- *Spectacular panoramic views*
- *Close to town & beaches*
- *Bush pathways, gardens & BBQ*
- *Peaceful, relaxing home*
- *Spacious ensuite bedrooms*
- *Claw-foot bath to soak in*
- *Self-contained cosy cottage*

Welcome to **Fraser Highlands** for Bed and Breakfast in a great New Zealand location! The hillside native bush property offers spectacular views of Tasman Bay and surrounding mountain ranges. Accommodation includes two Queen-size bedrooms with Ensuites, Family/Twin room, TV, tea/coffee facilities and wireless internet access. Alternatively, our fully furnished cottage is a wonderful retreat. Hosts Jim and Sue would be happy for you to settle in the lounge, with a cosy log fire during the cooler months. Sue provides fabulous home cooked food! Continental breakfast includes freshly baked bread, muffins, cereals, and delicious local fruits. Evening meals and lunches are available on request. Jim (experienced pilot) could fly you over the magnificent Kahurangi National Park and numerous Bays. Also, if you wish, he will play a wee tune on the bagpipes!

Fraser Highlands is less than 15 minutes to beachfront cafés, boating, kayaking, tramping, mountain biking, wineries, scenic drives and the local township Motueka.

THE RESURGENCE

Riwaka Valley Road, Motueka
Ph (03) 528 4664
email: info@resurgence.co.nz
www.resurgence.co.nz

Tariff : N.Z. Dollars	
Double	$395-675
Single	$395-675
Child	n/a

Bedrooms	Qty
Double	5
Twin/Double	5
Single	

Bed Size	Qty
Super King/Twin	4
King	
Queen	6
Double	
Single	

Bathrooms	Qty
Ensuite	10
Private	
Guest Share	

    Luxury Eco-Lodge

Features & Attractions

- Swimming pool and spa pool
- Gourmet dining
- Wilderness with bush tracks
- Sorry, no children under 18
- Abel Tasman National Park
- Nelson art and wine trails
- Golden Bay day trips
- Guided walks & Eco tours

One of New Zealand's leading luxury eco-lodges, **The Resurgence** is set in 50 acres of tranquil wilderness with 5km of bush tracks. Surrounded by birds, this relaxed and friendly Lodge is a perfect base for exploring the Nelson Region. Select Boutique Lodge Rooms or self-contained Bush Suites on Dinner B&B or self-clontained basis. Dinner is a highlight with superb 4-course lodge-dining showcasing Nelson wine and produce. **The Resurgence** is the closest 5-star accommodation to the Abel Tasman National Park and also offers easy day trips to Golden Bay, Kahurangi National Park or Nelson art studios and wineries. Let your well-travelled hosts help you plan activities such as kayaking, hikes and birding trips to winery and art tours. This child-free, smoke free resort with pool, spa and massage therapies is accessible by road, 45 mins from Nelson airport. Ideal for honeymoons and for active couples who enjoy good food and nature. Visit our website to Book on line.

DIRECTIONS: Follow SH 60 from Motueka, through Riwaka past the 2 turnings towards Abel Tasman National Park. After 2 km, justas SH 60 starts to go uphill, turn left down Riwaka Valley Rd. Continue towards the source of the river for 5.7 km.

COASTAL PALMS APARTMENTS

95 Trewavas Street, Motueka, Nelson
Ph (03) 528 0166, Fax (03) 528 0166
Mobile 021-217 6961
email: info@coastalpalms.co.nz
www.coastalpalms.co.nz

Tariff : N.Z. Dollars	
Double	$190-300
Extra person	$30-50
Child under 12	$30

Bedrooms	Qty
Double	4
Twin/Double	2
Single	2
Bed Size	**Qty**
Super King/Twin	2
King Single	1
Queen	2
Double Sofa Bed	3
Single	2
Bathrooms	**Qty**
Ensuite	2
Private	1
Guest Share	

   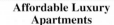

Affordable Luxury Apartments

Features & Attractions

- *Panoramic 270 degree views*
- *Absolute waterfront site*
- *Ideal romantic getaway*
- *Private deck or balcony*
- *Comfort & affordable luxury*
- *Close to restaurants & attractions*
- *Private entrance & car park*
- *Free Wifi – Broadband*

Coastal Palms is situated on the fringe of Motueka township overlooking Tasman Bay, with the waterfront at your doorstep and the gateway to Abel Tasman National Park. **Coastal Palms Apartments** offers comfort and affordable luxury with direct private access to the beach. All apartments have their own private deck or balcony, ensuite bathroom, fully self-contained kitchen, alfresco living, BBQ, TV/Stereo with CD Player, DVD, Library and private entrance and car park. With 270 degree views of the Nelson region from Tasman Bay to the surrounding mountain ranges, Coastal Palms attracts discerning guests from around the world wanting style and privacy in peaceful settings, and is the ideal romantic getaway! Escape to this undiscovered haven to enjoy serene beauty and tranquillity while relaxing on the private balcony with close amenities to restaurants and attractions. Warm, helpful hospitality assured.

DIRECTIONS: From **Nelson Airport** on SH 6, then SH 60 to Motueka. At 1st roundabout right to Wharf Rd, then left Trewavas St. From start of **Abel Tasman National Park** to Motueka approx 15 min. Through town left at roundabout and proceed as above. For map see our website.

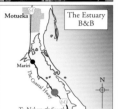

THE ESTUARY B&B

59 Easton Loop,
Tasman Coastal Highway, Mariri
Ph (03) 526 6213, Mobile 027-526 6213
e-mail: theestuarybandb@xtra.co.nz
www.theestuary.net.nz

Features & Attractions

- *Sea & river fishing*
- *Easy access to local attractions*
- *Outdoor BBQ, entertainment area*
- *Lovely estuary views*
- *Tennis, canoes & bikes available*
- *Abel Tasman National Park nearby*

	Quality B&B with Estuary Views					Double	$110-130
						Single	$80
						Child	

The Estuary B&B is set in a picturesque location on the Tasman Coastal Highway overlooking the Kina Estuary with views of the surrounding snow capped mountains. All rooms enjoy views, ensuites, flat screen television with built in DVD, free to air channels, electric blankets, heap pump and robes. There are comfortable facilities for guests including a guest lounge with large screen television and sky channels, guest kitchen with a range of equipment, dining room, laundry, internet room and spa. Extensive entertainment area with BBQ, tennis court, canoes and bikes are available for guest use. We have a very friendly Papillion "Teddy" who loves to play fetch and a sleepy cat called "Boots". Local attractions are too many to list and can be found on our website. Your hosts have an extensive knowledge of the area and are happy to advise of the best places to visit in the area.

Bedrooms	Qty
Double	3
Twin	
Single	1
Bed Size	**Qty**
King	
Queen	3
Double	1
Single	
Bathrooms	**Qty**
Ensuite	4
Private	
Guest Share	

OLIVES @ MARIRI BED & BREAKFAST

27 Johnstone Loop, Mariri, Tasman
Ph (03) 526 6775, Fax (03) 526 6775
Mobile 021-163 7610
email: margaret@olivesatmariri.co.nz
www.olivesatmariri.co.nz

Features & Attractions

- *Exclusive to you*
- *Peaceful rural setting*
- *30 mins to Abel Tasman*
- *Wineries / Artists*
- *Glorious beaches*
- *Golf courses*

	Countrystay Bed & Breakfast					Double	$180-200
						Single	$140
						Child	$20

You will be our exclusive guests when you stay at Olives @ Mariri and we will make sure you enjoy your time here. Our 90 year old renovated farmhouse is a peaceful retreat within a lovely rural garden and olive grove. Your comfortable suite includes indoor and outdoor space, bathroom, tea/coffee making facilities, refrigerator and TV. Wake to birdsong followed by a breakfast of seasonal produce - much of it from our own garden. Try our delicious olive oil. Olives @Mariri is a convenient staging post for local activites including wineries, beaches, potters and artists. (approx 30 minutes by car to Abel Tasman and Nelson city). You're assured of a warm welcome.

Bedrooms	Qty
Double	1
Twin	
Single	
Bed Size	**Qty**
King	
Queen	1
Double	
Single	
Bathrooms	**Qty**
Ensuite	1
Private	
Guest Share	

DIRECTIONS: Johnstone Loop exists Highway 60 immediately past Harley Road and enters again 300m further on. The B&B is signposted on the Loop.

ACCENT HOUSE BOUTIQUE B&B

148 Aranui Road, Mapua Village, Nelson
Ph (03) 540 3442, Mobile 027-540 3442
email: info@accentbnb.co.nz
www.accentbnb.co.nz

Tariff : N.Z. Dollars	
Double	$200
Single	$180
Child	

Bedrooms	Qty
Double	3
Twin	1
Single	

Bed Size	Qty
Super King	
King	2
Queen	1
Double	
King/Single	1

Bathrooms	Qty
Ensuite	4
Private	
Guest Share	

Boutique Bed & Breakfast

Features & Attractions

- Walk to nearby restaurants
- Outdoor giant chess
- Relaxed & friendly
- Elegant rooms & ensuites
- Guest lounge & laundry
- Access to outdoor seating
- Walk to art & craft studios/beach
- Abel Tasman Park/Nelson 30 min.

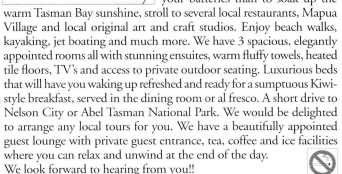

Welcome to our beautiful home, designed especially for your relaxation and comfort, and overlooking a private lagoon. Stay with us for a few days and check out all that our stunning region has to offer. What better way to recharge your batteries than to soak up the warm Tasman Bay sunshine, stroll to several local restaurants, Mapua Village and local original art and craft studios. Enjoy beach walks, kayaking, jet boating and much more. We have 3 spacious, elegantly appointed rooms all with stunning ensuites, warm fluffy towels, heated tile floors, TV's and access to private outdoor seating. Luxurious beds that will have you waking up refreshed and ready for a sumptuous Kiwi-style breakfast, served in the dining room or al fresco. A short drive to Nelson City or Abel Tasman National Park. We would be delighted to arrange any local tours for you. We have a beautifully appointed guest lounge with private guest entrance, tea, coffee and ice facilities where you can relax and unwind at the end of the day.
We look forward to hearing from you!!

KIMERET PLACE BOUTIQUE BED & BREAKFAST

78 Bronte Rd East, Off SH 60, Nr Mapua,
Upper Moutere, Nelson
Ph (03) 540 2727
email: stay@kimeretplace.co.nz
www.kimeretplace.co.nz

Tariff : N.Z. Dollars	
Double	$230-360
Single	$210-330
Child	–

Bedrooms	Qty
Double	4
Twin	
Single	
Bed Size	**Qty**
California King	1
King	3
Queen	
Double	
Single	
Bathrooms	**Qty**
Ensuite	4
Private	
Guest Share	

 Peace, Comfort and Personal Service

Features & Attractions

- *Stunning views*
- *Swimming pool & spa*
- *Self-contained cottage*
- *Elegant rooms & suites*
- *Art, craft & wine trails*
- *National Parks & beaches*
- *Award winning restaurants*
- *Space, peace, privacy*

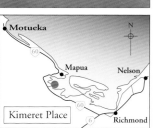

At **Kimeret Place B&B** the emphasis is on comfort and relaxation. Enjoy the peace of our secluded four acres overlooking the Waimea Inlet. Soak up the sun and the stunning views from our heated pool and terrace, or escape to the swing and the shade of mature trees. In the evening, after a delicious meal at a local restaurant, immerse yourself in the spa under a star-filled southern sky. What better way to recharge the batteries? Situated in the heart of Nelson's wine and craft area, **Kimeret Place B&B is** an ideal base to explore the diversity of the region, from the beautiful beaches of the Abel Tasman NP to the dramatic mountains of Kahurangi NP. Endless sandy beaches, trout filled streams, spectacular golf courses, horse riding and award winning restaurants are all nearby. Our accommodation options include two luxurious suites and two adjoining apartments (which can be booked as a 2 bedroom cottage, ideal for families or groups). All have complimentary tea/coffee facilities, fridge, mini-bar, hair dryers, toiletries, sitting area with TV, DVD and Hi-Fi as well as views from either balcony or deck.

DIRECTIONS:
From Richmond on SH 60 turn right
after 12 km into Bronte Road East.
From Mapua: 4 km on left.

KERSHAW HOUSE
BOUTIQUE ACCOMMODATION
10 Wensley Road, Richmond
Ph (03) 544 0957, Fax (03) 544 0950
Mobile 027-571 4300
email: bookings@kershawhouse.co.nz
www.kershawhouse.co.nz

Tariff : N.Z. Dollars	
Double	$175-295
Single	–
Child	–

Bedrooms	Qty
Double	3
Twin	1
Single	
Bed Size	**Qty**
Super King	1
King	2
Queen	
Double	
King Single	2
Bathrooms	**Qty**
Ensuite	4
Private	
Guest Share	

**Luxury Boutique
B&B Accommodation**

Features & Attractions

- *1920's Historic Home*
- *Luxury rooms & ensuites*
- *5 min. walk to restaurant*
- *Friendly NZ hosts*
- *Free NZ Scenic DVD*
- *Free off-street parking*
- *Free wireless Internet*
- *Abel Tasman Park 30 min.*

Pete and Jill welcome you to one of the finest historic homes in the Nelson region. Located 10 minutes from Nelson Airport and en-route to the Abel Tasman Park it is a great place to base yourself to explore the Tasman Region. **Kershaw House** is a registered historic home that has been extensively refurbished, it retains the charms of yesteryear and includes the comforts of today.

Each guest room is tastefully furnished and spacious, with ensuites. The guest lounge has a warm, welcoming atmosphere and opens out to a tranquil courtyard. The selection of restaurants less than 10 minutes walk from **Kershaw House** make evening dining very convenient. Breakfast is a scrumptious affair daily, with continental and cooked options on offer. Leave with a lasting memory of your NZ trip, receive a complimentary copy of 'Kiwi Country NZ' – filmed and produced by your host Peter.

We look forward to hosting you.

Nelson

YOUR HOSTS: Selene and Shane Ferguson — Ph: (03) 546 8770

A WOODSY HOUSE

121 Grove Street, The Wood, Nelson
Phone (03) 546 8770, Mobile 027-877 5696
email: gaiacot@hotmail.com
www.awoodsyhouse.com

Features & Attractions

- *Peaceful city haven*
- *Stunning 180 degree views*
- *Therapy spa and sauna*
- *Heritage listed house*
- *Close to town*
- *Optional home baked breakfast*

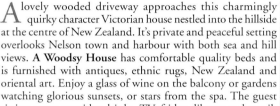

City Haven Bed & Breakfast

	Double	$105-125
	Single	$90-110
	Child	

A lovely wooded driveway approaches this charmingly quirky character Victorian house nestled into the hillside at the centre of New Zealand. It's private and peaceful setting overlooks Nelson town and harbour with both sea and hill views. **A Woodsy House** has comfortable quality beds and is furnished with antiques, ethnic rugs, New Zealand and oriental art. Enjoy a glass of wine on the balcony or gardens watching glorious sunsets, or stars from the spa. The guest sitting room provides drinks, TV, fridge, library and email. The city centre is a pleasant walk away. Well travelled hosts invite you to this idyllic spot. Optional delicious organic breakfast of fruit, yoghurt, juice, home made muesli, bread, muffins, jams, croissants and local cheese.

Bedrooms	Qty
Double	3
Twin	1
Single	1
Bed Size	**Qty**
Super King	1
King	1
Queen	1
Single	2
Bathrooms	**Qty**
Ensuite	
Private	3
Guest Share	

Nelson

YOUR HOSTS: Sherry and Warwick Bishop — Ph: (03) 548 2133

SERENDIPITY BOUTIQUE BED & BREAKFAST

2/4 Mount Pleasant Ave, Beachville, Nelson
Ph (03) 548 2133, Fax (03) 548 2183
Mobile 021-420 165
email: relax@serendipity.co.nz
www.serendipity.co.nz

Features & Attractions

- *Quiet garden setting*
- *Centrally heated home*
- *Stunning harbour views*
- *Only 1km to Nelson City*
- *Off-street guest parking*
- *Free internet & laundry*

Serendipity Boutique Bed & Breakfast

	Double	$150
	Single	$100-130
	Child	–

Serendipity - The gift of making fortunate discoveries by accident. Come and enjoy our warm and cozy, fully restored 1920's home. Guests have a comfortable, large queen-bedded room, private bathroom with bath and shower. We only take one set of guests at a time. Fully cooked or continental breakfast. Nelson city or harbourside restaurants are a 15minute walk away. We delight in helping guests plan their sight seeing. Free airport pickup offered. We have no kids or pets at home. We both enjoy films, theatre, books and travel. Join us for a wine, tea/coffee as we welcome you into our home and the beautiful Nelson region.

Bedrooms	Qty
Double	1
Twin	
Single	1
Bed Size	**Qty**
King	
Queen	1
Double	
Single	1
Bathrooms	**Qty**
Ensuite	
Private	1
Guest Share	

DIRECTIONS: It is important to contact us for detailed directions. We are on the private right of way between 23-25 Stanley Cres. First on left - with parking for guests.

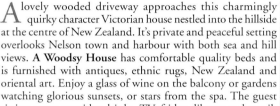

170

AMBLESIDE LUXURY BED & BREAKFAST

237 Annesbrook Drive, Tahunanui, Nelson
Ph/Fax (03) 548 5067, Mobile 021-214 5223
email: ambleside@paradise.net.nz
www.amblesidenelson.co.nz

Tariff : N.Z. Dollars	
Double	$160-200
Single	$130-160
Child	

Bedrooms	Qty
Double	3
Twin	1
Single	

Bed Size	Qty
Super King	1
King	1
Queen	1
King/Single	2
Single	

Bathrooms	Qty
Ensuite	4
Private	
Guest Share	

**Luxury
Boutique Accommodation**

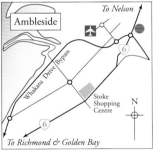

Features & Attractions

- *Purpose-built guest wing*
- *Off-street parking*
- *Laundry facilities*
- *Spa pool*
- *Tame eels and wildlife*
- *Phone, fax, wireless internet*
- *Beach & golf club*
- *Tea / coffee, refreshments*

Minutes from the CBD, on SH6, **Ambleside B&B** is a purpose-built, 4star-plus, spacious accommodation exuding comfort, style and ambience. Guests have own, private entrance off the deck, separate guest lounge and each room, beautifully appointed, has its own ensuite. Breakfasts, according to our guests, are "second to none" and served on the deck or the sunny courtyard. Choose from the extensive menu including delicious blueberry pancakes and dine when you choose. Settle in with a cuppa, yummy homemade baking and complimentary local wine/beer, also served throughout your stay. A spirit of gracious hospitality sets **Ambleside** apart and you are assured of warm and friendly service. Our central location affords you close proximity to the city, beaches, world-class restaurants and Abel Tasman Park. "*After enjoying all types and styles of accommodation in the S.I. were we able to appreciate just how good this B&B is. Ambleside sets standards others must strive to achieve, a jewel in the crown.*" David Ewing, UK.

SUSSEX HOUSE BED & BREAKFAST
238 Bridge Street, Nelson
Ph (03) 548 9972, Fax (03) 548 9975
Mobile 027-478 4846
email: reservations@sussex.co.nz
www.sussex.co.nz

Features & Attractions
- 5 min. walk to city
- 130-year-old residence
- Overlooking botan. gardens
- Riverside location
- Off-street parking
- Fluent French spoken

Quality Bed & Breakfast

	Double	$150-180
	Single	$110-150
	Child	neg

Situated beside the beautiful Maitai River, our charming Victorian family home has retained its original character and ambience. It is only minutes walk from central Nelson's award-winning restaurants and cafés, the Queen's Gardens, Suter Art Gallery, Botanical Hill (The Centre of New Zealand) and numerous river and bush walks. The five sunny bedrooms all have TV and are spacious and tastefully decorated. All rooms have access to the verandah and complimentary tea and coffee facilities are provided. Breakfast includes fresh and preserved fruits, home-made bread, hot croissants, home-made yoghurt, cheeses and a large variety of cereals. Our facilities include: a wheelchair suite, free email/Internet station, fax, laundry and complimentary port. We speak French, having lived for 25 years in New Caledonia.

Bedrooms	Qty
Double	3
Twin	2
Single	
Bed Size	Qty
King	
Queen	5
Double	
Single	2
Bathrooms	Qty
Ensuite	4
Private	1
Guest Share	

HAVENVIEW HOMESTAY
10 Davies Drive, Walters Bluff, Nelson
Ph (03) 546 6045, Mobile 027-420 0737
email: havenview@paradise.net.nz
www.havenview.co.nz

Features & Attractions
- Panoramic sea views
- 3 min drive to city centre
- Dinner by prior arrangement
- Welcome wine on deck each evening
- Wireless internet access
- New Zealand hosts

**Homestay
Bed & Breakfast**

	Double	$140-160
	Single	
	Child	

Welcome to our sunny, modern home, only three minutes from the centre of Nelson. Relax on our deck sipping a complimentary local wine and nibbles each evening while enjoying the panoramic views across the bay to Able Tasman Park. Join us for an evening meal or dine at one of Nelson's fine restaurants. We serve a light cooked breakfast at a time to suit you; and then during the day visit the National Park; do a wine tour; or have a game of golf. We both play golf and can recommend various courses. Our large queen ensuite has sea views, while our second queen room has a view of our garden. Come and let us make your stay a friendly, pampered experience.

Bedrooms	Qty
Double	2
Twin	
Single	
Bed Size	Qty
King	
Queen	2
Double	
King Single	
Bathrooms	Qty
Ensuite	1
Private	1
Guest Share	

DIRECTIONS: Exit motorway at Founders Park sign, 700m turn left up Walters Bluff, right into Davies Drive, look for homestay sign after 3rd house on right. (We are down right of way).

A CULINARY EXPERIENCE
LUXURY B&B
15 Seawatch Way, Atawhai, Nelson
Ph (03) 545 1886, Mobile 027-445 1886
email: stay@a-culinary-experience.com
www.a-culinary-experience.com

Tariff : N.Z. Dollars	
Double	$299-350
Single	$285-335
Child	

Bedrooms	Qty
Double	2
Twin	
Single	
Bed Size	**Qty**
Super King	
King	2
Queen	
Double	
King Single	2
Bathrooms	**Qty**
Ensuite	2
Private	
Guest Share	

Luxury B&B
Boutique Accommodation

Features & Attractions

- *Sauna, spa pool, massage*
- *Gourmet dinners & breakfasts*
- *Sculpture garden & art tour*
- *Organic gardens; free range chickens*
- *Stunning water views*
- *Pampered Holiday package*
- *Separate Self-contained apartment*
- *Wood-fired Pizza Oven*

Welcome to our lovely home filled with laughter, amazing views, original art and fabulous breakfasts and dinners. Completed in 2011, this purpose-built 5 star Luxury Bed and Breakfast was designed for you, the discerning traveller. Book one of our luxurious rooms: king-size beds, heated tile ensuites with two person shower or double spa bath, and all the amenities that you would expect in a luxury lodge. The media centre is located in the spacious guest library.

Enjoy the sea views from your private balcony or patio, the vineyard , the wood-fired pizza patio or the olive and lavender garden. Sip a complimentary glass of wine in the wine cellar. Celebrate sensational sunsets, exquisite bay and mountain views. Indulge yourself with a soak in the outdoor spa; relax in the infrared sauna; have a massage. Let us pamper you! With so much to do in the region, a stay of 3 or more nights is recommended.

AVAREST BED & BREAKFAST

33 Kerr Bay Rd, St Arnaud, Nelson Lakes
Ph (03) 521 1864, Fax (03) 521 1865
Mobile 027-430 5036
email: avarestbnb@xtra.co.nz
www.avarestbnb.co.nz

Features & Attractions
- *2 min. walk to lake edge*
- *& stunning views*
- *Single party booking*
- *Relaxed comfortable atmosphere*
- *Bushwalks, trout fishing*
- *Phone, fax, wireless internet*

Boutique Accommodation Bed & Breakfast

	Double	$220-260
	Single	$200-240
	Child	–

Avarest, in the heart of Nelson Lakes National Park, overlooks Lake Rotoiti, a 2 min walk to the water's edge. Our luxury mountain retreat is nestled amongst mature native forest filled with the sound of bellbirds and tuis. About 130 Rhododendrons flower progressively from September to January. Guest rooms are comfortable and tastefully decorated with the downstairs area only for our clients, which includes bathroom, lounge/library plus tea and coffee making facilities. **Avarest** breakfast is as simple or elaborate as your appetite requires. Pre-dinner drinks and finger food served around 5-ish. Lunches and dinner by prior arrangement. Kiri, the cat, will welcome you.

Bedrooms	Qty
Double	2
Twin	
Single	1
Bed Size	Qty
King	
Queen	2
Double	
Single	1
Bathrooms	Qty
Ensuite	
Private	
Guest Share	1

DIRECTIONS: Enter Kerr Bay Rd from SH63, travel past the Dept of Conservation HQ
towards the lake. We are the last driveway on the left.

AWAPIRITI LODGE

560 Shenandoah Highway, Murchison
Ph (03) 523 9889
email: idw1@farmside.co.nz
www.awapiritilodge.co.nz

Features & Attractions
- *Extensive native forest*
- *Swimming & fishing on site*
- *Dinner by arrangement*
- *Beautiful garden setting*
- *10 mins to adventure activities*
- *15 mins to excellent golf course*

Riverside Country Bed & Breakfast

	Double	$140-180
	Single	$125-140
	Child	

Dean and Maudie welcome you to our 116 hectares of mainly native forest, bordering a national park and the Maruia River, offering opportunities for trout fishing, swimming and kayaking. Come and enjoy the sights and sounds of the abundant bird life in our garden. We are situated only minutes from the Maruia Falls and the Buller Gorge which offers adventure activities such as jet-boating, whitewater rafting and gold panning at the Swingbridge. **The Lodge** is centrally located for day trips to Nelson Lakes or the Maruia hot springs, after which you can relax with a pre-dinner drink by the fire and enjoy an excellent home-cooked dinner. Our rooms have ensuites and a separate lounge with tv and complimentary port. Please phone for easy directions.

Bedrooms	Qty
Double	2
Twin	
Single	
Bed Size	Qty
Super King	1
Queen	1
Double	
King Single	2
Bathrooms	Qty
Ensuite	2
Private	
Guest Share	

MURCHISON LODGE

15 Grey Street, Murchison
Ph (03) 523 9196
email: info@murchisonlodge.co.nz
www.murchisonlodge.co.nz

Features & Attractions

- *Free wireless broadband*
- *Evening meals available*
- *5 mins walk to pubs & cafés*
- *Fishing, rafting, golf*
- *Children over 12 welcome*
- *Peaceful river setting*

$	Double	$155-215
	Single	$130-190
	Child	–

Comfortable B&B on Four Riverside Acres

Bedrooms	Qty
Double	3
Twin	1
Single	
Bed Size	Qty
King	1
Queen	2
Double	
Single	2
Bathrooms	Qty
Ensuite	3
Private	1
Guest Share	

Comfortable and quiet B&B with four spacious rooms, all with their own bathroom. Awake to the smell of fresh bread, and bacon on the BBQ. Breakfast on freshly collected eggs and homegrown fruit. Our four acres supports various animals (including a friendly dog) and borders the Buller River with its swimming holes and fishing access.

Relax with an evening meal at the **Lodge** - or take a short, pleasant walk to the township. The area is renowned for it's fly-fishing and white-water activities. Bike or walk local trails, or play golf (free use of bikes and clubs). Check your emails on our free WI-FI on the verandah or curl up with a wine in front of the cosy log fire.

DIRECTIONS:
To find Grey Street when entering town:
From south & west take 2nd left. From
north & east take 1st right.

NGAIO BAY ECOSTAY B&B
Ngaio Bay, French Pass Road, near French Pass,
Marlborough Sounds
Ph/Fax (03) 576 5287
email: welcome@ngaiobay.co.nz
www.ngaiobay.co.nz

Tariff : N.Z. Dollars	
Double	$260-370
Single	$175-260
Child	$90

Bedrooms	Qty
Double	3
Twin	
Single	
Bed Size	Qty
Super King	
King	3
Queen	
Double	
Single	5
Bathrooms	Qty
Ensuite	1
Private	2
Guest Share	

 **Remote Marlborough Sounds
Eco-homestay and Bed & Breakfast**

Features & Attractions
- *Sandy private beach*
- *Outdoor fire-heated bath*
- *Dolphins, seals, blue penguins*
- *Bush and farm walks, kayaks nearby*
- *Charter boats available*
- *Steadfast traditional sail*
- *Organic garden & orchard*
- *Stunning sunsets*

Experience something special at **Ngaio Bay**, on our own private beachfront, in a remote part of the Marlborough Sounds near the awesome waters of French Pass. Wilderness and physical beauty, warm

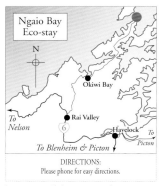

DIRECTIONS:
Please phone for easy directions.

welcoming hosts, scrumptious meals, homegrown organic fruit and vegies when available, stunning sunsets, private separate accommodation. Great for a romantic honeymoon, family get-together, peaceful holiday or wilderness adventure. **Ngaio Bay** is an authentic personal Kiwi experience. The small Garden Cottage and deck are hidden in the garden overlooking the beach, loft-style Rose and Dolphin is sunny and spacious, with deck overlooking bush, stream and sea, and Seabreeze Cottage is new, with full kitchen if you wish, very spacious and sunny with large decks and stunning views, a tempur bed. A special treat is the outdoor fireheated bath on the beach, enjoyed at sunset or under the stars, prepared with care by Roger. Dinner is included in the tariff. Two loveable old labradors. *Arrive as strangers, leave as friends.*

TIRIMOANA HOUSE
257 Anakiwa Rd, Tirimoana, Picton
Ph (03) 574 2627
Mobile 021-135 9708
email: bookings@tirimoanahouse.com
www.tirimoanahouse.com

Tariff : N.Z. Dollars	
Double	$200-330
Single	enquire
Child	n/a

Bedrooms	Qty
Double	5
Twin	
Single	
Bed Size	**Qty**
Super King	
King	
Queen	5
Double	
Single	
Bathrooms	**Qty**
Ensuite	5
Private	
Guest Share	

This Is Our View!
Luxury Waterfront Accommodation

Features & Attractions
- *Swimming and spa pools*
- *Walks & boat trips arranged*
- *Stunning sea views*
- *Free WiFi, internet*
- *Marlborough wine train tours*
- *Kayaking/horse trekking in sounds*
- *Queen Charlotte Track*
- *Winter rates May 1st-Sept 30th less 10%*

Our two-storey home sits on an elevated waterfront site and enjoys superb sea views of the Marlborough Sounds, **Tirimoana House** is located a convenient 30 min drive from Picton, Havelock a short 20 min drive and close to many of Marlborough wineries and restaurants. All 5 sumptuous bedrooms are en-suite, have queen size beds, TV, own deck, tea & coffee making facilities, fantastic views of the Sounds. One suite sleeps 4 and has its own private lounge and deck. Our guest lounge has WiFi, internet access, Sky TV, in winter relax in front of the log fire before enjoying a gourmet dinner of local fare and wines. Note: Evening meals are available by arrangement. Close by is the renowned Queen Charlotte Track (walk out - water taxi back), kayaking, mountain biking and famous wineries. Boat trips from Picton and wine tours, with collect and return to **Tirimoana House** can be arranged. After a full day of activities you can relax in our swimming or spa pools.

QUEENS VIEW B&B

259G Anakiwa Road, Anakiwa, Picton
Phone (03) 574 2363, Mobile 021-0229 2864
email: enquiries@queensview.co.nz
www.queensview.co.nz

Features & Attractions

- *Mountain biking*
- *Boat mooring available*
- *Art, craft & wine trails*
- *Kayaking & boat cruises*
- *Stunning scenery & sunsets*
- *Queen Charlotte Track 5min.*

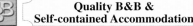

Quality B&B & Self-contained Accommodation

Double	$145-180
Single	$90-120
Child	neg

Queens View B&B has arguably some of the best views of the Queen Charlotte Sound and with Picton only 30 min. and Havelock a mere 20 min., it's the ideal central location to enjoy the "Top of the South".

Our home has 3 tastefully decorated guest rooms, beautiful gardens, where you can enjoy that evening glass of wine and a BBQ. The self-contained facilities include a fully equipped kitchen, TV/DVD, modest library, internet access and private boat mooring. From the house it's a mere 6-minute drive to the local Country Inn. Note: evening meals can be arranged, if sufficient notice given. Activities are plentiful, be it water sports, golf, mountain bikes, walks or the attraction of the wineries. All are within easy reach from **Queens View B&B.**

Bedrooms	Qty
Double	2
Twin	1
Single	
Bed Size	Qty
King	
Queen	2
Double	
Single	2
Bathrooms	Qty
Ensuite	1
Private	2
Guest Share	

TANGLEWOOD BED & BREAKFAST

1744 Queen Charlotte Dve, The Grove, Picton
Ph (03) 574 2080, Fax (03) 574 2044
Mobile 027-481 4388
email: tanglewood.hearn@xtra.co.nz
www.tanglewood.net.nz

Features & Attractions

- *5km to Queen Charlotte Walkway*
- *Fifth generation Kiwi hospitality*
- *Delicious full breakfast*
- *Glowworms*
- *Four person Spa/Jacuzzi*
- *Home cooked meal - $50pp*

Superior Bed & Breakfast Self-contained Accommodation

Double	$155-185
Single	$120-140
Child	neg

Our modern architectural home is nestled amongst the native ferns overlooking the stunning Queen Charlotte Sounds. Enjoy one of our new luxury super king/twin ensuite rooms each with balcony and views; or our self-contained private guest wing which includes a queen and two single beds (each with ensuite), lounge, kitchen and sunny balcony/ BBQ area.

After a busy day you can relax in our spa/jacuzzi surrounded by our beautiful native garden and birds, or take an evening stroll to view our glow worms. Generous breakfasts are provided and dinners are available by arrangement. Make **Tanglewood** your base for Marlborough wineries, swimming, fishing, cycling, kayaking or walking the Queen Charlotte Walkway. Kiwi hospitality at its best!

Bedrooms	Qty
Double	3
Twin	1
Single	
Bed Size	Qty
Super King	2
Queen	1
King/Single	2
Single	2
Bathrooms	Qty
Ensuite	4
Private	
Guest Share	

A Sea View B&B

424 Port Underwood Road,
Whatamonga Bay, Picton
Ph (03) 573 8815, Mobile 021-155 1890
email: info@aseaview.co.nz
www.aseaview.co.nz

Tariff : N.Z. Dollars	
Double	$170-215
Single	$150-180
Child	

Bedrooms	Qty
Double	3
Twin	
Single	
Bed Size	**Qty**
Super King	
King	2
Queen	1
Double	
Single	
Bathrooms	**Qty**
Ensuite	3
Private	
Guest Share	

        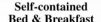 **Self-contained Bed & Breakfast**

'A Sea View'

Features & Attractions

- *Breathtaking views*
- *Secluded, terraced garden*
- *Two rooms have kitchenettes*
- *WIFI Available*
- *One courtesy pick-up from Picton*
- *Outdoor activities & wine tours*
- *Delicious full breakfast*
- *Private entrance to rooms*

Share with us our wonderful view of Queen Charlotte Sound. **A Sea View** is set among trees and offers unimpeded, awe-inspiring views of the Queen Charlotte Sounds. From your room or the deck, experience the ever-changing moods of the Sounds. Enjoy the peace and tranquility that a large garden with its great variety of plants and wildlife offer. Enjoy a continental or full breakfast including home made, home grown and locally sourced ingredients. All rooms are warm with large comfortable beds, ensuites and tea and coffee facilities. Come any time of year and discover the many activities that Marlborough is famous for: wine tasting, kayaking, boating, fishing, diving and trekking or a cruise on the Sounds visiting the many beautiful bays. At day's end, while relaxing on the deck with a cool drink and enjoying the sunset on the hills around the bay, take the opportunity to discuss with us your plans for your time in Marlborough and your onward journey through New Zealand.

DIRECTIONS: From High St in Picton take Waikawa Bay Rd for 9km, continue for 1km past Karaka Point until you see **Sea View** sign on your right (12-15 min Picton)

179

VIEWFORTH

6 Okiwa Place, Tirimoana, Picton
Ph (03) 574 2341, Mobile 021-152 9406
e-mail: viewforth@xtra.co.nz
www.charmingaccommodation.co.nz

Features & Attractions

- *Tranquil, restful environment*
- *5 minutes to waters edge*
- *Sea kayaking, mountain biking*
- *Courtesy transfers*
- *Queen Charlotte Track*
- *Local wine trails, boat cruises*

 Quality Bed & Breakfast Self-contained Accom.

Double	$145
Single	$100
Child	n/a

Relax in peaceful native bush surroundings which are enhanced by views to the Sounds and a 2 mins walk to the waters edge. Our well appointed self-contained Suite has a private entrance from north facing decks, and affords absolute privacy. Facilities include open plan kitchenette, living and bedroom, with an adjoining ensuite bathroom. We are situated in Tirimoana/Anakiwa within easy driving to local restaurants, in Picton (30 mins), Blenheim (50 mins) and Havelock (20 mins). Queen Charlotte Track is 5 mins away where you can walk all or part of the track and water taxi back. Ferry/water taxi available to/from Anakiwa, and other local bays from Picton. Visit local wineries, enjoy fishing, golf, kayaking, cycling, boat cruises and many other outdoor activities.

For easy directions Phone 021-152 9406

Bedrooms	Qty
Double	1
Twin	
Single	

Bed Size	Qty
King	
Queen	1
Double	
Single	

Bathrooms	Qty
Ensuite	1
Private	
Guest Share	

Baxter Bed & Breakfast

28 Elisha Drive, Blenheim, Marlborough
Ph (03) 578 3753 Mobile 021-129 2062
email: baxterart@xtra.co.nz
www.baxterhomestay.com

Tariff : N.Z. Dollars	
Double	$175-240
Single	
Child	

Bedrooms	Qty
Double	4
Twin	
Single	
Bed Size	**Qty**
Super King	2
King	
Queen	1
Double	3
Single	1
Bathrooms	**Qty**
Ensuite	3
Private	
Guest Share	1

Quality Bed & Breakfast
Panoramic Views

Features & Attractions

- *Panoramic views*
- *Private and peaceful*
- *Close to wineries*
- *4 mins. from town centre*
- *Discounts for 3+ nights*
- *Laundry/wireless internet*
- *Adjacent to walking tracks*
- *Set in prize winning gardens*

Warm and friendly hospitality awaits you at our sunny, comfortable, modern home. Enjoy panoramic views over Blenheim and nearby vineyards or watching native birds in our prize winning garden. Share our spacious lounge with piano, large screen TV or relax in your private suite with TV, tea and coffee making facilities and either attractive garden outlooks or spectacular elevated views with balcony. Our luxury self-contained suite has a fully equipped kitchen. Brian, a renowned New Zealand artist, has a gallery. His paintings also adorn walls of our home. As we have lived in Blenheim over 50 years, our local knowledge will be valuable when helping you arrange visits to local attractions, e.g. wine tours, restaurants, Sounds cruises, drives etc. Adjacent to Wither Hills walking tracks. Our interests include: sport, travel, gardening, art, music, photography and video production.

"Many thanks. You are fantastic hosts and made me feel at home" Dame Malvina Major.

BLUE RIDGE ESTATE VINEYARD HOMESTAY

50 O'Dwyers Road, Rapaura, Blenheim
Ph (03) 570 2198
email: stay@blueridge.co.nz
www.blueridge.co.nz

Tariff : N.Z. Dollars	
Double	$220-265
Single	$220-265
Child	

Bedrooms	Qty
Double	2
Twin	1
Single	
Bed Size	**Qty**
Super King	
King	
Queen	2
Double	
Single	2
Bathrooms	**Qty**
Ensuite	1
Private	2
Guest Share	

Boutique Vineyard Homestay

Features & Attractions

- *Quiet and peaceful*
- *Stunning rural views*
- *Warm, friendly hospitality*
- *Excellent restaurants nearby*
- *Award winning home*
- *Comfort and privacy*
- *Tastefully furnished*
- *Heart of the wine region*

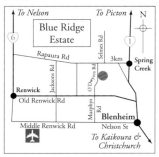

Set on a twenty acre purpose-designed homestay property, **Blue Ridge Estate**, 2002 Master Builders' House of the Year, enjoys a rural setting with stunning views across vineyards to the Richmond Range. Close to many of Marlborough's fine wineries, restaurants, gardens, only twenty five minutes from Picton, and seven minutes to the airport or Blenheim. Bedrooms and bathrooms are tastefully furnished– electric blankets, tea and coffee facilities, high quality linen, hair dryer, heated towel rail. Spend a winter evening in front of our open fire. Our home has proven popular with both international and New Zealand visitors. Come and share our home, where comfort and privacy will ensure your Marlborough visit is indeed a memorable one. In consideration for other guests, this property is not suitable for children. Wireless internet access available. **Reservations essential.**

182

OMAKA HEIGHTS B&B COUNTRYSTAY

199 Brookby Road, Omaka Valley, Blenheim
Ph (03) 572 7402, Mobile 027-276 9791
email: omakaheights@netz.co.nz
www.omakaheights.co.nz

Tariff : N.Z. Dollars	
Double	$180-215
Single	$135-170
Child	neg

Bedrooms	Qty
Double	1
Twin	1
Single	
Bed Size	**Qty**
Super King	
King	
Queen	1
Double	
King/Single	2
Bathrooms	**Qty**
Ensuite	2
Private	
Guest Share	

        Countrystay Bed & Breakfast

Features & Attractions

- *Outstanding views*
- *Wine & sightseeing tours*
- *Art and craft visits*
- *Scenic flights*
- *Golf, fishing, boating*
- *Whale & dolphin watching*
- *Skiing and tramping*
- *Excellent dining nearby*

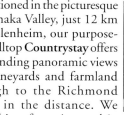

DIRECTIONS: From Blenheim take Middle Renwick Rd, after passing the airport take 1st left into Godfrey Rd. Then take 1st right into Dog Point Rd and first left into Brookby Rd.

Positioned in the picturesque Omaka Valley, just 12 km from Blenheim, our purpose-built hilltop **Countrystay** offers out-standing panoramic views over vineyards and farmland through to the Richmond Range in the distance. We are within a few minutes drive of over thirty wineries. There are numerous restaurants and cafés, offering world class cuisine, located within Blenheim town and the surrounding vineyard area. Our self-contained **Countrystay** wing offers two guest rooms with private ensuite facilities and private decks plus a guest lounge. The twin room/ensuite is completely wheelchair accessible. The lounge provides tea/coffee making facilities, refrigerator and television. The bedrooms are fully equipped with hairdryer and electric blankets. Guests are offered a hearty breakfast and complimentary pre-dinner beverages. Wireless broadband available. You may enjoy a stroll around our eight hectare property on which we farm alpacas.

OLDE MILL HOUSE B&B & CYCLE HIRE

9 Wilson Street, Renwick, Marlborough
Ph/Fax (03) 572 8458
email: info@oldemillhouse.co.nz
www.oldemillhouse.co.nz

Features & Attractions

- *Stunning views Richmond Ranges*
- *Numerous vineyard cellar doors*
- *Tripadvisor rated* ☆☆☆☆☆
- *Free guest bikes*
- *Outdoor spa/ BBQ*
- *Free Wireless Internet*

Homestay
Bed & Breakfast

Double	$156	
Single	$120	
Child u/12	$40	

Diane welcomes you to your "***Home away from Home***". Our character home is set in beautiful, peaceful gardens and has been refurbished to provide quality accommodation while retaining its 'olde world' charm. We offer three guest rooms, all with ensuites, quality linen, hairdryers etc. Complimentary cycles are provided for guests to tour the vineyards – there are approximately 25 cellar doors within a 5 km radius of **Olde Mill House**. Relax and enjoy a glass of wine in our elevated spa with views of our gardens and the Richmond Ranges.

Complimentary: wireless broadband internet access, travel to and from local vineyard restaurants and airport/bus transfers. We look forward to meeting you soon.

Bedrooms	Qty
Double	3
Twin	
Single	

Bed Size	Qty
King	2
Queen	1
Twin/Single	2
Single	

Bathrooms	Qty
Ensuite	3
Private	
Guest Share	

THE STREAM ESTATE COTTAGE

856 Rapaura Road, Rapaura, Blenheim
Ph (03) 570 5838, Mobile 021-1511 021
email: shireen@xtra.co.nz
www.thestreamestate.co.nz

Tariff : N.Z. Dollars	
Double	$250
Single	
Child	

Bedrooms	Qty
Double	1
Twin	1
Single	
Bed Size	**Qty**
Super King	
King	
Queen	1
Double	
King/Single	2
Bathrooms	**Qty**
Ensuite	
Private	1
Guest Share	

Self-contained Vineyard Cottage

Features & Attractions

- *Self-contained privacy*
- *Located in vineyard*
- *Set beside natural spring*
- *Trout fishing at cottage door*
- *Town and airport 10 minutes*
- *Heart of wine trail region*
- *Close to many cafés and restaurants*
- *Beautiful views*

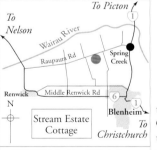

DIRECTIONS: From Picton (SH1) take Rapaura Road towards Nelson. From Nelson (SH6) turn left into Rapaura Road, immediately after Main Wairau River Bridge.

Set beside a natural spring creek, renowned for its fantastic trout fishing, **The Stream Estate Cottage** offers total privacy within the vineyard. From the front patio, surrounded by vines and the natural fast flowing spring, the views are breathtaking. **The Stream Estate Cottage** is self-contained and well appointed with separate lounge, dining and kitchen area, featuring a large open fire and double doors which open onto the front patio from the lounge and main bedroom. Two double bedrooms, plus a share ensuite complete the cottage. Being very centrally located on the Rapaura Road, the 'Golden Mile' of the Marlborough wine industry, **The Stream Estate Cottage** is within ten minutes of most wineries, restaurants and the town centre of Blenheim.

"A little piece of paradise at your door"

185

BEACHFRONT FARMSTAY

3578 Karamea Highway, Karamea
Ph/Fax (03) 782 6762, Mobile 027-249 8827
email: farmstay@xtra.co.nz
www.westcoastbeachaccommodation.co.nz

Features & Attractions

- *Private access to beach*
- *Peaceful rural setting*
- *Clear night sky*
- *Espresso coffee*
- *Mouthwatering wholesome cooking*
- *Complimentary internet & laundry*

 Farmstay Bed & Breakfast

Double	$160-180
Single	$140
Child	neg

Bedrooms	Qty
Double	2
Twin	
Single	1

Bed Size	Qty
King	1
Queen	1
Double	
Single	

Bathrooms	Qty
Ensuite	2
Private	
Family Share	

Our 500 cow dairy farm has 2.5kms of coastline, a 2min walk and you will be on a sandy beach usually all to yourself. Relax in elegant rooms with your own private deck. Special farmhouse breakfasts, home preserving, tasty fish, bacon and egg dishes, espresso coffee. Join us in the evening for mouthwatering wholesome cooking, farm grown meat, fresh fish, organic vegetables, homemade desserts served with NZ wine. Gluten free catered for. Enquire about a BBQ and bonfire on the beach, a unique Kiwi tradition, (weather permitting) or a fishing experience with Russell and his Kentiki Torpedo. Experience nature at its best, the Oparara Basin is one of Kahurangi National Park's special places. Day 1: visit the Limestone Caves and Arches. Day 2: walk the new Oparara Valley Eco Walk. Day 3: walk for a couple of hours along the Heaphy track.

DIRECTIONS:
Karamea Beachfront Farmstay
is 84 km north of Westport
and 3 km north of Little Wanganui.

HAVENLEE HOMESTAY

76 Queen Street, Westport
Ph (03) 789 8543, Fax (03) 789 8502
Mobile 027-627 2702
email: info@havenlee.co.nz
www.havenlee.co.nz

Features & Attractions

- *Warm friendly welcome*
- *A garden oasis*
- *At home atmosphere*
- *Self-contained annexe*
- *Closest to town*
- *Denniston Heritage Site*

Best Choice for First Class Hospitality

Double	$120-170
Single	$100
Child	neg

Bedrooms	Qty
Double	3
Twin	
Single	

Bed Size	Qty
King	1
Queen	2
Double	
Single	2

Bathrooms	Qty
Ensuite	1
Private	1
Guest Share	1

Peace in Paradise – this is **Havenlee**. From the moment you arrive you will feel at home right away. A warm, welcoming greeting at our relaxed, spacious, quality Homestay will introduce you to the fine hospitality you will receive during your stay with

DIRECTIONS: Along Palmerston St turn right at Wakefield Street, left at Queen Street, 1st home on left.

us. We were born and bred in the Westport area and very proud of our West Coast heritage. **Havenlee** is centrally located: minutes from the Tasman Sea, and idyllic base from which to explore the environmental wonderland.

Check out the numerous adventure experiences, local attractions and heritage sites. Soak up the nature to rest and restore body and soul. Breakfast is delicious; continental-plus with a cooked option as required using locally sourced produce wherever possible. Ensuite, private or guest share bathroom facilities available. WiFi and laundry facilities are available to guests.

BREAKERS BOUTIQUE ACCOMMODATION
Nine Mile Beach, Coast Road,
SH 6, Greymouth
Ph (03) 762 7743, Fax (03) 762 7733
email: stay@breakers.co.nz
www.breakers.co.nz

Features & Attractions

- *Fantastic sea views*
- *Al-fresco dining*
- *Warm, inviting hospitality*
- *Private access to beach*
- *Separate guest lounge*
- *Relaxing atmosphere*

Double	$215-355	
Single	–	
Child	n/a	

Seaside Bed & Breakfast

Bedrooms	Qty
Double	4
Twin	2
Single	
Bed Size	Qty
Super King	1
King	1
Queen	2
Single	2
Bathrooms	Qty
Ensuite	4
Private	
Guest Share	

Stunningly located on 2 acres of native bush and landscaped gardens overlooking the Tasman Sea. All rooms guaranteed a magnificent sea view. Private track for access to the beach below. Meander along the beach or fossick in the rock pools. Breakfast is included at **Breakers** and alfresco dining is available as well as local beer and wine. Warm, relaxing environment and a helpful hostess await you. Enjoy a magnificent West Coast sunset out over the sea in the comfort of your room or outside on the balcony. Sit back, relax and enjoy the wonderful views. Lie in bed and watch the rolling surf and be lulled to sleep by the sound of the breaking waves. You may never want to leave this little slice of paradise.

DIRECTIONS: 14kms north of Greymouth on SH6. After Strongman Mine Memorial directly on the left after crossing Nine Mile Creek bridge. 30kms south of Punakaiki and the Pancake Rocks at Nine Mile Creek. Look out for other creeks 14 mile, 13mile and 10mile. On right before crossing Nine Mile.

OAK LODGE
286 State Highway 6, Coal Creek, Greymouth
Ph (03) 768 6832
Mobile 027-222 1192
email: relax@oaklodge.co.nz
www.oaklodge.co.nz

Features & Attractions

- *Delightful rural setting*
- *Spa pool/sauna*
- *Swimming pool*
- *Tennis court/pool table*
- *Sheep, hens and eels*
- *B&B and self contained*

Double	$150-245	
Single	$150-205	
Child	$25-45	

Rural Boutique B&B & Self-contained Cottage

Bedrooms	Qty
Double	5
Twin	1
Single	
Bed Size	Qty
Super King	3
Queen	2
Double	
Single	4
Bathrooms	Qty
Ensuite	5
Private	1
Guest Share	

Truly a home full of character and charm, this quality B&B is only two minutes north of Greymouth. Our guest accommodation is upstairs and includes 5 spacious well appointed bedrooms, 4 with ensuites and one with a private bathroom. The guest lounge has tea and coffee making facilities and microwave. Relax on the balcony or rejuvenate in the spa pool or sauna. There is also the tennis court, swimming pool and billiards room for your enjoyment. Take a stroll around the garden, feed the sheep and eels or collect the eggs. Continental and cooked breakfasts are served. Wireless internet available. Alastair and Shirley have been sheep and cattle farmers in the past and extend a very warm welcome to you.

DIRECTIONS:
3km north of Greymouth State Highway 6. **Oak Lodge** is on the right, an elevated section.

Paroa Homestay Bed & Breakfast

345 Main South Road, Paroa, Greymouth
Ph (03) 762 6769, Fax (03) 762 6765
Mobile 027-323 3118
email: paroahomestay@xtra.co.nz
www.paroahomestay.co.nz

Features & Attractions

- *Home away from home*
- *Off street parking*
- *Superb breakfast*
- *Seaview and mountain views*
- *Three minutes walk to beach*
- *Spacious rooms, separate guest lounge*

Bed & Breakfast Overlooking the Sea		Double	$145
		Single	$120
		Child	neg

View incredible sunsets and mountains whilst relaxing on terraces overlooking the sea - just three minutes walk to beach. Large modern home (with antique furniture) surrounded by native trees and bush. View Pam's unique tub/barrel organic vegetable garden whilst relaxing in back garden. Enjoy superb breakfast (waffles, fresh fruit salad, yoghurt, homemade muffins, cheese/nuts/dried fruit). Food is Pam's forte as previously owning a busy café/restaurant. Homemade baking served on arrival. Tea/coffee making facilities also available. Visit Punakaiki (Blowholes/Pancake Rocks), Shantytown Heritage Village, Monteiths Brewery Tour, view Coal Creek Waterfall through rainforest bush walk, fish for trout. Courtesy car to restaurants for evening meal. Secure off street parking.
Guest comments - "*best breakfast in New Zealand*" A.N, Canberra, "*Our host was just so welcoming*" L.G, UK. Pam has welcomed guests for 16 years. Stay two nights at a reduced cost of $140.00 per night.

Bedrooms	Qty
Double	2
Twin	
Single	1
Bed Size	**Qty**
Super King	1
King	1
Double	1
Single	
Bathrooms	**Qty**
Ensuite	1
Off Suite	1
Guest Share	1

Rosewood Bed & Breakfast

20 High Street, Greymouth
Ph (03) 768 4674, Fax (03) 768 4694
email: stay@rosewoodnz.co.nz
www.rosewoodnz.co.nz

Features & Attractions

- *Character home*
- *Spacious rooms*
- *Separate guest lounge*
- *Courtesy pick-ups*
- *10-15 min walk to restaurants*
- *Ensuite or private facilities*

Superior Bed & Breakfast		Double	$190-240
		Single	$150-250
		Child	$25

Whether you've just got off the Trans Alpine or are travelling through Greymouth between Christchurch, Nelson or the Glaciers, or just want a few days away, **Rosewood Bed & Breakfast** is the ideal place to stop and recover from your journey and the activities of the day. Rhonda and Stephan await you with a warm friendly welcome in their restored 1920's character home that has retained its grand features of wood panelling and leadlight windows. You will enjoy relaxing in the window seat in the guest lounge/dining room with a cup of tea or coffee and some of Rhonda's home-made biscuits before taking a wander into town for dinner in one of the cafés or restaurants. Spacious, well equipped bedrooms with private facilities will let you have a great night's sleep in a very comfortable bed. Full continental and cooked breakfast awaits you next morning to give you that perfect start to the day. Rhonda and Stephan appreciate all that the West Coast region has to offer, and would love to make your stay a memorable one for you!

Bedrooms	Qty
Double	4
Twin	2
Single	1
Bed Size	**Qty**
King	1
Queen	4
Double	
Single	1
Bathrooms	**Qty**
Ensuite	3
Private	1
Guest Share	

SUNSETVIEW HOMESTAY

335 Main South Road, Greymouth, Westland
Ph/Fax (03) 762 6616, Mobile 027-475 5218
email: sunsetview@xtra.co.nz
www.charmingaccommodation.co.nz

Features & Attractions
- *Sea & mountain views*
- *Short walk to beach*
- *Swimming pool/barbeque*
- *Relaxed & friendly*
- *Children welcome*
- *Generous breakfasts*

**Homestay
Bed & Breakfast**

Double	$100-140
Single	$90-100
Child	neg

Bedrooms	Qty
Double	4
Twin	
Single	
Bed Size	**Qty**
Super King	1
King	2
Queen	1
King/Single	2
Bathrooms	**Qty**
Ensuite	2
Private	1
Guest Share	

Welcome to our sunny home with amazing sea and mountain views. We offer well appointed queen and king bedrooms with Sky TV.

Full continental and cooked breakfasts, other home cooked meals available by prior arrangement. Our home is centrally heated. Internet, laundry/dryer facilities available. We have for your use an indoor pool which is heated from November till April. Beach is a 3min walk.

Downstairs we offer an apartment with its private entrance and two bedrooms, ensuite, kitchen/ dining/ lounge area. It can sleep up to 5 and can be enjoyed either as a regular B&B facility or as a self-catered basis. Fishing trips can be arranged. Courtesy car service to and from local restaurants and travel centres. Plenty of off-street parking.

DIRECTIONS:
Approx 5km South of town centre

AWATUNA BEACHSIDE BED & BREAKFAST

1209 Kumara Junction Highway,
Awatuna, RD 2 Hokitika
Ph (03) 755 6060, Mobile 027-404 6658
email: awatuna-beachside@xtra.co.nz
www.westcoast.net.nz

Features & Attractions
- *Scenic coastal views*
- *Historic gold trail walks*
- *Adventure activities arranged*
- *A taste of the country*
- *10 min from town*
- *Beach walks*

Double	$125-155
Single	$75-100
Child	

**Bed & Breakfast
Homestay**

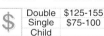

Bedrooms	Qty
Double	2
Twin	1
Single	
Bed Size	**Qty**
King	1
Queen	1
Double	
Single	2
Bathrooms	**Qty**
Ensuite	3
Private	
Guest Share	

Awatuna Beachside Bed & Breakfast is nestled between the highway and the beach, in park-like grounds and with splendid views of the coastline and the Alps. We offer indoor and outdoor relaxation and ease. Walk along a lonely beach, or just soak up the views from our veranda, while enjoying a quiet drink. For the more active there is tramping, exploring the gold field trails, or a spot of fishing. A host of activities can be arranged.

The best of country living within minutes of town. Our house has been purpose-built – mixing modern living with traditional West Coast hospitality. Meet the friendly sheep, goats and our cat Max. Complimentary transport offered when appropriate.

189

NEW RIVER BLUEGUMS B&B/COTTAGES

985 Main South Road, Camerons, Greymouth
Ph (03) 762 6678, Fax (03) 762 6678
email: mail@bluegumsnz.com
www.bluegumsnz.com

Tariff : N.Z. Dollars	
Double	$145-195
Single	$115-155
Child	$25

Bedrooms	Qty
Double	3
Twin	
Single	

Bed Size	Qty
Super King	
King	1
Queen	2
Double	2
Single	2

Bathrooms	Qty
Ensuite	3
Private	1
Guest Share	

**Special Rural Retreat
& Self-contained Bed & Breakfast**

Features & Attractions

- *15 min walk to beach*
- *Two self-contained cottages*
- *Tennis court*
- *Log & Stone home*
- *Away from main highway*
- *Short drive to cafés & attractions*
- *Feed farm animals*
- *Outdoor bath-tub*

Situated on a small farm **New River Bluegums** offers quality self-contained and in-house accommodation, while providing the base for a relaxing West Coast stay. Enjoy full breakfast, complimentary refreshments, wireless internet, feed farm animals, play tennis and soak in the outdoor bathtub. Coco, our friendly chocolate lab will entertain you.

Laundry and BBQ facilities. s/c cottages: 2 accessible units, each with queen bedroom, lounge with single bed and double sofabed, kitchen dining, TV/DVD, large tiled bathroom. Tui Room main log house: king bed, TV, lovely ensuite bathroom. We are 10 minute drive south of Greymouth and under 2 hours to Franz Josef Glacier. "*Terrific place, tranquil, very good breakfast - wonderful hosts, loved it.*" - guest comment.

AWATUNA HOMESTEAD
9 Stafford Rd, Awatuna, Hokitika
Ph (03) 755 6834, Fax (03) 755 6876
Mobile 027-310 1329
email: rest@awatunahomestead.co.nz
www.awatunahomestead.co.nz

Tariff : N.Z. Dollars	
Double	$290-370
Single	$250
Child	neg

Bedrooms	Qty
Double	2
Double/Twin	2
Twin	1
Bed Size	**Qty**
Super King	
S.King/Twin	2
Queen	2
King Single	
Single	2
Bathrooms	**Qty**
Ensuite	3
Private	1
Family Share	1

Luxury Bed & Breakfast
& Self-contained Apartment

Features & Attractions

- Dinner by prior arrangement
- Extensive NZ wine list
- Organic vegies, enviro gardens
- Maori cultural story telling
- Vintage cars on site
- Open fire beach picnics
- WIFI Guest Internet
- Beach, bush walking

Map: Awatuna Homestead, To Greymouth, Taramakau River, Tasman Sea, Awatuna, Stafford Rd, Stafford Loop Rd, To Hokitika, To Christchurch

A Gold Enviro. Award winning family home since 1874, on the sea coast between Greymouth and Hokitika, **Awatuna Homestead** is only 2 hrs drive from the Glaciers, 2 hrs from Punakaiki Rocks and 3.5 hrs from Christchurch. Base yourselves at the Homestead for a few days and take relaxing short day trips to the interesting and exciting places on the West Coast. On your return to the **Homestead**, enjoy a relaxing wine or beer and, if you wish, listen to Mäori cultural storytelling with Hëmi, followed by an al fresco style or pre-booked full evening dinner of country fare, prepared and cooked at the **Homestead** by Pauline. At evening's end make your way to your ensuited bedrooms and sink into the luxurious warmth and comfort of fabulous beds for a great sleep. Wake up feeling refreshed to enjoy a breakfast of homemade muesli, fruit, organic yoghurt, fresh-baked bread and fresh eggs from the **Homestead** chickens. Vintage cars, outdoor hot tub and extensive gardens compliment your special experience at the **Homestead**.

TEICHELMANN'S BED & BREAKFAST

20 Hamilton Street, Hokitika
Ph (03) 755 8232, Fax (03) 755 8239
Mobile 027-255 8232
email: teichel@xtra.co.nz
www.teichelmanns.co.nz

Features & Attractions

- *Quiet, central location*
- *Close to restaurants/cafés*
- *Heritage, character house*
- *Beach & shops nearby*
- *Walks, golf and fishing*
- *Craft & heritage trails*

	Boutique Bed & Breakfast			Double	$195-250
			$	Single	$120-195
				Child	–

'History.....With a Touch of Class' - **Teichelmann's** is a long established, iconic Bed & Breakfast accommodation located in the central heritage area of Hokitika. Frances & Brian place a strong emphasis on the personal side of our business and have created an environment where guests feel welcome and at home in an historic building. Five ensuite guest bedrooms on two levels as well as a guest lounge. Teicheys Garden Cottage offers a spa bath with a private fern garden outlook. **Teichelmann's** location ensures a short walk to interesting craft galleries, restaurants or visit local attractions, including great sunsets at the beach. Breakfast is not to be missed. A buffet selection of fruits, yoghurt, cereal, followed by cooked choice of local free range eggs and bacon.

Bedrooms	Qty
Double	5
Twin	
Single	1
Bed Size	Qty
Super King	3
King	2
King/Single	1
Single	1
Bathrooms	Qty
Ensuite	5
Private	1
Guest Share	

DIRECTIONS: Turn left at Town Clock, then first right. Booking in advance is recommended.

THE GARDEN B & B

136 Fitzherbert St, Hokitika
Ph (03) 755 5418, Mobile 021-025 54249
email: gardenbandb@xtra.co.nz
www.gardenbandb.co.nz

Features & Attractions

- *Off-street parking*
- *Wireless internet*
- *Well travelled hosts*
- *Character home and garden*
- *Walk to town, beach, glow-worm dell*
- *Complimentary cuppa on arrival*

	Affordable Quality Bed & Breakfast		Double	$120-160
			Single	$90-140
			Child	u10$10-u16$20

"Great stay, superb breakfast and great hospitality- the best…" from our guest book.

Enjoy warm hospitality in a character 1930s villa, only five minutes walk from restaurants, shopping and a wild West Coast beach. Your hosts, David and Glenis, have lived and hiked all over the South Island and are a mine of information on travel destinations. Explore the West Coast glaciers, Punakaiki, Shanty Town and the Lake Kaniere/ Hokitika Gorge loop from a central base. Start the day with a delicious cooked and continental breakfast with four menu options including the popular "Scrambled Eggs on Fire". Home made bread, jams and muesli are a feature. A relaxing outdoor spa is available.

Bedrooms	Qty
Double	3
Twin	1
Single	
Bed Size	Qty
King	
Queen	2
Double	1
Single	2
Bathrooms	Qty
Ensuite	1
Guest Share	1
Family Share	1

DIRECTIONS:
On SH6 opposite 4 Square Store.

HOKITIKA HERITAGE LODGE

46 Alpine View, Hokitika
Ph (03) 755 7357, Fax (03) 755 8760
Mobile 027-437 1254
email: info@hokitikaheritagelodge.co.nz
www.hokitikaheritagelodge.co.nz

Features & Attractions

- Spectacular mountain views
- Magnificent sea views
- Heritage character home
- Replica heritage cottage
- Restaurants/glowworms close
- Beach & bush walks close

Double	$195-250	
Single	$140-180	
Child		

Bed & Breakfast & Self-catering

Bedrooms	Qty
Double	5
Twin	
Single	
Bed Size	**Qty**
King	2
Queen	3
Double	
Single	1
Bathrooms	**Qty**
Ensuite	3
Private	1
Guest Share	

Hokitika Heritage Lodge

NZ hospitality at its best! Our B&B Lodge overlooks extensive views of Tasman Sea, Hokitika, the Southern Alps, including Mount Cook. 'Bank House' provides full Bed & Breakfast, with 3 spacious ensuite rooms and guest lounge. Historic and stylish décor with attention to detail is used throughout the Lodge to reflect NZ, West Coast and family history, including **Gold**, **Jade** and **Heritage** themed rooms. **Gatehouse Cottage** is a self-catering holiday home and includes 2 beautiful bedrooms with private bathroom; lounge with TV, dining and full kitchen. Dianne, (Literacy Teacher) and Chris, (Property Consultant and Rotarian) enjoy chatting with guests over a welcoming drink and home-baking. Broadband Internet and wireless network are available. Dinners available with pre-booking. Stay a night, or more. Relax, or explore the beautiful West Coast.

WOODLAND GLEN LODGE

96 Hau Hau Rd, Blue Spur, Hokitika
Ph/Fax (03) 755 5063, Mobile 027-201 6126
email: woodlandglen1@gmail.com
www.hokitika.net

Features & Attractions

- Quiet private surroundings
- 3 mins. from tourist centre
- Wonderful gardens & Mt. views
- Lake Kaniere/Hokitika Gorge 20 mins.
- Separate guest lounge & dining
- Internet & digital TVs in rooms

Double	$180-200	
Single	$150-180	
Child		

Quality Bed & Breakfast close to Hokitika

Bedrooms	Qty
Double	5
Twin	2
Single	
Bed Size	**Qty**
King	
Queen	5
Double	
Single	2
Bathrooms	**Qty**
Ensuite	3
Private	
Guest Share	1

DIRECTIONS: From Main St into Hokitika turn east into Hampden St. Proceed straight for approx. 2km until sign on right. Advance booking recommended.

Woodland Glen Lodge is a large homestead located on 21 acres, providing that country setting with peace and quite only a few minutes drive from the centre of Hokitika. **Woodland Glen** is set in tranquil surroundings amongst beautiful established native gardens and trees with an abundance of native bird life, offering the ideal retreat or just time out. Woodland Glen is a beautifully presented lodge with exceptional facilities to make your stay so pleasurable. Our hearty Kiwi breakfast will ensure you get through your day ahead. Laurie is a 4th generation West Coaster, a retired Police officer and now commercial pilot. Janette is from Edinburgh Scotland and is employed locally as a health professional, she has an active interest in the craft of quilting. You need to stay at least 2 nights to cover our local attractions.

PARAMATA LODGE
Bold Head Road, Ross, West Coast
Ph (03) 755 4250, Mobile 027-367 2699
email: stay@paramatalodge.co.nz
www.paramatalodge.co.nz

Tariff : N.Z. Dollars	
Double	$290-350
Single	$200-250
Child	n/a

Bedrooms	Qty
Double	3
Twin	2
Single	

Bed Size	Qty
Super King	2
King	1
Queen	
Double	
Single	6

Bathrooms	Qty
Ensuite	3
Private	
Guest Share	

  Ecological Sanctuary / Luxury Lodge

Features & Attractions

- *Fine dining our specialty*
- *Guided wilderness tours*
- *Beach access*
- *Free canoes and walks*
- *Trout/salmon fishing*
- *Free wireless internet*
- *Central regional location*
- *Luxurious features*

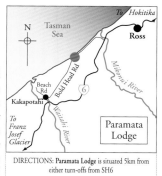

DIRECTIONS: **Paramata Lodge** is situated 5km from either turn-offs from SH6

Peace and tranquility in a natural forest setting where the Southern Alps provide a dramatic backdrop and the Tasman Sea, a moody western expanse. Paramata Lodge is an arts and craft style luxury accommodation with three guest bedrooms, spacious lounges and library, all with views. Your personal hosts provide guided wilderness tours into the surrounding forest and coastal wetland environments offering interesting historic perspective while exploring nature's dynamic interplays. Wildlife encounters may suggest that things haven't changed for centuries! Tours (with a conservation permit) are conducted either walking or by boat, and miles of remote sandy beach can be explored at your leisure. All meals are created from home grown produce using Central European influences and fresh Pacific flavours. Paramata Lodge is centrally located for exploring the region's main attractions. 30mins drive to Hokitika, 1.10 hour to Franz Josef Glacier. There are 3 fishing rivers within five km from the lodge.

Fox Glacier Lodge

Sullivan Road, Fox Glacier
Ph (03) 751 0888, Fax (03) 751 0026
email: foxglacierlodge@xtra.co.nz
www.foxglacierlodge.com

Tariff : N.Z. Dollars	
Double	$130-255
Single	$95-180
Child	

Bedrooms	Qty
Double or Twin	8
Twin	
Single	
Bed Size	**Qty**
Super King	
King	1
Queen	7
Double	
Single	6
Bathrooms	**Qty**
Ensuite	8
Private	
Guest Share	

**Alpine Chalet Lodge
Bed & Breakfast**

Features & Attractions

- *Warm & friendly hospitality*
- *Magestic mountain views*
- *Tranquil rainforest setting*
- *Mountain bikes available*
- *Double spa bath units available*
- *Winter warmth from gas log fires*
- *Central to cafés, restaurants & shops*
- *Wireless internet*

Experience our warm hospitality, mountain views and awake to the smell of freshly made bread and filter coffee. Our modern, solid timber, purpose-built lodge is in the heart of Fox Glacier Village. We are the closest accommodation to the glacier and only a one minute stroll to all cafés, restaurants and shops. Enjoy our tranquil setting, surrounded by unique temperate rainforest with majestic mountain views. Close by glow worm forest walk. We would be more than happy to offer our local knowledge in helping you book any local activities like glacier walks and scenic helicopter/fixed wing flights.

Laundry facilities and mountain bikes are available for your use. We also have 3 apartment-style units, self-contained/ self-catering with spa baths and fires. We will endeavour to make your stay a comfortable and memorable experience. We look forward to meeting you and sharing our little slice of heaven.

Map:
To Franz Josef
Lake Matheson Rd
N
Sullivan Rd
BP Petrol Station
Fox Glacier Lodge
To Haast
DIRECTIONS: Sullivan Road is off SH 6, opp BP Petrol Station.

REFLECTION LODGE

Cook Flat Road, Fox Glacier
Ph (03) 751 0707
email: raelene@reflectionlodge.co.nz
www.reflectionlodge.co.nz

Tariff : N.Z. Dollars	
Double	$150-210
Single	$130-150
Child	$45

Bedrooms	Qty
Double	2
Twin	1
Single	

Bed Size	Qty
Super King	
King	
Queen	2
Double	
Single	3

Bathrooms	Qty
Ensuite	1
Private	1
Family Share	

Homestay
Bed & Breakfast

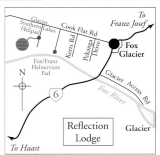

Features & Attractions

- *Spectacular views*
- *Peaceful and tranquil*
- *Lake Matheson nearby*
- *Free wireless broadband*
- *Stunning scenic walks*
- *We arrange helicopter flights & heli-hikes*
- *Breakfast with lake views*
- *Dinner by arrangement*

Welcome to the Glacier Region!
Reflection Lodge offers panoramic views of Mt Cook and Mt Tasman, New Zealand's two highest peaks reflected in our private lake. Colin, a local helicopter pilot and Raelene, a fourth generation 'West Coaster' have lived in the Glacier region for over eighteen years. We have been hosting since 1992 and pride ourselves in friendly and homely hospitality in a relaxed atmosphere.

We offer quality evening meals by arrangement. Alternatively a wide range of restaurants are available within a 10 minute walk. We are more than happy to assist you with any activities in our region, scenic helicopter flights, glacier walks, Lake Matheson, Gillespie's beach seal colony.

Arrive as a guest, depart as a friend! Families very welcome.

Quotes:

"Location is beautiful, stunning views! We leave on our journey refreshed and nourished. Thank you for your warmth and kind hospitality! We shall be back! !" California, USA.
"Hospitality and hilarity know no bounds here!!"
Herts, UK.

Austin Heights Quality Bed & Breakfast

19 Austin Street, Kaikoura
Ph (03) 319 5836, Fax (03) 319 6836
email: stay@austinheights.co.nz
www.austinheights.co.nz

Features & Attractions

- *Spectacular views from rooms*
- *Handy to all activities/amenities*
- *Luxury Hydro Therapy Spa*
- *Prize-winning gardens*
- *Private parking/entrances*
- *Courtesy bus/train transfer*

Double	$169-285	
Single	$169-269	
Child	u/12 $30	

Private Self-contained Apartments

Bedrooms	Qty
Double	4
Twin	
Single	
Bed Size	**Qty**
Super King	1
Queen	3
Double	
Single	
Bathrooms	**Qty**
Ensuite	3
Private	1
Guest Share	

Love Kaikoura, but hate the noise of the traffic? – Here's the answer. Situated on the Kaikoura Peninsula and handy to all attractions **Austin Heights** offers tranquility, friendly Kiwi Hosts, plus one of the best views available in Kaikoura. Two elevated and spacious apartments opening out onto a balcony. Luxury super-king and queen beds each fitted with electric blanket and wool rest. Lovely kitchenette with tea and coffee facilities, microwave, fridge, toaster, cutlery, dishes etc. 32" flat screen satellite TV/DVD/movies, stereo/CD player, wireless internet available in each room. Shower ensuites with toiletries, bathrobes, heated towel rails, hairdryers and luxury towels. Complimentary wine and beer, chocolates and biscuits. These two suites are ideal for two couples travelling together. Our self-contained apartment downstairs on the ground level has a luxury queen size bed plus a ¾ sofa bed. Bath/shower. 1 cot and highchair. Books/toys. Also a private bedroom and bathroom in hosts home with a comfortable queen bed and a great view. A generous continental breakfast included in tariff. Cooked available.

YOUR HOST: **Alison Taylor**   Ph: (03) 319 7075 ◁   *Kaikoura*

Awatea Country Bed & Breakfast

29 Skevingtons Road, Kaikoura
Ph/Fax (03) 319 7075, Mobile 021-318 759
email: info@awatea.co.nz
www.awatea.co.nz

Features & Attractions

- *Amazing mountain & sea views*
- *Minutes to town, Whale Watch etc*
- *Spacious guest lounge*
- *Close to good restaurants*
- *Tranquil, quiet, private*
- *Walking distance to beach*

Double	$160-200	
Single	$125-150	
Child	$50	

Bed & Breakfast

Bedrooms	Qty
Double	3
Twin	1
Single	
Bed Size	**Qty**
King	
Queen	3
Double	
King/Single	2
Bathrooms	**Qty**
Ensuite	4
Private	
Guest Share	

Only minutes from all of Kaikoura's tourist attractions, with spectacular mountain and sea views, **Awatea** offers quiet country accommodation for the discerning traveller. Relax by the fire in the spacious guest lounge or enjoy your cup of tea on the sunny patio. All rooms have ensuite facilities, TV, electric blankets, hairdryers and are warm and welcoming. Laundry done at your request. You can walk to the beach on quiet country roads. There is a courtesy car service and I will help you arrange your activities so that you don't miss a thing while in Kaikoura. Travelling with your horse? Grazing is available and there is plenty of parking for floats or horse trucks. Is your dog with you? Kennels are available. **Awatea** is a pet friendly place to stay.

ARDARA LODGE

233 Schoolhouse Road, Kaikoura
Ph (03) 319 5736, Fax (03) 319 5732
Mobile 027-448 8641
email: ardara@xtra.co.nz
www.ardaralodge.com

Tariff : N.Z. Dollars	
Double	$135
Single	$120
Child	$25

Bedrooms	Qty
Double	6
Twin	
Single	

Bed Size	Qty
Super King	
King	1
Queen	5
Double	
Single	

Bathrooms	Qty
Ensuite	6
Private	
Guest Share	

 Bed & Breakfast Self-contained Accommodation

Features & Attractions

- *Spectacular mountain view*
- *Whalewatch/dolphins 5min*
- *Quiet & tranquil*
- *Hot-tub / spa*
- *Walk to 'Donegal House', Irish restaurant and bar*
- *Guest lounge with Sky TV*
- *Off-street parking*

DIRECTIONS:
Driving North, 4kms from Kaikoura
on State Highway 1, turn left into
Schoolhouse Road and continue
1.5kms until Ardara Lodge sign.

Ardara Lodge is conveniently located in a two-acre rural atmosphere with stunning alpine views and provides classic New Zealand Bed & Breakfast accommodation in Kaikoura. Our modern **Lodge** and self-contained **Cottage** are set on two acres surrounded by farmland. After an exhilarating day exploring the natural splendours of Kaikoura, unwind in the tranquillity of **Ardara Lodge** on our viewing deck or in our spa. Here you will experience the magic of the beautiful Kaikoura mountains. The changing cloud formations, sunrises and sunsets make this area unique. We are conveniently located 100 metres from Donegal House Restaurant and Bar. Self-contained **Cottage** $170-245.

198

ENDEAVOUR HEIGHTS BED & BREAKFAST

1 Endeavour Place, Kaikoura
Ph/Fax (03) 319 5333, Mobile 027-224 0549
email: dreavers@xtra.co.nz
www.endeavourheights.co.nz

Tariff : N.Z. Dollars	
Double	$160-200
Single	$150
Child	neg

Bedrooms	Qty
Double	1
Twin	
Single	
Bed Size	**Qty**
Super King	
King	1
Queen	
Double	
Single	
Bathrooms	**Qty**
Ensuite	1
Private	
Guest Share	

Boutique Bed & Breakfast

Features & Attractions

- *Sky TV – Free Broadband*
- *Whale watching*
- *Dolphin swimming*
- *Cafés, restaurants & shops nearby*
- *Spectacular sea & mountain views*
- *Close to Peninsula Walkway*
- *View the magnificent Albatross*
- *Gourmet continental breakfast*

Endeavour Heights truly portrays excellence in hospitality, quality accommodation and scenic views. Centrally located amidst Kaikoura's major tourist attractions, such as the popular Seal Colony the Peninsula Walkway and the Kaikoura township, all of which are accessible by foot. The "Te Moana" suite is a separate private apartment, with comfortable living space; king sized bed, quality bed linen and a luxurious bathroom with a deep welcoming bath.

The room embraces the breathtaking views of "Kaikoura where the mountains meet the sea" from its own private balcony. A gourmet continental breakfast is serviced to your room. Grant and Janice welcome you to Endeavour Heights, warm, relaxing and peaceful. Easy to find but hard to leave.

| *Kaikoura* | ▷ YOUR HOSTS: **Julie and Kerry Howden** | Free Ph: 0800 107 770 |

BENDAMERE HOUSE BED & BREAKFAST

37 Adelphi Terrace, Kaikoura
Ph (03) 319 5830, Fax (03) 319 7337
Mobile 027-543 2559
email: bendamerehouse@xtra.co.nz
www.bendamere.co.nz

Tariff : N.Z. Dollars	
Double	$160-220
Single	$160-200
Child	n/a

Bedrooms	Qty
Double	5
Twin	2
Single	3

Bed Size	Qty
Super King	
King	5
Queen	
Double	
Single	2

Bathrooms	Qty
Ensuite	5
Private	
Guest Share	

  Quality Accommodation / Superb Ocean & Mountain Views

Features & Attractions

- *5 ensuite rooms enjoy sea views*
- *Quiet, private & peaceful*
- *5 min. walk to township*
- *Expansive gardens & lawns*
- *Free wireless Broadband internet*
- *Courtesy bus/train transfer*
- *Communal breakfast/dining room*
- *Ample, secure off-street parking*

Kerry and Julie Howden and 3 sons welcome you to Kaikoura's **Bendamere House B&B** which boasts 5 quality ensuite rooms all with balconies and breathtaking ocean and mountain views! Enjoy

relaxing in our expansive lawns and rose gardens. All rooms have first class facilities, quality sleepyhead beds, TV, Tea/coffee facilities, silent fridges, heatpumps, bathrobes, hairdryers, iron/ironing boards and homebaked shortbread, a treat with a cuppa. Wireless broadband internet and laundry facilities available. Secure offstreet parking and courtesy pickup/dropoff to trains and buses and 5 minutes walk to the Kaikoura Township! A delicious continental breakfast served in our communal dining room includes cereals, fresh fruit salad, yoghurt, toast, spreads and homebaked muffins, orange juice, tea and coffee. Cooked breakfast available at extra cost!

Guest Comments - Bob & Moira Brewer, England - Friendly helpful hosts, very comfortable room, superb views! Judy & Bob Buntin, England - Lovely place, beautiful views, excellent breakfast. Best B&B in New Zealand!

200

BUSH & SEA BOUTIQUE BED & BREAKFAST

14 Takahanga Terrace, Kaikoura
Ph (03) 319 6789, Fax (03) 319 6709
Mobile 027-481 3150
email: info@bushandsea.co.nz
www.bushandsea.co.nz

Tariff : N.Z. Dollars	
Double	$185-235
Single	$165-205
Child	

Bedrooms	Qty
Double	2
Twin	
Single	

Bed Size	Qty
Super King	1
King	
Queen	1
Double	
Single	

Bathrooms	Qty
Ensuite	2
Private	
Guest Share	

**Panoramic Sea Views
Central Location**

Features & Attractions

- *Free wireless internet*
- *Private guest suite access*
- *Delicious breakfast menu*
- *Comfortable beds*
- *Stunning sea views over bush reserve*
- *Intimate B&B with just 2 suites*
- *Whale watch & dolphin swimming*
- *Guest decks and outdoor furniture*

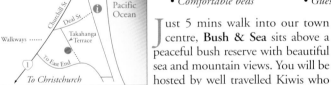

Just 5 mins walk into our town centre, **Bush & Sea** sits above a peaceful bush reserve with beautiful sea and mountain views. You will be hosted by well travelled Kiwis who enjoy family, the outdoors, music and running our B&B! With outdoor decks surrounding our home, you can relax and enjoy the views from many vantage points. With just 2 suites (with private access), you'll feel truly welcomed! Both suites have tiled ensuites with excellent showers, underfloor heating, sound insulation, a CD/DVD player (and selection of disks), silent fridges, tea and coffee (fresh). The wonderful comfort of our beds is always mentioned by our guests! Our **Bush Suite** has a queen bed, our **Sea Suite**, a super-king, or twin bed. Both suites look out over our native garden setting, to the mountains, with stunning sea views from the main deck. Enjoy a delicious cooked and continental breakfast, while overlooking incredible views of Kaikoura's sea, bush and mountains. **Bush & Sea B&B** is an excellent base for local and regional tourist attractions so allow for at least 2 nights stay.

MIRA MONTE COUNTRY HOMESTAY B&B
324 Woodbank Road, Hanmer Springs
Ph (03) 315 7604, Mobile 021-065 7531
email: relax@miramonte.co.nz
www.miramonte.co.nz

Features & Attractions
- *Village centre 5min drive*
- *Swimming pool*
- *Quiet and peaceful*
- *Large garden with mountain views*
- *Grand piano, selection CD's*
- *Golf course nearby*

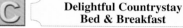

Delightful Countrystay Bed & Breakfast

	Price
Double	$150-165
Single	$120-140
Child	neg

Tastefully peaceful – the ideal place to relax and enjoy a unique part of New Zealand. Near Hanmer Springs, a popular sub-alpine tourist resort, we offer delightful, warm, affordable accommodation. Lovely country garden setting. Relax in our swimming pool and enjoy the mountain outlook. We have it all! Our rooms are attractively decorated with your comfort in mind. Withdraw to your own sittingroom or join us for a coffee, wine or chat. After 20 years in the hospitality trade we know how to pamper you. We have travelled widely and have many interests. Music, tramping and golf are some of our hobbies. We speak Dutch and German. Mindy, our Jack Russell, is part of our family.
We'd love you to stay with us!

Bedrooms	Qty
Double	2
Twin	
Single	
Bed Size	**Qty**
King	2
Queen	
Double	
Single	1
Bathrooms	**Qty**
Ensuite	2
Private	
Guest Share	

CHARWELL ECO LODGE
82 Medway Road, Hanmer Springs
Ph (03) 315 5070, Fax (03) 315 5071
Mobile 021-347 905
email: charwell.countrystay@xtra.co.nz
www.charwell.co.nz

Features & Attractions
- *Awesome views from all room*
- *Great breakfasts*
- *Large log fire in lounge*
- *8 mins to famous hot pools*
- *Private & peaceful*
- *A magical mountain retreat*

Boutique Countrystay

	Price
Double	$200-240
Single	$190-210
Child	–

On a sunny private hillside in the Hanmer basin, **Charwell Eco Lodge** offers the perfect place to relax and enjoy a little luxury. We can guarantee the views from your rooms are unsurpassed by any other accommodation provider in the Hanmer area. Situated 1, 1/2 hours from Christchurch international Airport, 8 minutes from Hanmer Springs Village & Thermal Resort. 2hours from Kaikoura and the famous Whale & Dolphin watch activities, 40 minutes from the Waipara Wine region. Ours is the perfect place to either start your holiday or Honeymoon or just relax for a couple of days before flying out of Christchurch at the end of your trip to NZ.

DIRECTIONS: Cross historic ferry bridge over Waiau River. 1km turn right before Hanmer River bridge, signposted to Charwell Eco Lodge. 100m from campground take steep drive on right. Keep left on drive at fork, we are 1st turn-off on right.

Bedrooms	Qty
Double/Twin	3
Twin	
Single	
Bed Size	**Qty**
Super King	1
King	1
Queen	1
Single	
Bathrooms	**Qty**
Ensuite	3
Private	
Guest Share	

ALBERGO HANMER B&B AND LUXURY VILLA

88 Rippingale Road, Hanmer Springs,
North Canterbury
Ph/Fax (03) 315 7428, Mobile 021-228 8194
email: albergo@paradise.net.nz
www.albergohanmer.com

Tariff : N.Z. Dollars	
Double	$160-250
Single	from $120
S/C Villa	$250-500

Bedrooms	Qty
Double	6
Twin	1
Single	
Bed Size	**Qty**
Super King	1
King	2
Queen	5
Double	1
Single	2
Bathrooms	**Qty**
Ensuite	4
Guest Share	1
Family Share	1

**A Place Where
Magic Happens**

Features & Attractions

- *All day sun, views from all windows*
- *3-course breakfast, over 10 choices*
- *Perfect fusion of NZ & Swiss cuisine*
- *Hot pools, cafes & shops 2 min.*
- *S/C villas with cinema & hot tub*
- *Underfloor heat & aircon*
- *Attractive 'Day Spa' packages*
- *In house massage & spa treatment*

Arrive to dramatic alpine views, blitz your senses in fresh n' fun eclectic interiors. Stretch out on super-king beds in main lodge rooms, with TV/fridge/teas and spacious ensuites – choose the spa suite for that bubble bath delight! Relax in cosy corners or Feng Shui courtyard with soothing waterfall. The Luxury Alpine Villa, with 'wow' views from the high panorama window, while you shower. Slip on a fluffy bathrobe and wander out to the private jacuzzi and soak up Hanmer's starry night skies. Awesome projection TV/DVD American king bed and kitchen/lounge. Served at a time to suit you, **Albergo's** breakfast features: Designer fruit

DIRECTIONS:
At junction before main village, 300m past Caltex Garage, take Argelins Road (centre branch), take 2nd left Rippingale Road Albergo Hanmer is 800m down on left (sign at drive).

platters or Swiss Birchermuesli, French fluffy omelettes, wafer-thin crepes, '**Albergo** Egg Nests', all with crunchy Swiss bread and Italian coffee!

Whatever you chose you will arrive as a guest and leave a friend. "*Albergo is the most warmest, adorable and fun place we have ever visited. Your kindness and spirit shine through in everything*" – Marcia & Paul, Colorado, USA.

203

PAHAU DOWNS
Pahau Downs Rd, Culverden, North Canterbury
Ph/Fax (03) 315 8224
Mobile 021-227 0040
email: pahaudowns@xtra.co.nz
www.pahaudowns.co.nz

Features & Attractions

- *Self-contained private cottage*
- *Heated swimming pool*
- *Sheep & beef farm tour available*
- *Walks, tours, mountain bikes*
- *Excellent trout/salmon fishing*
- *Dinner by arrangement*

**High Quality Farmstay
Self-contained Cottage**

Double	$245	
Single	poa	
Child	poa	

This romantic self-contained cottage is available for your exclusive use. Superbly equipped with two large bedrooms, a shower and bathroom and a sunny sitting/dining room with woodburner. Use it as a base for trips to local attractions such as Hanmer Springs, Mount Lyford, Kaikoura, and fishing on the Waiau or Hurunui rivers. **Pahau Downs** is a tranquil working farm set amidst stunning scenery of the Amuri Basin. Enjoy the mountain views from the heated swimming pool, walk over the 6000 acre farm or tour the working sheep and beef station with the owner. Free Tour for guests who stay two nights or more.

Bedrooms	Qty
Double	1
Twin	1
Single	
Bed Size	**Qty**
King	
Queen	1
Double	
Single	2
Bathrooms	**Qty**
Ensuite	
Private	1
Guest Share	

DIRECTIONS: In Culverden turn past school till you reach a T-junction; turn right and follow the road till you reach a sign 'Pahau Downs Road', follow unsealed road till you reach the farm. (30 min from Hanmer Springs)

HIELAN HOUSE COUNTRYSTAY B&B
74 Bush Road, Oxford
Ph/Fax (03) 312 4382
Mobile 027-435 9435
email: hielanhouse@ihug.co.nz
www.hielanhouse.co.nz

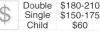

Features & Attractions

- *Quiet, private, rural setting*
- *A view from every room*
- *Tasty dinners & breakfasts*
- *Free e-mail, internet, fax*
- *Laundry, spa, sauna*
- *Gateway to everywhere!*

**Countrystay
Bed & Breakfast**

Double	$180-210	
Single	$150-175	
Child	$60	

Shirley and John offer quiet quality accommodation on 6 acres just 3 minutes from Inland Scenic Route 72. Elevated above the township enjoy beautiful views and comfortable beds away from traffic noise. Two well appointed upstairs guests rooms with relaxing areas, ensuites. TV/DVD's, tea/coffee making facilities, fridges, hairdryers, slippers etc. Menu breakfasts. Dinner available on request. Free wireless internet, emails, laundry, sauna, spa, inground swimming pool (summer) ladies/men's golf clubs available for your use on our local panoramic golf course. Bush walks, safe parking. Stay longer and make us your base for day trips to Arthurs Pass, Hanmer Springs, Akaroa, Christchurch City, Waipara wineries. Christchurch and International airport an easy drive. We enjoy meeting people and would love to host you.

Bedrooms	Qty
Double	2
Twin	1
Single	
Bed Size	**Qty**
Super King	1
Queen	1
Double	
Single	2
Bathrooms	**Qty**
Ensuite	1
Private	1
Guest Share	

Okuku Country Estate & Cottage

2 Rakahuri Road, Rangiora
Ph (03) 312 8740
email: enquiries@okukucountryestate.co.nz
www.okukucountryestate.co.nz

Tariff : N.Z. Dollars	
Double	$200-400
Single	$200-250
Child	neg

Bedrooms	Qty
Double	8
Twin	
Single	1
Bed Size	Qty
Super King	
King	3
Queen	3
Double	2
Single	1
Bathrooms	Qty
Ensuite	6
Private	1
Guest Share	

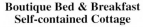
Boutique Bed & Breakfast
Self-contained Cottage

Features & Attractions

- *Peaceful rural setting*
- *Self-cater cosy cottage*
- *Gracious historic home*
- *Generous hospitality*
- *Garden walks*
- *Mountain bikes*
- *Food & wine trail*
- *Great base for exploring*

DIRECTIONS: From Christchurch travel north to Rangiora then follow road to Loburn. Turn left into Hodgsons Rd [Okuku Country Estate is AA signed] Travel 18 km, crossing Okuku and Gary rivers. Turn left into Rakahuri Rd

Set amongst magnificent parkland and stunning gardens, this gracious, historic 1920's homestead and cottage is secluded yet extremely accessible, just 50 mins from Christchurch. The newly refurbished, fully equipped self-contained cottage has magnificent views of snow capped Alps and farm paddocks housing pet goats. Relax on the private verandah or in the cosy warmth of this 3 bedroom romantic and inviting country escape. Homestead guests enjoy the ambience of beautiful furniture, fine china and art works in the reception rooms, billiards room, or Pool and Spa House. The ensuite bedrooms, have picturesque views of the 100 acre grounds. **Okuku** offers a self-catering cottage through to a fully catered option in the Homestead. All guests are warmly welcomed by the owner hosts of this grand historic estate. Prior bookings essential.

PETE'S FARM STAY BED & BREAKFAST

45 Mairaki Road, Fernside, Rangiora
Ph (03) 313 5180, Fax (03) 313 5182
Mobile 027-221 8989
email: petesfarm@xtra.co.nz
www.petesfarm.co.nz

Tariff : N.Z. Dollars	
Double	$160-180
Single	$120
Cottage	$200-280

Bedrooms	Qty
Double	4
Twin	2
Single	

Bed Size	Qty
Super King	1
King	1
Queen	2
Double	1
Single	4

Bathrooms	Qty
Ensuite	1
Private	3
Guest Share	

Quality Farmstay and Self Contained Cottage

Features & Attractions

- *Free sheep shearing demo*
- *Free farm tour*
- *Pet animals to feed*
- *Children welcome*
- *25 mins from Christchurch Airport*
- *Laundry facilities*
- *Spectacular mountain views*
- *Free wireless internet*

Welcome to **Pete's Farm**. Enjoy great views of the mountains and countryside from our new house or cottage while taking in the peacefulness and quietness of the area. Just one minute off Scenic Inland Route 72. Experience up close Pete shearing a sheep. Feed our pet sheep, calves and alpacas. Watch our friendly dog Meg round up our mob of sheep.
Pete's House: Four bedrooms. Private TV lounge. Sunny and warm with two outdoor terraces. **Cottage:** Two bedrooms with lounge, kitchen and bathroom. Private deck with mountain views.
Hosts Pete and Gaye offer you a homely atmosphere where you can relax after a day sightseeing and enjoy the panoramic views of the mountains or countryside. Great place to base yourself for day trips to Kaikoura, Arthurs Pass, Hanmer Springs, Akaroa. Check out what our guests are saying about us on trip advisor or our webpage. Children welcome. Please ring or email for reservations.

OAKHAMPTON LODGE

24 Keetly Place, Ohoka, Kaiapoi
Ph/Fax (03) 312 6413, Mobile 021-027 92097
email: info@oakhampton.co.nz
www.oakhampton.co.nz

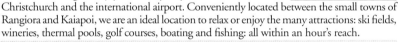

Features & Attractions

- *Beautiful 4 acre garden*
- *Delicious breakfasts*
- *Country walks*
- *7 km from northern motorway*
- *7 km to Kaiapoi & Rangiora*
- *Drinks, dinner & good company*

$		
	Double	$150-180
	Single	$130-150
	Child	

Boutique Country Stay
Bed & Breakfast

Bedrooms	Qty
Double	2
Twin	
Single	
Bed Size	**Qty**
Super King	1
Queen	1
Double	
King/Single	2
Bathrooms	**Qty**
Ensuite	1
Private	1
Guest Share	

"Thank you so much for helping us make a smooth transition to NZ - a truly soft landing! We couldn't have asked for more caring hosts!" Shuli & Eran, Israel.

Enjoy the peace, tranquility and friendly hospitality in our spacious, modern home and beautiful gardens. **Oakhampton Lodge** is in the heart of Ohoka village, North Canterbury. Oak lined roads, mountain views and lush, green farmland provide the perfect location for those wishing to enjoy a country stay within 20 minutes of Christchurch and the international airport. Conveniently located between the small towns of Rangiora and Kaiapoi, we are an ideal location to relax or enjoy the many attractions: ski fields, wineries, thermal pools, golf courses, boating and fishing: all within an hour's reach.

DIRECTIONS: Driving north from Christchurch over Waimakariri River, take 2nd Kaiapoi exit and follow signs to Ohoka, 7 km from the motorway. Keetly Place is 1st on right past Jacksons Rd., just before the Ohoka Hall and service station.

OBERAU

9 Jacksons Road, Ohoka, North Canterbury
Ph (03) 312 6867, Mobile 021-262 5855
email: oberau@xtra.co.nz
www.oberau.co.nz

Features & Attractions

- *4 acres, pond and truffiere*
- *Potager vegetable garden*
- *Cooked or light breakfasts*
- *15 minutes to Airport*
- *2 hours to several ski fields*
- *Dinner by arrangement*

$		
	Double	$150-170
	Single	$120
	Child	

European Country Stay
Bed & Breakfast

Bedrooms	Qty
Double	2
Twin	
Single	
Bed Size	**Qty**
King	1
Queen	1
Double	
Single	
Bathrooms	**Qty**
Ensuite	1
Private	1
Guest Share	

Oberau provides guests with the opportunity to stay in a beautiful environment within 20 min of Christchurch and its international airport. The house is set in a large garden with pond, potager and a truffiere, plus uninterrupted rural views from all bedrooms. The hundreds of overseas guests who have stayed with Sara and Rod still regularly correspond and many rate their stay at **Oberau** as a highlight of their New Zealand visit. The two local towns of Rangiora and Kaiapoi are within 10 min drive. **Oberau** is the ideal base for those who wish to explore the ski fields, wineries, thermal pools, fishing and golf courses which make North Canterbury a delight to visit. Come and stay with us and allow Sara to assist you in planning your day while enjoying a leisurely breakfast.

DIRECTIONS: Drive north out of Christchurch. Immediately over the Waimakariri River take the exit onto Tram Rd. 6km up Tram Rd turn right into Jackson's Rd. The 2nd house on your left is **Oberau**.

Burwood - Christchurch

 YOUR HOSTS: **Fay and Lindsay Turner**   Ph: (03) 385 1012

Finlay Banks Boutique B&B
7 Banks Avenue, Burwood, Christchurch
Ph (03) 385 1012, Fax (03) 385 1014
Mobile 027-485 1015
email: finlaybanks@xtra.co.nz
www.finlaybanks.co.nz

Features & Attractions

- *Kiwi hosts*
- *Private and peaceful*
- *Warm relaxed hospitality*
- *Evening meal, BBQ, picnic baskets*
- *Courtesy transfers*
- *Off street parking, wireless internet*

**Boutique
Bed & Breakfast**

Double	$180-200	
Single	$130-150	
Child	POA	

Our family home 'Finlay Banks' with its private rose gardens is perfectly located in the heart of the picturesque garden city. Kiwi hosts Fay & Lindsay offer two comfortable en-suite rooms, quality beds and linen, bathrobes and complimentary toiletries, delicious continental or cooked breakfasts with home preserved fruits and jams, complimentary drinks on arrival, friendly and relaxed atmosphere, evening dining options, off street parking, close to CBD and International airport and courtesy transfers. Make **Finlay Banks** your preferred accommodation, it's the ideal base for regional day trips, for arrivals and departures from your South Island holiday or while in the area on business. **Finlay Banks** is a smoke free property.

Bedrooms	Qty
Double	2
Twin	
Single	
Bed Size	Qty
Super King/Twin	1
Queen	1
Double	
Single	
Bathrooms	Qty
Ensuite	2
Private	
Guest Share	

Westhaven - Christchurch

YOUR HOSTS: **Juanita and Graeme Wilson**   Ph: (03) 385 2343

Granita Bed & Breakfast
17 Lytham Green, Westhaven, Christchurch
Ph/Fax (03) 385 2343, Mobile 027-205 5807
email: wilson@granita.co.nz
www.granita.co.nz

Features & Attractions

- *Quiet, peaceful environment*
- *Spacious rooms*
- *Relaxed & friendly hospitality*
- *Close to shops & restaurants*
- *Outdoor spa*
- *Private outdoor spa*

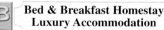

**Bed & Breakfast Homestay
Luxury Accommodation**

Double	$195	
Single	$165	
Child		

We welcome you to our architecturally designed B&B in a quiet suburb close to the airport, beaches, golf courses, shops and restaurants, yet only 10 min. drive to city centre. The accommodation has been purpose built to a high standard - with you, our guest, in mind. We only accept exclusive one party bookings, i.e. one or two couples travelling together, or two singles. Separate guest lounge and dining, two queen rooms attractively decorated, each with private facilities. Cooked and continental breakfast is provided. Take the opportunity to relax in the private outdoor spa. We provide laundry facilities, internet access, LCD TV's in each bedroom and garaging.

Bedrooms	Qty
Double	2
Twin	
Single	
Bed Size	Qty
King	
Queen	2
Double	
Single	
Bathrooms	Qty
Ensuite	
Private	2
Guest Share	

DIRECTIONS: From city centre travel north on Colombo St, right onto Edgeware Rd, left onto Hills Rd. On to Akaroa St, then Briggs Rd, At traffic lights cross Marshlands Rd onto Lake Terrace Rd. Turn left onto Fairway Drive. Lytham Green is 2nd on right.

AIRPORT STABLEFORD B&B

2 Stableford Green, Burnside, Christchurch
Ph (03) 358 3264, Mobile 021-883 804
email: stableford@xtra.co.nz
www.stableford.co.nz

Features & Attractions

- *Closest B&B to airport*
- *Off-street parking*
- *Good restaurants nearby*
- *Courtesy airport transfers*
- *Friendly, relaxed, comfortable*
- *Adjacent Russley Golf Course*

Double	$140	
Single	$130	
Child		

**Airport Accommodation
Bed & Breakfast**

Bedrooms	Qty
Double	2
Twin	1
Single	
Bed Size	**Qty**
King	
Queen	2
Double	
Single	2
Bathrooms	**Qty**
Ensuite	2
Private	1
Guest Share	

Welcome to **Airport Stableford**, the closest B&B to the Christchurch Airport, making it ideal for arriving or departing visitors. Airport transfers and city bus-stop at door. We are situated adjacent to the Russley Golf Club. **Airport Stableford** is new, clean, warm and comfortable with a separate guest lounge. All bedrooms have their own ensuite or bathroom with a powerful shower. Secure off street parking available. Good restaurants nearby.

Our interests are travel, sport, music, and antiques. Cat and small dog in residence. Ask about our winter rates.

Come and enjoy our beautiful home.

SHAMROCK GARDEN BED & BREAKFAST

358 Sawyers Arms Road, Harewood, Christchurch
Ph/Fax (03) 359 5375, Mobile 021-0261 5589
email: shamrockbnb@hotmail.com
www.shamrockbnb.co.nz

Features & Attractions

- *10,000m² park like garden*
- *Walk to mall, restaurants & bar*
- *Bus service at gate*
- *Luxury honeymoon suite*
- *Wireless broadband*
- *Courtesy airport transfers*

Double	$140-200	
Single	$120-170	
Child	$30-40	

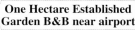

**One Hectare Established
Garden B&B near airport**

Bedrooms	Qty
Double	3
Twin	1
Single	
Bed Size	**Qty**
Super King	2
Queen	2
Double	
Single	5
Bathrooms	**Qty**
Ensuite	1
Private	1
Guest Share	1

Shamrock Garden B&B is set on one hectare of established park-like garden and surrounded by more than 150 large Rhododendrons. A private stream runs quietly through the garden... Guests are free to enjoy the whole day sun on the decks, relax in the lounge, or just walk leisurely among trees or paths through the garden. Breakfast is served out in the garden. We are located 5 mins drive from Christchurch Airport, 10 mins from Cathedral Square, walking distance to Papanui Club Restaurant and Bar, coffee shop, Sweethearts Restaurant, 1500m to Bishopdale Mall, 2 mins to Willowbank Wildlife Reserve, 4 mins to Clearwater Resort, Northland Mall and....Please visit our Website...

DIRECTIONS: Arriving from the North along SH 1, drive along Main North Rd. Turn right into Johns Rd. At the first roundabout, turn left into Sawyers Arms Rd. Arriving from the South along SH 1, in Hornby, turn left into Carmen Rd. Turn right at the 4th roundabout on Johns Rd into Sawyers Arms Rd.

HAREWOOD HOMESTAY
489 Sawyers Arms Road, Harewood, Christchurch
Ph (03) 360 2590, Mobile 027-471 4651
email: jenkerr.home@gmail.com
www.charmingaccommodation.co.nz

Tariff : N.Z. Dollars	
Double	$170-250
Single	$170-220
Child	Neg

Bedrooms	Qty
Double	2
Twin	
Single	

Bed Size	Qty
Super King	1
King	
Queen	1
Double	
King Singles	2

Bathrooms	Qty
Ensuite	1
Private	1
Guest Share	1

Elegant Homestay - B&B
In Great Location

Features & Attractions

- *Courtesy pick up/return*
- *Rural setting in city boundry*
- *Modern guest suite with extra's*
- *Close to several golf courses*
- *Tours & evening meals by arrangement*
- *Gateway to International attractions*
- *10 mins to/from Airport*
- *Wifi internet available*

DIRECTIONS:
From Christchurch Airport head north on Durey Rd. At roundabout take 2nd exit onto Memorial Ave. At roundabout take 1st exit onto Russley Rd/State Highway 1 and go through two roundabouts. At the next roundabout take third exit onto Sawyers Arms Rd heading to Casebrook. Travel for about 1 minute and you will find **Harewood Homestay** is on the right down a long driveway.

Welcome to Christchurch and our home. Situated less than a ten minute drive from the airport we are the ideal place for you to base yourself and explore Christchurch and its surrounds.

Our home is semi-rural but all attractions and amentities are very close by and easity accessible. Our rooms offer tea/coffee making facilities, television and little extras to help make your stay more pleasurable. Wireless internet is available to guests, as is a well equipped laundry. Close by is a variety of dining opions, or you may, at an extra cost to you, wish to dine 'at home' where you will enjoy fresh and creative food. We share our home (inside) with 'Ruby' - a happy Jack Russell. We look forward to meeting you.

230c GLENVEAGH B&B

230c Clyde Road, Fendalton, Christchurch
Ph (03) 351 4407, Fax (03) 351 4406
Mobile 021-883 283
email: boyd45@xtra.co.nz
www.glenveagh.co.nz

Tariff : N.Z. Dollars	
Double	$140-190
Single	$140-190
Child	$30

Bedrooms	Qty
Double	2
Double/Triple	1
Twin	1
Bed Size	**Qty**
Super King	1
King	
Queen	1
Double	
Single	3
Bathrooms	**Qty**
Ensuite	1
Private	1
Guest Share	

 **Delightful Bed & Breakfast
Close to Airport**

Features & Attractions

- *Email, laundry facilities*
- *Courtesy pickup airport, bus, train*
- *Located between airport & city*
- *Restaurants, shops, parks nearby*
- *Off-street parking*
- *On bus route to city*
- *Guest lounge, courtyard*
- *House u/floor heating*

Ian and Alison have named their B&B, **Glenveagh**, which is a castle in Donegal, Ireland where Ian's ancestors came from. Our B&B is well designed for guests, with three upstairs bedrooms and downstairs a separate lounge and an outside courtyard. **Glenveagh** is off the main road (Memorial Ave.) from the airport to the city. There are four restaurants within walking distance. The central city is 5 minutes by car, alternatively there is a bus stop nearby. Off-street parking. Courtesy car available from bus, train and airport.

Alison, ex-librarian, enjoys gardening, reading, bridge. Ian taught in secondary schools, designed and built houses, plays golf, bowls and we like to travel. Attractions: Cathedral Square, Art Centre, Art Gallery, Hagley Park, Botanical Gardens, Gondola, Antarctic Centre, Willowbank Wildlife Reserve. Wireless Internet available. Killybegs Cottage, Kaikoura available. See our website. No smoking inside house please. We look forward to your company.

ALUMNI HOUSE

51A Middleton Road, Riccarton, Christchurch
Ph (03) 980 9000, Mobile 021-056 9825
email: alumnihouse@paradise.net.nz
www.alumnihouse.co.nz

Tariff : N.Z. Dollars	
Double	$140-160
Single	
Child	$20

Bedrooms	Qty
Double	3
Twin	
Single	
Bed Size	**Qty**
Super King	
King	3
Queen	
Double	
Single	
Bathrooms	**Qty**
Ensuite	3
Private	
Guest Share	

Boutique Bed & Breakfast
Self-contained Luxury

Features & Attractions

- *Family-Unit option*
- *Private external access*
- *Free wireless broadband*
- *Laundry facilities*
- *Secluded and spacious*
- *Sustainability focused*
- *Walk to Uni, malls, cafés*
- *Off-street parking*

Alumni House provides quality accommodation for visitors to Christchurch. We are conveniently located within easy walking distance of shopping malls, cafes and restaurants, an extensive network of bus routes and Canterbury University. **Alumni House** boasts three spacious and stylish guest suites as well as private lounges for guests. Two suites offer private external access and open out to a spacious, sunny courtyard and lawn. One guest lounge, the Common Room, features a small kitchen as well as dining facilities that allow for self-catering if required. In addition this room contains heat pump, TV/DVD, and telephone. Delicious and nutritious - continental breakfasts included in the daily tariff. We are a family and eco-friendly destination located within a large and private garden setting and immediately adjacent to one of Christchurch's gorgeous parks. Philippa, Brad and family look forward to welcoming you and to ensuring that you have a relaxed and comfortable stay.

LEINSTER BED & BREAKFAST

34b Leinster Road, Merivale, Christchurch
Ph/Fax (03) 355 6176, Mobile 027-433 0771
email: brian.kay@xtra.co.nz
www.leinsterbnb.co.nz

Tariff : N.Z. Dollars	
Double	$150-180
Single	$120
Child	neg

Bedrooms	Qty
Double	2
Twin	1
Single	1
Bed Size	Qty
Super King	
King	
Queen	1
Double	1
Single	1
Bathrooms	Qty
Ensuite	1
Private	1
Guest Share	

**Bed & Breakfast
Homestay**

Features & Attractions

- *Airport 10 mins, City 5 mins*
- *Centrally located, easy to find*
- *Quiet comfortable rooms*
- *Excellent local restaurants*
- *Courtesy transfers*
- *Off-street parking*
- *Laundry & email facilities*
- *Gluten-free food on request*

A t **Leinster Bed & Breakfast** we offer a friendly, hospitable stay in our modern, sunny home. We pride ourselves on creating a relaxed, friendly atmosphere. Comfortable, quiet rooms with television, tea & coffee, electric blankets and heaters. Having travelled to many countries and most places in New Zealand, we enjoy meeting like-minded travellers and helping with their ongoing travel plans. This can be done around the breakfast table or in the evening whilst enjoying a good wine (or two). By car we are only five minutes to all the city attractions and ten minutes from the airport. For evening dining convenience there are excellent restaurants and wine bars at Merivale Village which is a leisurely stroll to the end of the street. So why not come and stay and see if you can agree with Jim and Jo from Colorado, who wrote and said: *"Kay and Brian are a big #10. I hope we get to visit them again. We stayed longer than intended because of them and because of the beauty of Christchurch"*.

213

ELIZA'S MANOR ON BEALEY

82 Bealey Avenue, Christchurch
Ph (03) 366 8584, Fax (03) 366 4946
email: info@elizas.co.nz
www.elizas.co.nz

Features & Attractions

- Listed heritage home
- Secluded courtyard
- Restaurants close
- Flat walk to Cathedral Square
- Day trip to Akaroa/Hanmer
- Smoke-free environment

Classic Heritage Boutique Accommodation

	Double	$230-345
	Single	$210-325
	Child	

Eliza's Manor on Bealey offers quality Bed & Breakfast accommodation in a beautifully restored 1860's homestead. Each of the eight rooms combines historic ambience with modern ensuite conveniences. A sumptuous breakfast is served as part of the room rate and includes a selection of fruits, cereals, yoghurts, breads as well as a choice of cooked breakfasts. Enjoy personal service as you unwind at a 'home away from home', where service and attention to detail are a priority. A guest computer on the ground floor provides free high-speed access to the internet. Wireless internet access is also available. Free off-street parking is available.

Eliza's Manor on Bealey is a totally smoke-free environment. Situated in Bealey Avenue on the northern boundary of the Christchurch CBD, 15 minutes by taxi from the airport and the railway station, a 15 minute walk to the downtown city centre, arts activities and botanical gardens.

Bedrooms	Qty
Double	8
Twin	
Single	
Bed Size	Qty
Super King	4
Queen	4
Double	
Single	1
Bathrooms	Qty
Ensuite	8
Private	
Guest Share	

VISA · MasterCard · AMERICAN EXPRESS · Diners · bankcard · eftpos

Charming **Places to Stay** in New Zealand

"Charming Places to Stay is a lovely book, the best presented of all the B&B books we have ever seen, it is crisp, clear and every advert looks enticing. We have stayed all over the world and it is by far and away the most accurate book we have ever used as well."

Robin and Linda Spiller, Cornwall, UK

214

LILAC ROSE

172 Blighs Road, Strowan, Christchurch
Ph (03) 354 4683, Mobile 027-221 5219
email: info@lilacrose.co.nz
www.lilacrose.co.nz

Tariff : N.Z. Dollars	
Double	$145-175
Single	$120-150
Child	$30

Bedrooms	Qty
Double	2
Twin	1
Single	

Bed Size	Qty
Super King	1
King	
Queen	2
Double	
Single	2

Bathrooms	Qty
Ensuite	1
Private	2
Guest Share	

  Delightful Boutique Accommodation

Features & Attractions

- *Convenient location*
- *Restored heritage villa*
- *Generous hospitality*
- *Gazebo with outdoor hot tub*
- *Complimentary transfers*
- *Secure off-street parking*
- *Spacious guest lounge*
- *Wi-Fi, guest laptop, Sky*

The **Lilac Rose** is a charming heritage villa that has been completely renovated to offer luxury accommodation. We are located a convenient 7 minutes from both Christchurch Airport and the city centre, and a short stroll to shops, restaurants, cinemas and public transport. As a guest at the **Lilac Rose** you can enjoy generous hospitality, spacious rooms with stylish decor, antiques and fresh flowers. Our beautifully furnished guest rooms have comfortable beds, luxury linen, robes, LCD TV/DVD players, bar fridge & tea/coffee making facilities. Each has a private modern bathroom (one with claw foot bath), heated towel rails, plush towels and luxury toiletries. The Lilac Rose is a romantic retreat. You can relax outdoors on the veranda and admire our stunning landscaped garden or really indulge and enjoy a hot spa in our outdoor pool - bliss! Our beautiful private guest lounge is the perfect place to enjoy a drink, SKY TV, or use the guest laptop with complimentary Wi-Fi. Let us tempt you with a sumptuous breakfast, home baking, bottomless fresh coffee and complimentary wine and nibbles.

215

ONUKU BED & BREAKFAST
27 Harry Ell Drive, Cashmere, Christchurch
Ph (03) 332 7296
email: bob.wilkinson@paradise.net.nz
www.onukubedandbreakfast.co.nz

Features & Attractions

• *Families welcome*	• *Golf & bridge arranged*
• *Hill walks*	• *Warm friendly hospitality*
• *Hiking tours arranged*	• *Dinner by arrangement*

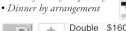

Luxury Bed & Breakfast

Double	$160-180	
Single	$100	
Child		

O nuku Bed & Breakfast is a stunning, newly created upmarket home, specifically designed for the comfort of guests. It has panoramic views from Banks Peninsula over the city and plains to the sea and mountains. The ground floor (with two bedrooms, two bathrooms and living area) is most suitable for a family or group. Bob is involved in the tourism industry and can arrange and accompany guests on golf and hiking tours.

Jenny is a New Zealand bridge representative and is happy to arrange a friendly game of bridge either at home or in one of the local clubs. They have both travelled extensively and promise fellow travellers a warm and friendly welcome.

Bedrooms	Qty
Double	2
Twin	1
Single	
Bed Size	**Qty**
King	
Queen	2
Double	
Single	2
Bathrooms	**Qty**
Ensuite	2
Private	1
Guest Share	

GOVERNORS BAY B&B
851 Governors Bay Road, Lyttelton
Ph (03) 329 9727
email: eva@gbbedandbreakfast.co.nz
www.gbbedandbreakfast.co.nz

Features & Attractions

• *Waterfront property*	• *Peaceful sanctuary*
• *Foreshore walking track*	• *Homemade organic breakfast*
• *Holistic treatments*	• *Catering for dietary needs*

DIRECTIONS: From Christchurch go south on Colombo St to Cashmere. Continue straight ahead through the round about, up Dyers Pass, over the top of the hill and down the other side. At the bottom of the hill you will be in Governors Bay.
Left now towards "Lyttelton". Continue along this road for 1km until you reach 851.

Organic Bed & Breakfast

Double	$130	
Single	$90	
Child	neg.	

R elax and rejuvenate in our eco-friendly home surrounded by bush. Enjoy the truly spectacular harbour views from the 20m² large ensuite room and listen to the sea and bell birds from the sunny balcony.

Wake up to see the sun rising out of the harbour and enjoy Eva's delicious organic homemade breakfast, she also caters for dietary needs.

Treat yourself to a deeply relaxing massage. Watch the quail, peacock and horse roaming around outside the house.

I look forward to welcoming you.

Bedrooms	Qty
Double	1
Twin	
Single	1
Bed Size	**Qty**
King	1
Queen	1
Double	
King/Single	1
Bathrooms	**Qty**
Ensuite	1
Private	
Family Share	1

Mt Pleasant Homestay

106A Mt Pleasant Road, Mt Pleasant, Christchurch
Ph/Fax (03) 384 1940, Mobile 021-253 5857
email: mtpleasantbnb@clear.net.nz
www.mtpleasanthomestay.co.nz

Tariff : N.Z. Dollars	
Double	$140-150
Single	$110
Child	neg

Bedrooms	Qty
Double	1
Twin	1
Single	

Bed Size	Qty
Super King	
King/Single	1
Queen	1
Double	
Single	

Bathrooms	Qty
Ensuite	1
Private	1
Guest Share	

     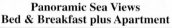

**Panoramic Sea Views
Bed & Breakfast plus Apartment**

Features & Attractions

- *Stylish contemporary design*
- *Rest, comfort, peace*
- *Wireless internet & laundry*
- *Private suite available*
- *Delicious breakfasts with sea views*
- *Guest lounge & kitchen*
- *Close to restaurants & cafés*
- *Courtesy transfers*

Jan welcomes you to **Mt Pleasant Homestay.** Simply park your car at the front door and prepare to enjoy warm hospitality in a new, modern home with breathtaking views. You can be sure of a quiet comfortable stay and enjoy sumptuous breakfasts while gazing out over the Pacific to distant mountains. All guest rooms open to the sheltered patio and garden of roses and perennials and Bellbirds in the near-by trees. Our road leads to a spectacular Scenic Drive, countless walkways and cycle tracks. Many attractions are in this immediate vicinity, an early settler village, Maori village and gondola. Ferrymead, three minutes by car, has a variety of cafés and restaurants, as does Sumner Beach (of Lonely Planet fame) an eight minute drive. Guests have a lounge and kitchen. Private Suite is available for a minimum 2 night stay at $230 per night including breakfast. Be prepared to lose your heart to my second in charge: Mollie, a personable Tibetan Terrier. Jan has travelled extensively in New Zealand and overseas and we enjoy chatting with like-minded guests over a glass of wine, and are always sad to say goodbye. Welcome to **Mt Pleasant Homestay**.

THE STABLES BED & BREAKFAST
562 Sandy Knolls Rd, West Melton, Christchurch
Ph (03) 347 9547, Mobile 021-633 181
email: stablesbandb@gmail.com
www.thestablesbandb.co.nz

Tariff : N.Z. Dollars	
Double	$150
Single	$130
Child	neg

Bedrooms	Qty
Double/Twin	1
Double	1
Single	
Bed Size	**Qty**
S King/Twin	1/2
King	
Queen	1
Double	
Single	
Bathrooms	**Qty**
Ensuite	2
Private	
Guest Share	

 Equestrian based Countrystay Bed & Breakfast

Features & Attractions

- *Broadband wireless internet*
- *Suites air conditioned*
- *30 mins to Mount Hutt ski-field*
- *Golf courses in vicinity*
- *Quiet rural setting*
- *Stabling/yards/grazing for horses*
- *Flat panel TV in suites*
- *Tiled private ensuite each room*

The Stables Bed and Breakfast is located approximately 30km west of Christchurch city just off the main West Coast highway (State Highway 73). The property is a six hectare equestrian training property with stables, arena, round pen and yards, along with a recently completed architecturally designed house. The two bed and breakfast rooms are in a self contained wing, along with a small breakfast sitting area where you also have a microwave. Both bedrooms have flat panel TV, personal minibar, free wireless internet, under floor heating and heat pump/air conditioning. Breakfast is Continental Breakfast.

We are within thirty minutes of the access road to Mount Hutt and other ski fields in the area. A number of golf courses within a short distance. Dinners are available as long as they are booked a minimum of seven days prior to arrival. Frozen pre-cooked dinners available for microwave heating.
"We look forward to welcoming you".

218

CEDARVIEW FARM BED & BREAKFAST

33 Barters Road, Templeton, Christchurch
Ph (03) 349 7491, Fax (03) 349 7755
Mobile 027-433 5335
email: cedarviewfarm@xtra.co.nz
www.cedarviewhomestay.com

Tariff : N.Z. Dollars	
Double	$135-185
Single	$120-135
Child	neg

Bedrooms	Qty
Double	2
Twin	1
Single	
Bed Size	**Qty**
Super King	
King	1
Queen	1
Double	
Single	2
Bathrooms	**Qty**
Ensuite	1
Private	1
Guest Share	1

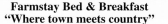

**Farmstay Bed & Breakfast
"Where town meets country"**

Features & Attractions

- *Airport 10min, City Centre 15-20min*
- *Highways, north, south, west, nearby*
- *Relaxed, tranquil atmosphere*
- *Restaurants, wineries, golf*
- *Factory outlet shopping*
- *Modern smoke-free home*
- *Lovely garden setting*
- *Antarctic Centre*

Welcome to New Zealand. We moved here from the UK in 1986 and simply love our lifestyle. Our bright modern smoke free home offers affordable high quality 4 star accommodation in a very convenient location close to the Airport and Central city. Highways 1 and 73 (north, south and west) are nearby. We keep beef cattle (except over the winter months), hens, sheep, 2 Shetland Ponies "Bella & Thomas". Our labrador dog "Ruby" and farm cat "Alfie" just love to be played with. We are close to local shopping areas, motor racing, golf, wineries and restaurants (enjoy a meal and see the kiwis at Willowbank Wildlife Reserve). Whatever your passion then we are ideally located for you. Enjoy Carol's home-made bread, jams and preserves. Free-range eggs (providing the girls get busy and lay some of course) and even our own honey. We look forward to getting to know you over a coffee, glass of wine or beer and helping you make the most of your stay in charming Christchurch.

Cedar Park Gardens B&B

"Cedar Park", 101B Lowes Rd, Rolleston, Christchurch
Ph (03) 347 7605, Mobile 027-436 5156
email: anne@cedarparkgardens.co.nz
www.cedarparkgardens.co.nz

Features & Attractions

- *Secluded 1.5 acre garden*
- *Warm, friendly hosts*
- *Close to airport/scenic train/city*
- *Secure off-road parking*
- *Superb breakfast*
- *Dinner by arrangement*

DIRECTIONS:
At Rolleston BP Station, turn from SH 1, onto Tennyson St, continue 1.5 km to 2nd roundabout, turn right onto Lowes Rd. We are 300m on left, at **end** of private lane - is signposted.

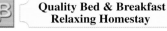

Quality Bed & Breakfast Relaxing Homestay

Double/Triple	$130-145
Single	$120-140
Child	$15-20

Bedrooms	Qty
Double/Triple	1
Twin	1
Single	
Bed Size	Qty
King	
Queen	1
King/Single	1
Single	2
Bathrooms	Qty
Ensuite	1
Private	
Family Share	1

Enjoy a relaxing stay in our peaceful, quiet, sunny home, set in beautiful country gardens on the southern outskirts of Christchurch. Conveniently situated 2km off SH1, and within easy reach of Canterbury skifields, Lincoln University, Burnham Military camp, Akaroa, wineries, golf courses, Christchurch attractions and International airport, **Tranzalpine Scenic Train**. Excellent restaurants 10 minute walk away. Main guest room has a private entrance, **no steps**, parking at door, park-like outlook, ensuite, tea/coffee making facilities, TV. Wireless internet available. **Some French spoken.** A welcoming "cuppa" provided on arrival. Children welcome. Enjoy a lavish breakfast-cooked or continental. Complimentary transport to/from **Christchurch Airport** and **Tranzalpine Scenic Train**. Anne and Ron have many varied interests, and along with Tigger their cat, take pleasure from making your stay comfortable, enjoyable and memorable.

Fantail Lodge on Greenpark

164 River Road, Lincoln - TaiTapu, Christchurch
Ph (03) 325 7572, Mobile 027-433 7706
email: fantaillge@netspeed.net.nz
www.fantaillodgegpk.co.nz

Features & Attractions

- *Genuine kiwi hospitality*
- *Abundant bird life*
- *Lincoln University 5km*
- *Selwyn Food & Wine Trail*
- *Little River Rail Trail*
- *Guided local tours*

Countrystay Quality Bed & Breakfast

Double	$130-155
Single	$110-130
Child	

Bedrooms	Qty
Double	2
Twin	
Single	
Bed Size	Qty
Super King	1
Queen	1
Double	
Single	
Bathrooms	Qty
Ensuite	1
Private	1
Guest Share	1

Enjoy our relaxing and Peaceful country environment in our modern architecturally designed home and beautiful landscaped gardens with views of the Southern Alps, nestled on 10 acre farmlet with Perendale Sheep and Beef cattle. Fantails, Bellbirds, Silvereyes, Pukeko's and other native birds often frequent our garden. Experience genuine Kiwi hospitality. with Pamela (Artist) and Doug (Photographer and Tour guide). Guests separate lounge for privacy, TV. Wireless internet available. Continental breakfast. Ample off road parking. Local award winning Restaurants and Wineries 5-20 km. Located on River Road (off Lincoln -TaiTapu Road) which meanders along the Halswell River. Airport 25 Km, Pickup available. 5km from Lincoln University. "Great place to start your South Island Tour". Information on Southern Routes and Attractions for Self-drive guests. Local day tour options by arrangement: Akaroa, Great Alpine Highway, Selwyn Wine Trail or a Phototour with Doug.

HAZELVIEW

1153 Springs Road, Lincoln, Canterbury
Ph (03) 325 3362, Mobile 027-253 4263
email: enquiry@hazelview.co.nz
www.hazelview.co.nz

Features & Attractions

- *Secluded orchard setting*
- *Self-contained apartment*
- *Complimentary orchard tours*
- *Free Wireless Broadband*
- *City/airport 17 minutes*
- *Near Lincoln University*

Double	$140
Single	$120
Child	neg

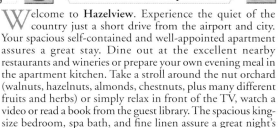

**Quality Bed & Breakfast
Orchardstay**

Bedrooms	Qty
Double	1
Twin	
Single	
Bed Size	**Qty**
King	2
Queen	
Double	
Single	
Bathrooms	**Qty**
Ensuite	1
Private	
Guest Share	

Welcome to **Hazelview**. Experience the quiet of the country just a short drive from the airport and city. Your spacious self-contained and well-appointed apartment assures a great stay. Dine out at the excellent nearby restaurants and wineries or prepare your own evening meal in the apartment kitchen. Take a stroll around the nut orchard (walnuts, hazelnuts, almonds, chestnuts, plus many different fruits and herbs) or simply relax in front of the TV, watch a video or read a book from the guest library. The spacious king-size bedroom, spa bath, and fine linen assure a great night's rest. Enjoy either a continental breakfast or by arrangement have a full cooked breakfast. Complimentary coffee, teas and nibbles.

LA BELLE VILLA

113 Rue Jolie, Akaroa
Ph/Fax (03) 304 7084, Mobile 021-045 9156
email: bookings@labellevilla.co.nz
www.labellevilla.co.nz

Features & Attractions

- *Friendly hospitality*
- *Central situation*
- *Historic house*
- *Garden with bird life*
- *Homemade breakfasts*
- *Great value*

  Bed & Breakfast

$	Double	$150-180
	Single	$130-160
	Child	

Situated in the heart of Akaroa makes **La Belle Villa** a great choice to explore our historic town and surrounding peninsula. Set in picturesque gardens with a trickling stream, our photogenic home offers an opportunity for visitors to enjoy the ambience of a by-gone era but with the convenience of en-suite bathrooms in all guest rooms.

Our special breakfast has received universal praise and includes homemade bread, muesli, preserves, filled croissants, local grapefruit, berries in season and a selection of teas and espresso coffee. Breakfast is served in the garden or beside warm open fires if the weather dictates. A separate guest lounge enables 24 hour tea and coffee making facilities. A child friendly home which offers warm hospitality. We also have a two-bedroomed self contained Apartment which is popular with families or two couples travelling together.

Bedrooms	Qty
Double	5
Twin	1
Single	
Bed Size	**Qty**
Super King	1
King	4
Queen	1
King/Single	2
Bathrooms	**Qty**
Ensuite	4
Private	
Guest Share	1

GARTHOWEN LUXURY WATERFRONT B&B

7 Beach Road, Akaroa
Ph/Fax (03) 304 7419, Mobile 027-437 1096
email: info@garthowen.co.nz
www.garthowen.co.nz

Tariff : N.Z. Dollars	
Double	$295-345
Single	$280
Child	

Bedrooms	Qty
Double	4
Twin	1
Single	

Bed Size	Qty
Super King	4
King	
Queen	
Double	
Single	2

Bathrooms	Qty
Ensuite	4
Private	
Guest Share	

    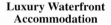

Luxury Waterfront Accommodation

Features & Attractions

- *Scrumptious cooked breakfasts*
- *2 minute walk to shops & restaurants*
- *Guest computer, wireless Broadband*
- *Place of tranquility*
- *Panoramic sea views*
- *Warm, friendly hospitality*
- *Finest linen, flowers, robes*
- *Picturesque cottage garden*

Sometimes you discover a beautiful place, Akaroa is such a place. **Garthowen B&B**, 5 star Qualmark and Qualmark Environment Gold will provide you with the perfect setting in which to relax, unwind and feel pampered. Situated right on the waterfront of Akaroa's main street, purposely built to the original 1890 guest house, **Garthowen** was opened in December 2005, this is an absolutely stunning house with harbour views from every room. Enjoy a gourmet breakfast from our scrumptious breakfast menu served in the dining room or on the balcony, savour the view, smell the sea air. All rooms have superking beds, ensuites, TV/DVD's, air conditioning, underfloor heating, personalised gowns, tea/coffee making, cotton embroidered bedlinen, fresh flowers and complimentary Port, Sparkling Mineral Water and chocolates. Akaroa's Information Centre and fine restaurants only a 2 minute stroll away. Meet Jessie our long haired Jack Russell, she would love to be spoiled by you.

We'll make your stay a memorable one.

Kawatea Farmstay

'Kawatea', 1048 Okains Bay Road,
Akaroa, Banks Peninsula
Ph (03) 304 8621, Fax (03) 304 8621
email: kawatea@xtra.co.nz
www.kawateafarmstay.co.nz

Tariff : N.Z. Dollars	
Double	$130-160
Single	$90-160
Child	neg

Bedrooms	Qty
Double	1
Twin	2
Single	

Bed Size	Qty
Super King	
King	
Queen	3
King/Single	1
Single	1

Bathrooms	Qty
Ensuite	1
Private	1
Guest Share	1

**Historic Homestead
Quality Accommodation & Dinner**

Features & Attractions

- *1400 acre sheep & beef farm*
- *Creative dinners, NZ wine*
- *Warm country hospitality*
- *Peaceful romantic retreat*
- *Safe swimming beach*
- *Seals, dolphins, birdlife*
- *Coastal walks, kayaks, golf*
- *Akaroa Village 20 min*

DIRECTIONS:
Take Highway 75 from Christchurch through Duvauchelle. Turn left at signpost marked Okain's Bay. Kawatea is 11 km on right.

Escape to the beauty and tranquillity of the country. Enjoy a unique holiday experience in a gracious historic homestead set in beautiful mature gardens, and surrounded by land, farmed by our family for five generations. **Kawatea** is an elegant, carefully renovated home, built in 1900 from native timbers; it features stained glass windows, handcrafted furniture and much olde world charm. Enjoy a relaxing day with a book on the verandah, or participate in seasonal farm activities and feed the pet sheep. Wander our hillside farm enjoying the panoramic views of Banks Peninsula, or walk along the scenic coastline to secluded swimming beaches and a seal colony. Learn about Maori culture and the life of early settlers at the acclaimed Okain's Bay Museum or visit Akaroa with its French influence, cafés and craft shops. Join us for dinner savouring seafood from the bay and creative country fare from our garden, whilst sharing experiences with fellow travellers. We have been hosting since 1988 and pride ourselves on thoughtful, personal attention and friendly hospitality in a relaxed atmosphere.

224

BOSSU FARMSTAY

Wainui, Akaroa, Banks Peninsula
Ph/Fax (03) 304 8421
email: bossu@xtra.co.nz
www.charmingaccommodation.co.nz

Tariff : N.Z. Dollars	
Double	$165
Single	$110
Child	neg

Bedrooms	Qty
Double	1
Twin	1
Single	
Bed Size	**Qty**
Super King	
King	
Queen	1
Double	
Single	2
Bathrooms	**Qty**
Ensuite	
Guest Share	1
Family Share	1

DIRECTIONS:
First property on seaward side
after Wainui with a stone entrance.

**Farmstay
Bed & Breakfast**

Features & Attractions

- *Panoramic views of Akaroa Harbour*
- *Viewing dolphins & sea birds*
- *French farm winery nearby*
- *Drinks, dinner & good company*
- *Farm tour & walks*
- *Hand feed pet sheep*
- *Golf course nearby*
- *Grass tennis court*

Our farm has 2 km of coastline overlooking the beautiful harbour of Akaroa with panoramic views to the historic town of Akaroa. Our house is situated near this coastline with a large garden, and a well used grass tennis court surrounded by lovely mature trees. The property runs sheep, some forestry and two small vineyards. We have been hosting guests since 1977 so obviously, love having people to stay, and taking them, we think, on an interesting farm tour. There are lovely walks and interesting bays to visit on Banks Peninsula. Our interests include tennis, golf (Akaroa golf course is nearby) and bridge and many of our guests come with us to our local club. We have both travelled extensively so enjoy hearing about other countries. We have a small well behaved Jack Russell terrier. Most guests join us for dinner where we offer pre-dinner drinks and our locally grown wine for $35 per person. We look forward to your enquiry and hopefully meeting you.

GLENTHORNE STATION
Harper Road, Darfield,
Lake Coleridge, Canterbury
Ph (03) 318 5818, Fax (03) 318 5819
email: info@glenthorne.co.nz
www.glenthorne.co.nz

Features & Attractions

- *62,352 acres (25,2333 hectares)*
- *1 1/2 hrs from Christchurch*
- *8 lakes & 4 rivers for fishing*
- *Walks and tramps*
- *Horse trekking*
- *Excellent base for skiers*

Self-contained Accommodation

Double	–
Single	$25-90
Child	neg

Glenthorne Station is a 62,352 acre sheep and cattle station nestled on the shores of Lake Coleridge near the Southern Alps. Enjoy amazing views of Lake Coleridge and the surrounding mountains. **Glenthorne** is perfectly situated in the centre of the South Island which makes an excellent stop-over when travelling to some of New Zealand's most popular destinations. Explore and experience the great outdoors by making the most of some of our outstanding walks and tramps. We have a range of self-contained options available, all fully furnished and fully equipped for self-catering.

DIRECTIONS: Turn off at SH 72 at Windwhistle, onto Coleridge Rd for approx. 20 min, after crossing Acheron River turn right onto Homestead Rd and then turn left onto Harper Rd. Coming from SH 73, turn off at Lake Lyndon onto Lyndon Rd, travel approx. 20 min nd then take your next right onto Harper Rd. From both directions Glenthorne is 10 mins once on Harper Rd.

Bedrooms	Qty
Double	5
Twin	2
Single	
Bed Size	**Qty**
King	
Queen	2
Double	4
Single	4
Bathrooms	Qty
Ensuite	2
Private	
Guest Share	2

TYRONE DEER FARM
646 Mt. Hutt Station Rd, Alternative Route
Methven to Rakaia Gorge
Ph (03) 302 8096
email: tyronedeerfarm@xtra.co.nz
www.charmingaccommodation.co.nz

Tariff : N.Z. Dollars	
Double	$150-160
Single	$105
Child	neg

Bedrooms	Qty
Double	3
Twin	1
Single	
Bed Size	**Qty**
Super King	1
King	
Queen	1
Double	1
Single	1
Bathrooms	**Qty**
Ensuite	2
Private	1
Guest Share	

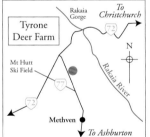

**Countrystay
Bed & Breakfast**

Features & Attractions

- *Centre of South Island*
- *Golf 18-hole courses, club hire*
- *Skiing MtHutt & heli-skiing*
- *Jet boating/hot air ballooning*
- *1 hour Christchurch Airport*
- *Tramping, alpine & bush walks*
- *Fishing, hunting guides available*
- *Mountain views*

Welcome to **Tyrone Deer Farm** centrally situated in the Mt.Hutt, Rakaia Gorge, Methven area, 5km from the Inland Tourist Route (SH72), an ideal stopover on the way to Queenstown and just 1hr from Christchurch International Airport. Enjoy beautiful views of Mt.Hutt and of our deer grazing just metres away. The ensuite bedrooms have electric blankets, wool underlays, duvets, heaters and hair dryers. The lounge has open fire, TV, tea/coffee making facilities and a guest fridge. Come and meet 'Gus' our pet deer, her daughter '$$s' and '10.30' our cat. Stay 2 or 3 nights, do some of our wonderful local walks, ski Mt.Hutt, laze in the garden, swim in the pool, but most of all **relax**! On arrival enjoy a cup of tea/coffee and home made muffins with your hosts. An evening meal, served with New Zealand wine, by prior arrangement.

Two self-contained townhouses available on Main St. Methven (Mt Hutt Village). Tariff for 2 persons $140.00. Extra adult $20.00, child $10.00 (summer rates).

227

GREEN GABLES DEER FARM

185 Waimarama Road, Methven
Ph (03) 302 8308, Fax (03) 302 8309
email: greengables@xtra.co.nz
www.nzfarmstay.com

Tariff : N.Z. Dollars	
Double	$140-180
Single	$110-140
Child	$55

Bedrooms	Qty
Double	2
Twin	1
Single	

Bed Size	Qty
Super King	2
King	
Queen	
Double	
King/Single	2

Bathrooms	Qty
Ensuite	2
Private	1
Guest Share	

**Ensuites – Super King Beds
Sumptuous Breakfasts**

Features & Attractions

- *International golf courses*
- *Fishing, jet boating, horse riding*
- *Trips to 'Lord of the Rings' film site*
- *Superb restaurants –4 km*
- *Sumptuous breakfasts*
- *Hot air ballooning*
- *Refreshments on arrival*
- *Skiing at Mt Hutt*

Green Gables
Deer Farm

DIRECTIONS:
Situated on SH77, 4 km north-west
of Methven. From Inland Scenic Route
72, turn into SH77 and travel 5 km,
Green Gables is on the right.

Set in tranquil surroundings at the foot of Mt Hutt, with many summer and winter activities close by, **Green Gables Deer Farm** is within easy reach of Christchurch (1 hr), Kaikoura for Whale Watching and Dolphins (3 hrs), Mt. Cook (3.5 hrs) and Queenstown (approx 5.5 hrs). Our stylish rooms have all the comforts you will require, with your own private entrance opening out onto the garden with a backdrop of graceful deer wandering in the paddocks and the ever changing colours of the mountain views. There is plenty of room to stroll, maybe feed the pet deer and meet our friendly dogs or just relax and unwind.

Dine in by arrangement and enjoy the fresh local produce used in our home-cooked meals and desserts, together with a complimentary pre-dinner drink.

CRICKLEWOOD HOUSE

120 Johnstone Street, Tinwald, RD 4, Ashburton
Ph (03) 307 1980, Fax (03) 307 1985
Mobile 027-223 1939
email: gdrobins@clear.net.nz
www.cricklewoodhouse.co.nz

Tariff : N.Z. Dollars	
Double	$140-180
Single	$100
Child	

Bedrooms	Qty
Double	2
Twin	
Single	1
Bed Size	**Qty**
Super King	
King/Twin	1
King	1
Double	
Single	2
Bathrooms	**Qty**
Ensuite	1
Private	
Guest Share	1

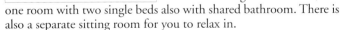

**Country Stay
Boutique Accommodation**

Features & Attractions

- *TV and tea making facilities*
- *One hour south of Christchurch*
- *Three-course dinner available*
- *Email facilities*
- *Quiet, comfortable rooms*
- *Smoke-free inside*
- *Local restaurants nearby*
- *Friendly hosts*

Cricklewood House is a house, purpose-built with guests' total comfort catered for. Formal dining room with period furniture makes our home very relaxing. We have one king-size bedroom with ensuite, one king/twin bed with shared guest bathroom, and one room with two single beds also with shared bathroom. There is also a separate sitting room for you to relax in.

When you arrive you will be greeted with a hot drink, and a very warm welcome. We will serve dinner with twenty four hour notice, alternatively you are only five to eight minutes to some fine Ashburton restaurants. We are situated just off Highway One, one hour south of Christchurch, well suited to travelling north or to Mount Cook, the Southern Lakes and Queenstown. We can also direct you to various activities in the district and further afield.

Our interests are gardening, sports, embroidery, and cooking. We are retired farmers who have been in the hosting business for over twenty years. We look forward to having your company at our place.

KEPPOCH HOMESTAY
39 Grayburn Road, Ashburton
Ph/Fax (03) 308 7818
Mobile 021-214 1936
email: keppoch@xtra.co.nz
www.keppoch.com

Features & Attractions

- *Friendly welcoming hosts*
- *Warm comfortable home*
- *Ground floor guest rooms*
- *Peaceful location*
- *Dinner by arrangement*
- *50 mins to Christchurch Int. Airport*

Homestay Bed & Breakfast		

Double	$100
Single	$60
Child	$25 u/12

Bedrooms	Qty
Double	1
Twin	1
Single	
Bed Size	**Qty**
King	
Queen	1
Double	
Single	2
Bathrooms	**Qty**
Ensuite	
Private	
Guest Share	1

Friendly and welcoming hosts, Valmai and Kenneth, are pleased to share their warm and attractive home with guests, situated in a quiet semi-rural area, yet handy to town with comprehensive shopping areas and many recommendable restaurants.

Being less than 1 hour from Christchurch Airport and NE to the town, **Keppoch** is a favoured place to stay arriving or departing the South Island. Stay longer and enjoy some of the many attractions of the area: braided fishing rivers (salmon and trout), mountains with tramping and skiing, the fertile rural farming area.

Being retired farmers, Ken and Valmai are well informed and farm visits can be arranged with prior notice.

RICHLYN PARK B&B

9 Tiplady Road, Geraldine, South Canterbury
Ph/Fax (03) 693 9681, Mobile 027-600 9951
email: rickpitelen@xtra.co.nz
www.richlynpark.co.nz

Tariff : N.Z. Dollars	
Double	$130
Single	$100
Child	

Bedrooms	Qty
Double	2
Twin	
Single	
Bed Size	**Qty**
Super King	
King	
Queen	2
Double	
Single	
Bathrooms	**Qty**
Ensuite	2
Private	
Guest Share	

Richlyn Park B&B

DIRECTIONS:
Richlyn Park Bed & Breakfast
is 3km south of Geraldine on SH 79.

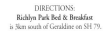

Charming and Friendly Bed & Breakfast

Features & Attractions

- *Friendly welcoming hosts*
- *Warm comfortable home*
- *Ground floor guest rooms*
- *Beautiful views of the countryside*
- *Dinner by arrangement*
- *1 Hour 45 mins to Christchurch*
- *Laundry/Email available*
- *Close to fishing and rafting*

Welcome to **Richlyn Park Bed & Breakfast**, located five minutes from the charming, picturesque town of Geraldine. Our purpose built home set on three acres of gardens offers all the comforts of home with spacious superior guest bedrooms, large ensuites, all situated in your own private wing. If you want to get away from the bustle of life and relax with a book and a wine or pull on your tramping boots or skis and get stuck into those mountains, maybe fishing, white water rafting, or even hobbit spotting in Lord of the Rings country. Whatever grabs your fancy, you will enjoy your stay at **Richlyn Park** where Evalyn and Rick will really look after you.

THE DOWNS BED & BREAKFAST

5 Ribbonwood Road, The Downs, Geraldine
Ph/Fax (03) 693 7388, Mobile 021-675 249
email:info@thedowns.co.nz
www.thedowns.co.nz

Tariff : N.Z. Dollars	
Double	$200-220
Single	$150
Child	

Bedrooms	Qty
Double	3
Twin	1
Single	

Bed Size	Qty
Super King	
King	
Queen	3
Double	
Single	2

Bathrooms	Qty
Ensuite	3
Private	1
Guest Share	

 Superior Bed & Breakfast

Features & Attractions

- Large garden setting
- Complimentary bar
- Free guest laundry
- Broadband internet

- Mini gym/pool room
- Handy to shops & restaurants
- Art studios
- High standard of facilities

The **Downs B&B** offers you quality accommodation in our large, modern home. A wander round the beautiful park-like garden is a lovely way to unwind after your journey. Peace, tranquillity and bird song are part of the surroundings here. The guest rooms are spacious. Each has its own TV, comfortable armchairs and ensuites, all furnished to a very high standard. A full Kiwi and continental breakfast is served in the guest lounge or on the balcony overlooking the garden. There is also a complimentary self-service bar and tea and coffee making facilities and home-baked cookies are available at all times. The region of Geraldine has much to offer in the way of arts, crafts, dining experiences, golf, fishing, 4 WD tours and skiing. We are only too pleased to assist you with your further sightseeing plans and accommodation if necessary.

VICTORIA VILLA

55 Cox Street, Geraldine
Ph (03) 693 8605, Mobile 021-0826 4212
email: sharonsmash@hotmail.com
www.geraldineaccommodation.com

Features & Attractions

- *100 year old restored villa*
- *Ensuites & private bathroom*
- *Mins to village & forest walks*
- *Molded ceilings & original features*
- *Wireless internet*
- *Continental or full english breakfast*

$	Double	$125-135
	Single	$90-100
	Child	$10-15

 Boutique Accommodation & Detached Studio

Bedrooms	Qty
Double	3
Twin	
Single	
Bed Size	**Qty**
King	
Queen	3
Double	
Single	3
Bathrooms	**Qty**
Ensuite	3
Private	
Guest Share	1

We welcome you to our historic beautiful villa which has an interesting and varied history. It has been a hospital, a maternity home, a lodge and an art gallery. We offer high quality accommodation with modern facilities that do not compromise the original integrity of the building.

We offer fine linen and delicious food featuring excellent local produce. Geraldine is a lovely South Canterbury village which has many attractions, cafes, restaurants, art gallery, vintage car museum, boutique picture theatre, outdoor pursuits and local forest walks. Geraldine is home to many well known artists and crafts people. We are within 75minutes of Mt Hutt and Mt Dobson and only 60 minutes to Lake Tekapo.

To Christchurch
Victoria Villa
Talbot St
Cox St
N
To Fairlie, Tekapo, Mt Cook, Wanaka & Queenstown
To Timaru

AMERICAN EXPRESS   VISA   MasterCard

www.phototrips.info

BLUEBERRY COTTAGE
72A High Street, Timaru
Ph (03) 684 3115, Fax (03) 684 3172
Mobile 027-636 4301
email: relax@blueberrycottage.co.nz
www.blueberrycottage.co.nz

Tariff : N.Z. Dollars	
Double	$115
Single	$75
Child	neg

Bedrooms	Qty
Double	1
Twin/Double	1
Single	

Bed Size	Qty
Super King	1
King Single	2
Queen	1
Double	
Single	

Bathrooms	Qty
Ensuite	
Private	1
Guest Share	1

 **Bed & Breakfast
Homestay**

Features & Attractions

- *Quiet sea-front setting*
- *Friendly home hospitality*
- *Sea to mountain views*
- *Gateway to Southern Alps*
- *Stroll to beach-walkways*
- *Relaxation at its best*

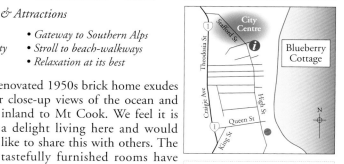

Our recently delightfully renovated 1950s brick home exudes comfort with spectacular close-up views of the ocean and

inland to Mt Cook. We feel it is a delight living here and would like to share this with others. The tastefully furnished rooms have television with access to separate outside patios.

Handy to hospital and gardens. It is a comfortable walking distance to

DIRECTIONS:
Timaru South on SH 1.
Turn into Queen Street.
Pass hospital and right into High St.
Blueberry Cottage entrance on left.

shops, cafés, bars, or eating place of your choice. Timaru is centrally situated on the east coast of the South Island, allowing easy access to many scenic spots, i.e. day trips to lakes, skiing in winter, Mount Cook, fishing rivers, bush walks, vineyards and other interesting towns. Shops display our high quality wool products and gifts of interest to overseas' visitors.

TE KITEROA LODGE

227 Point Bush Road, Waimate, South Canterbury
Ph (03) 689 1088, Mobile 021-576 868
email: info@tekiteroalodge.co.nz
www.tekiteroalodge.co.nz

Tariff : N.Z. Dollars	
Double	$150
Single	$125
Child	$25

Bedrooms	Qty
Double	5
Twin	
Single	

Bed Size	Qty
Super King	1
King	
Queen	3
Double	1
Single	

Bathrooms	Qty
Ensuite	3
Private	
Guest Share	2

**Boutique Vineyard
Accommodation**

Features & Attractions

- *Adjacent native bush & walkways*
- *Within Vineyard & winery*
- *Dinner by arrangement*
- *Wireless & WiFi Internet*
- *Coast to mountain views*
- *Nearby fishing & hunting*
- *Continental/english breakfast*
- *Spa bath available*

Te Kiteroa (long view) is exactly what you will experience staying at our Lodge as well as a memorable and relaxing stay. An Edwardian era Lodge, **Te Kiteroa** is located midway between Christchurch and Dunedin close to SH1. Break your journey and connect with local history. Step back in time and enjoy Waimate, a farming community with origins of Sawmill township and Edwardian heritage. **Te Kiteroa** is set in a peaceful and tranquil setting with nearby walkways, birdlife, and natural habitat for local wallabies. Enjoy a soak in the outdoor hot tub or enjoy a glass of our own local wine. We have expanded the Lodge to include a vineyard and winery and have produced our own wines since 2006. We welcome everyone... Gary and Ann have worked overseas for many years but now enjoying welcoming visitors to their unique Lodge.

235

CENTRE HILL COTTAGE

59 Howell Road, Totara Valley, Pleasant Point
Ph (03) 614 7385, Mobile 027-420 1120
email: centre.hill@paradise.net.nz
www.centrehillcottage.com

Tariff : N.Z. Dollars	
Double	$250-350
Single	$70
Child	$30

Bedrooms	Qty
Double	1
Twin	1
Single	

Bed Size	Qty
Super King	
King	
Queen	1
Double	
Single	2

Bathrooms	Qty
Ensuite	
Private	1
Guest Share	

**Luxury
Farmstay Retreat**

VISA   MasterCard

Features & Attractions

- Atmosphere of peace and tranquility
- Complimentary food hamper & wine
- Breakfast delivered daily
- Swimming pool, farm walks, tennis
- Laundry facilities
- Covered access from garage
- Sampling organic produce
- Cycles available

Your host, Ian Blakemore invites you to this special place. **Centre Hill**, naturally and brilliantly connects people and place. The Cottage is unpretentiously stylish and offers a cosy charm for those wanting a transforming experience. Drenched with stunning views, the cottage is nestled amongst mature trees on a Certified Organic Farm and features a large warm living area with a spacious deck a fully equipped modern kitchen, two bedrooms, a luxurious bathroom with under floor heating and a raised spa bath. Experience the fun of the outdoor bath while stargazing, or open the complimentary bottle of wine and indulge yourself in this magical setting. **Centre Hill Cottage** is the perfect place to unwind, relax, recharge your batteries and just be in the now.

DIRECTIONS:
From Pleasant Point Hotel turn into
Te Ngawai Rd, over bridge, left into
Totara Valley, next left into Howell Rd and
Centre Hill Cottage is first on the left,
5 km from Hotel turn-off.

236

RIVENDELL LODGE

15 Stanton Road, Kimbell, Fairlie
Ph (03) 685 8833
Mobile 027-481 9189
email: joan@rivendell-lodge.co.nz
www.rivendell-lodge.co.nz

Tariff : N.Z. Dollars	
Double	$130-160
Single	$85-100
Child	neg

Bedrooms	Qty
Double	4
Twin	2
Single	
Bed Size	Qty
Super King	
King	
Queen	3
Double	1
Single	2
Bathrooms	Qty
Ensuite	2
Private	2
Guest Share	

Bed & Breakfast Countrystay

Features & Attractions

- Peaceful rural retreat
- Families welcome
- Skifield 5 km
- Spa bath available
- Magnificent alpine scenery
- Guided walking & tramping
- Laundry & email available
- Ensuite rooms also have balconies

"They stayed long in Rivendell and found it hard to leave. The house was perfect whether you liked sleep, or work, or storytelling, or singing, or just sitting and thinking best, or a pleasant mixture of them all. Everyone grew refreshed and strong in a few days there. Merely to be there was a cure for weariness, fear and sadness." - Tolkien.

Welcome to my one acre of paradise – a haven of peace and tranquility offering quality country comfort and hospitality. As a well travelled writer I am passionate about mountains, literature and local history. I enjoy cooking and gardening, and delight in sharing home-grown produce. Take time out from the Christchurch-Queenstown route and enjoy our magnificent countryside. Fishing, walking, golf, watersports or skiing nearby. Relax in the garden, complete with stream and cat, or come exploring with me. Complimentary refreshments on arrival. Dinner $50.00pp by arrangement.

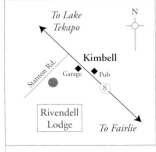

To Lake Tekapo
N
Kimbell
Stanton Rd.
Garage ◆ Pub
8
Rivendell Lodge
To Fairlie

DIRECTIONS:
100m up Stanton Road at Kimbell on SH 8, 8km west of Fairlie.

FREDA DU FAUR HOUSE

1 Esther Hope Street, Lake Tekapo, South Canterbury
Ph (03) 680 6513
email: dawntek@xtra.co.nz
www.fredadufaur.co.nz

Tariff : N.Z. Dollars	
Double	$180
Single	$100
Child	$90

Bedrooms	Qty
Double	2
Twin	1
Single	
Bed Size	**Qty**
Super King	
King	
Queen	1
Double	1
Single	1
Bathrooms	**Qty**
Ensuite	2
Private	1
Guest Share	

 Bed & Breakfast Homestay

Features & Attractions

- *Snowcapped mountains*
- *Crystal blue lakes*
- *Beautiful gardens & water feature*
- *Fishing and small game guide*
- *Handy to ski fields*
- *10 mins. to shops, restaurants*
- *1 hour from Mt. Cook*
- *Peaceful and quiet*

DIRECTIONS:
From SH 8 turn into Lochinvas,
right into Hamilton Drive,
then right into Esther Hope Street
where you will see our sign.
We are 2nd on the left.

When you come to this area you will experience Tekapo's tranquility and a touch of mountain magic. Dawn and Barry extend to you a warm and friendly welcome. Our home with beautiful mountain and lake views is warm and comfortable. Rimu panelling, heart timber furniture and an attractive decor are blending in with the McKenzie Country.
All guest bedrooms in their private wing are overlooking the garden,

two are opening onto a balcony.
Enjoy light refreshments on our patio surrounded by the scent of lavender and roses or view the ever-changing panorama from the lounge. In the morning you have the choice of either continental or special breakfast.

A ten minute walk takes you to the centre with shops and restaurants. There are several lovely walkways nearby and Mount Cook is only a one hour scenic drive from Lake Tekapo. "Bessy", the black labrador, and "Bella", our persian himalayan color fortè kitten, will welcome you.

238

GLACIER ROCK GALLERY AND B&B

35 Lochinver Ave, Lake Tekapo
Ph (03) 680 6669, Fax (03) 680 6661
Mobile 021-753 570
email: info@glacierrock.co.nz
www.glacierrock.co.nz

Tariff : N.Z. Dollars	
Double	$170-250
Single	
Child	

Bedrooms	Qty
Double	2
Twin	
Single	
Bed Size	**Qty**
Super King	
King	1
Queen	1
Double	
Single	
Bathrooms	**Qty**
Ensuite	2
Private	
Guest Share	

Gallery and Bed & Breakfast

DIRECTIONS:
From SH8 turn into Hamilton Drive. Turn first left. Timber and stone house on left as road starts to climb.

Features & Attractions

- *Breathtaking lake views*
- *Warm hospitality*
- *Well travelled, friendly hosts*
- *1 hour Aoraki Mt Cook*
- *Awesome night skies*
- *Quality accommodation*
- *Enjoyable walking tracks*
- *10 min. wildlife refuge*

Chris and Colin warmly welcome you to **Glacier Rock**. We enjoy sharing our knowledge and love of the MacKenzie Country with our guests. Designed and built by Colin on sustainability principles, our home offers panoramic views of Lake Tekapo and the surrounding mountains.

The two rooms each have ensuite, tea/coffee making facilities, TV, independent entry and direct access to a large sunny patio and breakfast/lounge room facing the view. The king room has spectacular views of the lake. The queen room overlooks the garden.

A healthy continental breakfast is served with fresh homemade bread and yoghurt. You are welcome to wander around the gallery to view Colin's paintings or you can ask to see Chris' weaving. The gallery exhibits and sells Colin's watercolour landscapes of New Zealand and a variety of land and cityscapes from Europe.

CREEL HOUSE

36 Murray Place, Lake Tekapo
Ph (03) 680 6516
email: creelhouse.l.tek@xtra.co.nz
www.laketekapoflyfishing.co.nz

Features & Attractions

- *Church of the Good Shepherd*
- *Scenic flights glaciers/Mt. Cook*
- *Easy access to walking tracks*
- *Stargazing on clear evenings*
- *Skiing/ice-skating - winter*
- *Wireless internet*

**Creel House
Bed & Breakfast**

Double	$160-175
Single	$105-110
Child	–

"Welcome." Our home, built by Grant, has three storeys with panoramic views of Lake Tekapo, Mt. John, Southern Alps and surrounding mountains, and has a native garden. There is a separate guest lounge and guest entrance, and all rooms are spacious. Walking distance to shops and restaurants is 10-15 minutes. We have two cats. Our living quarters are on the ground floor with guest's accommodation on the middle and upper floor. Breakfast is a lavish, healthy continental with home-made produce.

Grant is a registered member of the NZ Fishing and Guides Association. He is available for guided fly fishing for day tours and packages are available. Details on website.

Bedrooms	Qty
Double	2
Twin	1
Single	
Bed Size	**Qty**
King	
Queen	2
Double	
Single	2
Bathrooms	**Qty**
Ensuite	1
Private	2
Guest Share	

TEKAPO HEIGHTS

2 Sams Place, Lake Tekapo
Ph (03) 680 6528, Fax (03) 680 6532
email: tekapoheights@slingshot.co.nz
www.tekapoheights.co.nz

Features & Attractions

- *Magnificent lake views*
- *MacKenzie night sky*
- *Luxurious, spacious rooms*
- *Tranquil setting*
- *Walking distance to village*
- *Continental/English breakfast*

 **Panoramic Lake Views
Luxury Bed & Breakfast**

Double	$195-250
Single	$170-195
Child	$65

Hi, and welcome to our home. Come and relax and enjoy the spectacular views we have overlooking Lake Tekapo and the surrounding mountains. Enjoy the luxury of your room, with ensuites or a private bathroom, all with paved areas opening outside to great scenery. Tea/coffee facilities and satellite TV are available in all rooms, or come join us in our spacious lounge, where pre dinner drinks are served in the evening, restaurants are only 5 mins walk away. We are open all year round for the many activities available, in winter (skiing /ice skating/hot pools) and summer (fishing/tramping) just some of the things available. In the morning enjoy a cooked breakfast while taking in the tranquillity of the lake. We are half way between Christchurch and Queenstown with Mt Cook only 1hr away. We look forward to meeting you.

Bedrooms	Qty
Double	3
Twin	
Single	
Bed Size	**Qty**
Super King	2
Queen	1
Double	
Single	
Bathrooms	**Qty**
Ensuite	2
Private	1
Guest Share	

DIRECTIONS:
From SH8 turn left on to Aorangi Crescent (last street going out of Tekapo towards Mt Cook), then turn 2nd right, Andrew Don Drive, then next right, Sams Place-sign outside – Tekapo Heights.

TEKAPO HOUSE

8 O'Neill Place, Lakeview Heights, Lake Tekapo
Ph (03) 680 6607, Fax (03) 680 6691
Mobile 027-240 4974
email: rayntek@xtra.co.nz
www.charmingaccommodation.co.nz

Tariff : N.Z. Dollars	
Double	$140-160
Single	$80
Child	$35

Bedrooms	Qty
Double	2
Twin	1
Single	
Bed Size	**Qty**
Super King	1
King	
Queen	1
Double	
Single	
Bathrooms	**Qty**
Ensuite	1
Private	
Guest Share	1

 Bed & Breakfast
Boutique Accommodation

Features & Attractions

- *Outstanding lake views*
- *Excellent walking tracks*
- *Excellent choice of restaurants*
- *Christchurch/Queenstown, 3 hr. drive*
- *Fishing*
- *Round hill ski field*
- *Amazing clear skies*
- *Generous cooked breakfast*

Treat yourself to Tekapo. Just three hours from Christchurch and three hours from Queenstown, Lake Tekapo is one of New Zealand's most celebrated beauty spots. The ever-changing colours of the lake with snow capped mountains beyond draw artists and photographers from around the world every season.

Take time to relax at **Tekapo House**, with stunning views from almost every room and hearty breakfasts to start your day. Enjoy warmth, comfort and home-style hospitality. Jenny and Peter know the area well and can advise on all local attractions. At Lake Tekapo you can fish, hike, bird-watch, horse-trek, take scenic flights over the Alps, and ski and skate in winter. Or simply take in the beauty of the environment. Treat yourself to memories at **Tekapo House**.

HEARTLAND LODGE

19 North West Arch, Twizel, South Canterbury
Ph (03) 435 0008, Mobile 027-341 8943
email: heartlandlodge@xtra.co.nz
www.heartland-lodge.co.nz

Features & Attractions
- *Mountain views from all rooms*
- *Self-catering option*
- *Peaceful, rural setting*
- *Fly fishing*
- *Walks & bike rides*
- *Dinner available*

 Hosted Accommodation B&B and Self-contained Apartment

	Double	$160-290
$	Single	$160-250
	Child	–

H eartland Lodge is a purpose-built homestay forty minutes from the Aoraki Mount Cook World Heritage Park. Large guest rooms feature full size ensuite bathrooms with spa baths. We are minutes from the Twizel town centre and its services and restaurants. Mary and Jim are a fund of local knowledge and will help you plan activities and further travel. Dinner is available, made from fresh, local produce and special diets can be catered for. Self-catering option in self-contained apartment.

Bedrooms	Qty
Double	4
Twin	4
Single	4
Bed Size	**Qty**
Super King	3
King	
Queen	1
Long/Single	6
Bathrooms	**Qty**
Ensuite	4
Private	
Guest Share	

PINEGROVE COTTAGE

29 North West Arch, Twizel
Ph (03) 435 0430, Mobile 021-464 726
email: aljohpinegrove@hotmail.com
www.charmingaccommodation.co.nz

Features & Attractions
- *Extensive tranquil garden & pond*
- *Mountain & tree views*
- *Fishing, walks & scenic flights*
- *2 self-contained, spacious units*
- *Relaxing outdoor & BBQ area*
- *45 min. to Mt Cook / Aoraki*

 Bed & Breakfast Self-contained Cottage Units

	Double	$140-160
$	Single	$100
	Child	$10-20

P inegrove Cottage is situated in a sunny, tranquil location with alpine views. In the evenings the native birds come down to the pond. You can sit quietly by the water's edge to observe them. Feel free to wander through the garden and find a secluded spot to relax and contemplate.

We look forward to welcoming you to make your stay enjoyable and relaxing. Each cottage unit has 2 bedrooms, fully equipped kitchen, laundry, bathroom, living area with heat pump and outdoor area with BBQ.
A continental hamper breakfast with home-made goodies is included in the tariff.

Bedrooms	Qty
Double	2
Twin	2
Single	
Bed Size	**Qty**
King	
Queen	2
Double	1
Single	2
Bathrooms	**Qty**
Ensuite	
Private	2
Guest Share	

242

MATAGOURI COTTAGE

37 Elizabeth Street, Lake Hawea
Ph (03) 443 1987
email: info@matagouricottage.co.nz
www.matagouricottage.co.nz

Tariff : N.Z. Dollars	
Double	$140-170
Single	$95-120
Child	neg

Bedrooms	Qty
Double	1
Twin/Double	1
Single	

Bed Size	Qty
Super King	
King	
Queen	2
Double	
Single	1

Bathrooms	Qty
Ensuite	2
Private	
Guest Share	

Bed & Breakfast Homestay

Features & Attractions

- *Home away from home*
- *Secluded location*
- *Short walk to café and hotel*
- *5 min. walk to lake*
- *Relax on the verandah*
- *Dinner by arrangement*
- *Full breakfast*
- *17km to Wanaka*

Judith and Ian welcome you to charming **Matagouri Cottage**, which is nestled in trees in a tranquil part of Lake Hawea village. Judith has come back to the district where she was raised on a sheep station. Ian trained as a quantity surveyor and has lived in Hong Kong and also in England where he was involved in the running of a B & B. He's lived in New Zealand since 1987. **Matagouri Cottage**, apart from the fact of its peaceful location, is the centre of an area famed for its diversity. Ski fields abound, mountains and lakes with their immense opportunities are a great attraction and there is a vibrant wine growing industry virtually on the doorstep. **Matagouri Cottage** has two charmingly appointed ensuite bedrooms and all the comforts of a New Zealand country home including an open fire in the sitting room and wood burner in the kitchen/dining room.

AVALANCHE BED & BREAKFAST

74 Bill's Way, Rippon Lea, Wanaka
Ph (03) 443 6665, Fax 443 6701
Mobile 027-633 2364
 email: stay@wanakabedandbreakfast.com
www.wanakabedandbreakfast.com

Features & Attractions

- *Spacious private studio*
- *Lovely peaceful garden*
- *Short walk to restaurants*
- *Delicious home baking*
- *Close to lake & walking tracks*
- *Stunning rural & mountain views*

Bed & Breakfast / Self-contained				Double	$165-180
				Single	$160
				Child	$30

Bedrooms	Qty
Double	3
Twin	1
Single	

Bed Size	Qty
King	
Queen	2
Double	1
Single	3

Bathrooms	Qty
Ensuite	1
Private	
Guest Share	1

Avalanche B&B has spectacular views over farmland to the mountains. Admire Mt **Avalanche** and its glacier from your spacious, private self-contained studio. Relax in the lovely, peaceful garden setting. Delicious continental breakfast supplies and home baking are provided each day. Complimentary bikes, wireless internet and laundry facilities are also available. We are 2.5 km from the centre of town by the famous Rippon Vineyard, near three ski fields and close to scenic walking tracks. Enjoy staying within 10 minutes walk to the lake and two quality restaurants. We offer warm hospitality in our comfortable home and are happy to help with planning any activities in this wonderful environment. We have a small friendly dog, Roxy, and an adventurous cat, Tiggy.

Charming **Places to Stay** in New Zealand

"Superb! ...independent travellers, whether from overseas or locals, should never travel New Zealand without a copy of this guide..."

Colin Moore, NZ Herald.

ALPINE VIEW LODGE
23 Studholme Road South, Wanaka
Ph (03) 443 7111, Fax (03) 443 1723
Mobile 021-650 385
email: stay@alpineviewlodge.co.nz
www.alpineviewlodge.co.nz

Tariff : N.Z. Dollars	
Double	$160-180
Single	$140-160
Child	

Bedrooms	Qty
Double	
Twin	1
Single	
Bed Size	Qty
Super King	
King/Singles	2
Queen	2
Double	
Single	
Bathrooms	Qty
Ensuite	3
Private	1
Guest Share	

**Bed & Breakfast
Self-contained Accommodation**

Features & Attractions

- *Spectacular mountain views*
- *Quiet & peaceful setting*
- *Complimentary wireless internet*
- *Genuine Kiwi Hospitality*
- *Private patio or deck*
- *Own private BBQ's*
- *Close to 4 ski fields*
- *B&B or self cater*

Set on 4 scenic acres with stunning mountain views, **Alpine View Lodge** offers you something unique and special. Just minutes from the lake and hustle and bustle of town, Alpine View has a range of self-catering and bed and breakfast options that are specious, warm, and private.

With such a peaceful and quiet location many of our guests just do not want to leave. Michele and Craig pride themselves on their role as hosts and will happily share their local knowledge of the area and the activities on hand to make the most of your stay. **Alpine View Lodge** is the perfect place to enjoy a slice of paradise in the South Island's Southern Lakes, while experiencing authentic and genuine kiwi hospitality. We look forward to sharing our slice of paradise with you.

ATHERTON HOUSE

3 Atherton Place, Wanaka
Ph/Fax (03) 443 8343, Mobile 027-228 1982
email: roy.kate@xtra.co.nz
www.atherton.co.nz

Tariff : N.Z. Dollars	
Double	$200-250
Single	$150-175
Child	

Bedrooms	Qty
Double	2
Queen	
Single	
Bed Size	**Qty**
Super King	
King/Single	1
Queen	1
Double	
Single	2
Bathrooms	**Qty**
Ensuite	2
Private	
Guest Share	

 Luxury Lakeside Accommodation

Features & Attractions

- *Stunning lake and mountain views*
- *Quiet and peaceful*
- *Lakeside walk to township*
- *Complimentry aperitifs*
- *Wi Fi Internet available*
- *Free laundry facilities*
- *Generous breakfast included*
- *Dinner available with hosts*

Welcome to our home offering luxurious comfort and warm Kiwi hospitality, set in an acre of lawns and gardens on the shores of beautiful Lake Wanaka. Visitors can unwind in their own spacious and tastefully appointed private wing, which opens out to a peaceful courtyard and landscaped grounds running down to the lake. Our guests are welcome to share our living areas with its collections of antiques and New Zealand art or just relax in their own private lounge with tea/coffee facilities, Sky TV, a New Zealand library and writing desk. Enjoy the lakeside walk to the township accessible from our home.

After extensive experience hosting farm-stays we built **Atherton House** to provide tranquil and comfortable surroundings perfect for relaxing and enjoying the views. We enjoy art, antiques, travel, all sports especially golf, good food and wine, meeting and helping guests experience our wonderful part of the world.

246

BEACONFIELD B&B

251 Beacon Point Road, Wanaka
Ph (03) 443 2737, Mobile 021-150 5760
email: mikerackley@xtra.co.nz
www.beaconfieldbandb.co.nz

Tariff : N.Z. Dollars	
Double	$200-225
Single	$185
Child	$20-50

Bedrooms	Qty
Double	2
Twin	
Single	1
Bed Size	Qty
Super King	
King	
Queen	2
Double	
Single	1
Bathrooms	Qty
Ensuite	2
Private	
Guest Share	

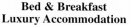
**Bed & Breakfast
Luxury Accommodation**

Features & Attractions

• *Private and tranquil*
• *Purpose built B&B*
• *Delicious, healthy breakfast*
• *Breathtaking lake & mountain views*
• *Warm friendly hospitality*
• *Well travelled hosts*
• *Complimentary refreshments*
• *Off street parking*

Welcome to our new Architect designed home set on an acre amidst a boutique vineyard and with breathtaking lake and mountain views. We invite you to share our Kiwi hospitality and local knowledge. Your spacious guest room with ensuite has French doors to a sunny veranda with stunning views. You will never tire of the beauty and tranquillity. Share our interests of food, wine, music, local art, antiques, travel and sports. Carla is a nurse and Michael was a lawyer and hospital manager. We are both widely travelled and have lived in UK, US, and Australia. A gourmet breakfast with home baking, and refreshments are included. Enjoy a glass of our **Beaconfield Estate** pinot noir. Laundry and email facilities are available as is our home cinema.

COLLINSONS COTTAGE
67 Manuka Crest, Wanaka
Ph (03) 443 7089, Fax (03) 443 7088
Mobile 027-443 0180
email: stay@collinsonscottage.co.nz
www.collinsonscottage.co.nz

Features & Attractions

- *Warm hospitality*
- *Wireless available*
- *Off-street parking*
- *Garden setting*
- *Painting gallery*
- *Golf experience*

Homestay Bed & Breakfast
SC. Studio & Apartment

Double	$140
Single	$100
Studio	$150

Bedrooms	Qty
Double	1
Twin	1
Single	
Bed Size	**Qty**
King	
Queen	1
Double	
Single	2
Bathrooms	**Qty**
Ensuite	
Private	1
Guest Share	

Your hosts Brian and Susanne welcome you to our relaxing home and garden. Situated minutes from the town centre with thirty odd restaurants at your disposal. A quiet walk around our large garden will entice your camera and with a painting gallery to view local scenery. All the perks of home are enjoyed at the Collinsons - tea/coffee making facilities with filtered water on tap, plus television in the Jasmine bedroom, and a secluded hideaway courtyard to enjoy in the summer evenings. Our interests are gardening, painting, sport and meeting people. Our passion is golf. The kids are gone and only our cat (Ping) is in residence. You may arrive as a guest but hopefully you will leave as friends having enjoyed all that Wanaka has to offer.

Collinson's Cottage

Lake Wanaka

Wanaka Township

PEAK - SPORTCHALET
36 Hunter Crescent, Wanaka
Ph (03) 443 6990
email: stay@peak-sportchalet.co.nz
www.peak-sportchalet.co.nz

Features & Attractions

- *High quality standard*
- *Fully equipped kitchen*
- *In-house massages*
- *Wireless/broadband internet*
- *Close to lake & walking tracks*
- *Drying room/ski storage*

Bed & Breakfast
Self-contained Chalet

Double	$120-175
Single	$100-120
Child	neg

Bedrooms	Qty
Double	2
Twin	1
Single	1
Bed Size	**Qty**
Super King	1
Queen	1
Double	
King/Single	2
Bathrooms	**Qty**
Ensuite	2
Private	1
Guest Share	

Welcome to **Peak-Sportchalet**, self-contained Chalet or Studio with kitchenette. Experience hospitality and high quality in a quiet area with mountain views, close to lakeside walking tracks. Enjoy fine furniture, bathrooms with underfloor heating, flatscreen TV, DVD and sound system in the lounge, WiFi access from all rooms. Sliding doors open onto private sundecks with great mountain views.

Awake refreshed on supreme quality beds. Our luxury Chalet can be converted into a 1- or 2-bedroom unit, sleeping up to 6 guests, and has fully equipped kitchen. A logfire rounds up the special alpine experience for you. In-house massages available. Breakfast buffet option with homemade goods in front of an open fire. We cater for special diets. Certified environmentally friendly accommodation.

Hunter Cres

Aubrey Rd

Peak - Sportchalet

Lake Wanaka

To Cromwell

WANAKA

LAKE WANAKA HOMESTAY

85 Warren Street, Wanaka
Ph (03) 443 7995, Fax (03) 443 7945
email: wanakahomestay@xtra.co.nz
www.lakewanakahomestay.co.nz

Tariff : N.Z. Dollars	
Double	$130-140
Single	$100
Child	-

Bedrooms	Qty
Double	2
Twin	
Single	
Bed Size	**Qty**
Super King	
King	
Queen	
Double	2
Single	
Bathrooms	**Qty**
Ensuite	
Private	1
Guest Share	1

**Homestay
Bed & Breakfast**

Features & Attractions

- *5 minutes town centre*
- *Relaxing garden setting*
- *Wireless internet*
- *Lake mountain views*
- *Private off street parking*
- *Full breakfast*
- *Friendly, helpful hosts*
- *Book your trips*

To Hawea
Lake Wanaka
Helwick St
Ardmore St
McDougall St
Warren St
Lake Wanaka Homestay
To Queenstown

Relax and soak up the breathtaking views of **Lake Wanaka Homestay**. Enjoy the very best in southern hospitality with your hosts Peter & Gailie. With over 20 years experience in Homestay and Bed & Breakfast we understand your needs and welcome you to our home. **Lake Wanaka Homestay** is a genuine home away from home ideally centrally situated, overlooking the lake and just 5 minutes walk to shops, restaurants and lake. Relax in our living area and patio, soak up the 180 degree lake and mountain views, Free WiFi access, complimentary tea, coffee, home baking anytime, continental and full cooked breakfast all included in price, private off street parking, two warm comfortable bedrooms, electric blankets and heaters in rooms. Share our home and we will share our passion

for fishing, golf, skiing, gardening and the great outdoors paradise we live in. Take time to enjoy the many roses in our garden and we will ensure you of a wonderful stay.

ROCKWOOD BED & BREAKFAST
6 Waimana Place, Wanaka
Ph (03) 443 7550, Mobile 027-247 4590
email: don.sal@xtra.co.nz
www.rockwoodwanaka.co.nz

Tariff : N.Z. Dollars	
Double	$160-210
Single	$150
Child	½ price

Bedrooms	Qty
Double	2
Twin	
Single	
Bed Size	**Qty**
Super King/Twin	1
King	
Queen	1
Double	
Single	
Bathrooms	**Qty**
Ensuite	1
Private	1
Guest Share	

**Homestay
Bed & Breakfast**

Features & Attractions

- *Close to skifields*
- *Wireless broadband internet*
- *Artist's residence*
- *3kms from town*
- *Mountain bikes & kayak available*
- *Off street parking*
- *Laundry facilities available*
- *Delicious breakfasts*

Sixteen years ago Sally and Don arrived in Wanaka and built their retirement home on a weed infested and wind battered block of land near the lake. Today it sits sheltered among mature trees and an established private garden with lovely dry stone walls and places to relax away from the crowds. Don flew ski planes and became an airline pilot, then he and Sally had a mixed-cropping and sheep farm before retiring to this idyllic spot with gorgeous mountain views and access to some of the best fishing and cycling/walking tracks in the world. Two bikes and a kayak are available for guests to use and three ski fields are close by. As there are so many pursuits and attractions, guests are given a warm welcome and help in deciding where to go or the option to just 'chill out' to make their holiday a very special one.

STUARTS HOMESTAY B&B

5 Mansor Court, Cromwell
Ph (03) 445 3636, Fax (03) 445 3617
Mobile 027-252 9823
email: ian.elaine@xtra.co.nz
www.stuartshomestaybandb.co.nz

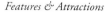

Features & Attractions

- *Dinner by arrangement*
- *Golf, fishing, walks, boating*
- *Wanaka & Queenstown 45 min*
- *Off-street parking*
- *Wine & gold trails*
- *Quiet garden setting*

$	Double	$110-130
	Single	$60-70
	Child	

**Homestay
Bed & Breakfast**

Bedrooms	Qty
Double	2
Twin	1
Single	
Bed Size	**Qty**
King	
Queen	2
Double	
Single	2
Bathrooms	**Qty**
Ensuite	1
Private	
Guest Share	1

Welcome to **Stuarts Homestay** which is situated within walking distance of most of Cromwell's amenities. We are semi-retired Southland farmers who have hosted for over twenty years. We enjoy sharing our modern sunny home and garden with visitors and a friendly stay is assured.

Have tea, coffee and homemade baking available at all times. Share dinner with us (prior booking please) or just Bed & Breakfast (full or continental).

We are also happy to transport you to and from buses.

Cromwell is a quiet and relaxed town which is known for historic gold diggings, vineyards, orchards, trout fishing, boating and walks, with Wanaka and Queenstown forty-five minutes away.

ARGYLL ON CLYDE

1 Annan Street, Clyde
Ph/Fax (03) 449 3268, Mobile 027-431 8241
email: argyllonclyde@yahoo.co.nz
www.argyllonclyde.co.nz

Features & Attractions

- *Central Otago Wine Trail*
- *Historic gold-mining town*
- *Relax in the spa*
- *Central Otago Rail Trail*
- *Fishing, golf, walks*
- *Warm, friendly hospitality*

$	Double	$120-160
	Single	$100-130
	Child	neg

**Homestay
Bed & Breakfast**

Bedrooms	Qty
Double	2
Twin	1
Single	1
Bed Size	**Qty**
King	
Queen	2
Double	
Single	2
Bathrooms	Qty
Ensuite	1
Private	1
Guest Share	1

Alan and Trish welcome you to their new modern home situated in the historic gold-mining town of Clyde and overlooking the Clyde Golf Course and Dunstan mountains.

Your friendly hosts are ex-farmers who enjoy meeting people, walking, cycling, golfing and fishing. They will make your stay a memorable one, pampering you with exquisite accommodation and cuisine.

Relax in the spa, and enjoy the comforable beds and the delicious cooked breakfast.

A friendly place to rest at the beginning or the end of the Central Otago Rail Trail.

HARTLEY HOMESTEAD BOUTIQUE B&B
23 Pyke Street, Clyde
Ph (03) 449 3307, Mobile 027-286 0438
e-mail: info@hartleyhomestead.co.nz
www.hartleyhomestead.co.nz

Features & Attractions
- *Guest lounge with library & Sky TV*
- *Private surroundings*
- *Wireless broadband*
- *Luxurious beds and linen*
- *Close to start/finish of Rail Trail*
- *Hot tub*

 Delightful Boutique Bed & Breakfast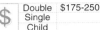

Double	$175-250	
Single		
Child		

Hartley Homestead Boutique Bed & Breakfast is a grand 1900s mud brick homestead surrounded by almost an acre of lawns and mature gardens on the banks of the picturesque Clutha River. A short stroll from restaurants, cafés and bars of the historic gold mining township of Clyde and within walking distance of the Otago Central Rail Trail, **Hartley Homestead** is the ideal base for spending time exploring Central Otago.

There are two beautifully appointed bedrooms with guest lounge in the homestead and a private super-king bed unit in the grounds. Join us, along with Mollie, our border collie, for a glass of local wine and cheeses or relax in the hot tub overlooking our pinot noir vines. **Hartley Homestead** is 15 minutes drive from Cromwell, one hour from Queenstown and Wanaka and two and a half hours from Dunedin.

Bedrooms	Qty
Double	3
Twin	
Single	
Bed Size	**Qty**
Super King	2
King	1
Double	
Single	
Bathrooms	**Qty**
Family Share	1
Private	2
Guest Share	

QUAIL ROCK
BED & BREAKFAST ACCOMMODATION
5 Fairway Drive, Alexandra, Central Otago
Ph (03) 448 7224, Fax (03) 448 5343
Mobile 021-259 5083 or 021-138 1383
e-mail: robyn@quailrock.co.nz
www.quailrock.co.nz

Features & Attractions
- *Dinner by arrangement*
- *Private guest entrance*
- *Breathtaking views*
- *Central Otago Rail Trail*
- *Handy to walking tracks*
- *Wine & gold trails*

Homestay Bed & Breakfast

Double	$150-180	
Single	$100-130	
Child	n/a	

Geoff and Robyn welcome you to **Quail Rock**. Come and relax in our home surroundings with lovely views overlooking the township and the mighty Clutha river and as far as the eye can see over the iconic Central Otago countryside. Our private guest wing has its own entrance and has been built for comfort surrounded by modern furnishings and local art and stunning views. You can choose from two rooms, queen bed with ensuite and French doors leading to the garden, or twin room with two king singles, private bathroom. Enjoy a tasty breakfast, fresh fruit available from our own orchard. **Quail Rock** is the perfect place to stay while exploring the delights of the Dunstan region. We will collect and deliver you and bikes to the Clyde end of the Rail Trail. We are within walking distance to the centre of town.

Bedrooms	Qty
Double	1
Twin	1
Single	
Bed Size	**Qty**
King	
Queen	1
Double	
King/Single	1
Bathrooms	**Qty**
Ensuite	1
Private	1
Guest Share	

BERNSLEIGH

21 Bracken Street, Arrowtown
Ph (03) 442 1550, Fax (03) 442 1540
Mobile 021-969 610
email: lindapeek@xtra.co.nz
www.charmingaccommodation.co.nz

Features & Attractions

- *Peaceful, private setting*
- *Southern hospitality*
- *Magnificent scenery*
- *Golf courses nearby*
- *Close to ski fields*
- *Near award winning wineries*

$	Double	$170
	Single	$130
	Child	neg

Homestay
Bed & Breakfast

Bedrooms	Qty
Double	2
Twin	1
Single	
Bed Size	**Qty**
King	
Queen	2
Double	
Single	2
Bathrooms	**Qty**
Ensuite	1
Private	
Guest Share	1

Welcome to our modern, comfortable home situated in a peaceful location overlooking world-class golf courses. Enjoy the panoramic views of mountain and rural scenes. Private entry leads to your tastefully furnished rooms, which are equipped with all facilities including robes and hair-dryers. **Bernsleigh** offers a sunny, private courtyard and a cosy indoor atmosphere. Relax in the spa bath or admire the night sky in the outdoor spa. Wireless internet, email, fax, laundry facilities are available along with assistance with further activity/sightseeing planning. Take a short walk to a range of cafés and restaurants. A stay at **Bernsleigh** will be the highlight of your visit to historic Arrowtown, where you will enjoy the warm hospitality of David and Linda as they open their home to you.

LAVENDER TERRACE

9a Fox's Terrace, Arrowtown
Ph (03) 442 1186, Mobile 027-378 3473
email: judy@lavenderterrace.co.nz
www.lavenderterrace.co.nz

Features & Attractions

- *Private guest entrance*
- *Peaceful town location*
- *20 minutes to Queenstown*
- *Great base for activities*
- *Wineries, golfing nearby*
- *Friendly & relaxed*

$	Double	$130
	Single	$100
	Child	

Delightful Cottage
Bed & Breakfast

Bedrooms	Qty
Double	1
Twin	
Single	
Bed Size	**Qty**
King	
Queen	1
Double	
Single	
Bathrooms	**Qty**
Ensuite	1
Private	
Guest Share	

A warm welcome awaits you at **Lavender Terrace** in historic Arrowtown. We are surrounded by mountains, walking trails, golf courses, ski fields, vineyards, artist galleries and breath-taking scenery. Town centre with restaurants, shops, quaint cafes and a cinema/bookstore is an easy 10 minutes stroll. The guest bedroom has French doors opening to the garden. Quality linens and a comfortable bed ensure a warm, luxurious sleep. Relax in the garden or in the cosy guest lounge with coffee/tea, biscuits, TV, fridge. Enjoy breakfast in the sunny breakfast room or in the garden. Complimentary wireless internet, laundry. Our interests include travel, hiking and service dog training. If you'd like, you can meet the mobility assistance dog we are currently raising.

WESTRANGE B&B
80 Cotter Avenue, Arrowtown
Ph (03) 442 1280, Fax (03) 442 1210
Mobile 027-436 1661
email: ijchamberlain@xtra.co.nz
www.charmingaccommodation.co.nz

Features & Attractions
- *Self contained apartment*
- *Beautiful views*
- *Close to wineries*
- *Historic Arrowtown*
- *Golf courses nearby*
- *Walking distance to restaurants*

 Self-contained Bed & Breakfast

Double	$150
Single	$100
Child	

Bedrooms	Qty
Double	1
Twin	
Single	
Bed Size	**Qty**
King	
Queen	1
Double	
Single	
Bathrooms	**Qty**
Ensuite	
Private	1
Guest Share	

Our luxurious new fully, self contained apartment has a rural outlook close to skifields, golf courses and wineries and superb views over the Wakatipu basin to the surrounding mountains. The centrally heated apartment has its own entrance, bedroom, lounge with TV & DVD, kitchenette, and bathroom with hairdryer.

A continental breakfast is provided. Off street parking. Fifteen minutes walk to town centre, twenty minutes drive to Queenstown.

Margaret enjoys meeting people and will do all she can to make your stay memorable.

WILLOWBY DOWNS
792 Malaghans Road, Queenstown
Ph (03) 442 1714, Fax (03) 442 1887
Mobile 027-222 0964
email: willowbydowns@xtra.co.nz
 www.willowbydowns.co.nz

Features & Attractions
- *Pick up airport or coaches*
- *Real southern hospitality.*
- *Limousine tours arranged*
- *Close to ski fields*
- *Golf courses nearby*
- *15 min to Queenstown*

 Homestay Bed & Breakfast

Double	$150
Single	$100
Child	neg

Bedrooms	Qty
Double	3
Twin	
Single	
Bed Size	**Qty**
King	
Queen	1
Double	
King/Single	2
Bathrooms	**Qty**
Ensuite	2
Private	
Guest Share	1

With Pam and David you are assured of a genuinely warm and friendly welcome, ex hoteliers they are passionate and practiced in the art of southern hospitality. Our home is off Malaghans Road, 500 metres down a driveway and approximately 5 km from the historic goldmining town of Arrowtown passing Millbrook Resort on the way. This B&B Homestay has features that will make you feel at home. With a coffee or tea on your arrival, you can relax in this warm and sunny home environment. **Willowby Downs** has lovely, well appointed guest rooms, electric blankets, TV, laundry options available, with the guests welcome to use the email, fax and telephone facilities. You have the choice of two master bedrooms with elevated views of Coronet Peak and the surrounding area. Pam and David are able to arrange any extra tours or special events you may require.

WILLOWBROOK B&B AND COTTAGES

Malaghans Road, Queenstown
Ph (03) 442 1773, Fax (03) 442 1780
Mobile 027-451 6739
email: info@willowbrook.net.nz
www.willowbrook.net.nz

Features & Attractions

- *Scenic, rural location*
- *Golf courses & vineyards*
- *Millbrook Resort - 3 mins*
- *Door to ski lift - 15 mins*
- *Guest lounge, open fire*
- *Free email & internet*

	Double	$165-185
	Single	$135-145
	Child	

 Rural Bed & Breakfast
Self-contained Accommodation

Bedrooms	Qty
Double	4
Twin	3
Single	
Bed Size	**Qty**
Super King	2
Queen	2
Double	
Single	8
Bathrooms	**Qty**
Ensuite	5
Private	1
Guest Share	

Willowbrook offers B&B and self-catering accommodation in an idyllic rural setting below Coronet Peak only 15 minutes from Queenstown. 4 acres of mature garden contain a tennis court (rackets available), a luxurious spa pool and some friendly sheep. The **Main House (B&B)** has double rooms with ensuite/private bathroom and guest lounge with open fire and complimentary email facilities. The **Barn (s/c)** is in a studio apartment style and has an adjoining **Annex** available for extra members of the same party. The **Cottage (s/c)** is a delightful 2 bedroom cottage with full kitchen/laundry facilities. All have wireless broadband for your laptop, Sky TV and BBQ on the deck. Expect a warm welcome from Trish and Tony, along with friendly advice and exceptional hospitality.

THE TURRET

712 Lake Hayes Arrow Junction Highway,
(SH6), Queenstown
Ph (03) 442 1107, Mobile 021-941 028
email: theturret@xtra.co.nz
www.theturret.co.nz

Tariff : N.Z. Dollars	
Double	$195-450
Single	$175-430
Child	$20

Bedrooms	Qty
Double	3
Twin	
Single	
Bed Size	**Qty**
Super King	
King	
Queen	2
Double	
King Single	1
Bathrooms	**Qty**
Ensuite	2
Private	1
Guest Share	

Bed & Breakfast
Luxury Accommodation

Features & Attractions

- *Close to wineries & golf courses*
- *Award winning garden*
- *Opposite the Lake Hayes Track*
- *Elegant cooked or continental breakfast*
- *Free Broardband access*
- *Close to four ski fields*
- *Stunning views*
- *Open log fire*

DIRECTIONS:
Overlooking Lake Hayes between
Queenstown and Arrowtown
on SH 6. Across the road from
the Lake Hayes Pavillion.

This distinctive lakeside retreat, ideally situated between Queenstown and historic Arrowtown, offers luxury accommodation with stunning garden, lake and mountain views. Privacy, comfort and relaxation with warm hospitality will truly make your stay a memorable one.

Two of the guest rooms have french doors opening out onto the terrace, while the Turret Suite has its own balcony.

All rooms have fabulous views and quality beds and linens. There is a separate dining room and a sitting room with a wood burning fire for guests' use.

Start your day with an elegant breakfast, served at a time convenient to you, then go out and experience all that Queenstown has to offer. Dinner is available upon request.

Larch Hill B&B/Homestay
16 Panners Way, Queenstown
Ph (03) 442 4811, Fax (03) 441 8882
Mobile 027-339 6483
email: info@larchhill.com
www.larchhill.com

Tariff : N.Z. Dollars	
Double	$160-230
Single	$140-200
Apartment	$260-340

Bedrooms	Qty
Double	2
Twin	1
Apartment	1
Bed Size	**Qty**
Super King	1
King	1
Queen	1
King/Single	2
Single	2
Bathrooms	**Qty**
Ensuite	2
Private	2
Guest Share	

Homestay/Bed & Breakfast
Superb Accommodation

Larch Hill
B & B

To Cromwell & Dunedin

Panners Way · Goldfield Heights

Sherwood Manor

Queenstown

Lake Wakatipu

Frankton

To Te Anau & Invercargill

DIRECTIONS:
From Frankton drive 2½ km on SH6A
(Frankton Rd) towards Queenstown.
At 'Sherwood Manor' turn right into
Goldfield Heights. Panners Way is 2nd left.
We are No. 16 at end of accessway.

Features & Attractions

- *Magnificent lake & mountain views*
- *Tranquil setting*
- *Generous breakfasts*
- *All rooms have their own bathroom*
- *Free wireless internet access*
- *In-room tea/coffee making*
- *Accredited tour booking agents*
- *S/c apartment available*

We offer you a warm welcome to **Larch Hill** in beautiful Queenstown. Featured in 'National Geographic Traveller' and Cathay Pacific's 'Discovery' magazines, **Larch Hill B&B/Homestay** is purpose built on an elevated site with all rooms and sundeck overlooking Lake Wakatipu and the surrounding spectacular mountains. Enjoy our comfortable, relaxing home with its panoramic views and sunny courtyard surrounded by cottage gardens. We are only a three minute drive from the centre of Queenstown and within walking distance of the lake. Public transport passes our street regularly. Our self-contained apartment is ideal for families or groups of four. Breakfasts are generous and include home-made bread, freshly baked croissants and pastries, fresh fruit salad, yoghurt, and freshly ground, percolated coffee. We encourage you to take advantage of our free booking service for Queenstown tours and activities, even before you arrive.

TURNER HEIGHTS TOWNHOUSES
14 Turner Street, Queenstown
Ph (03) 442 8383, Fax (03) 442 9494
e-mail: turnerh@queenstown.co.nz
www.turnerheights.co.nz

Features & Attractions

- *Fantastic views*
- *Close to town centre*
- *Quiet location*
- *Outdoor spa pools*
- *Wireless internet*
- *Golf courses & skiing nearby*

Self-contained Accommodation

	Double	$149-200
	Extra pp	$30
	Child	$15

Turner Heights Townhouses is located a two minute walk into the heart of Queenstown's vibrant centre yet is positioned for panoramic views and quiet location. We offer your choice of two bedroom townhouse, some with superior views and some with private spa pools. The townhouses will comfortably sleep four persons and the one bedroom apartments, two persons, with the option for extra persons in either if required. Each townhouse has it's own kitchen with full cooking facilities and washer and dryer. Barbecues are strategically located around the property and a communal spa pool is available for your pleasure. Your hosts are experts on all the activities and tours in the area and can even arrange these prior to your arrival.

Town Houses	Qty
Two Bedroom	9
One Bedroom	3
Single	
Bed Size	**Qty**
King	
Queen	12
Double	
Single	21
Bathrooms	**Qty**
Ensuite	
Private	12
Guest Share	

The 'Grand Old Lady' on Lake Wakatipu

PENCARROW

678 Frankton Road, Queenstown
Ph (03) 442 8938, Fax (03) 442 8974
Mobile 027-413 1567
email: info@pencarrow.net
www.pencarrow.net

Tariff : N.Z. Dollars	
Double	$595
Single	–
Child	–

Bedrooms	Qty
Double	4
Twin	
Single	
Bed Size	**Qty**
Super King	3
King	1
Queen	
Double	
Single	
Bathrooms	**Qty**
Ensuite	4
Private	
Guest Share	

**Luxury
Boutique Accommodation**

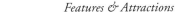

Features & Attractions

- *All rooms are suites*
- *Four acres of gardens*
- *Snooker, darts, horseshoes*
- *Spa pool, outdoor fireplace*
- *Stunning lake & mountain views*
- *Wineries, fishing, jetboat*
- *Skiing, golf, hiking*
- *Arrowtown, Glenorchy, Wanaka*

DIRECTIONS: From Cromwell, Invercargill
and Queenstown Airport take SH 6 (Frankton
Rd) towards Queenstown. 1 km past Shell
Service Station turn right at Greenstone Terrace
Apartments (two tone brown) and take the
middle drive up to Pencarrow on the hill.

Pencarrow is an all-suite country estate 2 miles from Queenstown offering 4 acres of elegance with stunning views of Lake Wakatipu and the Remarkables. Outdoors many sitting decks/patios, fireplace, spa pool, waterfall, tree, plant, and flower species. Indoors plenty of space and privacy. Guest lounge/bar with fireplace, concierge/library room, snooker/ games room, incredible views. Wine cellar, workout room, golf clubs, ski facilities, gold mining pans, horseshoes all free of charge. Suites have sitting room, writing desk, magazines/books, mini bar, tea/coffee facilities, homemade biscuits, fresh flowers, free WiFi (laptops provided), Sky (cable) television, DVD/Stereo/CD systems, direct-dial phones, iron/ironing board. En-suites equipped with oversized jet spa bath, separate shower, double vanity, heated towel rail, under-tile heating, hair dryer, bathrobes, slippers, guest amenity basket. Breakfast is a 4 course full on affair each morning at your personally requested time in the cosy dining room with antique fireplace and floor to ceiling bay windows. Welcome gift, afternoon "sweet in the suite", and drinks all included!

259

CORONET VIEW DELUXE BED & BREAKFAST AND APARTMENTS

30 Huff Street, Queenstown
Ph/Fax (03) 442 6766, Mobile 027-432 0895
email: stay@coronetview.com
www.coronetview.com

Tariff : N.Z. Dollars	
Double	$165-270
Single	$145-250
Child	$30

Bedrooms	Qty
Double	7
Twin	3
Single	
Bed Size	**Qty**
Super King	6
King	
Queen	1
Double	
King/Single	3
Bathrooms	**Qty**
Ensuite	10
Private	1
Guest Share	

   Deluxe Bed & Breakfast and Apartments A

Features & Attractions

- *Wireless internet facilities*
- *Full laundry facilities*
- *Barbeque and spa area*
- *Self-catering apartments*
- *Close to town centre*
- *Web booking service*
- *Guiding service & tours*

Centrally located just ten minutes walk from town, **Coronet View** enjoys superb views of Coronet Peak, The Remarkables and Lake Wakatipu. Beautifully appointed rooms offer every comfort in either hosted accommodation or private apartments. **Coronet View** offers ten luxurious guest rooms plus three fully self-contained private apartments. Guest common areas occasionally shared with gorgeous persian cats include elevated and spacious dining and living areas, outdoor decks, a sunny conservatory, outdoor barbeque, pool and jacuzzi area and computers with internet access.

Bed & Breakfast – A home away from home with true Kiwi hospitality. Most rooms feature super king beds and all have sheepskin electric blankets. Your hosts are knowledgeable local people who can recommend and book your activities at no extra cost.

Apartments – 1-6 bedroom on site apartments. Most configurations feature ensuites, super king beds, generous living areas, fully equipped kitchens and laundries.

TRELAWN PLACE

35 Watties Track, off Gorge Rd,
Arthurs Point, Queenstown
Ph (03) 442 9160, Fax (03) 442 9167
Mobile 021-101 5805
email: trelawn@ihug.co.nz
www.trelawnb-b.co.nz

Tariff : N.Z. Dollars	
Double	$275-400
Single	POA
Child	$65

Bedrooms	Qty
Double	5
Twin	4
Single	6
Bed Size	**Qty**
Super King	1
King	1
Queen	1
King/Single	3
Single	4
Bathrooms	**Qty**
Ensuite	2
Private	3
Guest Share	

Stunning Riverside Location

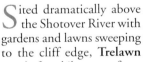

Features & Attractions

- *Unique location beside the Shotover*
- *Fantastic mountain views*
- *Broadband wireless laptop*
- *Outdoor jacuzzi, spa, guest laundry*
- *5 min from town centre*
- *Large private garden*
- *Wedding venue*
- *Walkway to river*

Sited dramatically above the Shotover River with gardens and lawns sweeping to the cliff edge, **Trelawn Place** is a superior country lodge only four kilometres from busy Queenstown. We have five comfortably appointed ensuite rooms, furnished with country chintz and antique style furniture. Our guest sitting room has an open fire and a well stocked library. Outdoors you will find quiet sitting areas and shady vine-covered verandahs. Generous cooked breakfast features home-made and grown produce. If you are missing your pets, a cat and friendly corgis will make you feel at home. A seventy two hour cancellation policy applies. Helpful information and bookings for all activities.

Three self-contained cottages, a honeymoon hideaway, with Juliet balconies, cosy fireside, and roses framing the door.

Rose 'n' Reel

89 Ben Loch Lane, Te Anau, Fiordland
Ph/Fax (03) 249 7582, Mobile 027-454 5723
email: rosenreel@xtra.co.nz
www.rosenreel.co.nz

Features & Attractions

- *Lake & mountain views*
- *Extensive garden*
- *Peaceful farm location*
- *Guided fishing available*
- *Feed tame deer*
- *Warm country hospitality*

DIRECTIONS:
Please phone or email for
bookings and easy directions.

**Deer Farm Bed & Breakfast
Self-contained Cabin**

Double	$120-130
Single	$75-100
Child	neg

Bedrooms	Qty
Double	2
Twin	
Single	1
Bed Size	**Qty**
King	
Queen	2
Double	1
King/Single	1
Bathrooms	**Qty**
Ensuite	
Private	1
Guest Share	1

Genuine Kiwi hospitality in a magic setting five minutes from Te Anau. Hand-feed tame fallow deer and meet our friendly cat and Meg the dog. Relax on the verandah of our fully self-contained cabin and enjoy watching deer with a magnificent lake and mountain backdrop. The two-room cabin has cooking facilities, refrigerator, microwave, television, one queen and one double bed plus bathroom. Our modern smoke-free home is set in an extensive garden and has two downstairs guest bedrooms. Lex is a keen fly fisherman and guide and is available for guiding on our beautiful local rivers. Lyn loves to garden and enjoys sharing her garden with guests. Fiordland is a special place and we will do all we can to make your time here memorable, including helping to plan and book your trips if you so wish.

New Zealand - a hiker's paradise.

WHITESTONES B&B

113 Pumphouse Road, Te Anau
Ph (03) 249 8279, Mobile 021-161 0853
email: info@whitestones.co.nz
www.whitestones.co.nz

Tariff : N.Z. Dollars	
Double	$240-280
Single	$200-240
Child	–

Bedrooms	Qty
Double	2
Twin	
Single	

Bed Size	Qty
Super King	
King	2
Queen	
Double	
Single	

Bathrooms	Qty
Ensuite	2
Private	
Guest Share	

  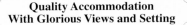

Quality Accommodation
With Glorious Views and Setting

Features & Attractions

- *Stunning mountain views*
- *Delicious full breakfasts*
- *Warm and friendly hospitality*
- *Quality accommodation*
- *Tranquility plus*
- *Private entrance*
- *Working deer farm*
- *Laundry facilities available*

Lake Te Anau — To Milford Sound — Te Anau — Whitestones B&B — Pumphouse Rd — Lynwood Rd — To Manapouri — To Mossburn — N

DIRECTIONS: Follow main SH 44. Turn right at Lynwood Road, turn left at Pumphouse Road. We are at 113.

Experience the comfort, tranquility and privacy of our purpose built guest area. We offer excellent accommodation on a working deer farm. Two private guest rooms and guest lounge area. All with their own entrances and deck areas. **Whitestones** has expansive mountain and countryside views from each room.

Both rooms are modern with King beds, electric blankets and heating, spacious bathrooms with under floor heating, mirror demisters, heated towel rails, lavender toiletries and luxury towels. We like to provide additional touches to make your stay enjoyable and memorable. Enjoy delicious homemade baking and other seasonal goodies with tea/coffee in the guest lounge. Choose from an extensive breakfast menu and/or continental breakfast at a time to suit you. We look forward to your stay.

ANTLER LODGE BED & BREAKFAST
44 Matai Street, Te Anau
Ph/Fax (03) 249 8188, Mobile 027-684 1385
email: antler.lodge@xtra.co.nz
www.antlerlodgeteanau.co.nz

Features & Attractions

- *Quality accommodation*
- *Close to restaurants & shops*
- *Trip bookings & pick ups*
- *2 fully self-contained units*
- *Continental breakfasts*
- *Mountain Views*

Bed & Breakfast Self-contained

	Double	$130-155
	Single	
	Child	

Antler Lodge B & B

Helen and Chris warmly welcome you to Te Anau. We offer the privacy, independence and relaxation of self contained units along with friendly helpful service. Our ground floor studio units have queen size beds, full kitchen facilities and ensuite. While our upstairs unit has its own entrance to an attractive dining area that includes a refrigerator and microwave, the spacious bedroom, featuring warm timber and mountain views, has a king size bed, a walk-in wardrobe and elegant ensuite. All our rooms have relaxing, comfortable furnishings with efficient heating and electric blankets and of course complimentary tea and coffee. Breakfast is provided in the rooms for guests to enjoy at their leisure.

We are looking forward to meeting you.

Bedrooms	Qty
Double	3
Twin	
Single	
Bed Size	**Qty**
King	1
Queen	2
Double	
Single	
Bathrooms	**Qty**
Ensuite	3
Private	
Guest Share	

BLUE RIDGE BED & BREAKFAST
15 Melland Place, Te Anau, Fiordland
Ph (03) 249 7740, Fax (03) 249 7340
Mobile 027-258 9877
email: info@blueridge.net.nz
www.blueridge.net.nz

Features & Attractions

- *Luxurious ensuite rooms*
- *Delicious full breakfast*
- *5mins walk to town centre*
- *Glorious mountain views*
- *Free broadband in rooms*
- *Hydrotherapy spa pool*

Boutique Accommodation & Studio Apartments

	Double	$225-275
	Single	$200-225
	Child	neg.

Blue Ridge

Phillip & Julia warmly welcome you to **Blue Ridge**. Our modern, sunny guest lodge containing 3 studio apartments is in a separate building from the main house. We also have one private suite of 2 rooms plus ensuite in our home. They have views of the Fiordland mountains and/or our lovely garden. We are often complimented on our tasteful decor and comfortable beds with feather duvets and electric blankets. All rooms have TV and DVD and modern tiled ensuite bathrooms with under-tile heating, heated towel rails and powerful showers. Organic lavender toiletries, hairdryers and robes are provided. A full gourmet breakfast is served in our dining room. Tea and coffee provisions, home baking, laundry service, high spec wireless internet and use of our heated spa pool are all complimentary. We have plenty of parking and storage and we able to book local activities and restaurants for you.

Bedrooms	Qty
Double	4
Twin	4
Single	4
Bed Size	**Qty**
King	3
Queen	1
Double	
Single	1
Bathrooms	**Qty**
Ensuite	4
Private	
Guest Share	

23 PATON

23 Paton Place, Te Anau
Ph/Fax (03) 249 9516, Mobile 027-680 5677
email: douglin@xtra.co.nz
www.charmingaccommodation.co.nz

Tariff : N.Z. Dollars	
Double	$140
Single	$120
Child	

Bedrooms	Qty
Double	1
Twin	1
Single	

Bed Size	Qty
Super King	
King	
Queen	1
Double	
Single	2

Bathrooms	Qty
Ensuite	
Private	1
Guest Share	

**Homestay
Bed & Breakfast**

Features & Attractions
- *Unimpeded mountain views*
- *Can book local trips*
- *Nearest fishing 300m*
- *Friendly helpful hosts*
- *Very peaceful secure setting*
- *Continental breakfast*
- *Lakeside walks*
- *Top outdoor/adventure destination*

We welcome guests to our warm sunny Te Anau home. We live within walking distance from Te Anau's restaurants and café's and offer you a very quiet and restful stay with uninterrupted views of the mountains and lake. There is a great veranda to relax on after a days travelling. We can help you plan your activities for your stay - some of the wonders of the world Milford Sound, Doubtful Sound and the Power House, Glow Worm caves, boat trips, kayaking, diving, great trout fishing rivers and several of the worlds greatest walks. We have an 18 hole golf course with magnificent vistas and good prices. Doug and Linda farmed in the area for 23 years so have a good knowledge of its attractions. Our interests include golf (Linda), lawn bowls (Doug) and back country horse trekking. You may meet Champ and Baldrick, our horses, various sheep and cattle and Grey the cat. We enjoy meeting people and being keen travellers we are aware of your requirements. Previous guests have found that at least two nights are necessary to enjoy this magnificent area properly.

COSY KIWI BED & BREAKFAST

186 Milford Road, Te Anau
Ph (03) 249 7475, Fax (03) 249 8471
email: info@cosykiwi.com
www.cosykiwi.com

Tourism Industry Association New Zealand

Features & Attractions

- *Breakfast buffet*
- *3 min. walk to town centre*
- *Immaculately clean*
- *Trip booking & pickup*
- *Email & fax facilities*
- *Off-street parking, laundry*

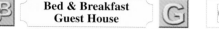

Bed & Breakfast Guest House

Double	$165-185
Single	$155-165
Extra person $45	

Cosy truly describes how you will feel within our warm modern Bed and Breakfast guesthouse. We provide privacy with comfort. Our quiet bedrooms are spacious, ensuited with top quality beds, flat screen televisions, individual heating and double glazed windows. Enjoy a sumptuous buffet breakfast of homemade breads, topped with homemade jams, marmalade, fresh fruit salad, dessert fruits, yoghurt, brewed coffee, special teas and our legendary pancakes sweet or savoury. We have a modern laundry, good off street parking and luggage storage for track walkers. Our warm guest lounge provides excellent space to relax, chat and a computer to access emails, we also have wifi available for guests with their own laptops. Relax outside on our sun-terrrace over looking the ever changing moods of the Murchison Mountains or stroll into the town centre to highly recommended restaurants (3 mins). We can recommend and book any sightseeing trips around Fiordland.

Bedrooms	Qty
Double	7
Twin	4
Single	7
Bed Size	**Qty**
Super King	1
King	3
Queen	3
Single	7
Bathrooms	**Qty**
Ensuite	7
Private	
Guest Share	

DUNLUCE BED & BREAKFAST

128 Aparima Drive, Te Anau, Fiordland
Ph (03) 249 7715, Fax (03) 249 7703
Mobile 027-330 2779
email: info@dunluce-fiordland.co.nz
www.dunluce-fiordland.co.nz

VISA
MasterCard

Features & Attractions

- *Private guest wing*
- *Luxurious ensuite rooms*
- *Contemporary styled home*
- *Lake and mountain views*
- *Laundry & wireless internet*
- *Delicious full breakfast*

DIRECTIONS: From Milford Rd turn left into Howden St and right into Aparima Dr. We are 300 mtres along Aparima Dr.

Bed & Breakfast Boutique Accommodation

Double	$230-295
Single	$205-270
Child	

Dunluce is a contemporary home which was architecturally designed and purpose built in 2005. We have a private guest wing of 4 ensuite rooms and a guest dining/lounge area. **Dunluce** has expansive views of Lake Te Anau and several mountain ranges from every room. All rooms are modern and uncluttered with king beds, electric blankets, heating TV/DVD. The ensuites have glass wall showers, underfloor heating, mirror demisters, organic lavender toiletries, hair dryers, robes and luxury towels. The Kepler deluxe room has a deep double soaking/spa bath. We provide many additional touches to make your stay memorable. We serve a delicious homemade buffet and also offer a breakfast menu of 3 cooked choices. There is a self serve tea/coffee in the dining room with home baking, fruit and complimentary wine. We have ample parking, wireless internet, storage and complimentary laundry. We can make bookings and give informed advice on local activities and dining.

Bedrooms	Qty
Double	4
Twin	
Single	
Bed Size	**Qty**
King	4
Queen	
Double	
Single	
Bathrooms	**Qty**
Ensuite	4
Private	
Guest Share	

266

HOUSE OF WOOD

44 Moana Crescent, Te Anau
Ph (03) 249 8404, Fax (03) 249 7676
Mobile 021-158 6686
email: houseofwood@xtra.co.nz
www.houseofwood.co.nz

Tariff : N.Z. Dollars	
Double	$135-155
Single	$115-135
Child	neg

Bedrooms	Qty
Double	3
Twin	1
Single	

Bed Size	Qty
Super King	1
King	
Queen	3
Double	
King/Single	2

Bathrooms	Qty
Ensuite	3
Private	1
Guest Share	

    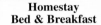

Homestay
Bed & Breakfast

Features & Attractions

- *Friendly and helpful hosts*
- *Town centre 2 min. walk*
- *Fishing, golf & tramping*
- *Hearty cooked breakfast*
- *Dinner by arrangement*
- *Fiordland World Heritage Park*
- *Mountain views*
- *Free wireless internet available*

We welcome you to our home, the **House of Wood**. Built of exotic timbers, it's conveniently located within two minutes' walk of our township with shops, restaurants, post office and cinema and a short walk to Lake Te Anau. Each room has comfortable beds, electric blanket, tea-making facilities, hairdryer, heater and outdoor table and chairs, so guests can admire the beautiful views from our balconies. We offer a delicious cooked breakfast and guests share a lounge. Dinner by arrangement. Our varied interests include golf, rowing, reading, gardening, fishing and boating. We can offer advice on tours available and can book them for you. For tourist trips you will be picked up from our gate. Two mountain bikes and luggage storage available. Laundromats nearby. We look forward to meeting you and sharing our slice of paradise. We would appreciate check-in after 2pm.

SHAKESPEARE HOUSE
10 Dusky Street, Te Anau
Ph (03) 249 7349, Fax (03) 249 7629
Mobile 027-225 1971
email: shakespearebnb@xtra.co.nz
www.shakespearehouse.co.nz

Features & Attractions

- *All ground floor units*
- *10 min walk to town centre*
- *Courtesy car*
- *Trip bookings & pick-up*
- *Continental & cooked breakfast*
- *Internet, payphone, wireless avail.*

**Guest House &
Self-contained Accommodation**

Double	$100-135
Single	$90-115
Child	$1-15

F iordland – the "Walking Capital" of the world – is right on your doorstep when you stay at **Shakespeare House**. Ray and Kylie extend a warm welcome to you and offer personal attention in a homely atmosphere. We are situated in a quiet residential area, yet are within walking distance of shops, lake, restaurants and attractions. Our units have their own private facilities, are warm and comfortable with tea/coffee, television and have the choice of king or twin beds. They open onto a sunny, relaxing conservatory where you may share your holiday experiences with other guests. We also have a two bedroom self-contained unit, which is popular with families or two couples travelling together. Our dining room catches the morning sun and has a lovely view of the mountains. Enjoy a substantial breakfast – either cooked from the menu or buffet-style continental. Good off-street parking, washing machine and dryers are available. We invite you to experience our hospitality.

Bedrooms	Qty
Double	4
Twin/Triple	3
Quad	1
Bed Size	Qty
Super King	2
King	4
Double	
King/Single	2
Bathrooms	Qty
Ensuite	8
Private	
Guest Share	

DIRECTIONS: Drive north on Lake Front Drive, carry on along Te Anau Terrace. Dusky Street is the last right turn before the boat harbour.

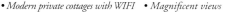

THE CROFT
Rapid 153, Milford Sound Road, Te Anau
Ph/Fax (03) 249 7393
Mobile 027-682 0061
email: jane@thecroft.co.nz
www.thecroft.co.nz

Features & Attractions

- *Modern private cottages with WIFI*
- *Tranquil surroundings*
- *Warm & friendly hosts*
- *Magnificent views*
- *On road to Milford Sound*
- *Small farm with sheep*

DIRECTIONS:
Follow the Te Anau-Milford Highway 94 for 3 km from Te Anau town centre. "**The Croft**" and "Bed & Breakfast" signs are at the gate. We are Rapid No. 153.

**Bed & Breakfast
Self-contained Accommodation**

Double	$160-195
Single	–
Child	–

W arm hospitality and quality accommodation are guaranteed at **The Croft**, a lifestyle farm, just two minutes from Te Anau on the Milford Sound Road. Our two modern self-contained cottages enjoy magnificent lake and mountain views, are set in large tranquil gardens. Timber ceilings, window seats, large ensuite bathrooms, elegant furnishings are some of the highlights of our two spacious cottages. Both have microwaves, refrigerators, CD/mini systems, DVDs and televisions. Enjoy a generous continental breakfast with Ross and Jane or have it served in your cottage at your leisure. We have a small flock of sheep and a cat called Kitty. Ross is a builder and Jane a past teacher. **The Croft** is an ideal base for all the many activities available in Fiordland. Sign at gate.

Bedrooms	Qty
Double	2
Twin	
Single	
Bed Size	Qty
King	
Queen	2
Double	
Single	1
Bathrooms	Qty
Ensuite	2
Private	
Guest Share	

LOCH VISTA B&B

454E Te Anau-Milford Highway, Te Anau
Ph (03) 249 7273, Fax (03) 249 7278
Mobile 027-455 9949
email: lochvista@xtra.co.nz
www.lochvista.co.nz

Tariff : N.Z. Dollars	
Double	$160-190
Single	$150-170
Child	

Bedrooms	Qty
Double	2
Twin	
Single	
Bed Size	**Qty**
Super King	
King	1
Queen	1
Double	
Single	
Bathrooms	**Qty**
Ensuite	2
Private	
Guest Share	

DIRECTIONS:
Travel along Milford Road 4.6 km
from the 80 km sign. Turn 1st right
after Sinclair Road and blue Lodge sign.
Travel 300m up the road,
turn right at the three letter boxes,
following driveway down to house.

Lakeside
Bed & Breakfast

Features & Attractions

- *Stunning mountain views*
- *Shops, cafés, bars - short drive*
- *Fishing & golfing*
- *Tramping & hiking*
- *On road to Milford Sound*
- *Overlooking Lake Te Anau*
- *Spectacular lake views*
- *Glowworm cave excursions*

Welcome to magical Fiordland. **Loch Vista** is situated on the Te Anau Milford highway just five kilometres from the town centre. **Loch Vista** is ideally positioned, overlooking Lake Te Anau and the stunning Murchison Mountains.

I have two rooms, one with king/twin bed and one with queen bed, both with ensuite, tea and coffee making facilities, refrigerator, television and hairdryer. French doors open onto the patio where you can sit and enjoy the spectacular views. Meet Mischief (my pet cat). Full cooked breakfast on request at $15 per person. Fiordland has a great deal to offer and I am more than happy to help my guests with any bookings to make their stay more relaxing.

269

CROWN LEA FARMSTAY

310 Gillespie Road, Te Anau
Ph/Fax (03) 249 8598, Mobile 021-168 0299
email: crownlea@farmstay.co.nz
www.crown-lea.com

Features & Attractions

- *Working sheep, cattle & deer farm*
- *Farmstyle dinners by arrangement*
- *Doubtful & Milford Sound day trips*
- *Farm tour available*
- *Local walking tracks*
- *Great fishing rivers*

 Farmstay

Double	$180
Single	$180
Child	

Bedrooms	Qty
Double	2
Twin	1
Single	
Bed Size	Qty
Super King	1
Queen	1
Double	
Single	2
Bathrooms	Qty
Ensuite	1
Private	2
Guest Share	

DIRECTIONS: Please phone for simple directions.

We warmly welcome you to **Crown Lea**, our 900 acre sheep, cattle and deer working farm, offering an informative farm tour, after 6pm, with spectacular views of Lake Manapouri, the Fiordland Mountains and Te Anau Basin. Following the farm tour, a traditional farmstyle dinner (NZ $40 per person) of home grown produce is served. Our large, modern family home has three bedrooms for guests, electric blankets on all beds, heaters in each room, ensuite and private bathrooms.

Crown Lea is within easy access of Doubtful and Milford Sounds, the glow worm caves, Milford and Kepler tracks or the superb fishing rivers in our area. We recommend at least two nights to enable relaxing days enjoying the Sounds, caves, tracks, sightseeing or fishing. Having travelled ourselves, we enjoy meeting guests from all parts of the world and we   look forward to meeting you.

Charming **Places to Stay** in New Zealand

"Simply the best B&B Guide I've come across anywhere. Superb choice of places, so easy to use, a delightful book. I eagerly recommend it to all travellers to New Zealand."

G. Wallis, Hampton, England

CATHEDRAL PEAKS B&B

44 Cathedral Drive, Manapouri, Fiordland
Ph (03) 249 6640, Fax (03) 249 6648
email: cathedralpeaks@ihug.co.nz
www.cathedralpeaks.com

Tariff : N.Z. Dollars	
Double	$200-250
Single	$200-220
Child	

Bedrooms	Qty
Double	3
Twin	
Single	
Bed Size	**Qty**
King/Twin	1
King	
Queen	1
Double	1
Single	
Bathrooms	**Qty**
Ensuite	3
Private	
Guest Share	

 Beautiful Lake Manapouri's Boutique Accommodation

VISA **MasterCard**

Features & Attractions

- *Smoke free*
- *Restaurant 3min. walk*
- *Spacious ensuite rooms*
- *Off-street parking*
- *Lake & mountain views*
- *Guest lounge/dining room*
- *Doubtful & Milford Sounds daytrips*
- *Fax, phone, computer & free internet*

Janice and Neal, your friendly hosts, warmly welcome you to share their recently built home. Take advantage of our lakefront location to relax and enjoy the majestic and stunning scenery from the comfort of your bedroom. Enjoy a continental or cooked breakfast in our guest shared lounge/dining room overlooking the lake. Rooms have tea/coffee making facilities, DVD, computer, free internet, iron and board, bathrobes, TV, heater, electric blanket, refrigerator and hairdryer. Looking towards the setting sun your view is rimmed with mountain peaks. Snow-capped in winter, unmarked by man's hand, their forested flanks lead your eyes to Lake Manapouri's edge. Forested islands blend into a silvered surface, which reflects mountain images, clouds, colours, stars, rainbows, the moon. Marvelous Manapouri, the mood ever changing, enchants – you may wish to never leave. 15 minutes drive to Lake Te Anau. 2 ½ hours drive to Milford Sound.15 minutes walk to the Doubtful Sound departure point.

HIGHWAY HOUSE
43 Lynn Street, Oamaru
Ph/Fax (03) 437 1066
email: breakfast@highwayhouse.co.nz
www.highwayhouse.co.nz

Features & Attractions

- *Historic Oamaru (stone)*
- *Harbour and blue penguins*
- *Idyllic rural scenery*

- *Free internet/email access*
- *English home/courtesy car*
- *French also spoken*

Traditional - Quality
King Beds and Full Breakfast

Double	$150-175
Single	$130-155
Child	neg

Bedrooms	Qty
Double	2
Twin	1
Single	
Bed Size	**Qty**
King	2
Queen	
Double	
Single	2
Bathrooms	**Qty**
Ensuite	1
Guest Share	1
Family Share	1

Highway House offers a very convenient location for the many attractions and dining facilities in Oamaru. It is easy to find from both the north and south (see map). This 1935 Arts and Crafts character house and garden have been redeveloped with professional interior design and horticultural expertise for the tourists' pleasure, comfort and convenience. Attention has been given to top-quality beds, large showers, internet access, garden seating and off-street parking, together with tasteful extras. We provide a cooked and/or a light Kiwi breakfast using appetizing and sustaining wholesome ingredients. Stephanie and Norman wish you to make the most of your stay in Oamaru and can assist with your travel plans.

So many attestations of quality and service.

GLEN DENDRON FARMSTAY

284 Breakneck Rd, Waianakarua, Oamaru
Ph/Fax (03) 439 5288, Mobile 021-615 227
email: stay@glendendronfarmstay.co.nz
www.glendendronfarmstay.co.nz

Tariff : N.Z. Dollars	
Double	$135-170
Single	$110-130
Child	$50

Bedrooms	Qty
Double	4
Twin	
Single	
Bed Size	Qty
Super King/Twin	2
King	
Queen	2
Double	
Single	
Bathrooms	Qty
Ensuite	2
Private	
Guest Share	1

DIRECTIONS:
Please phone for easy
directions.
Advance booking
recommended

Award winning Farmstay
With spectacular views

Features & Attractions

- *5 acre garden & views*
- *Feed sheep & alpacas*
- *Private golf course*
- *Bush walks, birds, waterfalls*
- *Penguin & seal colonies*
- *Moeraki Boulders nearby*
- *Wireless internet*
- *Dinner by arrangement*

Our modern award winning homestay is spectacularly sited on a hilltop with panoramic river valley and ocean views. Enjoy tranquillity and beauty when you stay in tastefully furnished bedrooms, two with ensuites. Explore the 5 acre garden and small farm. Feed sheep and alpacas, stroll through the forest or along the river, or play a round on our family's private 9-hole golf course. After a day exploring the delights of the area, join us for a three course meal with wine. We are keen gardeners, read widely and enjoy antiques. Anne is a floral designer and John a tree connoisseur. After a lifetime in large scale farming and forestry, before retiring to this 100 acre property, we now relish the opportunity to share our lifestyle with guests. With family living overseas, we travel frequently and have a great interest in other countries and cultures. An overnight stay is not enough to do justice to this area so plan to stay awhile! Attractions include Oamaru's historic architecture, heritage and fossil trails, beaches, seals, penguins and famous Moeraki Boulders. Take day trips to Mt Cook and Dunedin. We don't mind short notice!

BAYWATCH

Haven Street, Moeraki, Otago
Mobile 021-0233 2855
email: oceanbreezemoeraki@gmail.com
www.moerakioceanbreeze.co.nz

Tariff : N.Z. Dollars	
Double	$130
Single	
Child	

Bedrooms	Qty
Double	1
Twin	1
Single	
Bed Size	**Qty**
Super King	
King	
Queen	1
Double	
Single	2
Bathrooms	**Qty**
Ensuite	
Private	1
Guest Share	

 Spectacular Views of the Bay   VISA MasterCard

Features & Attractions

- *Spectacular sea & coastal views*
- *Great walking tracks around beaches*
- *5 min. drive to Moeraki Boulders*
- *Dolphins, seals & penguins close by*
- *Unspoilt fishing village*
- *Blue cod fishing charters avail.*
- *Close to Oamaru*
- *2 min. stroll to Fleurs Restaurant*

M oeraki is a unique, unspoilt fishing village which was once a thriving whaling station. It is now a restful place where you can relax and unwind and soak up the ambience.

To Oamaru & Christchurch
Moeraki Boulders
N
Moeraki Village
Baywatch
To Dunedin & Queenstown

The harbour is scattered with commercial, charter and pleasure boats. Charters can be arranged if required. Catch your own blue cod for dinner. The Moeraki Boulders are a five minute drive from the village

and the locals call them the eighth wonder of the world. The lighthouse is also a five minute drive, where yellow-eyed penguins can be seen coming in through the waves at dusk and calling to each other. Hector dolphins are regularly seen in the bay. Take a leisurely walk around the village, relax on your own deck, or enjoy the wonderful fresh fish straight from the boats at the world famous Fleurs Restaurant. Moeraki is a great place for a romantic getaway or a well deserved break.

BOUTIQUE BED & BREAKFAST

107 Jefferis Road, Waikouaiti, East Otago
Ph/Fax (03) 465 7239, Mobile 027-224 8212
email: info@boutiquebedandbreakfast.co.nz
www.boutiquebedandbreakfast.co.nz

Tariff : N.Z. Dollars	
Double	$160-190
Single	$160
Child	–

Bedrooms	Qty
Double	3
Twin	
Single	
Bed Size	Qty
Super King	
King	
Queen	3
Double	1
Single	
Bathrooms	Qty
Ensuite	3
Private	
Guest Share	

    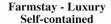

Farmstay - Luxury
Self-contained

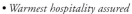

Features & Attractions

- *Warmest hospitality assured*
- *Home baking/sumptuous breakfast*
- *Complimentary deer farm tour*
- *Beautiful walks on reserves & beaches*
- *Ideal setting to relax*
- *Furnished for comfort & pleasure*
- *20 mins to Moeraki Boulders*
- *Surrounded by gardens & trees*

Indulge in tranquil garden surroundings as enjoyed by celebrity chef Rick Stein. Tastefully furnished rooms with ensuites, each with French doors opening on to verandas. Units separate from, but close to homestead are private and secure. Enjoy a hearty farm cooked breakfast in our homestead. Deer farm tour available. Tennis court on site. Close to two golf courses. A central location between Palmerston and Waikouaiti, (five minutes to each) with cafés, reserves and historic buildings. Make this your base to explore nature reserves with yellow eyed penguins, including the new ecosanctuary, Macraes gold mine, white sanded beaches, historic buildings and cafés and speciality shops. Five minutes from HW 85, gateway to Queenstown and Wanaka. Only twenty minutes to the famous Moeraki Boulders and Fleurs Restaurant. Thirty minutes to heritage city of Dunedin via beautiful coastal route. We endeavour to give our guests the best stay possible.

ATANUI
378 Heywards Point Road,
Port Chalmers, Dunedin
Ph (03) 482 1107
email: atanui@callsouth.net.nz
www.atanui.co.nz

Tariff : N.Z. Dollars	
Double	$150
Single	$120
Child	$60

Bedrooms	Qty
Double	1
Twin	1
Single	
Bed Size	**Qty**
Super King/Twin	1
King	
Queen	
Double	
Single	
Bathrooms	**Qty**
Ensuite	1
Private	1
Guest Share	

**Farmstay
With a Spectacular View**

Features & Attractions

- *Walking tracks and beaches*
- *Pet animals and spa*
- *30 minutes from Dunedin*
- *Spa bath*
- *Spectacular views*
- *Quiet and relaxing*
- *Dinner by arrangement.*
  $30 per person

We welcome you to our spacious renovated stone house, in a peaceful rural setting only 30 minutes from Dunedin. From our home, which is heated throughout with radiators off the rayburn range, you can enjoy sweeping 220° views of the Otago Harbour, Otago Peninsula and the Pacific Ocean. Relax in the spa pool or feed our animals – emus, alpaccas, pig and pet sheep.

Walking tracks and beaches are close by. Morning and afternoon teas with home baking are complimentary. Three course farm style meals are available by prior arrangement. We invite you to experience our hospitality and meet our cat Penny. You will love the unique awe inspiring setting of our farm and take back home lovely memories of this truly special place.

DIRECTIONS:
From north turn left at Waitati, follow sign to Port Chalmers till crossroads. Turn left (No Exit) on to next junction take Heywards Point Road (metal road) 4km on right. From south down to Port Chalmers Highway 88, follow sign up the hill to Long Beach till Heyward Point Road (metal road) 4km on right.

HARBOURSIDE BED & BREAKFAST HOMESTAY

6 Kiwi Street, St Leonards, Dunedin
Ph (03) 471 0690, Fax (03) 471 0063
email: harboursidebb@xtra.co.nz
www.charmingaccommodation.co.nz

Features & Attractions

- *7 minutes to city centre*
- *Overlooking harbour*
- *Children welcome*
- *Complimentary tea on arrival*
- *Home baking*
- *Dinner by arrangement*

$	Double	$100-120
	Single	$80-100
	Child	$30

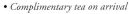

Bed & Breakfast Homestay
Spectacular Harbour Views

Bedrooms	Qty
Double	3
Twin	
Single	
Bed Size	**Qty**
Super King	1
Queen	2
Double	
Single	3
Bathrooms	**Qty**
Ensuite	1
Private	
Guest Share	1

We are situated in a quiet suburb overlooking Otago Harbour and surrounding hills. Handy to all local attractions - Larnach Castle, Olveston, Royal Albatross and Yellow Eyed Penguin colonies, harbour cruises, Taieri Gorge Excursion train. Bookings can be arranged. There are many lovely bush walks close to the city. Children are very welcome (lots of preloved toys). We have a generous amount of living space for you to relax in after a busy day. Cooked breakfast is included and with a little notice, we can arrange a three course meal. Courtesy pick-up from bus or train.

DIRECTIONS: On Northern Motorway turn left towards Port Chalmers (SH 88) from Anzac Avenue onto Ravensbourne Road. After 5km at St Leonards turn left into Moa Street, left into Kaka Road, straight ahead to Kiwi Street, turn left to No 6

277

LEITHVIEW

234 Malvern Street, Leith Valley, Dunedin
Ph (03) 467 9944, Mobile 027-490 7117
email: lvconstruction@xtra.co.nz
www.leithview.com

Tariff : N.Z. Dollars	
Double	$175-195
Single	neg.
Child	neg.

Bedrooms	Qty
Double	3
Twin	
Single	1
Bed Size	Qty
Super King	
King	1
Queen	2
Double	
Single	1
Bathrooms	Qty
Ensuite	3
Private	
Guest Share	

 **Delightful Country Living
So Close to Town**

Features & Attractions

- *Private native bush walk*
- *Large rambling gardens*
- *Five min. from town*
- *Home fed by spring water*
- *Peaceful location*
- *Prolific birdlife*
- *Glow-worm grotto nearby*
- *Spa pool under the stars*

Leithview

To City & Octagon

DIRECTIONS:
Once you reach our letterbox, follow
the gravel drive for 500m past the **Leithview** sign
up the hill.

Marja and Peter would like to welcome you to **Leithview**, a forty acre lifestyle property five minutes from the centre of

Dunedin. Our modern home is nestled on the northern slopes of the Leith Valley.

All bedrooms have a northerly aspect and their own private decks looking out over extensive gardens and native bush, including 200 year

old rimus and totara trees. Stroll around the property with our two retired sheepdogs and two cats, say hello to our friendly goats, cows, alpacas, ducks and chickens, then relax under the stars in the outdoor spa pool. The room rate includes a generous cooked or continental breakfast. These rates are subject to generous discounts during our off-peak season from April 1st to September 30th.
We have the internet available and there is a bus stop at the bottom of our driveway.

CITY SANCTUARY BED & BREAKFAST

165 Maitland Street, Dunedin
Ph (03) 474 5002
email: info@citysanctuary.co.nz
www.citysanctuary.co.nz

Tariff : N.Z. Dollars	
Double	$145-195
Single	$125-175
Child	neg

Bedrooms	Qty
Double	3
Twin	
Single	
Bed Size	**Qty**
Super King	
King	
Queen	3
Double	
Single	
Bathrooms	**Qty**
Ensuite	1
Private	2
Guest Share	

**Inner City Oasis
Bed & Breakfast**

Features & Attractions

- *Inner city location*
- *Elegant, spacious rooms*
- *Quiet and peaceful*
- *Personalised service*
- *Continental breakfast*
- *Ensuite & private bathrooms*
- *Set in a beautiful garden*
- *Spacious rooms*

Welcome to our attractive, restored villa in an oasis of cottage gardens and large trees, yet only 1 km to the city centre and all its attractions. Three lovely,

spacious rooms each have: queen bed with fleecy electric blanket, heater, writing desk, TV, radio/clock and fresh flowers. One room has an ensuite bathroom with spa bath and shower, the other two rooms each have their own private bathrooms. Relax in the guest lounge with large screen TV and DVD player, guest computer for emails and internet access, unwind with a stroll around the garden or simly enjoy the evening tranquility under the verandah eaves. Breakfasts include a delicious selection of home made bread, freshly baked croissants, cereals and fresh fruits, cheeses and condiments, juice, tea and coffee. One very friendly ginger cat in residence (Charlie). We look forward to welcoming you to the **City Sanctuary** and ensuring that you enjoy a perfectly relaxing and memorable stay.

Dunedin

YOUR HOSTS: **Kirstin Peacock and Ashley Grey**   Free Ph: 0800 268 252

DEACONS COURT
342 High Street, Dunedin
Ph (03) 477 9053, Fax (03) 477 9058
email: info@deaconscourt.com
www.deaconscourt.com

Features & Attractions
- *Spacious, sunny conservatory*
- *Very large & cozy bedrooms*
- *Cooked & continental breakfasts*
- *Close to city centre*
- *Friendly hospitality*
- *City & harbour views*

Bed & Breakfast Guesthouse

Double	$160
Single	$140
Child	$100

Bedrooms	Qty
Double	3
Twin/Double	2
Single	1
Bed Size	Qty
Super King	
King	2
Queen	1
King/Single	
Single	1
Bathrooms	Qty
Ensuite	2
Private	1

Welcome to our attractive Victorian spacious villa, which was built in 1891 and is on the city's heritage building register. It is an impressive building, with lovely views of the city and the harbour. We offer you friendly but unobtrusive hospitality in a quiet, secure haven. Guests can relax in our spacious and sunny, conservatory, enjoying our stunning and relaxing rose garden while watching and listening to native bird life. Breakfasts are delectable, cooked and continental. We are only 10 mins walk from the city centre and a wide selection of cafés, restaurants, bars and major city attractions. Bedrooms are very large and cozy and have ensuite or private bathrooms, heaters, TV and electric blankets. Complimentary 24 hour tea/coffee, parking and wireless broadband available.

Dunedin

YOUR HOSTS: **Janet and Alan Parker**   Ph: (03) 454 5568

EDGELEY BED & BREAKFAST
29 Spencer Street, Andersons Bay, Dunedin
Ph (03) 454 5568, Mobile 027-715 3635
email: edgeley@xtra.co.nz
www.edgeley.co.nz

Features & Attractions
- *Peaceful location*
- *Panoramic ocean view*
- *Off-street parking*
- *Large, private garden*
- *Spacious bedrooms*
- *Friendly, cheerful hosts*

Boutique Bed & Breakfast with Outstanding Sea Views

Double	$170-180
Single	$150-155
Child	–

Bedrooms	Qty
Double	2
Twin	
Single	
Bed Size	Qty
King	
Queen	2
Double	
Single	
Bathrooms	Qty
Ensuite	1
Private	1
Guest Share	

In 1923 Edgeley was described as "a superior class of house" and "one of the finest of the old homes round about Dunedin". With outstanding ocean views from the guest bedrooms and guests' lounge, we invite you to stay at the home of the Parker family and Penny our very friendly dog, in Anderson's Bay, the "Gateway to the Peninsula".

We offer an elite class of accommodation in peaceful surroundings. Listen to bellbirds and the sound of the Pacific Ocean whilst enjoying a sumptuous home-cooked breakfast. We have a maximum of five guests at any one time, so you can be assured that service and our guests' comfort is our top priority.

HIGHBRAE GUESTHOUSE
376 High Street, City Rise, Dunedin
Ph (03) 479 2070, Fax (03) 479 2100
Mobile 027-432 8470
email: stephen@highbrae.co.nz
www.highbrae.co.nz

Tariff : N.Z. Dollars	
Double	$120-140
Single	$90-110
Child	$25-35

Bedrooms	Qty
Double	3
Twin	1
Single	

Bed Size	Qty
Super King	
King	1
Queen	2
Double	
Single	3

Bathrooms	Qty
Private	1
Guest Share	1
Family Share	1

Bed & Breakfast & Guest House

Features & Attractions

- *Central location*
- *Warm hospitality*
- *Elegance with comfort*
- *Spectacular view of harbour*
- *Free wireless internet connection*
- *Free pick-up/dropoff to l ocal buses*
- *Grace and charm of a past era*
- *All the comforts of the present*

Highbrae Guesthouse

Imagine living in a stately home on one of Dunedin's most fashionable streets at the beginning of the 20th century! **Highbrae Guesthouse** provides first class bed & breakfast facilities with all the grace and elegance of a past era, combined with the comforts of the present. Centrally located within an easy walk to the heart of the city and with spectacular views over the harbour it is the ideal place to spend a few days or just for a quick stopover. Free wireless internet and a pick-up service from the train or bus station are available if required. Three double rooms share the beautiful Italian style upstairs bathroom, while a self-contained studio unit features a queen double bedroom, as well as a small kitchen, private bathroom and laundry. All rooms have television, heater and electric blankets. Hosts Stephen and Fienie, look forward to welcoming you into their lovely home.

281

HAZEL HOUSE BOUTIQUE BED & BREAKFAST

50 Hazel Avenue, Hazelhurst, Dunedin
Ph (03) 487 6550
Mobile 021-613 642
email: info@hazelhouse.co.nz
www.hazelhouse.co.nz

Tariff : N.Z. Dollars	
Double	$150-165
Single	$125-135
Child	neg

Bedrooms	Qty
Double	2
Twin	
Single	
Bed Size	**Qty**
Super King	
King	1
Queen	1
Double	
Single	
Bathrooms	**Qty**
Ensuite	1
Private	1
Guest Share	

**Boutique
Bed & Breakfast**

Features & Attractions

- *Elegant character villa*
- *Stunning guests lounge*
- *Warmth, comfort & luxury*
- *Quiet, peaceful location*
- *Friendly, welcoming hosts*
- *Close to top restaurants*
- *Free wireless internet*
- *5 minutes from city centre*

DIRECTIONS: Turn off Southern motorway at Caversham, off South Rd into Playfair St, left into Hazel Ave. Or from St Clair head along Forbury Rd, left at roundabout, left into Thorn St, left at Playfair St and left into Hazel Ave.

Hazel House is a classic 1900's villa located only five minutes from Dunedin's city centre. With the majestic rooms, ornate ceilings and lead light windows, it is an absolute delight to offer a peaceful and quiet location with warm inviting rooms, full continental and cooked breakfasts. A spectacular guests lounge, spacious king bedroom with private bathroom, or queen bedroom with ensuite, include quality linen and comfort. Enjoy Sky TV, wireless internet, tea and coffee or complimentary glass of wine, central heating, private courtyard, veranda, and warm welcome from hosts Sandy and Brent Ward. **Hazel House** is a short drive to outstanding restaurants, cafés, shops and historic buildings and attractions; including St Clair Beach, Dunedin Railway Station, Chinese Gardens, and the spectacular wildlife and Larnach Castle on the Otago Peninsula. Dunedin offers so much in art, fashion, sporting activities and history. Our aim is to make a real difference to your time in Dunedin, our fabulous "Edinburgh of the South".

282

ARTS CONTENT BED & BREAKFAST

1 Castlewood Road, Otago Peninsula
Ph/Fax (03) 476 0076
email: artscontent@hotmail.com
www.artscontentbnb.com

Tariff : N.Z. Dollars	
Double	$140-165
Single	$135-150
Child	$35

Bedrooms	Qty
Double	1
Twin	
Single	
Bed Size	**Qty**
Super King	
King	
Queen	1
Double	
Sofa-bed	1
Bathrooms	**Qty**
Ensuite	1
Private	
Guest Share	

 Absolute Waterfront B&B Self-contained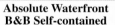

Features & Attractions

- *Absolute waterfront*
- *Panoramic harbour views*
- *Albatross, penguins & seals*
- *Larnach Castle - 5 min. drive*
- *Internet and Laundry*
- *Dunedin City - 15 mins.*
- *Fully Heated*
- *Sky T.V.*

DIRECTIONS: From Dunedin follow signs to Peninsula. We are 15min. drive along Portobello Road on the corner of Portobello Road & Castlewood Road in Company Bay. Look for Arts Content sign.

A rts Content is absolute waterfront, self-contained, cottage-style accommodation, ideal for a couple. Decorated in country style, it exudes charm and character. Warm, friendly hosts are ready to welcome you. The B&B adjoins our home, has private entrances and off-street parking. Enjoy sweeping, panoramic harbour views from the private deck. Leading off the spacious bedroom is your own ensuite. Upstairs is a lounge, dining, kitchen with comfortable seating including a sofa-bed which can accommodate an extra person. Heating is provided by heatpumps. Share our pleasure in our beautiful, 'secret' garden. A generous breakfast basket is provided. Within easy reach of the city, we are ideally located to access all the attractions of the Peninsula. The **Arts Content B&B** is the ideal base from which to access the stunning views, walking tracks, secluded beaches and the abundant wildlife for which the Peninsula is famous

Fantail Lodge

682 Portobello Road, Broad Bay, Dunedin
Ph (03) 478 0110, Mobile 027-415 6222
email: fantail.lodge@xtra.co.nz
www.charmingaccommodation.co.nz

Tariff : N.Z. Dollars	
Double	$145-155
Single	
Extra pp	$25

Bedrooms	Qty
Double	2
Twin	
Single	1
Bed Size	Qty
Super King	
King	
Queen	2
Double	
Single	2
Bathrooms	Qty
Ensuite	2
Private	
Guest Share	

**Harbourside
Self-contained Cottages**

DIRECTIONS:

From Dunedin take Portobello Rd
along harbour towards Taiaroa Head.
After 15 km (20 min) you will see
Broad Bay Boating Club and jetty.
Turn next right into Clearwater St and
turn again hard right in front of
two storey B&B house on corner.
Straight on to #682.

Features & Attractions

- *Harbourside cottages*
- *Exclusive spa pool*
- *Albatross, seals, penguins*
- *Larnach Castle*

- *Romantic hideaway*
- *Lush garden setting*
- *Free use of kayaks*
- *Breakfast opt. extra*

Fantail Lodge offers self-contained cottage accommodation set in a lush harbourside garden. We are situated centrally on the Otago Peninsula, within easy reach of unspoiled beaches, albatross, seals and penguins. Relax on the verandah and enjoy the company of native birds. Walk to the local castle or paddle a kayak on the harbour. With so much to explore we recommend you stay for at least two nights and we offer a discount for longer stays. We are five minutes drive to the local store and restaurants and twenty minutes from Dunedin. The cottages are equipped for self-catering with an optional continental breakfast hamper for busy travellers. There are two unique cottages for you to choose from:
'Fantail Cottage' offers queen bed accommodation with two singles on a mezzanine floor. Ideal for two, but comfortably sleeps four people.
'Bellbird Cottage' offers queen bed accommodation. Relax and enjoy the exclusive use of a spa pool under the stars. Perfect for a couple.

FERN COTTAGES - BROAD BAY

Broad Bay, Otago Peninsula, Dunedin
Mobile 027-228 3380, Fax (03) 476 1873
email: julzandlutz@xtra.co.nz
www.OtagoPeninsulaSeasideCottages.co.nz

Tariff : N.Z. Dollars	
Double	$160-180
Single	–
Child	–

Bedrooms	Qty
Double	2
Twin	
Single	
Bed Size	Qty
Super King	
King	
Queen	2
Double	
Single	
Bathrooms	Qty
Ensuite	2
Private	
Guest Share	

**Coastal Cottages
Bed & Breakfast**

Features & Attractions

- *Self-contained & private*
- *Penguins, Albatross and Seals*
- *Magnificent sea views*
- *Own fern grove*
- *Modern with warm ambience*
- *20 minutes from Dunedin*
- *Optional breakfast hamper*
- *Situated right by the water*

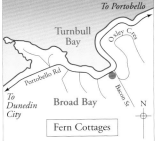

Situated about half way between Dunedin and the Penguin, Albatross, and Seal Colonies of the Otago Peninsula these two cottages are the ideal resting spot after your adventures during the day wildlife watching, tramping and beach walking, kayaking, boating, mountain biking, visiting Larnach castle; or having explored Dunedin with its sights, cafes, galleries, museums, theatres and entertainment. Enjoy the breathtaking views of Otago Harbour whilst sitting on the cottages' verandahs or take a stroll through our fern grove and listen to the native birds and the gurgling creek. The interior of the cottages is modern with a warm ambience. The modern kitchens invite to "cook up a storm". They are well stocked with spices and herbs, oils and vinegars, fresh ground coffee and teas muesli and cereals, milk and honey etc. Restaurants and cafes are only a short drive away. Our Special Breakfast Hamper with its scrumptious ingredients (Optional and at an extra cost) can be delivered by your hosts. Welcome orientation also available in German.

THE LODGE - BROAD BAY

Broad Bay, Otago Peninsula, Dunedin
Mobile 027-228 3380, Fax (03) 476 1873
email: julzandlutz@xtra.co.nz
www.OtagoPeninsulaSeasideCottages.co.nz

Tariff : N.Z. Dollars	
Double	$180
Single	
Child	

Bedrooms	Qty
Double	1
Twin	1
Single	
Bed Size	Qty
Super King	
King	
Queen	1
Double	
King/Single	2
Bathrooms	Qty
Ensuite	
Private	1
Guest Share	

**Coastal Cottage
Bed & Breakfast**

Features & Attractions

- *Modern with warm ambience*
- *Self-contained and private*
- *Optional hamper breakfast*
- *Magnificent sea views*

- *Close to wildlife*
- *Penguins, albatross and seals*
- *20 mins from Dunedin*
- *Situated right by the water*

Explore the Otago Peninsula - royal albatross, penguin and seal colonies, great walkways and beaches, galleries and hidden gems, and a castle! Enjoy the city life of Dunedin with its cafés and galleries, shops and museums, its theatres and entertainment.

Then come home to this fully self-contained and private haven, relax and enjoy the breathtaking views of Otago Harbour.

The modern kitchen invites you to "cook up a storm", or you might choose to dine out at the nearby restaurants. A scrumptious basket of ingredients for breakfast (optional and at extra cost) can be delivered by your hosts who live nearby on the Peninsula.

THE COTTAGE - BROAD BAY

Broad Bay, Otago Peninsula, Dunedin
Mobile 027-228 3380, Fax (03) 476 1873
email: thecottage@xtra.co.nz
www.OtagoPeninsulaSeasideCottages.co.nz

Tariff : N.Z. Dollars	
Double	$160
Single	
Child	

Bedrooms	Qty
Double	1
Twin	
Single	
Bed Size	**Qty**
Super King	
King	
Queen	1
Double	
Single	
Bathrooms	**Qty**
Ensuite	1
Private	
Guest Share	

**Coastal Cottage
Bed & Breakfast**

Features & Attractions

- *Olde-world charm*
- *Self-contained and private*
- *Optional hamper breakfast*
- *Sea views from verandah*
- *Close to wildlife*
- *Penguins, albatross & seals*
- *20 minutes from Dunedin*
- *Situated right by the water*

Whether you want to explore the wildlife of the Otago Peninsula with its great beaches and walkways, penguin, royal albatross and Seal colonies, harbour cruises and Larnach Castle or frequent the café scene, the galleries, the restaurants and city life of Dunedin, our **Cottage** is the ideal base for your adventures. Situated right by the water, this turn of the century fisherman's retreat is tucked among bush and trees with wonderful views of the harbour from the privacy of the verandah. **The Cottage** is full of old-world charm. It reflects the nostalgia of a bygone era whilst modern conveniences ensure a comfortable stay. The décor features the odd piece of original New Zealand art and numerous curiosities from yesteryear. Your hosts live nearby on the Peninsula. They are responsible for the scrumptious basket of ingredients for breakfast which is delivered to your cottage during the afternoon for the next morning (optional and at extra cost). "If you spend only one night... you'll be sorry... A few days is best."(Grace Magazine).

TREETOPS B&B

3 Treetop Drive, Portobello, Otago Peninsula
Ph (03) 478 0424, Mobile 027-773 8608
email:treetopsbandb@gmail.com
www.charmingaccommodation.co.nz

Tariff : N.Z. Dollars	
Double	$160-180
Single	$120-140
Child	

Bedrooms	Qty
Double	1
Twin	
Single	
Bed Size	**Qty**
Super King	
King	
Queen	1
Double	
Single	
Bathrooms	**Qty**
Ensuite	1
Private	
Guest Share	

Bed & Breakfast
with Stunning View

Features & Attractions

- *Set in native bush*
- *Cosy under-floor heating*
- *Close to wildlife attractions*
- *20mins from Dunedin*
- *Quiet & secluded*
- *Private access*
- *Beautiful local beaches*
- *8mins stroll to village*

DIRECTIONS:
Take Portobello Road alongside the harbour, or take Highcliff Road along the top of the Peninsula. Drive through Portobello village and turn right into Allans Beach Road. Take the second turn right into Treetop Drive.

Treetops B&B is set in native bush with wonderful views looking out over Portobello village and Latham Bay towards Quarantine Island. Quiet, tranquil setting where you can relax and unwind, enjoy the view, listen to the birdsong.

Handy to the various eco-tourism adventures and wildlife the peninsula is famous for – royal albatross, penguins, seals, sea lions and beautiful local beaches where you can wander at leisure.

Your B&B is self contained with cosy under-floor heating, ensuite bathroom with shower, queen bed with electric blanket; TV, DVD, laptop with internet access; board games and cards for your entertainment.

The kitchenette is equipped with fridge, toaster, microwave and tea/coffee making facilities. Continental breakfast basket is included (or optional). (Every 10th booking 50% discount). Two minutes drive into Portobello you can find the 1908 Restaurant, Portobello Hotel, Rics Galley Takeaways, Penguin Café and a very well stocked grocery store.

CAPTAIN EADY'S LOOKOUT
2 Moss Street, Portobello, Dunedin
Ph (03) 478 0537, Mobile 021-478 785
email: capteady@earthlight.co.nz
www.capteady.co.nz

Tariff : N.Z. Dollars	
Double	$160-195
Single	$150-185
Child	neg

Bedrooms	Qty
Double	2
Twin	1
Single	
Bed Size	**Qty**
Super King	
King	
Queen	2
Double	
Single	2
Bathrooms	**Qty**
Ensuite	2
Private	
Family Share	1

**Bed & Breakfast
Homestay**

Features & Attractions

- *Harbourside location*
- *Close to Albatross Colony*
- *Stunning Peninsula beaches*
- *Secluded garden*
- *Penguins, seals & native birdlife*
- *Special breakfasts, dinner available upon request*
- *Large character home, warm in winter*
- *Antiques, paintings by local artists*

Captain Eady's Lookout is a delightful Bed & Breakfast situated on the water's edge at Portobello on the Otago Peninsula, just twenty kilometres from Dunedin. This character house is set on a small bluff overlooking the Otago Harbour. It was built early last century by Captain Eady, a ferry master. The upstairs bedroom, with its own balcony, overlooks the water. The bedroom below opens onto a secluded garden.

You may have a special breakfast in the conservatory whilst taking in the splendid views of the harbour. The house has many antiques and on the walls are paintings by local artists. Feel free to enjoy our large jazz collection.

Captain Eady's Lookout is an ideal base from which to explore the Royal Albatross Colony, Larnach's Castle, and ocean beaches deserted, save for penguins and seals.

McAULEY GLEN BOUTIQUE B&B

13 McAuley Road, Portobello
Ph (03) 478 0724, Mobile 021-237 1919
email: maryandpat@clear.net.nz
www.mcauleyglen.co.nz

Features & Attractions

- *Getaway packages*
- *Kayak/bike, tours/hire*
- *Internet, laundry, parking*
- *Romantic retreat*
- *Spa pool, sauna*
- *Stroll to restaurants*

Boutique B&B

	Double	$195-240
	Single	$155-195
	Child	enquire

Located 20km from Dunedin centre on the magnificent Otago Peninsula, private, tranquil harbour side setting, lush gardens of colour, fragrance, bird song. Close to ocean beaches, albatross, penguin, seal and sea-lion colonies. Two elegantly appointed bedroom suites, purposely designed and furnished, separate courtyard entrance, luxurious beds, modern comfy loungers, LCD/TV, CD, DVD, mic/wave, fridge, teas/coffee, home baking, port, and chocolate treats. Beautiful en-suites, tiled, walk in shower, heated floor, heated towel rails, hair dryer, quality towels, robes, slippers and toiletries.

Your dedicated hosts are well travelled kiwis with a variety of interests, join us for refreshments and lively conversation, we proudly offer warm relaxed hospitality, delicious gourmet breakfast, rejuvenating spa/sauna, personalized tours, informative advice on attractions, evening meal by arrangement. See also www.bike-kayak.com.

Bedrooms	Qty
Double	2
Twin	1
Single	
Bed Size	**Qty**
King	
Queen	2
Double	
Single	2
Bathrooms	**Qty**
Ensuite	2
Private	
Guest Share	

CRABAPPLE COTTAGE

346 Harington Point Rd, RD 2,
Lower Portobello, Dunedin
Ph (03) 478 0103
email: kay@crabapple.co.nz
www.crabapple.co.nz

Features & Attractions

- *Close to wildlife attractions*
- *Pleasant, rural setting*
- *Private garden outlook*
- *5min. to restaurants & cafés*
- *25min. from Dunedin*
- *Restored settlers cottage*

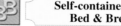
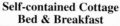

**Self-contained Cottage
Bed & Breakfast**

	Double	$115-140
	Single	
	Child	

Crabapple Cottage is a lovingly restored 1860s settlers cottage 25 minutes from Dunedin, on the beautiful Otago Peninsula. We are 10 minutes from the albatross colony, penguin beaches, Monarch Wildlife Cruises, off-road tours, the Portobello Aquarium, craft shops and beautiful beaches. Larnach's Castle is a 20 minutes scenic drive away. Our character cottage has a very comfortable queen-size bed, modern bathroom with all facilities, and a kitchen/lounge area equipped for basic self-catering. Enjoy a generous breakfast basket, which includes eggs from our own hens, and relax in an armchair or in the private herb garden with views of the hills and full afternoon sun. We are 5 minutes from restaurants, cafés and a general store with post facilities. We look forward to sharing our cosy cottage with you. - Sorry, no pets.

Bedrooms	Qty
Double	1
Twin	
Single	
Bed Size	**Qty**
King	
Queen	1
Double	
Single	
Bathrooms	**Qty**
Ensuite	1
Private	
Guest Share	

LESMAHAGOW

Benhar Main Road, Benhar, Balclutha
Ph (03) 418 2507, Mobile 027-457 8465
email: lesmahagow@xtra.co.nz
www.lesmahagow.co.nz

Features & Attractions
- *Historic home & gardens*
- *Catlins scenic area*
- *Quality & comfort assured*
- *Evening dining*
- *Centrally heated*
- *Spacious bedrooms*

$	Double	$160-190
	Single	
	Child	

   **Boutique Bed & Breakfast**

Bedrooms	Qty
Double	3
Twin	
Single	
Bed Size	**Qty**
King	
Queen	2
Double	1
Single	1
Bathrooms	**Qty**
Ensuite	
Private	3
Guest Share	

Lesmahagow offers excellent accommodation in an historic homestead and garden setting. Centrally situated, discerning travellers can make Lesmahagow their base to explore the Catlins region, Dunedin and the Otago Peninsula or the historic goldfields of Lawrence. Centrally heated, with delightfully furnished bedrooms and gorgeous bathrooms, you can be sure of wonderful hospitality, and a truly memorable stay. Feel free to explore and relax in our gardens or take time out to enjoy the guest lounge with an extensive range of books magazines and music. We offer evening dining utilising fresh produce from the garden and locally grown meats. Our special breakfasts, at a time to suit you, with freshly squeezed fruit juices, fresh fruits, home made breads, muesli and home baking will satisfy all taste buds! We love to help plan your day's activities and can arrange a variety of local trips for you. Come as strangers, leave as friends.

CURIO BAY BOUTIQUE STUDIOS
521a Curio Bay Road, Tokanui, Southland
Ph/Fax (03) 246 8797
email: accommodation@curiobay.com
www.curiobay.co.nz

Tariff : N.Z. Dollars	
Double	$140-220
Single	
Child	

Bedrooms	Qty
Double	3
Twin	
Single	

Bed Size	Qty
Super King	2
King	1
Queen	
Double	
Single	

Bathrooms	Qty
Ensuite	3
Private	
Guest Share	

Quality Self-contained Studios
Absolute Beachfront

Features & Attractions

- *Absolute beachfront*
- *Stunning seaviews*
- *Wildlife at your door*
- *Fossil forest, dolphins & penguins*
- *Romantic getaway*
- *Freshly ground coffee*
- *5 min. drive to cafe & museum*
- *Breakfast not included*

Our quality beachfront self-contained studios are situated right on the beach at Curio Bay. Roll out of your bed and you're on the beach, which is the home to a wide range of bird life, Blue and Yellow eyed penguins, seals and Hector's dolphins (Nov-April). Also, the fossil forest and camp shop are only a 10 minute walk away. We offer music, books, games, freshly ground coffee and a cosy place to put your feet up and relax in privacy. Our cell phone and TV-free studios have solar heated water, double glassing, fully equipped kitchen and spacious bathrooms. A great place for a romantic getaway!

Each Studio sleeps two to three people. Complimentary laundry facilities on site. Local Café/Restaurant only five minutes drive away.

Come and escape to Curio Bay!

CATLINS FARMSTAY & WATERSIDE WAIKAWA

174 Progress Valley Road, Catlins
Ph (03) 246 8843, Fax (03) 246 8844
email: catlinsfarmstay@xtra.co.nz
www. catlinsfarmstay.co.nz

Tariff : N.Z. Dollars	
Double	$185-270
Single	$160-200
Extra pp	$80

Bedrooms	Qty
Double	4
Twin/double	2
Single	

Bed Size	Qty
Super King	
King	3
Queen	2
Double	
Single	2

Bathrooms	Qty
Ensuite	5
Private	
Guest Share	

**Farmstay B&B and
Self-contained Accommodation**

Features & Attractions

- *5-10 mins to fossil forest Curio Bay*
- *Penguins, dolphins, sealions*
- *Waipohatu 3hr forest walk*
- *2km to Niagara Falls & Cafe*
- *Farmstay offers delicious breakfasts*
- *Real bacon & farm eggs*
- *1000 acre working farm*
- *Local hosts, local knowledge*

June and Murray welcome you to their 1000 acre sheep, cattle and deer farm with 2 sheep dogs. Excellent spacious accommodation - 3 ensuite rooms. In the morning enjoy a delicious breakfast in the dining room. **Catlins Farmstay** is an ideal location for exploring the Catlins being situated between Cathedral Caves and Curio Bay. June has lived on the Catlins coast all her life and loves to share her in-depth knowledge of this unique area. Curio Bay is just 10 mins drive away where you may see penguins, dolphins and sealions.

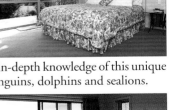

Waterside Waikawa is a wonderful holiday retreat situated overlooking the peaceful Waikawa harbour just five minutes drive from Curio Bay. It has two king rooms with ensuite and bathroom including a studio apartment with really great views. Quality furnishings and facilities including complimentary laundry facilities.

NITHDALE FARMSTAY
338 Nithdale Road, Kaiwera
Ph (03) 205 3586, Fax (03) 205 3587
Mobile 027-256 6642
email: nithdale@farmside.co.nz
www.nithdalefarmstay.co.nz

Tariff : N.Z. Dollars	
Double	$140-200
Single	$80-100
Child	$20-30

Bedrooms	Qty
Double	2
Twin	
Single	

Bed Size	Qty
Super King	
King	1
Queen	1
Double	
Single	2

Bathrooms	Qty
Ensuite	
Private	
Guest Share	1

 Farmstay Bed & Breakfast

Features & Attractions

- *Peaceful rural setting*
- *Friendly farm animals*
- *Farm tour & walk*
- *History of farming back to 1856*
- *Great fishing*
- *Centre of region*
- *Self catering available*
- *Evening meals by arrangement*

Come and enjoy the peaceful rural setting of **Nithdale Farmstay**. Located only 15 minutes drive south east of Gore in the heartland of Eastern Southland. Bring your rod and go fishing or take a day trip to the Catlins, Stewart Island, Fiordland or Queenstown. Or just relax, read, go for a walk over the hills or experience rural life. **Nithdale Farmstay** is part of the modern homestead recently built on Nithdale Station - a large property with a history of farming dating back to 1856.

Nithdale Farmstay contains a fully self contained unit with kitchen, bathroom, two double rooms. Bed and breakfast standard with evening meals available with prior arrangement. Farm tours are also available with prior arrangement.

B&B on Yarrow

167 Yarrow Street, Invercargill
Ph (03) 214 3124, Fax (03) 214 3126
Mobile 027-214 3125
email: b-and-b-onyarrow@woosh.co.nz
www.charmingaccommodation.co.nz

Tariff : N.Z. Dollars	
Double	$200-225
Single	$150-175
Child	

Bedrooms	Qty
Double	2
Twin	
Single	
Bed Size	**Qty**
Super King	
King	
Queen	2
Double	
Single	
Bathrooms	**Qty**
Ensuite	
Private	
Guest Share	1

**Bed & Breakfast
Boutique Style**

Features & Attractions

- *Centrally located*
- *Free bottle of wine*
- *Spacious and elegant*
- *Private and intimate*
- *Fax, email, laundry*
- *Off street parking*
- *Park & golf course nearby*
- *Mountain bikes available*

Geoff welcomes you to stay in his spacious modern two storey home. Sunny and warm with a european inspired interior design. Situated in the heart of Invercargill and only a casual stroll to town or Queenspark. The guest accommodation is upstairs and includes a spacious guest area with television and for those who want coffee or to chat in private. Alternatively you are welcome to use the large lounge downstairs.

Both bedrooms have nice views and have there own thermostat heating. Relax, unwind and enjoy your complimentary bottle of wine or take a leisurely bike ride through Queenspark. Continental breakfast is provided as part of your stay.

295

Glenroy Park Homestay

23 Glenroy Park Drive, Waikiwi, Invercargill
Ph/Fax (03) 215 8464, Mobile 027-376 2228
email: maggymae@xtra.co.nz
www.charmingaccommodation.co.nz

Features & Attractions

- *Warm hospitality*
- *Quiet retreat*
- *Dinner by arrangement*
- *Gateway to Fiordland and Catlins*
- *Invercargill - beautiful city*
- *Excellent golf courses*

Homestay Bed & Breakfast

Double	$120-130
Single	$85-110
Child	$12 u/12

Bedrooms	Qty
Double	1
Twin	1
Single	1

Bed Size	Qty
King	
Queen	1
Twin	
Single	3

Bathrooms	Qty
Ensuite	
Private	1
Guest Share	1

Exclusively Yours, in a quiet retreat, with parks, restaurants, and shops only a short distance away. We enjoy meeting people and love to cook. We both garden, play golf, with many courses nearby.

Be our special guests and share an evening of relaxation, and friendship. Dinner available. Invercargill, our garden city, has many historic buildings, lovely parks, and gardens, and a unique museum with live Tuatara lizards. Gateway to the pleasures of Fiordland, Queenstown, Catlins and Stewart Island.

DIRECTIONS: **From Queenstown:** Turn left at 2nd set of lights, Bainfield Road, travel 500m – we are 1st on left, Glenroy Park Drive, 3rd house on left. **From Dunedin:** Travel along Tay St; turn right at War Memorial towards Queenstown, travel approx 5km, turn right at traffic lights into Bainfield Road, then as above.

Braemar Farmstay

Rapid No 80, Highway 99, Invercargill
Ph/Fax (03) 235 8804, Mobile 027-273 9959
email: jean@braemarfarmstay.co.nz
www.braemarfarmstay.co.nz

Features & Attractions

- *Genuine southern hospitality*
- *Relaxed, rural setting*
- *7km from Invercargill city*
- *Golf courses nearby*
- *Friendly farm animals*
- *Evening meals by arrangement*

Homestay Bed & Breakfast

Double	$110-130
Single	$80-95
Child	$15-25

Bedrooms	Qty
Double	3
Twin	2
Single	

Bed Size	Qty
Super King	1
Queen	2
Double	
Single	4

Bathrooms	Qty
Ensuite	4
Private	1
Guest Share	

A warm welcome awaits you at **Braemar**, a working farm 10 minutes drive from Invercargill and located on the Southern Scenic Route (State Highway 99).

Guests are welcome to view the animals on the farm, dairy cows, calves, sheep, pigs, a cat or two or 'Little One', the donkey. Also on site is a small flower growing operation and farm shop. Local attractions include several nature reserves, wonderful Queens Park Museum and Art Gallery in Invercargill, several golf courses and two trout-fishing rivers. A hearty cooked breakfast is included. Internet access and laundry facilities available on request.

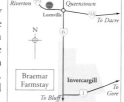

The location of **Braemar** is ideal for a stop-over between the Catlins attractions and the Lakes of Manapouri, Te Anau or the Queenstown area.

THE MANOR

9 Drysdale Road, Myross Bush, Invercargill
Ph/Fax (03) 230 4788, Mobile 027-667 0904
email: the.manor@xtra.co.nz
www.manorbb.co.nz

Tariff : N.Z. Dollars	
Double	$130-170
Single	$80-95
Child	neg

Bedrooms	Qty
Double	3
Twin	
Single	
Bed Size	**Qty**
Super King	
King	
Queen	3
Double	
Single	2
Bathrooms	**Qty**
Ensuite	1
Private	1
Guest Share	1

Homestay
Bed & Breakfast

The Manor
Kennington Roslyn Bush Rd
Drysdale Rd
Fairweather Rd
N
To Dunedin
Woodlands
To Invercargill
To Kennington

DIRECTIONS:
Signs on State Highway One
at Kennington Corner.

Features & Attractions

- *Quiet & peaceful*
- *Warm home*
- *City 5 minutes*
- *Wireless internet available*
- *Golf courses close by*
- *Dinner by arrangement*
- *Near Southern Scenic Route*
- *2.5hrs to Te Anau/Queenstown*

Relax and enjoy our warm comfortable home situated in a sheltered garden setting on our 10acre farmlet. There's a private guest area with television, refrigerator, tea/coffee making facilities alternatively you are welcome to join us in our lounge. We are retired farmers who enjoy golf, gardening, harness racing, travel and meeting people. Cooked and continental breakfast included. laundry facilities available. Free Wireless Internet available. Quality Beds. Hair dryer and bathrobes provided. Courtesy pickup from terminals.Four Golf courses in the Invercargill area. Enjoy Invercargill Shopping Restaurants and Historic buldings. A stop on your way to Stewart Island, Southern Scenic Route, Queenstown, Te Anau or Milford Sound. We would enjoy having you stay with us.

84 ON KING

84 King Street, Invercargill
Ph/Fax (03) 217 3919
email: 84onking@xtra.co.nz
www.84onking.co.nz

Features & Attractions

- *Friendly hospitality*
- *Dinner by arrangement*
- *Email & fax available*
- *Close to city centre*
- *Walking distance to park*
- *Gateway to Fiordland/Queenstown*

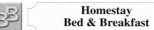
Homestay
Bed & Breakfast

	Double	$110
	Single	$80
	Child	

A warm welcome awaits you in our modern home situated in the popular Windsor suburb only metres from cafés, shops and restaurants and just a few minutes from the centre of Invercargill. Our home is warm and inviting with underfloor heating and a sunny outlook. We are semi retired farmers with interests in golf gardening, voluntary work in the community and meeting new people. Invercargill is a great place to spend a few days enjoying the green Southland farmland, bush walks, parks, golf courses and seashores on your way to Stewart Island, Fiordland or Queenstown. We have ample off street parking or alternatively are happy to collect you from the airport or bus terminal.

Bedrooms	Qty
Double	1
Twin	1
Single	
Bed Size	**Qty**
King	1
Queen	
Double	
King/Single	2
Bathrooms	**Qty**
Ensuite	
Private	1
Guest Share	1

VICTORIA RAILWAY HOTEL

3 Leven Street, Invercargill
Ph (03) 218 1281, Fax (03) 218 1283
email: vrhotel@xtra.co.nz
www.vrhotel.info

Features & Attractions

- *Private boutique hotel*
- *An Invercargill icon*
- *Old world charm*
- *Historic Places Trust Class I*
- *Broadband internet access*
- *Breakfast optional extra*

Boutique
Accommodation

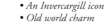

	Double	$145-195
	Single	$115-145
	Child	$15

Come and enjoy old-world charm, elegance and southern hospitality in a privately owned Boutique Hotel in the heart of Invercargill City. Built in 1896, the Hotel is a registered Class 1 New Zealand Historic Places Trust heritage building. We have completed significant refurbishment over the last three years: smoke detection, automatic fire sprinklers, CCTV, 24 hour PIR access, new bathrooms, broadband, etc. Internally we are now "modern" whilst retaining the building's atmosphere and character. In the evening come and relax in our Lounge Bar before dining and then enjoy traditional Asian Pacific Kiwi fare and a selection of local beers and fine New Zealand Wines. In the morning we offer both a continental and a full cooked "English" breakfast.

Bedrooms	Qty
Double	4
Twin	3
Single	4
Bed Size	**Qty**
King	
Queen	5
Double	5
Single	3
Bathrooms	**Qty**
Ensuite	11
Private	
Guest Share	

Stewart Island Lodge

14 Nichol Road, Oban, Stewart Island
Ph (03) 219 1085, Free Ph 0800 656501
email: info@stewartislandlodge.co.nz
www.stewartislandlodge.co.nz

Tariff : N.Z. Dollars	
Double	$290-390
Single	$290-390
Child	

Bedrooms	Qty
Twin/Double	5
Twin	
Single	
Bed Size	Qty
King Twin	5
King	
Queen	
Double	
Single	
Bathrooms	Qty
Ensuite	5
Private	
Guest Share	

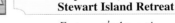

**Upmarket, Peaceful
Stewart Island Retreat**

Features & Attractions

- *Pick-up/drop-offs*
- *Central heating*
- *Wireless internet*
- *Private guest lounge*
- *Ensuites in all rooms*
- *Panoramic ocean views*
- *Native bird life*
- *Cooked/continental breakfast included*

S tewart Island Lodge is an up-market Bed and Breakfast accommodation nestled in native bush on Stewart Island. Located just five minutes walk from the island's village of Oban, the lodge is private and secluded with commanding views across Halfmoon Bay and Foveaux Strait. All guest rooms are king sized double or twin with their own ensuite bathroom and open onto an expansive balcony with stunning ocean views. A private guest lounge with an open fire provides an idyllic place to relax in the evening. The lodge's grounds are home to many native birds, including kaka (native parrots) which may be viewed from the terrace. Each evening guests are invited to enjoy a pre-dinner drink and appetisers with their hosts. Restaurants are available for evening dining in the township of Oban (at guest's expense). A continental or cooked breakfast is included in the tariff.

299

Comments

The
Translated Travellers' Pages

Herzlich Willkommen!

ようこそ！
歡迎 ！

"Lernen Sie das wahre Neuseeland kennen - die Neuseeländer selbst"

'Charming Places to Stay' in Neuseeland heißt Sie herzlich willkommen!

Eine überaus große Auswahl an Übernachtungsmöglichkeiten erwartet Sie in der Welt von "Bed & Breakfast" (private Übernachtung inclusive Frühstück) - vom einfachen Landhaus bis zum stattlichen Familiensitz. Überall werden Sie auf freundliche, aufgeschlossene Neuseeländer treffen. Manche von ihnen haben die Tradition des Gastgebens im Lauf der Jahre zu einer regelrechten Kunst entwickelt, auf die sie besonders stolz sind. Sogenannte "Home-stays", "Farmstays", Gastehäuser oder "Boutique"-Unterkünfte - sie alle fallen unter den Begriff "Bed & Breakfast". Hier lernen Sie das wahre Neuseeland kennen: die Neuseeländer selbst. - Ob Lehrer, Farmer oder ein pen-sionierter Angestellter, ob Künstler, Obstbauer, Heilpraktiker oder Schriftsteller, die Palette ist reichhaltig. Zum angenehmen Abenteuer kann die Übernachtung beispielsweise in einer Fischerlodge oder auf einer Schafsfarm im Hochland werden. Warum lernen Sie nicht nebenbei ein wenig reiten oder weben oder fühlen Sie sich einfach wie zu Hause in einem "Home-stay" oder "Countrystay" in der Stadt oder auf dem Land. Die Neuseeländer sind bekannt als warmherzige Gastgeber, Sie werden sich überall willkommen fühlen und unvergeßliche Reiseerinnerungen mit nach Hause bringen.

Was Sie erwarten können

Bed & Breakfast in Neuseeland ist bekannt für guten Service. Die Unterkünfte sind sauber, verfügen über bequeme Betten und bieten ein gutes, reichliches Frühstück an. Natürlich steht Ihr Wohlbefinden an erster Stelle. Ihre Gastgeber werden Ihnen gerne bei der Planung Ihrer weiteren Reise behilflich sein. Die Gastgeber wissen am besten darüber Bescheid, was die jeweilige Region zu bieten hat. Nutzen Sie diese unbezahlbaren Informationen aus erster Hand.

Was man von Ihnen erwartet

Ihre Gastgeber werden alles versuchen, Ihnen den Aufenthalt so angenehm wie möglich zu machen. Vergessen Sie jedoch bitte nicht, daß Sie in den meisten Fällen in Privathäusern zu Gast sein werden. Bedenken Sie auch die scheinbar unwichtigen Dinge. Es empfiehlt sich beispielsweise, um einen Hausschlüssel zu bitten, bevor Sie abends länger ausbleiben. Falls Sie ein Ferngespräch führen wollen, ist es besser, zuerst den Tarif abzuklären. Sagen Sie bitte auch so bald wie möglich Bescheid, wenn sich Ihre Ankunft verspäten sollte. Ein wenig Rücksichtnahme Ihrerseits wird so dazu beitragen, daß alle Beteiligten die Zeit auf eine angenehme Weise verbringen.

Praktische Hinweise

Besonders während der Sommersaison können Sie unnötige Enttäuschungen vermeiden, wenn Sie Ihre Unterkunft im voraus buchen. Es empfiehlt sich auch, die Gastgeber einen Tag vor Ihrer Ankunft anzurufen, um die Buchung zu bestätigen und die ungefähre Ankunftszeit mitzuteilen. Einige Bed & Breakfast Häuser bieten einen Abholdienst von Bus, Bahn oder Flughafen an - dieser Service ist oft im Preis mit eingeschlossen. Sagen Sie auch bitte rechtzeitig Bescheid, wenn Sie bei Ihren Gastgebern zusätzlich zur Übernachtung gerne ein warmes Abendessen hätten.

Boutique Accommodation

Der Begriff "Boutique" soll Ihnen sagen, daß es sich hier um ganz besonders schöne Bed & Breakfast-Übernachtungsmöglichkeiten handelt: eine geschmackvolle Inneneinrichtung, stilvolle Architektur oder ein romantisches Ambiente. Die Gastgeber dieser Häuser legen größten Wert auf gepflegte Gastfreundschaft.

Countrystay

"Countrystays" sind Bed & Breakfast-Unterkünfte in ländlicher Umgebung. Sie wohnen meist in nächster Nähe von dem, was Sie am typischen Landleben so schätzen. Ob Sie wandern gehen wollen, angeln oder einfach nur die unbeschreib- liche Natur pur genießen wollen, hier können Sie sich abseits vom Großstadtstreß in aller Ruhe erholen.

Luxury Accommodation

Die Luxusunterkünfte bieten eine hervorragende Ausstattung, exzellentes Essen und ganz besonderen Service. Oft sind diese Häuser archi- tektonische Glanzstücke oder sie liegen in einzig- artiger Umgebung. "Luxus" steht für außerge- wöhnliche Unterkunft und Gastfreundschaft.

Guesthouse/Inn

"Guest Houses" sind meistens Häuser, die eine größere Zahl von Gästen beherbergen, aber trotzdem eine persönliche Note aufweisen. Manche haben mehrere Aufenthaltsräume und einen speziellen Frühstücksraum. "Guest Houses" bieten im allgemeinen kein warmes Abendessen an.

Bed & Breakfast

Bed & Breakfast ist der Oberbegriff für alle Unterkunftsarten, die ein bequemes Bett, ein reichliches Frühstück und persönlichen Service im Preis einschließen. Während Ihres Aufenthalts werden Sie aufs Freundlichste von Ihren Gastgebern betreut.

Homestay

"Homestay" ist eine sehr beliebte Bed & Breakfast Variante. Sie wohnen in Privathäusern, die Gastgeber sind aufgeschlossen und freundlich und werden alles ihnen Mögliche tun, damit Sie sich "ganz wie zu Hause" fühlen nach dem Motto: "Sie kommen als Fremde und gehen als Freunde."

Self-contained Accommodation

Unterkünfte für Selbstversorger sind oft komplette Einliegerwohnungen oder einzeln stehende Häuschen mit eigenem Badezimmer und eigener Toilette und meistens mit Küche, Waschmaschine und Wäschetrockner. In manchen Fällen nehmen Sie das Frühstück zusammen mit der Gastfamilie ein. Es wird aber auch oftmals an die Haustür gebracht, oder Sie finden die Zutaten bereits in der Küche.

Farmstay

Wenn Sie echtes neuseeländisches Farmerleben hautnah genießen wollen, dann sind Sie im "Farmstay" gut aufgehoben. Üblicherweise können Sie bei der Farmtour mit auf die Weiden gehen und beim Füttern der Farmtiere mit dabei sein. Das Frühstück wird meistens mit der Familie zusammen eingenommen. Viele Farmstays bieten Vollverpflegung an.

"Auf einen Blick"

Kontaktaufnahme

Wer sind die Gastgeber und wo wohnen sie? Wie kommen Sie schnell mit ihnen in Kontakt?

"Auf einen Blick"

Übernachtungspreis

Alle Preise gelten für eine Übernachtung. **Double** *ist der Preis für zwei Personen in einem Zimmer,* **Single** *der Preis für eine Person in einem Zimmer. In einigen Fällen ist zusammen mit der Buchung eine Anzahlung erforderlich. Frühstück ist im Preis mit inbegriffen (falls nicht ausdrücklich anders erwähnt).* **Alle Preise gelten in $ NZ.** *Bitte lassen Sie sich die Preise von den Gastgebern bestätigen.*

"Auf einen Blick"

Symbole für Kategorien

Mit diesen einprägsamen Symbolen können Sie Ihre bevorzugte Unterkunftsmöglichkeit schnell ausfindig machen. Dieses System ist besonders hilfreich für Reisende, die die englische Sprache nicht fließend beherrschen.

"Auf einen Blick"

Kategoriestreifen

Die Gastgeber beschreiben ihre Kategorie in ihren eigenen Worten.

"Auf einen Blick"

Besondere Details

In Stichworten die attraktivsten Details der Unterkunft und der Sehenswürdigkeiten in der Umgebung.

"Auf einen Blick"

Kleine Straßenkarte

Im weißen Kästchen finden Sie den Namen des Hauses; der rote Punkt zeigt Ihnen die genaue Position. Im grünen Kästchen finden Sie die Wegbeschreibung.

Klar und übersichtlich

Schnell zu finden: Adresse, Telefon- und Faxnummer, E-Mail und Internetadresse.

"Ein persönliches Willkommen"

Dieser Text, von den Gastgebern persönlich verfaßt, beschreibt deren Lebensstil und Interessen, die Art der Unterkunft und was Sie als Gast erwarten können.

 Nichtraucher

Abkürzungen

SH – State Highway
h.p. – halber Preis
N.A. – nicht zutreffend
neg. – nach Vereinbarung
Qty – Anzahl
Tce – Terrace

Direkt buchen - Extrakosten vermeiden

Wenn Sie die Buchung selbst vornehmen, haben Sie von Anfang an persönlichen Kontakt mit Ihren Bed & Breakfast-Gastgebern in Neuseeland und vermeiden unnötige Kosten.

Wie wird dieser Reiseführer benützt – Zimmerdetails

Gästezimmer

Double = Zimmer mit Bett für 2 Personen
Twin = Zimmer mit 2 Betten für 2 Personen
Single = Zimmer mit Bett für eine Person

Bad/WC

Ensuite = Bad/WC mit Zimmer verbunden
Private = Eigenes Bad/WC, aber separat
Guest/Family Share =Bad/WC wird von Gästen oder der Gastfamilie mitbenutzt.

Bedrooms	Qty
Double	
Twin	
Single	
Bed Size	**Qty**
King	
Queen	
Double	
King/Single	
Bathrooms	**Qty**
Ensuite	
Private	
Guest Share	

Bettgrößen	
Super King	*180 x 200cm*
King	*165 x 200cm*
Queen	*150 x 200cm*
Double	*135 x 190cm*
Single	*90 x 190cm*
King Single	*90 x 200cm*

Kategorie Symbole

 Bed & Breakfast

 Boutique Accommodation

 Countrystay

 Farmstay

 Guest House / Inn

 Homestay

 Luxury Accommodation

 Self-contained Accom. & Cottages

Gängige Kreditkarten

 Amex – American Express

 Japanese Credit Card

 VISA

 Diners

 Bankcard

 MasterCard

 Maestro

 Eftpos

Mitgliedschaft in folgenden Verbänden und Gesellschaften

 Kiwihost

 Qualmark NZ

 @home NEW ZEALAND.

 Historic Places Trust

The @home NEW ZEALAND logo represents the leading organisation of Hosted Accommodation providers in New Zealand. It assures you of a warm welcome from friendly, helpful hosts. Accommodations displaying this logo have been assessed and meet the quality standards laid down by the association.

ニュージーランドの家庭生活を実体験！

～ニュージーランド・B＆Bへのお誘い～

ニュージーランド人は、旅行者に対する心暖まる、フレンドリーなもてなしを誇りとする国民として知られています。この「ニュージーランド風のもてなし」をじかに体験できるのが、Bed & Breakfast（ベッド・アンド・ブレックファースト、B＆B）です。これは一般のホテルとは一味ちがった、アット・ホームなサービスを身上とする宿泊施設の総称で、その具体的な中身はいろいろです。宿泊の場所でいうと、町中の一軒家・コッテージ・釣り場のロッジ・高原の牧場・乗馬や機織りの学校・お城（！）といった具合に多岐にわたっています。実際の名称としては、 Guest House（ゲスト・ハウス）、 Inn（イン）、 Boutique Accommodation（ブティック・アコモデーション）、 Countrystay （カントリーステイ）などがあります。また、安いものから高くて豪華なものまでありますので、予算に合わせて選ぶことが可能です。B&B のホスト（host, オーナー）は現役の教員・農家・芸術家・信仰療法家・作家、さらにはもと医師や弁護士など、実に多彩です。ホストの中には、単に話好き、という人から、専門的なサービスを提供する人まで、さまざまです。B&B は、「本物の」ニュージーランドを体験するのに恰好の機会といえます。ホストと、趣味や仕事の話などで盛り上がるのも楽しみのひとつではないでしょうか。

皆様の旅行が楽しく、思い出深いものとなりますように……

WHAT TO EXPECT

きれいな部屋、寝心地のよいベッド、おいしくて量もたっぷりの朝食、真心のこもったもてなし…ニュージーランドの Bed & Breakfast は、サービスの水準が高いことで知られています。さらに、ホストからは、その地域や周辺の見どころに関する詳しい「生の情報」を得ることができます。お客様の興味・関心をホストにお伝えください。ホストは皆様の旅行がすばらしいものとなる手助けができることを願っています。

― 宿泊者の心得

WHAT IS EXPECTED OF YOU

ホストは、お客様が楽しく思い出深いひとときを過ごすことができるよう、最大限の努力をしていますが、お客様の側にも配慮いただきたい点があります。それは、B＆Bは、基本的には「一般家庭」に泊まる、という形式をとっているという点です。ですから、ホストやその家族にたいする「ちょとした」気配りが大切です。たとえば、夜、帰りが遅くなる場合には、余裕をもって事前にその旨を伝えておき、「合鍵」を受け取っておくとか、電話を使用する際には、あらかじめ料金の確認をしておく、などです。こうした心遣いが、B＆Bでの滞在を成功させるカギなのです。

WHAT TO DO ― HINTS

B&B 宿泊の貴重なチャンスを逃さないためには、予約するのが一番です。（特に真夏は込み合います。）予約されましたら、到着の前日にホストに予約の確認をし、到着予定時刻を伝えておくことをおすすめします。ホストの中には、coach (コーチ、長距離バス)・飛行機・列車の発着場からの無料送迎サービスを行っている人もいます。また、到着日の夕食を希望される場合には、前日または前前日に、その旨をホストに伝えておきましょう。

BA　ブティック・アコモデーション

特色ある家屋を用いたB&B です。長い年月が醸し出す気品、優雅さ、ロマンス － Boutique Accommodation は、宿泊客の皆様をそうした雰囲気の中に包んでくれます。この雰囲気をいかに盛り上げるかが、ホストの腕のみせどころです。

C　　カントリーステイ

Homestay と同様、一般の家庭に滞在するものです。Countrystay の特徴は、場所が「いなか」にある点です。都会とはちがった、ニュージーランドの一面をじかに体験できます。

LA　ラクシャリー・アコモデーション

最高の立地条件のなかにある宿泊施設で、施設内外はさまざまな魅力でいっぱいです。豪華極まる設備や食事、それに群をぬいたハイ・クオリティーのサービスが特徴です。

G　　ゲスト・ハウス

通常、規模が比較的大きく、他のB&B の施設に比べ、より多くの宿泊客を泊めることができる施設ですが、B&B ならではの、フレンドリーなもてなしは変わりません。複数のラウンジや、朝食室が用意されているところもあります。夕食は出されないのが普通です。

Bed & Breakfast Categories

ベッド・アンド・ブレックファースト

一泊・朝食付きの宿の総称です。快適なベッド
と、たっぷりの朝食、それにホストの暖かいお
もてなしを存分にお楽しみください。

ホームステイ

ごく一般の家庭で、ホストによる身近なもてな
しを受けながら宿泊するものです。ホストは、
人と出会うのが好きで、宿泊客をまるで自分の
家にいるような、和やかな雰囲気にしてくれま
す。宿泊客の皆様が、初めて会った時には「見
知らぬ他人」でも、別れるときには「親しい友
人」となることを、ホストは心得ているのです。

セルフコンテインド・アコモデーション

宿泊者のための独立した入口・バスルーム・ラ
ウンジを含むのが普通です。独立した台所や洗
濯質室が用意されているところもあります。宿
泊施設は、一軒家のなかの一区画として存在す
る場合と、別棟の建物として存在する場合とが
あります。朝食はホストの家族とともにとる場
合、宿泊施設まで届けられる場合、朝食の材料
が宿泊所に用意されており、宿泊者が自分で用
意する場合とさまざまです。

ファームステイ

ニュージーランドの農業について理解を深めた
い、という人には理想的な機会です。動物たち
と身近に接しながら、農場での生活を経験して
いきます。牧場内のツアーを行っているところ
もあります。通常、朝食はホストの家族ととも
にとります。場所柄、近所にレストランなどが
ないため、多くのFarmstayでは昼食や夕食も出
されます。

How to use this guide – "at a glance"

"at a glance"

イージー・コントロール・パネル
ホストの氏名・所在地・連絡先など。

"at a glance"

ここに表示されているのは、一泊あたりの
料金です。**Double**（ダブル）は、一部屋
を2名で使用した場合の料金です。**Single**
（シングル）は、一部屋を1名で使用した
場合の料金です。予約の際に deposit
（ディポジット、料金の一部前払い）が
必要なところもあります。特に明記のない
場合、料金には朝食代が含まれています。
料金の表記は、すべて「NZドル」です。
料金に関する詳しい内容は、直接ホスト
までおたずねください。

"at a glance"

カテゴリー・シンボル
おさがしの B&B のタイプがすぐに見つか
るよう工夫されたマークです。お役立て
ください。

"at a glance"

カテゴリー・パネル
該当する B&B のカテゴリーの、ホスト自
身による定義・説明。

"at a glance"

フィーチャーズ＆アトラクションズ
宿泊施設およびその周辺のみどころのご紹
介。

"at a glance"

ロケーション・マップ
宿泊施設の位置が赤丸で示されています。
白のかこみの中に施設の名称が記されてい
ます。行き方の説明が追加で示されている
場合もあります。

クリアー・アドレス・ディーテールズ
宿泊施設の所在地・電話番号・Fax 番号・
e-mail アドレス・インターネット・ホーム
ページのアドレスといった、大切な情報は
こちらをご覧ください。

YOUR HOSTS: Katherine and Steve Whyte   Ph: (07) 332 2565   *Hamurana - Rotorua*

AT SPRINGWATERS LODGE
9 Te Waerenga Rd, Hamurana, Rotorua
Ph (07) 332 2565, Mobile 021-295 3652
email: info@springwaterslodge.co.nz
www.springwaterslodge.co.nz

Tariff : N.Z. Dollars

Double	$180-200
Single	$150-180
Child	$50

Bedrooms	Qty
Double	4
Twin	
Single	

Bed Size	Qty
Super King/Twin	1
King	3
Queen	
Double	
Single	

Bathrooms	Qty
Ensuite	4
Private	
Guest Share	

Affordable Luxury on Lake Rotorua's Doorstep

Features & Attractions

• Relaxed, friendly hosts
• Free wireless Broadband
• Spa pool, laundry
• Close to attractions

• Prime trout fishing spot
• Dinner guests welcomed
• 500m to golf course, springs
• Very generous breakfasts

Welcome to our spacious family home. Trout fishing, golf, walks and Hamurana Springs all within 500m of our doorstep. Spacious dining and lounging areas overlooking the lake allow plenty of space for relaxation. Newly refurbished throughout with quality furnishings. **Springwaters Lodge** is 1 level, offering rooms, each with ensuite, TV and DVD. Two rooms open onto their own patio, with lake views. A buffet-style breakfast can be enjoyed whilst a hot dish is being prepared. Join us for dinner and drinks or you may choose to dine at a local café. Home baking and refreshments available at any time. Our 2 senior school aged children, Nadia and Jaxon, share our passion for entertaining. Located just 10 minutes drive to many of Rotorua's leading attractions makes our location central. We are happy to help you with our local knowledge and assist you with booking your activities.

パーソナル・ウォーム・ウェルカム
ホストから読者へのひとことです。宿泊
施設の特徴や、ホストの人柄・ライフ・ス
タイルといったものを垣間見ることができ
ます。 No Smoking

宿泊予約申し込みは、B&B のホストに直接
なさいますと、ホストとそれだけ早くから
知り合うことができ、また中間業者を通し
た場合にかかる、さまざまな手数料を省く
ことができるので有利です。

ガイドのてびき － 客室・設備に関する記 述 について

Bedrooms

Double	= 二人用ベッドがある部屋
Twin	= 一人用ベッドが２つある部屋
Single	= 一人用ベッドが１つある部屋

Bathrooms

Ensuite	= 寝室に隣接
Private	= 各宿泊客専用
Guest Share/Family Share	= 他の宿泊客またはホストの家族と共用

Bedrooms	Qty
Double	
Twin	
Single	
Bed Size	**Qty**
King	
Queen	
Double	
King/Single	
Bathrooms	**Qty**
Ensuite	
Private	
Guest Share	

Bed Size

Super King	*180 x 200cm*
King	*165 x 200cm*
Queen	*150 x 200cm*
Double	*135 x 190cm*
Single	*90 x 190cm*
King Single	*90 x 200cm*

ガイドのてびき － カテゴリー・シンボル

 Bed & Breakfast

 Boutique Accommodation

 Countrystay

 Farmstay

 Guest House / Inn

 Homestay

 Luxury Accommodation

 Self-contained Accom. & Cottages

ガイドのてびき － お支払可能なクレジット・カード について

 Amex – American Express

 Japanese Credit Card

 VISA

 Diners

 Bankcard

 MasterCard

 Maestro

Eftpos

ガイドのてびき － B&B が提携している協会・団体について

 Kiwihost

 Qualmark NZ

 @home New Zealand.

 Historic Places Trust

 このマークは、ニュージーランド流の暖かく、フレンドリーで、質の高いサービスを保証するものです。Kiwi Host（キウ イ・ホ ス ト ）は、我が国をリードする顧客サービス・トレーニング・プログラムです。

介　紹

"體驗真正的紐西蘭──它的民族"

歡迎來到紐西蘭多樣化的旅店住宿簡介

紐西蘭的住宿，由小屋到別墅，從經濟單位到豪華大宅，您都會享受到在一個親切友善且好客的環境中居住。有多種不同的住宿方式：家庭住宿、農莊住宿、旅客之家、小客店、豪華旅店、鄉村住宿等等，他們一律提供給您一張溫暖的床以及香噴噴的西式早餐。這些都能讓您親身感受到紐西蘭的生活，認識居住在這裡的居民。您更可選擇嗜好與自己相似的家庭住宿，例如：老師、農夫、退休的專業人士、園藝專家、畫家、作家等等，住宿在他們的家，彼此交換心得，同時可享受獨特真誠的招待，體驗在漁村、郊外綿羊、海外之家的生活。不管是旅館或多樣化的家庭住宿，除了種類多之外，還充滿了紐西蘭獨特的友善及好客，不論您選擇那一種住宿，您將都是一位貴賓，盡情享受生活，讓日後有個難忘的回憶。

介　紹

期望什麼？

在紐西蘭床鋪及早餐享有標準服務的聲譽，住客會有最清潔、舒適的床，多種選擇熱烘烘早餐，及主人樂意友善的招待。除此之外，主人也會給於您居住地區的詳細資料。他們樂意幫您安排您在本地的旅遊計劃。他們豐富的經驗能增添您居住的樂趣。

對您的期望？

主人家會為您做任何的事，讓您享受一個難忘的停留。可是，請記得無論如何您只是一個客人。所以，請您注意一些事，例如，如果您晚歸的話，要向主人索取大門鎖匙，或當您要打長途、國內、本地電話時，應先詢問主人才可使用電話。請讓主人家知道您將夜歸。您處身置地的設想，會使您及主人都感到滿意。

給予您的建議

事先訂好一間房間，以避免屆時沒房間的失望，尤其在夏天時。除外，在您出發的前一天致電到主人家確定您訂好的房間及讓他們曉得您幾時會抵達。有些主人提供接送服務，如果您有需要的話。如果您需要他為您準備午餐的話，也請您早一、兩天前通知主人。

床鋪及早餐系列

 ## 家庭住宿

家庭住宿是最普遍的住宿方式，居住在溫暖、友善、好客的家庭中。主人喜歡認識不同的人，且樂意讓您有"家"的感覺，讓您曉得，您剛來的時候雖是一個陌生人，當您要離開時卻以朋友的身份離開。

鄉村居住

鄉村居住類似家庭住宿。您將居住於私人家庭中，慢慢地認識及接觸鄉村迷人的風景。許多鄉村住宿都靠近著名的旅遊風景區，能讓您最方便認識這些地方。

 ## 豪華大宅

豪華大宅代表了一流的設備，上等的餐飲和超水準的服務，許多此類住宿都有各自的特色，給予您額外一流的享受，它們代表了優越的住宿。

 ## 旅客之家

旅客之家通常能容納較多的旅客。雖然如此，主人仍會給您友善親切的招待。旅客之家可能會有數間的客廳及餐廳。旅客之家不常提供晚餐給住客。

床鋪及早餐系列

床 鋪 及 早 餐

床鋪及早餐是所有不同種類住所的代稱，供您選擇。除外，在您居住時間，主人更會給予您親切友善的招待，讓您有賓至如歸之感。

古 典 大 屋

在床鋪及早餐系列中，古典大屋的建築物具有古典氣息、整齊美觀、寧靜浪漫，是適合喜歡這類型的您來居住，主人將這些建築物的特質保持得非常好，確保您最佳的享受。

私 人 住 宿

此居住方式，通常包括了，私人的走道、浴室及客廳。它可以是一個家庭中隔出來的一部份或是一整間小屋。早餐可在主人家享用，也可送到您的門口或餐室。

農 場 住 宿

如果您選擇在農場居住，通常會由農場主人一家人接待您。如有需要，可為您安排參觀農場的行程，好讓您更加了解農場，您將跟農場主人一家人共同享用早餐；晚餐必須在事先通知，農場也將會為您準備，因為農場附近沒有餐館。

容易聯絡的範圍

您的旅店老闆；無論是何人，
身在何處，都能迅速與他們取
得聯絡。

價目表

價目表上的金額，表示住宿一晚的住宿
費。雙人（ Double ）表示兩人合用一間
房間的價錢。當您預定房間時，您可能要
預付訂金。價目表上的價錢通常包括早
餐，除非有特別註明不提供早餐。全部價
錢都以紐幣計算。請與旅店老闆確定住宿
明細資料。

各種住宿的代表符號

設計這些容易辨認的符號，是為了方便您
預約訂房，對於不太熟悉英文的遊客們，
這是絕對有幫助的。

住宿種類

旅店老闆會為您詳細介紹住宿種類。

地區特色及焦點

您住宿的四周環境以及您住宿區域的特
色與焦點，都會為您列出。

區域地圖

您所住宿的地點，在地圖上將以
紅點標示。旅店的店名，也會在
地圖上刊出。通常為配合找尋，
也都有方向圖來確認正確方向。

明確的地址

明確的地址，應包括住宿的地址，電話
和傳真號碼，電子郵件地址與網址。

"一項特別及溫暖的歡迎"

通常歡迎詞是由旅店老闆親自設計。有關
店內設備以及獨特的住宿方式，都會有清
楚的說明。

 No Smoking

縮寫

Cnr—角落
h.p.—半價
N.A. —無此設備
Qty—可磋商
Tce—陽台

直接預約—省錢

與紐西蘭"床與早餐"
旅店系列的老闆直接預約住宿，
您從一開始就會省了許多
不必要的附加費用。

如何使用這本指南 — 客房資料

房 間

Double = 一或二張床提供兩人住宿的房間
Twin = 提供二張床給兩人住宿的雙人房
Single = 提供一張床給單人住宿的單人房

浴 室

Ensuite = 浴室在您的房間內
Private = 提供您個人專用的浴室
Guest Share/Family Share = 公共浴室，必須與
　其他家庭或住客共同使用。

Bedrooms	Qty
Double	
Twin	
Single	
Bed Size	**Qty**
King	
Queen	
Double	
King/Single	
Bathrooms	**Qty**
Ensuite	
Private	
Guest Share	

床的尺寸

Super King
180 x 200cm
King
165 x 200cm
Queen
150 x 200cm
Double
135 x 190cm
Single
90 x 190cm
King Single
90 x 200cm

如何使用這本指南 — 代號種類

 Bed & Breakfast

 Guest House / Inn

 Boutique Accommodation

 Homestay

 Countrystay

 Luxury Accommodation

Farmstay

 Self-contained Accom. & Cottages

如何使用這本指南 — 旅店老闆接受信用卡付款

 Amex – American Express

 Bankcard

 Japanese Credit Card

 MasterCard

 VISA

 Maestro

Diners

Eftpos

如何使用這本指南 — 協會

 Kiwihost

 @home New Zealand.

 Qualmark NZ

 Historic Places Trust

 這個商標就是保證您是受本地人所歡迎的，以及獲得親切友善的服務。 Kiwi Host 是紐西蘭顧客服務訓練計畫的得獎者，我們確信我們對於您的重視，與您對於我們的肯定。

Special thanks to all of these friends who gave help and reassurance when deadlines loomed and spirits were low:

Joshua, Jamie, and Matthew Newman, photographers.
Katherine Richards, proof reader extraordinaire.
Tim Cornelius, Dunedin map designer.

Translations

German translation by *Uli Newman.*
Japanese translation by *Yoshi Isoyama at Transla NZ, PO Box 8069
Dunedin, New Zealand. isoyama@xtra.co.nz*
Mandarin (Chinese) translation by *Stephen Liu at Asian Communication Company Ltd
Dunedin, New Zealand.*

TRAVEL*wise* Ltd.

Index of Listings (by Regions)

Index of Listings (by Regions)

Index of Listings (by Regions)

Index of Listings (by Regions)

Index of Locations

Index of Locations

Index of Locations

Peter Shepherd CEO at TRAVELWISE would appreciate
your comments, favourable or otherwise. Your ideas
and suggestions will be used to further develop
"Charming Places to Stay".
So please, don't hesitate to send us your ideas,
suggestions, complaints or compliments.

Comments

For all enquiries please contact Peter at Travelwise Ltd
Ph: 0064-3-476 1515, Fax: 0064-3-476 1514
email: admin@travelwise.co.nz
www.travelwise.co.nz

You can book online at –www.charmingplacestostay.co.nz

Notes

For all enquiries please contact Peter at Travelwise Ltd
Ph: 0064-3-476 1515, Fax: 0064-3-476 1514
email: admin@travelwise.co.nz
www.travelwise.co.nz

You can book online at –www.charmingplacestostay.co.nz

Notes

For all enquiries please contact Peter at Travelwise Ltd
Ph: 0064-3-476 1515, Fax: 0064-3-476 1514
email: admin@travelwise.co.nz
www.travelwise.co.nz

You can book online at –www.charmingplacestostay.co.nz

Notes

For all enquiries please contact Peter at Travelwise Ltd
Ph: 0064-3-476 1515, Fax: 0064-3-476 1514
email: admin@travelwise.co.nz
www.travelwise.co.nz

You can book online at –www.charmingplacestostay.co.nz

Notes

For all enquiries please contact Peter at Travelwise Ltd
Ph: 0064-3-476 1515, Fax: 0064-3-476 1514
email: admin@travelwise.co.nz
www.travelwise.co.nz

You can book online at –www.charmingplacestostay.co.nz

Notes

For all enquiries please contact Peter at Travelwise Ltd
Ph: 0064-3-476 1515, Fax: 0064-3-476 1514
email: admin@travelwise.co.nz
www.travelwise.co.nz

You can book online at –www.charmingplacestostay.co.nz